Unruly Media

Unruly Media

YouTube, Music Video, and the
New Digital Cinema

CAROL VERNALLIS

OXFORD
UNIVERSITY PRESS

Oxford University Press is a department of the University of Oxford.
It furthers the University's objective of excellence in research,
scholarship, and education by publishing worldwide.

Oxford   New York
Auckland   Cape Town   Dar es Salaam   Hong Kong   Karachi
Kuala Lumpur   Madrid   Melbourne   Mexico City   Nairobi
New Delhi   Shanghai   Taipei   Toronto

With offices in
Argentina   Austria   Brazil   Chile   Czech Republic   France   Greece
Guatemala   Hungary   Italy   Japan   Poland   Portugal   Singapore
South Korea   Switzerland   Thailand   Turkey   Ukraine   Vietnam

Oxford is a registered trade mark of Oxford University Press
in the UK and certain other countries.

Published in the United States of America by
Oxford University Press
198 Madison Avenue, New York, NY 10016

Library of Congress Cataloging-in-Publication Data
Vernallis, Carol.
Unruly media : YouTube, music video, and the new digital cinema / Carol Vernallis.
pages   cm
Includes bibliographical references and index.
ISBN 978-0-19-976699-4 (alk. paper)—ISBN 978-0-19-976700-7 (alk. paper)
1. Music videos—History and criticism. 2. Digital media—Technological innovations. I. Title.
PN1992.8.M87.V48   2013
302.23'1—dc23   2013000191

This volume is published with the generous support of the Manfred Bukofzer Endowment of the
American Musicological Society.

9 8 7 6 5 4 3 2 1

Printed in the United States of America
on acid-free paper

For my husband, Charles Kronengold

CONTENTS

ACKNOWLEDGMENTS

I'd like to thank most my husband, Charles Kronengold. Thoughtful, witty, caring, and equanimous, he's better than I could've ever hoped for as a partner and fellow academic. I'd also like to thank three who have, over the years, been consistent and close readers of my work, and central to my imagination of what criticism can be—Les Brill, Alan Cameron, and George Toles. I'd also like to thank my dear co-editor Amy Herzog, as well as Claudia Gorbman and John Richardson. Together, we embarked on an endeavor—which sometimes felt daunting—of bringing 83 scholars to press in *The Oxford Handbook of New Audiovisual Aesthetics* and *The Oxford Handbook of Sound and Image in Digital Media*. That project ran alongside this one. And I'd like to thank our authors who contributed to these volumes: by being in close dialogue with their work, I came to new understandings of what thinking and writing can be, and my book is greatly enriched by this experience. My students, too, were often assigned chapters, and patiently read the work; and, with alarmed expressions, they let me know I had left out an important band, or spelled it incorrectly, or helped me with the crux of an argument. I'd also like to thank the directors who generously granted interviews to me. I tried out many of my theories on them, and they answered, sometimes with bemusement, but more often with great depth of feeling. I hope to bring their work to print in a book called *Transmedia Directors: Mavericks of Music Video, Commercials, and Film*. Thank you Jonas Åkerlund, Abteen Bagheri, Timur Bekmambetov, Jesse Dylan, Alan Ferguson, Francis Lawrence, David Fincher, Lorin Finkelstein, Charles Bigelow, Kevin Kerslake, Arev Manoukian, Melina Matsoukas, Dave Meyers, Chris Milk, Vincent Morisset, Marcus Nispel, Mark Pellington, and Floria Sigismondi.

I'd also like to thank many friends and fellow grapplers with text. Those listed read a chapter or influenced one. While I'm sure I've left people out, I'd like to include: Mark Applebaum, Caetlin Benson-Allott, Jonathan Berger,

Talya Berger, David Bordwell, Joseph Borrell, Ximena Briceno, Leslie Brill, Warren Buckland, Jim Buhler, Lori Burns, Lee Anne Callahan, Allan Cameron, Theo Cateforis, Dale Chapman, Will Cheng, Norma Coates, Lisa Coulthard, Georgia Cowart, Sean Cubitt, Daphna Davidson, Annette Davison, Kay Dickinson, Wheeler Winston Dixon, Kevin Donnelly, Nina Eidsheim, Marc Evans, Stephanie Ferneyhough, Alan Finke, Jonathan Flatley, Caryl Flinn, Joan Friedman, Simon Frith, Charles Hiroshi Garrett, Daniel Goldmark, Claudia Gorbman, Tom Grey, Dan Hallin, Heather Hendershot, Amy Herzog, Ken Hillis, Héctor Hoyos, Tim Hughes, Anthony Kaes, Ann Kaplan, Jaroslaw Kapuscinski, Selmin Kara, Henry Keazor, Mark Kerins, Bernard Kobes, Mathias Bonde Korsgaard, Richard Leppert, George Lewis, George Lipsitz, Jean Ma, Saikat Majumdar, Laura Marks, Richard Mook, Alan Moore, Anna Morcom, Mitchell Morris, Paul Morris, Tony Newcomb, Mark Nye, Jann Pasler, Megan Parry, Carole Piechota, John Richardson, Jesse Rodin, Ron Sadoff, Anna Schultz, Steve Shaviro, Jacob Smith, Jeff Smith, Katherine Spring, Sianne Ngai, Jason Stanyek, Garrett Stewart, Will Straw, Mathew Sumera, Philip Tagg, George Toles, Hannah Ueno, Blakey Vermeule, Margaret Vernallis, Marguerite Waller, and Aylish Wood.

And I'd like to thank my editor, Norm Hirschy. Many years ago he took me to lunch at a Society for Cinema and Media Studies conference and told me he wanted to publish my next book. No editor matches Norm. Other authors will concur! Responsible, fast, and graceful. A good fortune in my life. This beautiful book comes from the contribution of many: Marc Schneider, my production editor, Kay Kodner, my copyeditor, and Robert Swanson, my indexer. A special thank you, too, to Ian Bailey, Chuck Bigelow, Lee Anne Callahan, Yvette Noel-Schure, Niko Pfund, and Suzanne Ryan.

Unruly Media

Introduction

UNRULY MEDIA: YOUTUBE, MUSIC VIDEO,
AND THE NEW DIGITAL CINEMA

I love the media swirl: its accelerating aesthetics. mingled media, and memes that cross to and fro. For a young person today, this swirl, I imagine, suggests never being bored. It all seems new—the ever-present buzzing, switching, and staccato thinking, the horizons that open onto friendship networks. Much has changed too, for labor, global flows of capital, and forms of power and leisure. *Unruly Media* takes seriously the ways moving media shape our experience. Many of us traverse from the videogame "Angry Birds" on a cell phone, to a YouTube clip, to a feature film in a big theater or on a desktop computer, to Facebook, and then a music video. It's all scrambled. But we might try to grasp this condition while we still have the chance. What *is* a YouTube clip? What's a music video, or a post-classical film?

We might think about the media swirl in several ways. One is to focus on genre. For each form I'm considering—YouTube, music video, and digital post-classical cinema—I'd claim we have a concept of what the primary stylistic features are and the purest example can be. YouTube provides a whoopee-cushion effect; music video conveys a brief state of suspended bliss; and post-classical cinema creates a continuous sense of traversal but also bewilderment, as if much has transpired too quickly or too opaquely. Where were we again? These films can make you feel like you've been pummeled or blindly led. A definitive YouTube example might be "The Sneezing Baby Panda"; for music video it might be Lady Gaga's "Paparazzi"; a quintessential post-classical film might be *Bourne Ultimatum*. But today each genre's influences ripple out maddeningly, creating interference, blendings, loosenings of boundaries in ways we've never seen. Beyoncé's music video "Countdown" looks like a clip on You-Tube, as does Lana Del Rey's "Video Games." Segments from Edgar Wright's *Scott Pilgrim vs. the World*, Richard Kelly's *Southland Tales*, and Julie Taymor's *Across the Universe* could be placed on YouTube and inadvertently experienced

3

as music videos, prosumers' mashups, art students' class-projects, or trailers. So we might try to understand a media object differently now—through its length, level of gloss, platform, viewing audience, or budget. YouTube often has short, sophomoric clips. Vevo has well-rounded, conservative, corporate-identified music videos. Netflix has longish high- and lowbrow Hollywood, foreign, and independent films. But, of course, these categories blur. I wouldn't be surprised to find a music video on Netflix, perhaps as part of a curated collection, or a feature film on YouTube. Vevo's boundaries are also soft. It screens documentary "makings of," musicians' interviews, and strings of thematically linked clips.

We could instead see all these media as similar. They've all been influenced by the same technologies and socioeconomic pressures. We're in the midst of an international style that has heightened sonic and visual features; they've been intermedially reconfigured and accelerated. A range of contemporary global media, including viral web media, music video, South Asian cinema, and the feature films of music video directors who have crossed over to cinema, have changed in similar ways, though this new intensified style has also permeated these forms unevenly. International genres with long traditions, such as British police procedurals and Hong Kong action films, have embraced the new style to stunning effect, while soap operas and the Metropolitan Opera's HD-simulcasts have been among the slowest to assimilate change. Focusing on sound/image relations in an era of intensified audiovisual aesthetics, we might chart the ways new digital technologies like free-downloadable editing software, 10.1 surround-sound, digital intermediary and computer-generated imagery shape the new style.

These new technologies provide the ground for the stylistic transformations that have unfolded in the last fifteen or so years. For today's media practitioners, the new technologies present exciting opportunities: all of a YouTube clip, music video, or film can be present and available, simultaneously, until the moment of release. One can fine-tune the sound and image; move blocks of footage forward or back; sub in new backgrounds or new actors. This is different from working on one of the first *Star Wars* films and having to send your assistant to the vault to locate two reels of film to splice together.

Today's media relations become malleable and volatile in a "mixing-board" aesthetic. Our accrued knowledge about how to work fluidly with this material is informed by music video. Music video's major contribution to today's audiovisual turn stems from the fact that ways of placing music and image together are *learned*: they form genealogies. One can't just speed up Godard and put music against it. Today's unique audiovisual relations developed through music video directors' and editors' experiments at reconfiguring images and sounds. Music video used new technology (cheap, reusable videotape) and had new commercial and social demands (make it fast, creative, musical, different, wild). Today the soundtrack in toto has become "musicalized": sound effects and dialogue are now shaped alongside composed music into musical phrases. Sonic features can also adopt leading roles, driving the film; or sound can mediate, enabling individual film parameters to come to the fore. The image acquires a sense of speed and flexibility: the image's contents can seem as if they had been poured from one shot into the next. Cutting, too, can bestow an almost percussive rhythmic drive. An image in the new digital cinema often avoids a ground because the sound wafts it along.

These audiovisual forms of knowledge were shaped by music video. In the eighties music video was *the* laboratory: while commercials and films in that era tended toward tightly controlled client-author supervision and careful storyboarding, a music video director or editor might try anything. (Turn the image on its head and abut it with some red.) In the nineties music video directors streaming into cinema helped drive the new, audiovisually intensified, post-classical cinema. A second wave then immigrated, as industry funding, in response to free downloading, dried up in the 00s. Music video directors have flourished in the industry because they're especially attuned to the new technologies and the new audiovisual relations.

Many scholars of film, television, and new media have sought to address the nature and causes of our media swirl. David Bordwell claims that new production practices and media technologies like nonlinear editing systems and the video assist have engendered new approaches, but he emphasizes continuities with past media practices. Lev Manovich, on the other hand, believes we're now in an era of animation rather than pure cinema, and that database structures will supplant traditional narratives. This book focuses on the audiovisual turn. I argue that the sound-image practice developed in music videos, along with new audio software technologies that meld seamlessly with visual software, help produce a mediascape that foregrounds musical feature.[1] Multitracked, heavily produced popular music, especially, provides a model. Imagine it this way: new digital technologies allow a filmmaker to redraw an image of a house every time it occurs in a film. She can change its color in each iteration, and modify other parameters, like the texture of the forest behind it, or the sounds of crows sitting on its roof. This closely worked aesthetic is a popular music-industry practice. The soundtrack can be modulated to work with the scape of the image, and then the image, modulated once again.

This mixing-board aesthetic transforms much media, extending past YouTube and music video into post-classical cinema. Through an analysis of *Moulin Rouge!* and *Eternal Sunshine of the Spotless Mind*, this book shows the ways intensified audiovisual aesthetics can override traditional Hollywood film structure, turning "the five acts" into mere scaffolding that becomes hidden, slackened, or overwritten by more prominent musical forms. YouTube clips are altered too, in part, to compete with the website's most popular content, music videos. And music videos, like Lady Gaga and Jonas Åkerlund's "Paparazzi" and "Telephone," now shimmer between traditional narrative and musical structures in ways never before possible.

"Musicality", of course, and "audiovisuality" can be elusive concepts. We might describe musical and audiovisual processes as fluid, flexible, heterogeneous, and affectively rich. Henri Bergson felt music could have a special relation to time, rhythm, memory, and attention.[2] Listeners may wish to hold onto what has unfolded in the past, while simultaneously staying in the saddle of time and reaching for the future. It can also seem "musical" when a media object switches sections around so that *before*s and *after*s shift. To be aware of everything happening in the moment, the heterogeneous slice from top to bottom, is also a condition of music and music video. Suzanne Langer wrote that music can be a subjective as well as a temporal art: it can show us the ebbs and flows of our emotions.[3]

Intensified audiovisual aesthetics and a parameter-by-parameter analytical approach can help us understand today's music video and digital cinema. Music videos are musical and so are sections of today's films, through their music-heavy accompaniments and bombastic or finely grained diegetic and nondiegetic sounds. The odd one out might appear to be YouTube. I'd argue that YouTube's most viewed content is music video, and many clips, though they're not quite music videos, function similarly (the 2008 Obama campaign clip "Yes We Can" is one example). User-generated content like mashups and remixes count as well. Brief verité clips like "Haha Baby" and "The Sneezing Baby Panda" also reflect intensified audiovisual aesthetics. YouTube clips become popular under tremendous Darwinian pressures. Those that come to the fore often showcase close, audiovisually heightened, parametric aesthetics even if they also reflect a more direct rendering of the world. A clip like "Evolution of Dance" possesses an uncanny rightness of proportion, color, scale, and graphic values that could be modeled as an animation, and the interaction between dancer and played-back, popsong-medley is musical. In sum, much media, across platforms and genres, driven by close audiovisual relations, are not what we grew up with.[4]

Because so many media are linked across genres and platforms, it is worth considering larger, virtual structures that stretch across the web. We might also seek to situate these chains of associations and technological and aesthetic shifts in relation to socioeconomic and cultural factors like capital flows, work speedup, and just-in-time labor. Recent scholarship has considered the ways mainstream Hollywood crystallizes the culture's most pressing contradictions into myth. Today's media, however, are dispersed across many forms and platforms, so that we instead understand ourselves in relation to gender, class, race, sexual identity, labor, and power through constellations of sounds and images. Studies show that our ways of thinking, feeling, and dreaming have been transformed as well.[5] We might focus on the ways the new styles and techniques, most often *audiovisually intensified*, are contributing to a global experience.

I began with the question of identifying post-classical cinema, music video, and the YouTube clip. Even those we'd place at the center of their respective genres can seem riven and striated by the others. The following section describes what each genre is like *now*, and seeks to give a sense of its departure from the past. I'll conclude with examples of competition among genres.

Digital Cinema's Intensified Audiovisual Aesthetics

The Bourne Ultimatum, Eternal Sunshine of the Spotless Mind, and *Moulin Rouge!* are films I consider post-classical; globally there's *Breaking News, Day Watch, Hot Fuzz,* and *Yuva.* Debates among film theorists center on whether these films break with the past or revamp older practices. In the historical-continuity-with-a-twist camp, David Bordwell argues that classical narrative structures endure alongside minor variants like "puzzle" films. Camerawork and editing, such as bipolar extremes of lens-lengths, a reliance on close shots, wide-ranging camera movements, and rapid editing, define this new "surface" style.[6] In the other camp, Eleftheria Thanouli claims that broader shifts have taken place: today's plots slacken as characters pursue diverse goals, and stories divide into intertwined subplots. These multigeneric films adopt a self-conscious stance, and realism becomes hypermediated.[7]

I'll add that I map the borders of the post-classical style through sentiment. From 2000 to 2007 cinema's horizons seemed wide open. Any film might be a surprise. Post-classical films seemed intended to make you say "Oh! Really?" while feeling savvy or sophisticated. It included several strands of filmmaking, not only those with Bordwell's "intensified continuity," puzzle plots, or a preponderance of audiovisual sequences. Specifically visual techniques played a role as well: an overpreening of the image (à la Wes Anderson, enabled by DI), extensive use of CGI (often inspired by comic books, as in *300* and *Watchmen*), and possibly HD. Perhaps these developments were not closely related, but at the time it felt like they were. Enabled by digital technologies, their surprise factor—often created through mannerist showboating and strings of affectively rich audiovisual sequences—separated them from seamless classical Hollywood.

Zack Snyder's 2011 *Sucker Punch* is a post-classical film, in part because it has five layers, two possible realities and another three possible dreamscapes, all contradicting one another. The film ends like a music video. We don't understand what took place and we may feel driven to go back for another viewing. Perhaps *Sucker Punch*'s truths are locked somewhere in the soundtrack or between the soundtrack and the image (we're instructed to seek a key and there's much music and dancing). In *Sucker Punch* a heroine we know almost nothing about, incarcerated in a 19th-century insane asylum, is brought before "the theater," a large circular space, containing a stage, fellow inmates, an antique reel-to-reel tape player playing odd sound collages, and a schoolmarm advising performers to "sing away all the pain and guilt." This sounds like a pastiche of post-classical filmmaking and YouTube (à la "broadcasting yourself"), and as the protagonist defiantly heads the other way, she changes from one person into another and from one environment into another, while an alternative band sounding like seventies Genesis sings, "Where is my mind?" What's this got to do with anything? *Sucker Punch* exhibits post-classical tendencies turned musical: a music-video audiovisual passage in an overstylized setting, where sound effects both suture and make strange the image and the soundtrack. We shuttle back and forth across genres and media. We may want to argue that post-classical films employ pop songs to increase revenue streams, but why use one in *this* way? The scene is foregrounded here. "Where is my mind" seems to ask where we are in the media swirl. We're at a historical moment when directors and industry practitioners don't fully grasp their relation to revenue, audiences, or rights. They're bewildered and perhaps anxious. The scene seems to say, "It's wild, but stay here. Watch *this*." (See figure Intro.1.)

As another example, the trailer for *Abraham Lincoln: Vampire Hunter* cues viewers that it's for a post-classical film. A former music video director known for extremely heightened audiovisual relations, Timur Bekmambetov, directed the film. In the trailer, many films seem to be echoed in its opening images: *Notorious*, *Birth of a Nation*, *The Matrix*, *Independence Day*, *Inception*, and, most importantly, *Inglourious Basterds*, the last because it presents a revisioning of a historical event. Perhaps the most strongly post-classical touch is the fusing of Lincoln and vampire killers in a fantastical setting, where anything might happen, including time travel . . . why not zombies, ET, or an alien spacecraft? As with many post-classical films we're led through a changing landscape by the soundtrack. We simultaneously follow the *Inception*-like, repeated, honking bullhorn and a high-pitched ringing (has anyone yet capitalized on

Intro.1 "Where is my mind," from *Sucker Punch*. How do the song, the viewer, and the film relate to the media swirl?

Intro.2 Timur Bekmambetov's *Abraham Lincoln: Vampire Hunter* trailer as an example of post-classical aesthetics.

these two sound tropes?). We're encouraged to listen carefully. The tick-tick-tick at the trailer's end reminds me of the Westerns I've seen and what an authentic antique clock might sound like; meanings here are so contingent that everything seems up for grabs. Audiovisual relations carry enormous weight. The soundtrack is allowed to bear the truth (see figure Intro.2).

YouTube's Intensified Audiovisual Aesthetics

YouTube is vast and uncharted; I make no claims of comprehensiveness. But hopefully the reader will agree that part of what separates YouTube from other media are the clips' brevity and the ways they're often encountered through exchange with other people: a clip's interest derives from its associations with colleagues, family, friends, and contexts within communities. Often clips get forwarded because there's an intensity of affect that can't be assimilated: humorous or biting, only forwarding it will diffuse its aggressiveness or power to hold us fast.

"The Badger Song" may be one of the best YouTube exemplars, even though it has an unusual past, and its view count isn't as high as the more popular Llama and Mango songs. I was, however, able to get musicology professors to sing it along with me, and my students have shared with me many fond, touching associations with the clip. Does the "The Badger Song" possess any special aesthetic or cultural richness? I'd claim it has that first important thing, which is an affect that is hard to assimilate. "Badger" can hold us in a state of suspension, as if we were caught in the beam of a low-voltage Taser. It thus may work for tedium-inducing activities like riding on subways and being stuck in phone-bank queues. It may also excite primitive brain alarm systems. The Badger Song might reanimate deep-seated fears: some Neanderthal self sees badgers as potential foes. Though the badgers look cute and beckoning with their outstretched arms, they're regimented and pop up suddenly—a badger army gathering (even if they're doing calisthenics). Mushrooms are risky as well—their poison looms. And of course snakes. Why a badger and not a muskrat? (Are badgers cuter but also more threatening than mole rats?) What do badgers have to do with those snakes and the mushrooms, and what do they ask of me? (See figure Intro.3.)

Intro.3 "The Badger Song": YouTube aesthetics.

I've identified nine features that tend to structure popular YouTube clips. They are (1) pulse and reiteration; (2) irreality and weightlessness (tied to low-resolution and the digital); (3) graphic values; (4) a sense of scale that matches the medium; (5) unusual causal relations; (6) intermediality and intertextuality; (7) sardonic humor and parody; (8) condensation; (9) and formal replication of the web.

Let me discuss the first feature for "The Badger Song": pulse, reiteration, musicality. Besides the threatening or ominous signs of badgers, some are friendlier: the clip has a musicality that places it within the genre of music video. There's a game of fort-da or peek-a-boo based on a pulse. This is the kind of cognitive play that toddlers enjoy—the disappearance and appearance of objects, set to a familiar pattern, but here there's enough challenge for adults because there are so many badgers that one really needs to pay attention. What audiovisual relations enable this aesthetic? The swelling and terraced calls of "badger" hold one in a state of ruffled alarm, even as elements add a bit more intensity or release (the mushroom or snake); nevertheless, the buzziness remains. And yet there's also some pleasurable camp—some German dude singing "Shnake! Ooh!." High above the low conga-like drumming is a wheezy metallic sound, perhaps an artifact of the low-fi recording that gets stuck like an earworm. The tune shifts between major and minor. The mushrooms build intensity on the upbeat of three; the snake comes in on four, rephrasing measures into a bar of three and three. In some versions, there's a glitch that results from lengthening the clip's duration by looping the original. This inadvertently adds one measure of 9/8, which can sideline anyone trying to follow the pulse. Camera and movement within the frame may set up a looming response and then release us from it. Badgers pop, mushrooms lurch forward, and then, as a laughing but perhaps still threatening snake gently rolls to the right, the background glides left—a hop-hop-hop-slide. The looping creates odd aural and visual effects. We might watch and listen for small differences like additional badgers, an engorged mushroom, or more Badger calls. We're probably caught in a loop but our minds encourage us to find greater nuance. Is it the tape? Is it us? Do we want to be a swarming badger? Similar modes of audiovisual analysis can be applied to YouTube clips from "Haha Baby" to "The Sneezing Baby Panda."

Music Video's Intensified Audiovisual Aesthetics

What is a music video today? And, as a corollary, how different is a Lady Gaga video from one by A Flock of Seagulls? For the first question, I'd claim at one time we knew what a music video is, but no longer. The context in which music videos circulated in the eighties and nineties is different from now. Then clips were primarily seen on a few satellite services—like MTV; censorship was high, and it was difficult for directors and record companies to get their work on the air. Today music video clips are dispersed across a number of commercial websites as well as on YouTube. There's little vetting and access is much wider.

We used to define music videos as products of record companies in which images were put to recorded pop songs in order to sell songs. No longer. On YouTube individuals as much as record companies post music-video clips, and many prosumers have no hope of selling anything. The image can be taken from a variety of sources and a song recorded afterward: a clip might look like a music video, but the music can be neither prior nor preeminent. Clips can range from ten seconds to several hours. Interruptions may occur, and material from other genres can infiltrate. Music videos appear in new and unexpected media, like interactive games and iPhone apps. There's also a dizzying array of user-based content that ranges from vidding and remixes to mashups.

We can thus define music video, simply, as a relation of sound and image that we recognize as such. Such a broad definition might seem too sweeping—it applies to the clips I've just discussed like *Sucker Punch*, *Abraham Lincoln: Vampire Hunter*, and "The Badger Song," but it's the most we can say. Seeming to reside at the web's center, music video incorporates both post-classical cinematic techniques and YouTube. In the late 90s and early 00s budgets dried up and directors fled for more lucrative gigs in films and commercials. Some money has flowed back, both through the major's support of Vevo and new opportunities for product placement within clips. Returning directors incorporate their cinematic and commercial experiences. Jonas Åkerlund, Lady Gaga, and Beyoncé's "Telephone" is an amalgam of a music video and something else—B-movie, Tarantino-affair, *Natural Born Killers*. And Åkerlund's subsequent "Girl Panic" for Duran Duran is a 15-minute mockumentary. My guess is that as the web becomes further monetized, music videos will continue to fragment and blur boundaries.

Hype Williams, Lady Gaga, and Beyoncé's "Video Phone" is an example that draws on both YouTube and cinema. The opening cites *Reservoir Dogs* and then YouTube's "frontal address," stripped-down graphics, shallow space, low-res kaleidoscope effects, and rapid stutter. A new type of popular songwriting, enabled by software like Pro Tools, makes possible this more fragmented cell-phone-friendly

Intro.4 Beyoncé's "Video Phone": music video as mashup.

imagery. On YouTube, repetition is often combined with boredom and tedium. Repetition, of course, can also be paired with a kind of jacked-up, unrelenting excitement, like the songs of Katy Perry, but the music for "Video Phone" is a case of the former. The finger snaps are desultory, often lagging behind the beat. The synthesizer patch in the upper register spends most of its time cycling among three pitches. It conveys ennui. The exotic melody in the mid-range sounds like an inexpensive eight-bit Casio sound from the mid 80s—thin and tinny. The drums in the rhythm section seem cheap—sometimes sounding like banging on trash-can lids, and sometimes like tapping on heavy plastic. In the rhythm track the more muffled drum hits sound like an irregular heartbeat. This arrangement does not suggest money or luxury (there are no live strings, for example). "Watch me on your video phone" sounds like a corporate slogan we're consigned to hear over and over.

The song supports the image's dense web of signification. The music is un-settling and exotic: a listener might feel a bit anxious, but can't attribute its causes. The Morricone opening features a G-Phrygian ostinato (Bb, G, Ab, G), a mysterious, dark figure that hovers over the song like a cloud. An open, more flexible arrangement, where things pop in and out—are there menacing ele-ments at the periphery?—makes possible a prismatic visual scheme.

Beyoncé's earlier videos share little with the clashing models of good and bad sexuality in "Video Phone." We may be surprised to find in "Video Phone" that its female performer is allowed to take pleasure from bondage, be the around-the-way pinup for our boys overseas, move to an even redeemed state of near-pure whiteness, and then turn it all around again by vulnerably approaching orgasm while at the same time performing the role of a bored sex-worker and military trainer. This is really a mashup (see figure Intro.4).

Intensified Audiovisual Aesthetics across Genre and Platform

As mentioned earlier, much media, across platforms and genres, are not what we grew up with. Practices developed out of music video and new technologies have shaped the new style and close audiovisual analysis provides a way into

Intro.5 *Bourne Ultimatum* and reiteration.

Intro. 6 Beyoncé's "Countdown": unstoppable drive.

this work. My project has also been to describe each genre as other media have interpenetrated with it. Let me give one quick example of what analysis across the media landscape might look like. Perhaps our engagements with media are increasingly based on smaller units. We remember a fragment from a film and connect it to a moment in a YouTube clip or a music video. The low horn-blast from *Inception* has seeped into many trailers and action television shows.[8] Similarly, we often come across the image of falling off a cliff, scanning an empty horizon, breaking through a wall, or the "emergency kiss." Maybe these moments are a way to grapple with global warming and global capitalism. (Time's up. Watch for the nefarious 1 percent. Reproduce while you have a chance.) These sounds and images may work like visual and aural koans, at the same time as they're linked to advances in post-production software.

With so much media, there may be an impulse to coordinate it all. At some intuitive level we seek audiovisual material that syncs up; we seek a pulse. Consider the fast, rhythmic cutting in the *Bourne Ultimatum*, the repeated chants in the YouTube clip "Badger," and the music video for Rihanna's "Birthday Cake": the last revels in the word "cake," iterating it 90 times. If we attain synchronicity, will it be apocalyptic? I take the countdown sirens and ticking pulse in these works seriously (see figure Intro.5).[9] But I'm also counting on Beyoncé's energy and ebullience to help get us through (see figure Intro. 6).

Where Did We Come From and Where Are We Going?

Each of these media trends and genres possessed its own arc as it unfolded over the decade of the 00s. Between 2000 to 2007, digital cinema appeared to be ascending—references to films like *Babel* (2006), *Bourne Ultimatum* (2007),

Eternal Sunshine of the Spotless Mind (2004), *Memento* (2000), and *Moulin Rouge!* (2001) were dropped into many conversations. Film form no longer seemed set—every film could be a one-off—and while intensified continuity was peaking, no end seemed in sight. But then something happened. My guess is that, with the global economic crash, people had had enough of frothiness and uncertainty.[10] More "grounded" films like *No Country for Old Men* (2007) and *Revolutionary Road* (2008) took up the cultural space. Later accelerated films like *Sherlock Holmes—Game of Shadows* (2011), though intensified, seemed not to call for a rejoinder. At the same time, a crossfade occurred. YouTube hits like "David after Dentist" (2008) and "Haha Baby" (2006) started to garner millions of views; this coincided with Google's purchase of YouTube and the posting of ads. But there were losses—a once joyous, communal, ham-radio DIY spirit shared by prosumers and viewers when the site was ad-free evaporated. Suddenly music video became a jewel on the top of YouTube's heap. Music video, recently drained of revenue by the music industry, and with no place to call home, suddenly busted out with videos like Beyoncé and Lady Gaga's "Telephone."[11]

But like cinema's post-classical turn and the sudden preeminence of YouTube, this "return" to music video was sparked by corporate support.[12] Several record companies had banded together to create the site Vevo. Directors could now incorporate products that generated revenue, like Polaroid and PlentyOfFish. Music video had become electric. We remain in the midst of this, and can't fully understand it. The swirl is both centrifugal and centripetal.

YouTube, music video, and the New Digital cinema have become intertwined in surprising ways. We may not be able to guess in what ways the media swirl will develop, but accelerating rates of interpenetration and intertextuality suggest increasingly blurred boundaries among platforms and genres. Here are a few examples of the cauldron from which makers and audiences will draw new forms.

YOUTUBE-IFICATION

All media—from post-classical cinema to music videos and commercials—start to resemble or refer to YouTube. YouTube's style (a do-it-yourself look or aesthetic) infiltrates everything. In the "Johnny Cash Project," fans across the world each contributed one hand-drawn frame to a preexisting music video, thereby creating a new kind of crowd-sourced work. (The YouTube *Star Wars* remakes function similarly.) Ridley Scott produces *A Day in the Life*, a feature film made up of YouTube contributions by global prosumers. Then *Babies* appears, a film sparked by the YouTube babies-and-cats-documentary gold rush.[13]

As I previously mentioned, I thought the post-classical drive would continue forever, but I think the style has been tempered by the global downturn. (It's hard to dream expansively when everyone's hunkering down underneath austerity measures.) But even if the convoluted storytelling has abated, the process of YouTube-ification continues. The film *Scott Pilgrim vs. the World* may best embody YouTube aesthetics circa 2011: there's a brief holographic segment in which Bollywood dancers appear, for example, and then there's a new segment with ninjas! Though there's been a return to "slow" cinema and traditional cinema, like *Never Let Me Go* and *The King's Speech*, these still reflected contemporary media obsessions. *The King's Speech*, for example, could be said to engage with YouTube. It's about broadcasting yourself, about overcoming your resistance to putting yourself out there for millions to view, flaws and all. The final speech takes place in a small room draped in blankets with a single mic. It's a dream substitution for the lonely bedroom of today—the home space of video bloggers.

Today's genres converse with one another, but YouTube often feels like the driver. Here's one example. An average prosumer posts the now famous, cheap, fairly amateurish music video "Friday," and it goes viral. Superstar Katy Perry crafts a remake called "Friday," and then print media amplify its reach by inviting the songwriter of "Friday" to speak on one of the most vaunted platforms, the *UK Guardian*. Television and print media are an echo chamber for YouTube (which is vast, free, and semitrackable).[14] YouTube features film trailers on the top of their homepage. These seem more exciting than anything to be experienced in the theater. YouTube takes you to music videos. Sometimes, however, viewers are unsure where they are in the media streams; where a phenomenon was initiated or where to find content. An example: No longer a network watcher and never a football fan, I found myself befuddled when Madonna performed for the 2012 Super Bowl. How do I catch the performance even after the event? (Out of the loop along with 858,000 others, I watched a clip uploaded by someone with a shaky handheld camera, with the lens slanted sideways at a flatscreen.) Google and the web's Tower of Babel may add to YouTube's mystery and allure. Where is *that* clip?

CONFUSIONS OF PLATFORM, FORMS, AND TECHNOLOGIES

A viewer can become confused about what platform and genre they're participating in. I've watched feature films broken up on YouTube as 15-minute segments. Fans skip the censors by using acronyms (instead of *Sweet Smell of*

Success we have "SSOS Part 1," "SSOS Part 2"). Often a whole reel goes missing. All sizes and lengths of clips are being created today. Jonas Åkerlund makes a 15-minute Duran Duran video, which feels like a quasi-documentary overlaid or merged with a music video.[15] Kanye West posts a half-hour hip-hop opera. Others post teaser clips of 10 seconds, each intended to work like trailers for music videos.

Also, almost every new technology designed for the big film screen has been adapted for the cell-phone screen and vice versa. Audiences not only want their media to interpenetrate, they want to share methods for making things, both with technologies and across platforms. I've watched "how to" YouTube clips with miniature blue-screen boxes, with which prosumers claim they can compete with large-scale blockbuster films' CGI. There's "how to make 3D-HD for YouTube clips with cellophane and paper glasses." Filmmakers on the other hand are making films with light, cheap, low-res cameras. Renowned director Park Chan-wook (*Old Boy*) recently directed a full-length feature for the iPhone entitled *Paranmanjang*. Media objects also often echo one another simply through their production tropes. When watching Romero's *Dawn of the Dead*, the image started skipping and stuttering. I couldn't tell if my DVD was skipping, or if the image was referring to the stutter I frequently encounter on YouTube. The film *Chronicle* intensifies this (its digital artifacts are more extreme), setting off a string of connections that take me across genre and platform. It doesn't seem so odd when music assimilates noise, decay, and other refuse (think of John Cage and Cologne Techno); but it seems stranger when images from mainstream media do so (thereby becoming hyper-self-reflexive).[16]

A matrix helps show the ways that exchanges among genres and platforms flow in all directions:

Music Video. Beyoncé's "Countdown" and Lady Gaga's "Telephone"—influenced by YouTube and cinema.

"Countdown" contains multiple frames and suggested temporalities; animation, dance, and the Hollywood musical; a mashup.

"Telephone" alludes to B-movies, Tarantino's *Kill Bill* and *Natural Born Killers*; a mashup.

Film. Scott Pilgrim vs. the World—influenced by music video and YouTube.

Musical numbers from Bollywood to anime.

YouTube. "Michael Bay so fast your eyeballs burn," "Scary Mary," and "Total Eclipse of the Heart: Literal Video Version" clips; influenced by film and music video.

Fan-based remixed clips of cinema, trailers, and music videos.

MIXING IT UP?

But perhaps the multiple streams of media can be assimilated. We have a finely honed ability to determine a clip's genres and origins, one that matches our skills at discerning differences among faces or types of food. (My model here is sheep. They can remember up to 50 individual sheep faces over two years. A sheep can pick out another from a crowd even if its head is turned upside down. For humans and sheep such skills may be biologically hardwired. Caryl Flinn has written about the ways the musical, when fragmented into individual numbers and streamed on YouTube, becomes pocket-sized, remade, and staged in different contexts, on the go and ready for use; her remixed and mashed-up *The Sound of Music* clips don't promise utopia, but give us enough to get through. I'd argue that we can still sniff out the orginary sources (or tribes) where these clips belong.[17]

A good question arises, however. Why would we recognize a clip from, say, Julie Taymor's musical *Across the Universe* (like the remake of the Beatles' "Strawberry Fields") once it had migrated onto YouTube as a musical and not as a music video? Similarly, Annette Davidson's close analyses of openings of television shows like *Dexter* and *The Sopranos* seem able to get at much of why these are openings and not trailers, though what makes them so still seems ineffable, especially when pulled out of context on YouTube. (Similarly James Deaville and Vivian Sobchack write beautifully about trailers, but they don't fully capture why they aren't openings. These too remain elusive.)[18] Clips that intentionally work as mixed genres may be particularly mysterious. A country singer makes a clip for a song called "United Destroys Guitars." We know it's a performance document, a music video, a YouTube viral joke video and a direct letter to the airline, audiovisually inspired, but meant as a surrogate for the "contact us" reply email. Think about how discerning we can be with the nuances of food and wine. Do we respond in the same ways to media?[19]

YOUTUBE'S AUTHORIAL DEEP POCKETS

YouTube provides a reservoir of materials for practitioners and viewers. One could imagine it playing a role like Wikipedia's. Someday consumers will be fully trained as curators and will assess links according to their educational merit, truth-value, historical accuracy, and so on. YouTube and community-based web research might become our cultural touchstone. One of the best-known examples of music video and deep online study concerns the music video "Single Ladies" by Beyoncé and Jake Nava. Surfing YouTube, Nava's assistant, Justin Purcer, stumbled across an old Bob Fosse dance routine from the *Ed Sullivan* show and screened it for Nava, who forwarded it to Beyoncé.

Nava and Beyoncé collaborated on a fast, cheap video as part of what's known in the industry as a "twofer": in this case a director receives a sum to direct two videos, with the permission to allocate the money where she chooses. The resources went to the video everyone really cared about, "If I Were a Boy"—a rich, densely structured video that consumed an elaborate, multiday location shoot. "Single Ladies," on the other hand, was produced as a single-day studio knockoff. But YouTube's viewers latched onto "Single Ladies" sonic earworm ("All the single ladies!") and dance routine, both of which were good for jazzercise workouts and performances in front of one's bedroom mirror. Much to the chagrin of the makers, "Single Ladies" rather than "If I Were a Boy" shot to the top of the viral charts.[20] Fans found the original Fosse clip and strings of later spinoffs.

A second example. *The King's Speech* focuses on Prince Albert's attempt to cure himself of stuttering as he was being elevated at the beginning of World War II. After watching the film I immediately went to YouTube to hear a recording by the real king (and sure enough actor Colin Firth did a good imitation). In the film, when his coach Lionel Logue (Geoffrey Rush) says, "You let the w's go," I think the makers knew they'd have to be accountable: this fact was one that fans could quickly confirm on YouTube. When Jonas Åkerlund made the video "Moves Like Jagger" for Maroon 5, he knew viewers would riffle through YouTube's databases to check. Hanson's video "Thinkin' about Something" and Soulja Boy's "Superman" have auxiliary YouTube videos to help teach the dance steps; viewers can quickly guess whether the moves have merit. Directors, too, turn to YouTube for authority. Many read the comments about their work and they may tailor their work accordingly. How could Michael Bay not resist a fan's dare to one-up him when the fan releases, "Michael Bay so fast your eyeballs burn," a mashup of Bay's work that goes faster than Bay ever has himself? These practices can make for a more engaged public.

CULTURAL CAPITAL AND REPUTATION

YouTube, films, and music videos can make stars or butts of jokes out of almost anyone or anything. A clip from Oliver Hirschbiegel's *Downfall* with Bruno Ganz playing the Führer screaming is remixed with new subtitles proclaiming his desire for his Nintendo or his Big Mac. The film becomes ludicrous. Prosumers gleaning from YouTube's archives find spoofs like a mock Werner Herzog reading "Where's Waldo" juxtaposed against the real Herzog rant about a depressed penguin. Kanye West gets drunk during the MTV awards and disparages Taylor Swift, but he makes a 30-minute hip-hop opera posted to YouTube and seems suddenly rehabilitated. Britney Spears too has a quickly undulating arc of infamy and fame. Pundits even predict her rise and fall as if she were a stock market. And I'm not just talking about *People* magazine here: her music videos and bloggers chip in too. Jonas Åkerlund's music video "Hold It Against Me," for example, even depicts her as an alien sent to earth via meteor (in other words, she's meteoric). Cultural capital quickly rises and falls.

COMPETITION AMONG GENRES

How do music video, YouTube, and the new cut-up cinema shape one another? One part may just be pure competition between media. Eyes skitter across variously sized screens; how to catch and hold them? Digital technologies and the web make many genres and forms available instantaneously. Competition is fierce. Would Beyoncé's "Countdown" be so hopped up—its music going way too fast, almost like Alvin and the Chipmunks on speed, the herky-jerky movements and everything taken over almost by a seizure—if Beyoncé and crew weren't trying to beat out everyone else? But the clip also has brief stretches of quiet. We too need to find such fleeting moments of repose in the onslaught of work speedup.

SEGMENTATION

Films like *Melancholia* and *Sherlock Holmes: A Game of Shadows* have beautiful isolated segments that internally suggest multitemporality. Parts of the image create stillness while others present extreme slow motion, real time, and the quick. *Melancholia*'s opening, and *Sherlock Holmes*'s scene with gunshots in the forest, have recent precursors, like the film *300*. The technology that made these scenes possible (the ultraslow 20,000 fps camera) has been assimilated quickly. But these films' multitemporality may also reflect a response to the speeds we're experiencing in work and leisure. The ways these segments jut out from these films, as islands, may tell us something about our need to bracket experience or our willingness to try things out. It's only today that we have become so comfortable with such a variety: give me a bit of this and a bit of that. This can be a one-off. And even within the segment, we may be willing to parse things into fractured elements.

DIGITAL SPEEDUP

YouTube and online media are a swirling vortex that draws makers and viewers. A student in my class screened a clip I found quite striking—something that had been making the rounds on the independent festival circuit, Arev Manoukian's "Nuit Blanche." I contacted Manoukian and secured an interview. He told me he and his friend had been working at an ad firm and dropped out for two years, as hungry twentysomethings, to make "Nuit Blanche." An enormous gamble and a painstaking labor of love, the small film reflected fine, obsessive detail. But what if the two years had come to naught? Luckily the clip had a terrific "meme" and throughline: a couple who brave all, even death, to find one another and share a kiss. When I interviewed Manoukian I commented that I was working on the Russian director Timur Bekmambetov. Manoukian enthusiastically replied that Bekmambetov had already contacted him and the two were considering producing a film. Another film company had also approached him, telling him if he could produce so much intimacy in three minutes, surely he could do a film. Sony, too, contracted Manoukian to make a nearly exact replica of "Nuit Blanche" as a color 3-D commercial. In the past, such fortune would be unheard-of for someone in their 20s with a three-minute first film. For Manoukian, Sony quickly put digital technologies and global connections at his service. Staff and the director held Skype auditions globally; the recordings were used as screen tests. Two actors were flown in for the job. Today, knowledge, influence, and work spread in lightning-fast and unpredictable ways. (I emailed the clip to a colleague who wryly noted, "Oh my students have already showed it to me." Yet many other colleagues have not seen the work.) The paths of dissemination of a director's work and those who come in contact with it are unpredictable.

Unruly Media's Organization

It's hard to determine how much weight to grant each form of media. Trying to cover all three definitively—YouTube (or video online), music video, and post-classical cinema—is a little absurd. It's a media sublime. As quickly as I write in one area, something else can shift. YouTube, for example, now wants to screen well-financed, long-form content, and Google, its corporate owner, might try to promote a new platform, though nearly all of the planet can't be asked to make the switch. Netflix has started to produce its own films, including David Fincher's *House of Cards*. When I finished my music video book in 2004, I never envisioned we'd be here.

I freely admit that this book leaves many flanks open. I don't discuss video-games and television, which have their own forms of churning and transfiguration, though these surely have directed my genres. Nor do I consider 3-D much. But an approach that looks at just these three genres, at the same time, may catch something different, as well as something of the time's zeitgeist. Part of my goal is to register the sensation of trying to respond to the media's impossible call to experience everything—it's all coming at us at the same time.

I hope the engagements I aim to describe here will also be appreciated by my readers.

This book primarily covers a time span from the coming of digital technologies in the early 90s until the present (2013).[21] I hope this book poses useful questions—ones these newly intensified, unruly media may be encouraging us to ask for the first time. At what speed does the media object seem to move and does this speed hold fast or shift? What is the object drawing from, and what might it contribute to in the future? What sorts of affect does it aim to elicit? Is it made by professionals or amateurs? Who is watching it and who aims to profit by it? How quickly will it be abandoned? What kinds of pleasures is this object providing, and how might I use it with different media? Has my way of watching this clip changed?

We might imagine *Unruly Media* as three short books. Digital cinema first, before YouTube and finally music video, because this reproduces the order in which they peaked in the public consciousness. That ordering also follows the money, as I'll make clear below. I begin with post-classical cinema, also, because it remains one of the most engaging and ornate of these media. Music video makes sense as an endpoint because it synthesizes the genres of post-classical film and online viral media.

Chapter 1 introduces post-classical cinema with a treatment of some of the ways it departs from classical Hollywood's. One post-classical mode relates to what David Bordwell has called "intensified continuity": stylistic markers come to the fore, including prowling cameras, wipe-bys, constant reframing, and rapid-fire editing.[22] Angela Ndalianis, on the other hand, identifies another stream as neo-baroque. These films emphasize seriality, polycentrism, spectacle, and a dependence on technology.[23] While much has been written on these new films' visual gambits, not enough has been written on their accompanying soundtracks, even though developments like 5.1 surround-sound have shaped their changes. I'll point to some local ways that music and sound help structure this new prismatic cinema. For example, these films can showcase a wide variety of musical styles, often mingling American pop music and classical Hollywood scoring with other musical practices at a far remove. These films can also include heightened sequences in which lighting, dialogue, gesture, music, and sound effects all work musically. I'll begin to describe the ways foregrounded audiovisual relations can deform a film's large-scale structure, and I'll exemplify these through films like *The Bourne Supremacy*, *Bringing Out the Dead*, and *Day Watch*. These recent films possess multiple strands and place the viewer "too close" to characters who do not fully comprehend their predicaments. In the songs and musical interludes, the music reflects the characters' psyches but also provides a bird's-eye view that works to provide large-scale form for highly kaleidoscopic material.

Have the techniques and technologies of the digital era so transformed cinema that they've changed the nature of viewers' experiences? Chapter 2 considers a variety of films to address this question. It looks at the ways several films (like *Summer of Sam, SLC Punk!, Run Lola Run, Se7en, Transformers, Death Proof, Kill Bill, (500) Days of Summer, Day Watch,* and several by Johnnie To) exploit new technologies such as previsualization, CGI, Avid editing, and Pro Tools; recent shifts in cinematic practices like acting, music composition, and lighting; changing forms of industry organization and production culture; varied modes of distribution and reception; and the many styles shared globally and across genres. This chapter pays special attention to the relations between image and sound. It makes the bold claim that musical structures can overlay or supercede narrative ones.

Chapter 3 provides the strongest claims for the ways music video has shaped today's intensified digital cinema and YouTube. There hasn't been much scholarly discussion of this question. But the influence has been profound—perhaps more than we realize. Framed as a counterargument to Marco Calavita's, the chapter charts a genealogy of influences from the eighties until today, taking into account music video, Hollywood musicals, Asian action films, and European art cinema.

Chapter 4 takes seriously *Moulin Rouge!*'s claim that "we could steal time, just for one day." A variety of techniques—the characters' moves to apotheosis; a viewer's phenomenological experience of whirligig dizziness; the camera's passage through ornate, prismatic spaces; the film's peaks and valleys that overshadow its plot points; medleys; and a densely interwoven sound and orchestral score—make this seem possible. I argue that *Moulin Rouge!,* with more than the eye and ear can take in, points to new forms of filmmaking.

What is the most emblematic post-classical film of all time? Off the record, David Bordwell has proposed *Eternal Sunshine of the Spotless Mind,* and I concur. Chapter 5 focuses on how this remarkable film establishes structure and projects a sense of musicality. In *Eternal Sunshine,* the story's lacunae are built up through a bewildering number of flashbacks as well as process-oriented and mood-based events, all which make a space for the soundtrack. Alongside these lacunae are carefully refined structures. These include connections between shots based on visual or aural associations, and short sequences that undergo repetition and intensification. At least 30 visual motifs—like the skeleton posada figures, lamps, and hair dye—crisscross the film, playing a variety of roles. These motifs and the lattices that hold them are structured to connect with the soundtrack in an intimate fashion. The film's soundtrack contains much music. But even when music is absent, the dialogue and environmental sounds are designed to work musically. In *Eternal Sunshine,* a latticework of sound-image relations help to create new kinds of characterization, affect, and story.

Bollywood musical sequences circulate widely but they have inspired very few analyses that consider dance, costume, and cinematography in relation to song. In chapter 6, I'll argue that the musical numbers in Ratnam's *Yuva* problematize what the film draws from North American music videos and traditional Hindi cinema—two traditions that are already hybridized. (Neepa Majumdar marks the mid-80s as the moment when music video started shaping Hindi cinema; several recent North American music videos reflect a Bollywood aesthetic, like Shakira's "Hips Don't Lie" and the Pussycat Dolls' "Jai Ho.")[24] Chapter 6 acknowledges the limits to these cross-cultural intersections and mutual influences in order to get at each practice's specificity. Musical sequences in Hindi cinema reveal genre markers that may not be compatible with North American videos, including rapid shifts among lush locations, lip-syncing, a sharply etched choreography, an iconography of textiles, a layering of figures in the frame, and characters who focus on each other rather than address the viewer. Many features of North American music video appear in Bollywood cinema, although music video's reliance on sexual display has not been fully adopted in Bollywood. Does *Yuva* produce aesthetic results not possible in North American music videos?

Part II focuses on YouTube, a genre so vast and uncharted, it seems impossible to claim comprehensiveness. The number of clips on YouTube stretches to the sublime—YouTube streams 1.2 billion videos a day. Among the most popular clips, a large proportion foreground rich audiovisual aesthetics: music videos are among the most viewed. Once we attend closely to others like "Haha Baby," "Kung Fu Baby," "Evolution of Dance," or "The Sneezing Baby Panda" we'll discover that they too possess sound and image relations worthy of close analysis.

Chapter 7 provides attentive readings of several popular YouTube videos with an eye toward how they demonstrate broader aesthetic practices of the medium and genre. New aesthetic features differing from those found in earlier genres on television or cable include (1) pulse and reiteration; (2) irreality and weightlessness (tied to low-resolution and the digital); (3) graphic values; (4) a sense of scale that matches the medium; (5) unusual causal relations; (6) intermediality and intertextuality; (7) sardonic humor and parody; (8) condensation; and (9) formal replication of the web. I've claimed that music video is strange and on YouTube it's getting stranger. Trolling the web, however, produces unusual experiences. As we come across clips set adrift between election news tidbits, exhortations about how to keep your mate sexually engaged, and the newest fad diets, or click among streams of text, snapshots, and other YouTube links, music videos and audiovisually rich clips can now become the anchor rather than the source of discontinuity.

Chapter 8, focusing on audiovisual viral web media distributed during the 2008 presidential campaign, registers a cultural shift in which political debate now happens online. The chapter analyzes clips like "Yes We Can" and the presidential debates on YouTube for the ways they work aesthetically and intertextually. A close analysis of will.i.am's music video "Yes We Can," for example, shows the ways this clip may have shifted the trajectory of Obama's campaign. I'll account for the video's persuasiveness by providing a close reading of parameters like harmony, lyrics, and gesture and underscoring the subtle audio and visual references to nation, religion, death, and rebirth. I'll also show the ways this video became incorporated into multiple venues including the DNC convention and claim it foreshadowed the McCain-Obama debates as screened on YouTube. Through split-screen, two speakers fused at the shoulders, flowing and sputtering graphics, and McCain's nervous blinking, these clips conveyed a music-videocentric experience. The 2008 presidential campaign was about sentiment and sense; campaigns will never again be waged the same way.

Chapter 9 provides a case study of a generic hybrid—Beyoncé and Lady Gaga's "Video Phone," a music video subsumed by YouTube aesthetics. How does the web's simultaneous multitude of windows and oscillating, jumpy advertising shape music video aesthetics? Within a webpage, music videos must compete with lurid, flashing pop-up ads and other scrolling devices. Does the song and image, in response, project further than it once did? Often enframed by advertising content, clips like "Video Phone" more than ever want to assert a libertory otherness (sings Katy Perry, "I kissed a girl and I liked it"). Chapter 8 asks whether the music video has now become the supertext. Music video's prolongations and instances of condensation, along with its alternating flurries, thickets and wide-open spaces, map onto larger experiential and technological structures.

Part III focuses on music video. Chapter 10 begins by posing the question of how different a Lady Gaga video is from one by A Flock of Seagulls. Music video has been through shifts in technologies, platforms, periods of intense cross-pollination with other media, booms and busts, and changing levels of audience engagement. In the 00s, music videos, however, hit a true nadir as budgets dried up, only to suddenly reemerge today as a key driver of popular culture. Music video is financially viable again as directors and musicians embed product placement in clips, and YouTube clips link directly to the industry-driven site Vevo. Music video's moment of resurgence resembles MTV's first moment: there seems to be a question of what music video can do and where it fits.

Chapter 10 considers what it means to look back on this 30-year history. A comparison of the beginnings and the present shows vast differences in performance style, formal conceits, editing, spatial depictions, and the showcasing of new technologies. The older definition—that a music video is a product of the record company in which images are put to a pop record in order to sell the song—no longer fully applies. A definition that better reflects today's clips might hold that music videos contain heightened sound-image relations we recognize as such. This characterization presents new problems, however. In response, chapter 10 expands current analytic methods to include relational models: What are the image and music asking of one another and what do they want of me? Videos by today's auteurist directors reflect a technical proficiency that suggests anything could be accomplished, often without difficulty. In the eighties, however, an attempt at an audiovisual connection left a trace of the performers' and director's effort (just as we can feel the work of an electric guitarist in heavy metal or a sax player in jazz). The work of the image to meet the music gave early videos a special charm, a charm perhaps never to be produced again. Today's videos, however, may also reflect a full flowering of the genre. Many directors have labored in the industry and weathered its transitions—their knowledge and experience informs today's music videos.

While film studies has long debated the meaning and value of auteur studies and has created a canon of its own, no similar corpus exists for music video. When describing music video directors, some approaches may be borrowed directly from film studies, for example, the concept of style—a director's trademark use of camera, settings, and actors, as well as his or her political bent or worldview. Some film approaches will need to be modified, however, such as the relation of the director to collaborators and obstructionists, as well as to finances, technology, and time constraints and to questions concerning commercialism and high art. Some approaches will need to be specially tailored to music video. How does the director understand and approach a song? How does he or she work within musical genres and musical histories, and music video genres and music video histories? How does the director deal with music video's particular requirements—its short form, lack of dialogue, and need to showcase the star?

Chapter 11 addresses these questions through an analysis by the work of two music video directors. Director Dave Meyers's work seems to succeed through semiotic overload, sometimes abrasively overturning viewers' expectations about sexuality, gender, and race. His video for Missy Elliott's "One Minute Man," for example, shows the rapper Ludacris rocking a woman in a giant cradle and catching her drippings in a pan. In "Bombs over Baghdad," Outkast frolics among some of the most stereotypical images of blackness—gospel singers in purple robes, blaxploitation's dancing heroines, even orangutans and chimpanzees. But perhaps Meyers's imagery in combination with these particular songs create new meaning. A closer look at sonic, visual, and textual codes in Meyers's oeuvre will give us a more richly nuanced understanding of his clips. Francis Lawrence's classical and restrained attention to a song's musical surface, on the other hand, and his concern with the history of visual representation within music video provides a good counterpoint to work by Meyers.

Music video aesthetics have seeped into other genres, and music video directors like Michel Gondry and Spike Jonze are altering the landscape of feature films. But there are no archives for music video, and music video's history remains uncharted. Considering the recent work of eight directors—Mark Romanek, Michel Gondry, Chris Cunningham, Spike Jonze, and Hype Williams—provides an opportunity to reassess the genre. Through a close look at these directors' work in chapter 12, I'll show that music video has become a viable site to develop style and technique, and to discover means for communicating musical experience. We see that music video directors have a hand in every phase of production: the making of storyboards, the casting of extras and the selection of props, the shooting, the editing, and many other processes normally considered purely mechanical in other genres. Directorial styles diverge because there are no film schools for making music videos or industry internship programs, nor is there something akin to musical culture, like rehearsing in garages or spinning records at parties.

Unruly Media's afterword makes the claim that contemporary digital media present forms of space, time, and rhythm we haven't seen before. These new forms bear some similarities to contemporary experiences like work speedup, multitasking, and just-in-time labor. I can only guess why this is happening and its causes and effects. A Frankfurt School perspective might note that forms of entertainment replicate labor so we can better toil under our oppressive conditions. McLuhan might claim that the digital has infiltrated entertainment, finance, and labor, and hence there's a homology between them. My intuition is that both perspectives grasp something. I wonder if becoming more aware of the patterns of space, time, and rhythm in media and in work speedup might help us to adapt to social change. We might even work to train our forms of attention so that we can handle the shocks of contemporary society with more grace, care, and awareness.

Seeking to disentangle today's media swirl, we might track the style of each reconfigured medium through its emergence and peak. Though post-classical, intensified cinema takes many forms, I focus on films like *Eternal Sunshine*, *Life Aquatic*, and *Moulin Rouge!*, which foreground stylistic markers like prowling cameras, wipe-bys, constant reframing, and rapid editing. I'm especially interested in audiovisual passages that deform conventional narratives (such that the film resembles an archipelago more than a story with a throughline). Watching these films we can seek as much to immerse ourselves in color, camera, sound, and spectacle as to follow character. Music video, on the other hand, has changed as digital editing, new modes of sound-compression and -recording, and post-production tools like digital intermediary (a means to control each pixel's color as it shifts in time) make possible a hyper-control of sound-image relations.[25] With the relaxation of censorship and the end of strictures against product placement, along with platforms like the lucrative site Vevo, novel forms of narrative have emerged. More broadly music videos no longer have to fit the short lengths of pop songs, or present them without interruption, or attempt to "sell" or even showcase them: we may be able to say only that a music video is a relation of sound and image we recognize as such. By contrast the YouTube clips that resemble music videos, most often low-res and short, vie with millions of other clips, the body of the webpage, and other computer screens. The most popular YouTube clips share a collection of features: strange causal relations (wherein the viewer imagines a potential control over the frame), a strong sense of pulse, reiterative forms, anthropomorphism, stratified bands of information, and a sharp iconography and graphism for *both* sound and image.

How do these intensified aesthetics map onto our social structures? Here are a few conjectures, most somber, a few hopeful. Mark Augé argues that in today's society we move from non-place to non-place (the mall, the school, the prison, the home, the warehouse); we might say similarly that we pass through affective experiences as we traverse across jobs and relationships.[26] Even when we remain in one relationship or work situation, we may feel at some level we should be readying for the next opening. The variety of media we move across and through gives us a chance to practice this transitory mode of experience. (As Adorno argued, art and entertainment tend to be structured in ways that train us to perform labor and various social responsibilities.[27]) The most successful media seem complex in new ways: they forestall closure but remain open, encouraging us to move from one media object to the next. Here again, music provides a sense of continuity, almost a guardrail, as we cross genres.

Today's media elicit affects different from those of the past, and practicing these responses helps us negotiate our present moment. Sianne Ngai argues that our aesthetic categories, today, are smaller and more mixed than nineteenth century categories like the beautiful, sublime, and the picturesque. Most prevalent are the cute, interesting, and zany. These new aesthetic categories map onto commodity culture, the endless circulation of information, our failures to succeed at work speedup, and overproduction.[28] We can locate these affective modes, as they come forward and recede, mingle and recombine, across the genres of YouTube, music video, and film. Angela Ndalianias argues that we're in a neo-baroque mannerist era. Today's producers, both professional and amateur, find themselves in social relations similar to those of artisan laborers in the fourteenth century who suddenly discovered

themselves cut off from patronage and labor and craft organizations. A surface style and hyper self-referentiality help artisans sustain themselves on
craft alone.[29] Lauren Berlant argues that many citizens today fall outside of
the desired norm, and simply tread water, without a place to rest. The pressure to perform different identities at work, which requires an instrumental
approach, and in the home, where one must receive some acknowledgment
for being moral, creates a more schismed subject. How do we create a sense
of self when so much seems contingent?[30] We may no longer craft our lives as
artworks, as Alexander Nehamas claims we might.[31] Perhaps the shifting
surfaces and shimmering stories in contemporary media match the ways we
configure our own lives. Just as we can no longer create stable narratives for
our own life stories, today's media shimmer among multiple patterns.

Today's media comprise many intertextual associations. They also tend to
be built up through vast databases of material. Many of us too experience ourselves as extended out to Facebook, videogames, and the web. And the fast-
switching mobile attention our work receives, gets to be played out again in
leisure as we move across the media.

Most of this sounds pressured and a little grim, but my students seem
hopeful. They think the new media landscape, with so much material in
reserve, allows a person to think more creatively. New relations are constructed. Most charming to me are the grandparents and great grandparents
who have shared with me music videos and other clips their grandchildren
and great grandchildren have made. (Some shared clips skip generations,
passing over parents.) As Bordwell has pointed out, a stylistic norm within a
particular era makes some things possible and others not.[32] I find today's possibilities exciting.

How have music video, YouTube, and the new digital cinema shaped one
another? What will their interactions look like and sound like as the mediascape
around them continues to change? I've provided several examples, but let me
give one more that may work on a different register. In a 2012 conversation
with J. D. Conners about his work, I found myself thinking again about how
film moments are also tied to the audiovisual. J.D. Connors has argued that
many recent films grapple with questions concerning storage and retrieval of
information and digital rights. He notes these concerns are often visually figured as libraries (containing standing reserves of occult knowledge).[33] But he
doesn't point out that many of these film moments foreground the *soundtrack*.
Wall-E wants to catalog and preserve a song number from *Hello Dolly*. Hulk (in
Hulk) wants to keep a little homunculus of himself (his own little prosumer
YouTube clip?). *Indiana Jones and the Kingdom of the Crystal Skull* bewitched
metal dust (from oxidized tapes?) tracks through the warehouse in search of
the alien carcass; the soundtrack also drives to locate *Indiana Jones's* original

theme music, switching rapidly and abruptly through a sonic biblioteca ranging from Brahms, Strauss, Wagner, Bruckner, Berg, and snippets of *The Wizard of Oz* to *Star Wars*. These instances reflect a desire to hold on to the musical numbers in classical and post-classical film, audiovisually rich You-Tube clips, and yes, I'd say, music videos. The films themselves want to preserve and understand the archive. We too are drawn to a similar impulse: the audiovisual swirl both constitutes the unruliness of our present mediascape and gives us a way to understand it.

NEW DIGITAL CINEMA

CHAPTER 1

The New Cut-Up Cinema

Are we at the crest of a global wave, in which all film parameters are heightened, reconfigured, and accelerated? Examples of what I'm calling "intensified audiovisual aesthetics" include American films like *The Bourne Ultimatum, Bringing Out the Dead, Eternal Sunshine of the Spotless Mind,* and *Moulin Rouge;* globally we could point to *Breaking News, Day Watch* and *Night Watch, Hot Fuzz,* and *Yuva.* Debates among film theorists center on whether these sped-up, fragmented, "post-classical" films break with the past or revamp older practices. In the historical-continuity-with-a-twist camp, David Bordwell argues that classic narrative structures remain in place with minor variants like "puzzle" films. Camerawork and editing, such as bipolar extremes of lens-lengths, a reliance on close shots, wide-ranging camera movements, and rapid editing, define this new "surface" style. In the other camp, Eleftheria Thanouli claims that broader shifts have taken place: today's plots slacken as characters pursue diverse goals, and stories divide into intertwined subplots. These multigeneric films also adopt a self-conscious stance, and realism becomes hypermediated through intensified continuity, visual layers, and windowed worlds onto subjective experience. I place myself with those who locate a departure with the past: as narrative shapes have become more complicated, bulletholed, and deformed, our relationship to cinema has changed. A cluster of techniques have provoked a new way of experiencing film. I'll also ask what is lost when these theorists focus almost entirely on the *visual.* I argue that new sound/image relations—a phenomenon I call "the audiovisual turn," and that I like to identify as "the soundtrack and its image"—defines today's style.

Since Bordwell and Thanouli first argued about post-classical cinema, others have added to the discussion.[1] My contribution begins by noting that the post-classical style is rooted in sentiment: it stems from viewers' responses. From 2000 to 2007 there was a sense that the cinema's horizons were wide open. Any film might be a surprise. We might say post-classical films were intended to make you say, "Oh! Really?" while feeling savvy or sophisticated. This style included films that demonstrated Bordwell's "intensified continuity,"

puzzle plots, or a preponderance of audiovisual sequences.[2] Other visual techniques seemed to play a role as well, such as an overpreening of the image (à la
Wes Anderson, enabled by digital intermediary), the extensive use of CGI
(often inspired by comic books, as in *300* and *Watchmen*), and possibly 3D and
HD (high-definition). Perhaps these developments were not so closely related,
but at the time it felt like they were. Enabled by digital technologies, their surprise factor—often created through mannerist showboating and strings of affectively rich audiovisual sequences—separated them from seamless classical
Hollywood films. They seemed to share a structure of feeling.

From 2012 to 2013, the post-classical sentiment seems to have abated for
several reasons, including the economic downturn, the closing of several independent studios, the waning of an influx of new global film practices, and traditional Hollywood's assimilation of these "post-classical" techniques.[3] A new
strand has returned to a hyperclassicism (*Never Let Me Go*, *The Lives of Others*,
Winter's Bone). If we look carefully, however, we'll see that many post-classical
features remain prominent. Terrence Malick's *Tree of Life* and Lars Von Trier's
Melancholia, for example, contain unusual formal structures. *Inception* seems
like a culmination of the puzzle plot. Films with intensified continuity, like
Melancholia and *Sherlock Holmes: A Game of Shadows*, exhibit new ways of
articulating multitemporal passages. Perhaps post-classicism's strikingness
has lessened, but this style may be only momentarily submerged, soon to reassert itself. My contribution to the debate will highlight how strongly *audiovisual* these new shared styles are, and how thoroughly cinematic parameters
(from acting to set design) and formal structures have changed. I'll argue that
music video was the true precursor to these shifts.[4] These films can abandon or
hide the traditional 5 act narrative while incorporating musical structures.

Many theorists have tried to account for these stylistic shifts. David Bordwell, more than any other, has written on the topic, and he notes a wide variety of influences are important, most particularly new technologies like Avid
editing, the television's need to refresh, and expensive shoots on remote locations. Lev Manovich's account is similarly a technological one, pointing out
that computer technologies allow a shift from traditional narratives to database ones. My contribution is to say that music video is one of the most important influences. Why would I claim such a "popular art" could have contributed
so much? Since the early nineties critics have been complaining that films look
like music videos. Again, except for some grousing over film's perceived role as
a way to increase pop music sales, descriptions tend toward the visual—a new
"glance" aesthetic instead of a "deep gaze," a frenetic style of editing. Though a
focus on the visual reinscribes a failure to account for audiovisual relations,
I think these critics' intuitions were actually right. Music video style has colo-
nized contemporary cinema much more than we know, but in ways critics

haven't been able to identify. Music videos often showcase a mixing-board aesthetic, fluid, flexible forms in which individual parameters—a gesture, lyric, melodic hook, rhythm, edit, costuming touch, or prop—will come to the fore and fade away within a network of interlaced connections. It's the way that musical materials are worked with on the mixing board. Film, though bound by narrative traditions and more pressing economic imperatives, has an even greater chance to realize this multivalent ideal.

Why does a music-video-like aesthetic appear in contemporary media now? There are several reasons. Though the Internet makes gauging music video's current influence difficult, we should not forget that videos once seemed central to the culture. They were subject to frequent viewing and topics of conversation, and their effects only now are coming to fruition. Many of the preeminent filmmakers today, like Paul Thomas Anderson, Michael Bay, Timur Bekmambetov, David Fincher, Michel Gondry, Spike Jonze, Francis Lawrence, Spike Lee, and Martin Scorsese, directed and watched music videos.

Music video's production practices are similarly central. Since the early 80s music video directors most often film tons of footage within high shooting-to-editing ratios; use an array of dolly, handheld, crane, tracking, and off-angle camera techniques; drag the most gripping images onto the timeline; edit playfully and freely; cut and remix the soundtrack; and then re-colortime, calibrate, and generally fine-tune the image to the soundtrack, all at a breakneck pace to follow the song's path up the pop charts.

Economics, production practices, and technological developments are critical. But the *aesthetics* of music video is equally important. First on video, then on film, and now digitally, music video directors produce vast amounts of imagery within a hothouse environment densely saturated with experimentation. It's an industry truism that there's no right image for a pop song: the receptive soundtrack allows for a wide variety of audiovisual realizations. Let's make a video with those Quantel boxes, take out all of the color except for isolated spots of red, turn the footage upside down and place bold print against it, or move everything around except for the performer. The language of music video is a template for recent intensified continuity.

Of course, for post-classical cinema and music video, this ideal becomes possible through shared technologies. These often appear in music video before they break into film, as in the case of new devices that enable fluid camera movements: David Fincher's burrowing snorkel camera appeared in his Steve Winwood video "Roll With It" before his film *Fight Club*. The shared technologies most crucial today are Avid editing, where, as J. P. Geuens poignantly puts it, "images are but colorful rectangles sharing a flat space"; ProTools and Logic with their 240 tracks and zoom functions to modify the millisecond; and digital intermediary, which allows visual areas to be clustered in groups and connections to be made both motivically across time and instantaneously with the soundtrack. Similarly, 5.1 surround sound and better compression algorithms, as Mark Kerins points out, place sound materials as points in space, or seamlessly meld them into immersive environments.[5]

All of Bordwell's intensified techniques have long been foregrounded in music video, because they illuminate musical form: free-ranging camera movements like dollying, hand-held, reframing, and crane shots reflect music's flowing, processual nature. Blocks of image highlight song structure; intense colorization illuminates features like a song's harmony, sectional divisions, and timbre; and visual motifs speak to musical ones. Editing and editing-like effects such as strobing, flash frames, and superimpositions not only show off the song's rhythmic strata, and form aesthetic sequences on their own, but also function as a switch among elements like narrative, dance, lyrics, or a musical hook, letting none take the upper hand. Contemporary heightened media look and function somewhat similarly.

Of course we should place music video's influence in relation to other media developments, like the television remote, DVD extras, the TV's need to refresh the image, multiplexes, filming stars on location in the 80s with lots of cameras, independents and blockbusters, "belatedness," aggressive corporate profit-seeking through music and film rights, Hong Kong cinema (though 80s Kung Fu is frenetic and noisy, it's shot wide, and aurally stiff), New Wave and experimental (though Jean-Luc Godard and Orson Welles employed isolated effects; how much do you think directors have watched experimental filmmakers like Godard over music video?). Most importantly, this new aesthetic is music video's ideal.

Encompassing all parameters, music video's and heightened audiovisual's aesthetics are hard to encapsulate quickly. As mentioned, elements can fragment and interact moment by moment in a voluble fashion. An ideal is to traverse media from image to music to sound effect to voice and back, creating a moving line or trajectory. In music video we're continually taken out of and back into the music, resuturing ourselves to the soundtrack, which produces a moment-to-moment mode of attention. Our experiences of the body, self, time, and narration then shift. Music video is a *musical* genre. Videos can seem to imitate sonic properties like ebb, flow, and indeterminacy of boundaries. One can claim that popular music and music videos support modular forms and cell-like, motivic construction. They can be said to be more abstract, context-dependent, episodic, and less narratively driven than comparable popular written and visual genres.[6] Transferable to cinema, music video's stylistics can include unusual representations of time, space, and causality; an emphasis on texture, color, and mood; and a highlighting of ephemerality, process, and condensation.

Paul Greengrass's *Bourne Ultimatum* shows off this fluid and flexible use of materials, all of which, rendered digitally, become what Lev Manovich considers to be exchangeable data.[7] For *Bourne*, cinematographers were encouraged to shoot out of focus and to keep in mind that images could be reframed in post. Color timers worked simultaneously with footage and large swatches of empty black. The DI technicians posted in effects like eye lights, trumping the DP's work, and timers again mixed up that steely grey and milky blue color palate with splashes of red. Vast sound-effects libraries, by-the-yard, out-of-the-sequencer-boxes, easily recomposed music, and extensive dialogue loops all contribute to a wide, voluble mix.

Let me provide a few examples from the film. In *Bourne*'s opening, Jason, passing through an infirmary, knocks over some glass vials, with a sound so piercing it claims the status of a sound bridge. (In our new genre, film functions often shift.) On the cut the sound lingers as the images cross into another space and suddenly the camera framing cants (as if it were a music video— sound and music here in tandem with the limping body seem to exert forces on the image, and cause-effect relations become aural). Soon the frame's edge adopts a milky white overlay, as the wire mesh surrounding Bourne dissolves and memories flood in. In these moment-by-moment painterly elaborations we're pushed away from the narrative; *that* remains in the distance, the music and sound is what's close at hand. Listen to the sound design in this later clip: Bourne, knocked out after a bomb explosion in Tangiers, returns to consciousness. Within this passage, environmental sounds like dangling keys and police sirens act as stand-ins for the riq (a small tambourine) and ney (a wood flute). The entrances of traditional instruments, brought in underneath these concrete sounds, create a musical soundscape. When Bourne jumps on his motorcycle, the three pink posted-in flash frames recall the riq's rhythm, and rhyme with a series of camera wipes, making color, light, movement, sound, and music "musical" and Bourne heroic for negotiating a real and a musical world. The police sirens help shift the rhythm away from its 4/4 meter toward groupings of three: (tap the soundtrack's fast eighth notes and then [over that rhythm] sing "1 2 3, 1 2 3, 1 2 3, 1 2 3," alternating between the high and low pitches of the siren). This new rhythmic pattern carries through the section.

Another example: as Bourne runs through the city of Tangiers in pursuit of an assassin, the reiterative electronic dance music, along with the cinematographer's running/trawling in and after our protagonist's wake, keep us in the moment. *Bourne*'s average shot length of 2 seconds nests within the music's tempo of roughly 120 beats per minute (one shot per measure). The characters' sharply etched movements, the camera's rapid change of focus among them, and the jagged editing can bring forward musical materials—a beat, a beginning of a musical hook. The electronic dance music's constant pulse means any beat, and any offbeat as well, can be brought to the fore. Here, the meter is changing, and the pulse is *jointly* constructed by image and music. Listen also to how the low growl and then chorus of male voices might sound to Western listeners like a heavy metal music video.

Do I care if Bourne meets Big Daddy Programmer, or Godzilla? No. The narrative pay-off is only a placeholder, a marker I know will be coming. I've already learned a way of waiting, a mode of inhibition, from music video. In this genre we never know whether or not we'll even *get* a narrative. Maybe instead there'll be a big dance sequence or an explosive flurry of color. To be true to the film, we must attend consistently to a changing visual surface, which links itself moment by moment to the volubly reemerging musical materials. We stay in a narrow, bounded space of now.

The *Bourne* examples make clear that in intensified audiovisual aesthetics all parameters can become heightened, not just editing or narrative. The prismatic, in-flux mix is music video's legacy.

Lighting: In Johnnie To's *Election*, faces are placed in shadow; in Edgar Wright's *Hot Fuzz*, faces are revealed in stark, half-white/half-shadow; and in Michel Gondry's *Eternal Sunshine*, blurred faces obscure and complicate the image, thereby intensifying it and inciting new places to cut.

Gesture and Performance: Pantomimic, dance-like movements or deadpan expressions playing against rapid bi-focal lens shifts and editing, as well as one-liner zingers like "I snore?" are featured in Timur Bekmambetov's *Day Watch*. Or lines of dialogue like "This isn't some story you read in a newspaper, this is real!" in *Bourne* "pop" through the texture.

Sets and costumes: Those dangling cotton balls or glinting CDs alongside flamboyant oddball clothing in *Day Watch* speak to the soundtrack's layered textures. A yam or a photograph in To's *Breaking News* may seem both free-floating and at home, yet also carry more narrative weight than a key in *Notorious*.

Color: Splotches of red or a lone touch of yellow lead us through the bluish grays, encouraging the viewer to seek out and skip across images in To's *Breaking News* or Greengrass's *Bourne Ultimatum*.

Graphic typography: Freely placed anywhere on the screen, displaces the traditionally subdued subtitles; these vie for attention in *Day Watch*, dissolving and melting.

Sound: Whooshes, never instantaneously clear whether it's only about the camera movement, a noise in the environment, a character's subjective feeling, or a heightened effect designed to bind us to the music and disambiguate the soundtrack's role. As in music video, systems start signifying simultaneously. Near the opening of *Day Watch*, in the street fair scene, a child vampire telepathically sucks blood through a straw and a small box of orange juice. In this scene props, sound, movement, and framing, as well as slash-like neon lights, work to create heightened audiovisual relations. Much like in music video, the length of this segment and what roles its elements play remain unstable.

Post-classical can be more than just a surface style. I depart from Bordwell's claims when I argue that audiovisual intensified aesthetics create rifts in the form that permeate all the way to deep structure. Here are some examples.

More sequence than scene. As Bordwell claims, film scenes change as characters pass through doors.[8] No longer. Contemporary intensified films can be more experientially defined by their movement among different swatches of music, just as a music video does among verse, chorus, and bridge. In To's *Breaking News* or Greengrass's *Bourne Ultimatum,* heroes and villains traverse up, down, through, and across stairs, tall storied office and apartment buildings, streets, bridges, and/or subways, while the most fragmentary narrative information is relayed via cell phone; it's the music that defines an intensification, a shift of pace.

An effect of these films is that, like music video, they resist memory. (I dare anyone to recount a generic music video's shot sequence.) *Bourne's* traversals of blue/green stairwells and buildings, and the exchangeable panoramic overheads of the country's cityscapes, blur in our memories, obscuring the film's form. Does that color palate switch to pink in Tangiers? Isolated, momentary exchanges, such as "Pam, you look tired. Get some rest," swim up, but at a distance. They form tiny points in a momentarily performer-based archipelago set off by the more consistently rushing images.

Let's look at the large scale. Soundtracks today can showcase a wide variety of music, ranging from the jarringly disruptive to seamless, classic Hollywood film scoring. Sometimes an early music cue will jut out of the structure so that viewers are obliged to remain on soundtrack alert for the film's duration. In *Eternal Sunshine* the stop-starting of the nursery-room music that accompanies the lovers' first meeting on a train commands as much attention as the imagery. In *Day Watch,* the *Peter and the Wolf* light-ballet music against a coven of vampires eating flesh in a restaurant kitchen claims attention. Such shifts in role, such that the soundtrack takes preeminence, changes the status of the actor, often into someone who is more allegorical or inscrutable. Characters and camera begin to engage in what might be called a "paradance." In Martin Scorsese's *Bringing Out the Dead,* for example, Nicholas Cage no longer resembles a paramedic but rather The Clash's Joe Strummer.

In these new films, the musical ecosystem starts exerting its own weight and the film takes on music video's attributes.[9] These contemporary films feature an array of music, each often different from one another, creating an archipelago-like effect. In Scorsese's *Bringing Out the Dead,* punk, Aretha Franklin, merengue, Frank Sinatra, 80s Irish alternative pop music, 50s American Modernism, Doo Wop, Bernard Herrmann updated and sedated, Stravinsky,

Janis Joplin, the Rolling Stones and more play semidiagetically alongside ambulances and work and living room interiors. This sound world, even if it were to be purely diagetic, with its allusions to so many places, spaces, temporalities, and histories threaten to fracture the picture. An example: Frank, Nicholas Cage, enters a drug dealer's lair to clean up a bad shootout; blood red soaks the red carpets as the UB40 song "Red Wine" plays nondiagetically. Nothing could cue us into a druggy vibe more quickly than this pop song; but in a second Frank's outdoors, rescuing the dealer who's impaled on the high-storied porch ledge's ironwork. Fireworks, Gershwin's "Rhapsody in Blue," and proclamations of "I love this city!" ring out. The moments, even though they occur within a few minutes, seem dramatically separated in time. They're disjunct from one another. They seem to elicit E. Ann Kaplan's observation about music video's odd form. In her analysis of Madonna's "Papa Don't Preach," she notes that "whore/teenager" and "star performer" appear intermittently, personas having little to do with one another, yet existing simultaneously, each with its own truth value, neither annihilating the other nor offering a way to square the differences. Characters and music also in *Bringing Out the Dead* are unpredictable and act against type. The close of *Bringing Out the Dead* resembles Michael Jackson's "Thriller." Just like Michael Jackson's, we imagine Cage's serpent eyes malevolently widening, even as Cage cradles his paramour within a Pieta tableau.[10]

Similarly to *Bringing Out the Dead*, in *Life Aquatic with Steve Zissou* we pass through many musical excerpts: an eclectic group of pop songs from the 60s until today including New Order, The Zombies, Devo, and Sigur Rós; "Here's to You" by Ennio Morricone featuring Joan Baez; Pac-Man like music with low-bit-rate pop; Brazilian singer Seu Jorge performing David Bowie songs; Mark Mothersbaugh's "Scrapping and Yelling" played backward; theme music from the 1970s Australian TV documentary series *Inner Space*; and Bach. We also move through many visual settings including a diorama, documentary, heist, fancy ball, slapstick, animal nature film, the sea adventure, and animation. This unpredictable flow makes characters unfathomable. We must follow along for the ride, enjoying how a character moves against a changing landscape. The analysis of *Eternal Sunshine of the Spotless Mind* (see chapter 4) explores how these new cinematic structures reflect late-modern identity.

Music video aesthetics is only just taking shape globally, so it's hard to envision all its potential iterations, but some new stylistic features have emerged. Sound-image relations in Bekmambetov's *Day Watch*, a Russian CGI blockbuster, is a casebook of how to extend every one of Chion's music-image principles, and for the soundtrack to poeticize the image and vie for the film's center. The film's audiovisual-centrality creates a music video effect—images and sounds repeat, mirror, and echo one another to rhythmic effect. *Day Watch* may achieve its effects, in part, by drawing on the same techniques as the surrealist film *Un Chien Andalou*, with its imagery of a castrated eye and confusion about gender, thereby piercing directly into the viewer's unconscious. The image fragments into cell-like materials amenable to musical relations—birds, glyphs, eyes, breasts. Sounds reiterate the wind, the strum of a guitar. Passages through walls offer sound a past and future and markers to build aural palindromes.

The film possesses large-scale visual and aural pathways that cross between visual and aural. In the film's fifteen-minute opening we are pitched forth into space, flung forward on horses, tumbling, passing through a thicket of images and cuts, suspended, floating, the hands away from the body, the body partial in space. Within this cognitively and sensorially overloaded scape, sound chases and leads visual events, often rhyming with images, suggesting an inside and outside, a slowed-down and sped-up time, a past and future, and then suddenly we've found a switch-point, a new track, where a varied, richly articulated aural thread carries us from one place to another. The final high-pitched ear-ringing forms the section's apex. We discover, to our shock, that we've been chasing neither a character, nor an object, but a pitch.

I claim that these new films present a different sort of experience. Like music videos they express a human physicality that can unfold and expand in discovery, alongside the camera's and the music's trajectory. Camera, sound, and even CGI can each have their own ways of knowing the world, so we might call this new style pantheistic, or multi-perspectival-techno-embodied. Even if classical structures remain in place, it's not clear they do much more than mark an absence. When humanism surfaces, it can come in intense, isolated instances—a personal moment for each viewer—often bound up in some sort of music-image cryptogram.

In the next chapter, I'll discuss how post-classical films can adopt structures that depart completely from classic Hollywood films, at all levels of form— surface, middle-ground and deep-structure. In this way they may be able to hold on to the traditional five-act structure, but within that all formal con-straints become changed, and they approach a condition of music. For now, we might wish to decry this new "glance aesthetics," which destroys the Bazinian "world of looking." But this aesthetic also makes the image, sound, and form more fluid. Often, this new visual style, based on dislocation, free-association, flux, color, and texture, leaves us with a sense of sometimes being grounded in, sometimes hovering over our bodies. The new audiovisually intensified cinema may yet help us learn something about ourselves.

CHAPTER 2

The Audiovisual Turn and Post-Classical Cinema

I imagine a film that feels like a string of music videos and trailers. While watching it, I unexpectedly come across a sublime passage. I don't care about the past or the future. I'm happy being lost—as if I'd been running a maze and suddenly climb over a dead-end curlicue. How close are we to such a film? Perhaps not very. Film requires money and a substantial audience base, so most producers wouldn't depart from Hollywood norms so dramatically. But if I were to point to some provocative moments and techniques from post-classical films, perhaps viewers and makers will make this happen. Here's a thought-experiment in the service of this post-classical ideal.

I'd like to make a sharp turn here. I don't know about you but I multitask a great deal. I don't believe the literature that it's dangerous.[1] I'll happily work on something, put it down, do something else, and then come back to it. What if we let this multitasking serve as a mode of analysis? This chapter contains ten segments from films that might drive a new approach to post-classical cinema. Each segment below describes a particular technique, but I leave it to the reader to assemble these as she reads. (My hope is that by the end she will have built her own structure.) I then offer a recap. I attempt to characterize this style more broadly in the chapter's conclusion.

Post-classical film possesses a range of features, including disorienting storytelling devices like puzzle plots; forking-path, draft, and database narratives; a dazzling surface made up of shots with changing lens-lengths, wipe-bys, and handheld camera movements; and—what I hope to add to the description—audiovisual passages, musical numbers, and striking audiovisual effects, all of which can further distort classical Hollywood narrative filmmaking.

Getting Totally Lost—the Film Steps out of Itself for a Moment—Spike Lee's Summer of Sam *and James Merendino's* SLC Punk!

Summer of Sam records a serial killer's spree in New York in the hot summer of 1977. In the scene I admire, mobsters and cops meet at a diner to plot the capture of the rampaging murderer. (The film's conceit resembles Fritz Lang's *M*, but this time with the police and underworld joining forces.) To convince the head mobster of the need for a unified front, the cop begins reading aloud from one of Sam's letters detailing how Sam can't stop himself. As this narration unfolds, the film switches from the printed word to Sam's world, showing his bloody deeds and hapless victims. Sam's signoff is read and the men return to their linguine, then suddenly there's a cut to a close-up of the mouth of Sam's gun-barrel, with loaded bullets whirring at us. This moment is completely unannounced. It's as if Sam's dark psyche has suddenly seeped through subterranean conduits into wherever it chose. Either that or the editor felt frisky. We don't know. The film has other odd moments but none so strange as this. Perhaps these other moments provide a texture that makes this one rupture possible. For example, Sam sits in his abject rented hotel room and suddenly his huge, black, cow-sized dog starts talking to him; we see the pet's mouth move and hear a stentorian male voice speaking in English. *Summer of Sam* never returns to such stylish moments— unexplained punctures in the film's texture. These are one- or two-offs, like many contemporary films contain.

Besides these singular events, other more naturalized techniques contribute to the film's lumpy surface. For example, *SOS* has set-off music and music-video-like performance segments that jut out, such as those by the young Aaron Brophy, deliriously banging out The Who's "Baba O'Riley" on his electric guitar in his garage, accompanied by the camera's sudden colored-up surfaces that blur into fuzzy kaleidoscopic patterns. There's also a dreamy orgy sequence at Plato's Cave accompanied by disco. Though they fall within the film's vocabulary (a shift to music-driven activity, slightly encouraged by the diegesis), these moments overshadow almost everything else in the film, including the mayhem the murderer unleashes. Also appearing are a few peaks of fine, over-the-top theatrical acting: for example, a couple's quarrel in a cemetery under Sam's watchful eye; a raucous, drug-frenzied argument in an apartment by the same couple; and some nice chatter among men sparring on a dock. *Summer of Sam*'s oddness stems from the fact that it seems like it should foreground a long hunt for the killer, like David Fincher's *Zodiac* or Fritz Lang's *M*. By the film's close, however, details fall away and all that remains is a handful of sharply etched moments, an archipelago of unconnected events.

SLC Punk provides another case of inset narratives taking over a film—where time, space, and flow become out of joint. A low-budget independent featuring two punk-identified friends who take drugs and perform anarchic acts in the Mormon part of Salt Lake City, this film is a sort of *Trainspotting* American style. Like *Summer of Sam*, it contains striking scenes in which the inset narrative or musical moment breaks from the film and creates its own sense of time, so much so that when we're returned to the primary narrative we're completely disoriented. We're jostled around for a good few seconds while we try to acclimate; the characters too. In one such scene in *SLC Punk*, one male character lies on a cement abutment on the grass while another towers over him. The stoned friend above starts narrating a story with some inscrutable allusions to Napoleon and Waterloo. Suddenly we find ourselves in his memory—a drug deal: all the boys hover around the school quad. Perhaps because this is a quasi-reconstructed event they are dressed oddly, a little too stylized, with a mix of Asian action-adventure, British punk, and jaunty worker. A boy buys some tabs of acid and heads off with his bounty. A policeman charges after him. As the boy sprints across a lawn with rows of streaming sprinklers, the tabs begin to dissolve. The music changes to a Rolling Stones song, his running shifts into a dreamy slow-mo, and all of a sudden we're in a musical set-piece. The camera pierces through the boy's pants to document a moving diorama of ruddy-red plastic muscles and white bone (like you might see in a fifties high-school science class), the muscles absorbing the green LSD. Cut to this same boy now perched on top of a snow bank in front of his home. He talks to his friend, but clearly his brain is so dismantled he thinks he's Jesus—he's spewing pretty spacey dialogue. This moment seems as dreamy as a Fellini sequence—like the moment when a peacock spreads its feathers in the snow. Is this because the earlier allusions to Napoleon and Waterloo were prophetic, because the young male now reigns over his own private icy wasteland? Where are we and where have we been? We're as disoriented as anyone else—his friend can't believe his companion's brain is fried—but we're gently complicit, because we were pulled along by the pleasures of the young man's sprint for freedom (see figure 2.1).

I'm familiar with these two clips because my students posted them on my class's online blackboard site long before I saw the movies. Since I've watched these excerpts several times, I have a more intimate relationship with them than the rest of the film. When I watch these films these moments pop as disjunct sections outside the narratives (a double pop—both for their heightened effects and because I've watched them so many times!). Isn't that how many of us watch films today—we've gone to YouTube or IMDb and reviewed fragments? What would a film look like if it were built on its "trailerness"?

Figure 2.1 SLC Punk! picks viewers up, carries them, and drops them elsewhere.

It's engaging to re-view older films in the same light, seeking isolated, heightened moments that depart from the film's texture, especially now that we attend to surfaces differently, with a post-classical eye. In Josef von Sternberg's *The Scarlet Empress*, a wacky section features Marlene Dietrich as a young princess listening to a bedtime story read by her nurse. As the story unfolds the pages turn psychedelic—suddenly the frame brims with floggings, beheadings, the rack, and inset narratives. Her eyes widen in sadistic pleasure and perhaps so do ours. Busby Berkeley's "By a Waterfall" sequence from *Footlight Parade* is also transformed by my history of watching CGI and intensified aesthetics. I've always loved the sequence but now I'm riveted by the plastic elements of the women's fake hair and their stylized multiplications as they mesh with the mountain fountain's rivulets. Too much *Pan's Labyrinth* and *Lord of the Rings* have forever altered the past for me.

Speed—Running—Tom Tykwer's Run Lola Run

Simply put, *Run Lola Run*'s ebullience derives from its patterns of speed—falling, traversing, heading through. Its surface is dense and multitemporal. With intensified films we often feel we've crossed varied terrain, almost like the videogame hero Mario; the cartoon figure seemingly keeps moving while sometimes remaining still, as do his bricks. Lost at some key moments, we might feel many temporal stands coursing by and that the past falls away as does the future. *Run Lola Run* I'd claim is simply a repeated loop jiggered to restart each time, a run blocked by obstacles, *not*, as David Bordwell suggests, a narrative structure based on what I find to be the flimsiest of details. Lola, between runs, Bordwell argues, learns how to uncock her gun's release (so she can shoot it) as well as to control her voice so she can direct the roulette wheel's ball down a gutter;[2] she therefore becomes a reflective, active agent who shapes the diagesis.[3] But I would never have caught these details even after many viewings. They're too subtle. They leave almost no mark on the film.

A brief synopsis: Lola's drug-dealer boyfriend misplaces the payoff, and finds he only has one hour to return the money or forfeit his life. He calls her on the telephone, desperate for help. Lola then launches into what resembles a video game: she spins around like an avatar, with potential futures before her. She races through scenarios—begging her father for cash, robbing a bank, and playing roulette to deliver the winnings and save her man. Twice, in the process, she is killed, but then reboots.

We might say that instead of a narrative, *Run Lola Run* foregrounds a more playful formal schema. When Lola passes over a bridge, just like in *SLC Punk!*, her running slows to a graceful, lilting slow-motion, turning the film into a music video. There is no past, no future. The film has forgotten itself. The still images of people she passes are, before any plot element, tears in the surface of the film. In the orange-tinted scenes comprised of a single overhead shot of Lola and Mani with their heads nestled on pillows, they absent the film almost entirely. (The image here suggests the characters post-sex, viewing themselves lost in ruminations, in limbo, or beyond death—each possibility situates itself outside the film.) In one sequence, when Lola runs to meet Mani at the grocery store, she sprints from stage-right to stage-left, heading toward the border of a split-screen across which is a more purely graphic image of a turning clock, pushing her back. Here she's bound by pattern and the film curls back upon itself. At another point Lola morphs into a cartoon and runs down curving, moving stairs as if she were stilled on a turning hamster's wheel. Here, at least for a moment, viewers don't quite know where we are. The film's overhead shots of labyrinthine streets and ground-level obstacles (the ambulance breaking before a life-sized plate of glass, for example), morphs the film into a map. We might think of the film as a pinball machine. We might say that a ball through such a machine makes a narrative (the ball wants to reach the end), but on the other hand it's simply an object that moves around corners (see figure 2.2).

The film's intro underscores this commitment to design over story. In some purgatorial world outside the film, people mill about and the policeman announces: "The ball is round. The game lasts 90 minutes. . . . Everything else is pure theory," before a cartoon of a tunnel, clock, and spider web swallow the image up. Another nonteleological element is the electronic dance music soundtrack, comprised of synthesized sounds set in a loop. These keep us in

Figure 2.2 Run Lola Run: as Lola runs, the past and future fade away and all that remains is the present.

the moment rather than drive us forward, as Michael Wedell has argued.[4] The music's genre also imports a nonnarrative social context. Imagine this construct: you're at a rave, on drugs, and lost in light all night. At the end you come across $50 and the possibility of a trip home with someone. Is this a narrative? I'd argue this experience is more a freeform dance with a sudden fortuitous closing turn, and the same is true of *Run Lola Run*. The film's formalisms may also be supported by gender. Though Lola is a strong agent, we may still perceive her more as "within the moment" than a man. *Run Lola Run*'s arabesques push the film toward something else—a music video or an experimental film. Like *Run Lola Run*, a few contemporary films showcase formal structures superimposed on traditional plot devices. (Spike Jonze's *Adaptation* is first simply a meditation on flowers—four distinct, essayistic pieces on how to raise flowers.)[5] *Run Lola Run* is first a loop, in which Lola spans the city and the day. You can turn the film in another direction momentarily, but much of it resides here.

Tweaking the Frame—Change Your Film's Message through Postproduction Techniques— David Fincher's Se7en

David Fincher's *Se7en* is a grizzly, neo-noir police procedural. Detectives Sommerset and Mills chase after murderer John Doe as he progresses through his master plan of killing seven victims, each staged as one of the seven deadly sins. The film was greatly admired for its craft and detail, as well as its gritty opening credits that were set to music by Nine Inch Nails.[6]

Fincher is commonly known as the industry's most obsessive technician. For every minute he spends shooting or editing, twenty are devoted to repainting each frame. Directors have also told me they wait until Fincher tries out a new technical device before they do—he's the community's resident tech-geek. In *Se7en*'s rerelease (New Line Platinum Series, 2000), digital intermediary makes it possible for Fincher to direct the film's end away from sin toward Christian redemption. He achieves this partly through the film's setup. True, the murderer's crimes seem almost unthinkably atrocious (hence the film's strong pull), but perhaps most startling is that viewers are encouraged to adopt several subject positions toward the atrocities, including stances that are sympathetic and/or complicit. The mapping isn't exact, but one might interpret the viewer as interpolating herself into the killing spree through a variety of roles resembling Freud's "A Child Is Being Beaten." In Freud's recounting of a story frequently narrated for him, the patient fantasizes watching the father beat a sibling. The patient would imagine being the sibling, the parent, and then the onlooker, the last position evoking shame for having escaped punishment but having done nothing. In *Se7en* the crime scenes of Gluttony and Pride might place the viewer in the same position as the beaten child (this happened to him/her and, I can imagine, me). Sloth is that of the child who looks on. (In this case a drug user's body is chained to a bed. The delirious victim's mind most likely at some point is psychically split, with a spacing out, a looking on from above upon his damaged body, like Freud's sibling.) Lust may place the viewer in the position of the abuser imagining what pleasure/fear might be afforded to the perpetrator and enabler (even if the initial directive to harm comes from Doe). *Se7en* teaches us not to distance ourselves from these scenarios that interpolate us in multiple subject positions, because as Detective Somerset repeatedly makes clear, this is part of ordinary events. He notes that these atrocities are connected to our daily activities. We learn, at least we women, to say "fire" rather than "rape"; to pass over people in need on the street; to respond to crimes by saying, "It's always that way." We're encouraged to see terrible acts as lying on a continuum of behaviors that also includes our own.

Near its final confrontation, *Se7en* turns toward a valorization of human connection and interdependency. During a long-awaited shared drink in a bar, Somerset and Mills shift roles and an opening becomes possible. We suddenly see the two characters differently: we realize the older detective Somerset may be too passive, and the younger Mills more committed. Mills might be the one we should admire for fighting evil. Somerset sees it too, and in that instant, there's a rapprochement between the two men. We next see three scenes of intimacy: (1) a recumbent Detective Mills, wearing Somerset's white napkin (from the first dinner) and cradling Tracy Mills (a marked woman who wears red); (2) Somerset listening to the metronome as if it were a mother's heart (he then rejects it, turning aggressive); and (3) Somerset and Mills shaving together before they don wireless mics—a strongly homosocial or homoerotic moment. The film has established Mills's homophobia (during Greed he recoils from "taking it up the ass," and expresses anxiety about sitting next to Somerset in a diner), so this moment suggests a character arc. Perhaps this turn toward acceptance could suggest we're bound to one another on a fundamental level. One might say these touches only work to heighten the pathos and strengthen the impact of the great fall, but I don't think so.

Se7en's end turns *both* darker and lighter: as much as the film turns downward, it drives toward ascendance.[7] In the final scene, the towering pylons in the arid fields might possibly suspend or buoy characters. Doe looks beatific in this final sequence; he and Tracy might remind one of Falconetti's *Joan of Arc*. Somerset too, projects a transcendent mode, repeatedly looking heavenward. The digital remastering has tinged the image yellow (as well as green). Interlaced

Figure 2.3 John Doe's apotheosis in *Se7en*.

throughout the film proper have been fine-art images of floating women's heads. The film's end showcases Mills's vision of flash frames of Tracy, desaturated and ghostly white. It's been prepared for by several earlier match-cuts across scenes, including a photograph of Greed's wife's eyes darkened by graffitied glasses and Tracy rising off a pillow. In the closing scene, there's a movement from Doe's beatific head, to the whitish frames of Tracy, to Doe again. We might read this as if Tracy were Doe's apotheosis. Fine preproduction values and the film's interpolation of the viewer into multiple ethical vantage-points might have set this up. A moral shift is enabled by post-production technologies governed by color and light. Suddenly a director can nudge a film toward transcendence from one direction to another even after a final edit (see figure 2.3).[8]

Only the Soundtrack Situates Us—the Mercurial World of Monsters, Their Cityscapes and Intergalactic Scapes—Michael Bay's Transformers

I don't know why I'm besotted by the *Transformers* monsters. When I'm feeling a little enervated or lethargic, when I don't have a strong drive to face the world, one of *Transformers* action scenes in New York City helps me re-experience life as enchanted.[9] *Transformers* possesses a ferocious, obsessive commitment to color, line, motion, and gesture and this gives me arcs with which to align. A synopsis: Michael Bay's film features good and bad robots who arrive from outer space to fight it out among the diminutive humans. They tussle over a valuable cube called "The AllSpark." The robots have special powers, they can morph from dust to cars to giant autobots. Funding by Hasbro.

I'd claim Bay has not received the critical acclaim he deserves. Manny Farber once quipped that Nicholas Ray's films were absurd, but just look at the mise en scène in *Party Girl*.[10] No renowned film critic has similarly valorized Bay (though Manohla Dargis has claimed Bay has the mark of an auteur—simply for his onomastic obsessiveness).[11] Look, however, at these beautiful shots and the ways they collide into one another. Red streaks smashed against others with a touch of blue and yellow. The commitment to color is reminiscent of Yves Klein, the motion and the lines, of Willem de Kooning (see figure 2.4).

And much of *Transformers'* meaning and power stems from the soundtrack. Without sound, the Transformers' appendages seem jerky and fast. Some are budding, lurching, whip-unfurling here and there—while the trunks ebb and sway. We also follow groin-based swivelings, and then underbellied rampings-up, often captured by a low-angle camera. One can't get a good read on the figures. One might wish to call them "cubist," as some wild realization of the gray-brown period of Braque and Picasso. But with music, the monsters' lines are true. Is this because music suggests arc, shape, and drive, and we project these attributes onto these figures, fantasizing their exoskeletons, complete with spines and sets of joints and femurs—sound coordinates the brutes? (See fig. 2.5.)

The Transformers are sound-dependent. They're mercurial and underdetermined, often amalgamated out of dust, wiry miniatures, stalactite metal, pieces of car (tires and lug-nuts and so on), and more fully wrought cars—sometimes with odd parts (that's a dainty bonnet formed of a rake or a propeller!) and jewel-boxes (for heads). It's uncertain what will transform into

Figure 2.4 Streaks of line and color: *Transformers* breaks the 180-degree rule with the help of some trash and rocks in the foreground.

Figure 2.5 Transformers: the monster's underbelly swiveling.

what, at what angle and at what scale. As Transformers leap upward or fall down, they might dissolutely fracture or coalesce—sound helps us track their trajectories. Isn't this visual volubility the perfect corollary for these novel, fluid, mercurial, digitally enabled sounds? The Transformers are also dream-like constructions. I see phantom images as the Transformers rise up: a tiny, ghostly fairy-queen-like figure that rides on the back of—a dog! I'm sure the bored animators have been playing Rorschach tricks with me.

The soundtrack structures *Transformers* on many levels. In the opening some sounds are identified with good robots and some with bad ones. In the images good and evil remain distinct, but in the soundtrack they begin to mingle, tele-graphing some subconscious message that these elements can cavort with and contaminate one another. Elements of the soundtrack become musical. In *Trans-formers* dialogue becomes sung and object-like: "Your bling," and "You're a sol-dier now!" (perhaps echoing *Lord of the Rings* Gollum's catchy plaint of "Precious, precious"). The hero's songlike "no, no, no, no, no!," with an upward rolling in-flection, matches the *Transformers'* sonic "rise-up," as the monsters drive from the ground to the vertical. The monsters are also audio-sensitive: attuned to their environs, they mimic back mechanical frequencies, including those from the local radio stations, the infectious musicality of static and jingles. Sound scoring too tints the visual landscape of *Transformers*. The exploding and colliding bang-it-up visuals of the New York City sequences are luscious and awe-inspiring, but the marvelous may first emerge from the soundtrack—within the sound collages come struck, crashing, and fracturing metal; para-animal cries; and car's, plane's, and other mechanical devices' engines, wheels, and other innards skittering and squealing—sonic pitched kernels like "Kuhng!," "Puhng!," "bwawk-bwawk"; and a high-pitched "twee-twee-twee-whipple-whipple-whir-whir" as if the sounds were parts of a melodic line played on timpani and marimba. There are also the nervous, brisk, and brittle strings; the dialogue that emerges like zeppe-lins ("Megatron—come here!"); and the terracing, elegiac Wagnerian horns (low, melancholy, unresolved, and often backed by a singing chorus or strings), the last offering a firmament that rolls like undulating grassy hills and valleys. How central to the film's sense is this soundtrack? Look at the segment in the NYC scene after Bumblebee gives the hero the cube. The camera's framing and the editing of people running up and down streets give almost no indication of where anyone's going or where anyone is in space. But with the music, we im-mediately know the affective connections and the spatial coordinates of people and places. Sound defines the Transformers.

The soundtrack—its frightening and gentling influences—helps explain why *Transformers* beguiles me. Almost all other work belonging to the action genre—car races, male fight sequences with knives or guns—leave me rather cold. But the appeal of *Transformers* may lie in how it exploits primitive cognitive processes. First, the visuals. Watching the monsters go after one another—their monumental size and our minimal one—perhaps awakens primal fears of being eaten (though *Godzilla versus Mothra* doesn't do it for me). Perhaps *Transformers* then exploits an incommensurability. At the same time that the monsters are ferocious they're nurturing and cute. Monstrous puppies wrestling—this is Jeff Koons on the grand scale. They're like Mark Morris's dancers in ballerina tights but they're knocking down buildings. They hop across the buildings as if these were stairsteps. Even though the Transformers are wreaking major metropolitan damage, if you look closely at the human characters who are running and fleeing, you may notice many are bent over one another in gestures of care. More car doors fly open than should for the catastrophe at hand. This beckoning (mimicking the people) makes the scene tender. So too the warm golds, pinks, and teals that permeate the image.

I *like Transformers'* bull-in-a-china-shop construct. The film's grand battle in the desert does nothing for me—perhaps I'm drawn to the first of the franchise because this one is an urban id without real costs. There's an aspect of grace when the *Transformers'* monstrous metal chomps into those prewar buildings, and there's even more graciousness and responsiveness in the soundtrack. The Wagnerian horns give way to a field of just as orchestrated musical sound effects; then there's silence and space for a kind of faux, generic heavy-metal music. The horns in the soundtrack then break through and take on their most heightened melodic tropes as the girl says, "No. I've got to stay for Bumblebee," or thanks Sam by saying, "No matter what happens. I'm glad I got into that car with you."

But all this is not enough to earn my devotion. *Transformers* rules through its sublime music video aesthetics. Michael Bay was a commercial music video director before he crossed into cinema, and his later clips were especially finely crafted. As mentioned, *Transformers'* audiovisuality stems partly from the fact that we can't guess the sound the monsters might make, so every instant offers an opening for the soundtrack. The moments when the Transformers take off and land are phrased. Some of their trajectories are short, some long, some possess much articulation within the span between their beginnings and ends, some drive low or high, but all together, as a series, they become musical. Similarly in the soundtrack, the music rises and falls in wavelike fashion. These crests or sonic swells tend to run in sync or in a canon with the image. Together we have a beautiful, audiovisual, synesthetically enlivened motet.

I know *Transformers* is bad stuff. It's racist and prowar. The military devoted huge resources to the film—locations, equipment, guidance. It's a recruitment tool.[12] The film's imagery of loyalty, love, and America is hackneyed. Yet perhaps I can love these inset scenes for something related to line, sound, and color. I'll only watch these.

Extended Audiovisual Passages Support the Film's Heightened Texture—the "Dave Dee, Dozy, Beaky, Mitch & Tich" from Tarantino's Death Proof and Kill Bill's "House of Blue Leaves" Sequences

First a bit about these films' genres and storylines. *Kill Bill* is a mashup of kung fu, B-movie action, spaghetti western films, and cartoons. Nearly murdered at her own wedding while pregnant, the bride takes revenge on her former lover and head honcho, Bill, and his far-flung band of killers. She travels across continents and retrains to secure her revenge. *Grindhouse* is a remake of a 70s film genre known for flesh, sex, gore, and low production values. Tarantino lovingly includes the missing reels and film scratches. The film's conceit is that the killer has built a specially fortified car that, when crashed, kills his victims and leaves him relatively unscathed.

Tarantino's films' "musical" numbers are so amped up they tend to support the over-the-top qualities in his films proper. Lisa Coulthard has focused on the ways these scenes' soundtracks demand that we enjoy the action—the pop music and rambunctious Foley sounds spritz everything up, much like a laugh track. Miguel Mera has noted the care with which Tarantino assembles his soundtracks, how attentive he is to these musical excerpts' connotations, and how much space and time he gives them.[13] There have been monographs on Tarantino's visual style, but little that looks closely at an individual scene. I'll discuss two scenes that will reveal consistent elements in Tarantino's approach.

Both the women in *Death Proof*'s "Dave Dee, Dozy, Beaky, Mitch & Tich" scene and in *Kill Bill's* "House of Blue Leaves" sequence could be said to call for their deaths. In *Death Proof* no one should hang a leg out of a car window. Nor should the girls in the back seat be slapping one another with hair all astream. (We've been warned by our parents.) Seeming to acknowledge her mortality, Uma Thurman, in *Kill Bill's* "House of Blue Leaves," steadies herself for an inevitable encounter with her would-be assassins: her legs strongly planted for balance, she surveys the four corners of the space, as the sword-wielding marauding Crazy Eights stream toward her through multiple entryways. In both films the women seem to conjure up their mortal opponents. In *Grindhouse*, Jungle Julia's musings on a band's dismemberment (Bill, Deasy, Dozy, Mitch, and Tich will soon absent Pete Townsend); her wayward call for a dangerous boy ("growl!"); and her errant leg out a window establishes a context for an intruder who will rend asunder the momentarily coalesced girl band. In "House of Blue Leaves," Thurman and Lucy Liu acknowledge their destiny: "Is that what I think it is?" "You didn't think it was gonna be that easy, did you?" "You know, for a second there, yeah. I kinda did." Besides projecting a prescient knowledge of fate and death, both of these violent sequences foreground a moral element: Thurman refuses to fight a prepubescent boy, throwing him back to the pack. Her well-defined boundaries lead us to assume she practices only just warfare. In *Death Proof*, each woman envisions her death differently, encouraging us to consider how we might approach our own deaths. Both films also offer the consolations that wrongful deaths will be avenged.

These two sequences aestheticize the characters, settings, and actions. The bloodstained patterns on Thurman's outfit echo those the expiring Crazy Eight men draw with their own spurting blood onto the walls and floors. A reflecting pool stained with blood, and a beautiful Frankenthaler-like mural, smear the colors of red, orange, and blue into a vibrant site-specific artwork. This scene's bloody struggle will unfold on top of a glass floor under which lies a Zen garden. On the ceiling above emerge jutting geodesic chandeliers, a mirroring of the rocks below. Together, glass, rock, and garden resemble tide pools and suggest a fragile balance, perhaps a near-at-hand possibility for wisdom and beauty. The ceilings' decorative pattern of starbursts could be said to foreshadow the angular, splayed patterns Thurman and her opponents form as they engage with swords and bodies in motion. Thurman, for example, flings three adversaries over her shoulder, each flying away from her at 30-degree angles; swords will later cross to form an asterisk. The scene's aestheticized space makes it more possible to discover beauty in violence: Thurman will admire a handsome weapon whooshing past her—an ax, before she catches it in her bare hands. (Part of its attractiveness derives from its sound.) *Death Proof* too has a handsome beauty—the four women in their car are so varied and pretty they may be all we desire. The car also seems cocoon-like with its dappled rain, glowing reds, and regularly passing headlights—rhythmic enough to rock a baby to sleep. A lone, aestheticized sneaker similar to the ax in "House of Blues Leaves" flies free in *Death Proof*; it spins past a woman during the car crash, as if it were a pigeon suddenly taking flight (though ominously it's likely from one of the women's bare feet left below the dashboard). Might this scene encourage a foot fetish? Several severed feet linger toward the end of the "House of Blue Leaves" fight (see figure 2.6).

Figure 2.6 Uma Thurman and the Crazy Eights prepare to battle in *Kill Bill*'s "House of Blue Leaves."

Both film sequences modulate affect by cycling through peaks established through long periods of rising intensity before returning to a brief quiet. The gentle smile of Lucy Liu and the steeling of the death-proof killer before he revs his car are two examples of such quiet. And both films cycle through a second set of arcs that suggest how heightened states of danger can support exalted consciousness. Thurman's battle in "House of Blue Leaves" carries her into the most keen mode of attention. She takes a bead from a reflection of men in her sword. She and we hear the swirling chains as they come closer before they appear as a vision within the setting. Thurman moves and the men move, forward and away, like a gigantic, underwater anemone. The sleepy women in *Death Proof* too, though dreamy, still seem preternaturally intertwined and intimately aware of one another. Their attention moves forward together until they sync with the music.

Besides the leads, both films possess an array of highly defined, semiotically overdetermined minor characters. The girls sitting in the car in the "Dave Dee, Dozy, Beaky, Mitch & Tich" scene suggest different types. The woman in the front driver's seat looks a bit butch and also as if she's from the early eighties (so she's closest to the time of the accompanying songs). She bounces up and down rigorously, catching the 16th-note pulse. To our left lounges a femme fatale with long permed tresses, and a beauty mark by her temple, who catches the offhandedness of the singing. In the car seat's back left perches a more seventies type, a countrified, virginal girl, with Guinevere-like braided hair and full, rounded circle insignia across her small breasts. She sports a drummer's wristband and "air drums," showing she controls the beat. In the passenger side's right seat is the woman who seems, more than the others, to represent the scene's center. Is her charisma only an effect of the rhythms of shot/countershot, or does she more subtly control our attention in other ways? She's urban and nearest to our era. On her T-shirt is what looks like the Brooklyn bridge running across her breasts. Perhaps in *Death Proof*, urbanity trumps small-town locales.[14] In the back seat we have the split between the citified, sexually knowledgeable woman and the good girl; so too with the women in front (the languorous seductress and butch types). We might feel they ought to (and, as we'll soon discover, will) be rent apart. Similarly, the Crazy Eights are a varied pack. Some of the assailants are women, some of them look more punk. Thurman will split one apart, as if to find out what kind of person stands before her (see figure 2.7).

Both films emphasize poised, well-matched antagonists and a careful raising of the stakes. Our backseat female protagonist and *Death Proof*'s killer will soon meet. Her full pouty lips are teed off by the killer's Donald Duck insignia on the hood of his car. As in a cartoon, the two will meet in a big kiss—although in *Death Proof* it's also a fatal death-lock. A similar face-off

Figure 2.7 The ill-fated women in *Grindhouse*.

occurs in the "House of Blue Leaves." Masked, and resembling an inscrutable Yul Brynner, Thurman's opponent stands to meet her. Both adopt dance positions as if they might as well waltz as fight. These moments of intensity are heightened by earlier images of the weapons. The head Crazy Eight elegantly rotates the wood of his sword, and the gas pedal and the wheels of the death-proof car receive much screen time. We hear and see what these objects can do; they receive as much focused attention as any character.

Both the *Death Proof* and "House of Blue Leaves" scenes build cleverly and inexorably: in *Death Proof*, an extra small, red, luminous eye painted into the car window's righthand corner underscores our killer's bad-wolf persona. Its red glow rhymes with the red in the women's back-seat window. Like the girls our murderer is a music fan. (He has a CD on his car that echoes the smaller ornament hanging in the girls' car.) Both parties fiddle with their dashboards. "Raise it louder!" calls out one of the women, sounding like a blues howler who sings on the soundtrack. The red flourish of the dashboard's logo spells out the danger and speed our girls will meet. "House of Blue Leaves" similarly intensifies. Thurman becomes increasingly illuminated in glowing white light, as if her vengeance assumes messianic proportions.

Both the song and the scene for *Grindhouse* could be said to have the patterns of some acts of sex: a tightening of the stakes, dispersals, and a grand release. There's a harmonic shift rising up to the chorus, and the cars come to meet it. Our death chariot crests the hill. For the pop song, the dispersal is "ay ay ay ay ay," which the girls will echo with their heads circling, hair in front of their eyes. As we approach the collision, heads will become unrealistically crossed, shot implausibly close. Tools for ripping have been foreshadowed: the death-skull on the death-proof car's hood and the duck's beak are sharp weapons for dismemberment: in our vision the headlights of the girl's car nearly converge. But the point of impact is hard to witness, at least for me. An overhead shot, remote from the scene of action, records the cars as they lunge at one another almost as if they were in a dogfight. But I can't bear to watch this repeatedly.[15] Nevertheless I'd like to understand this moment. I like the flow of the cars, the tinkling of glass like wind chimes, the building of the scene.

Similarly to the "Dave Dee, Dozy, Beaky, Mitch & Tich" scene, the heightening of the stakes in "House of Blue Leaves" is terraced. Assassins point and prod in patterns almost as if they were performing the hokey-pokey—foot-foot-knee-knee-neck-chest. Uma Thurman leaps not only upon shoulders but up toward the balcony, capitalizing on a long arc to surmount space in multiple directions—onto the floor, the sides of the room, the ceiling. Too, the patterns of revving and cresting, alongside the song's chorus and verse, make *Death Proof*'s scenes oddly "musical."

As if to counterbalance the violence, both films also possess an elegance and a restraint. Everything seems poised and controlled within the normal confines of generic violence and then suddenly the scenes, briefly, go a bit too far—perhaps Tarantino is toying with us: in "House of Blue Leaves" Thurman and the men fight valiantly but then, birdlike, Thurman plucks out a Crazy Eight's eye, pinching it among her taut, talon-like fingers as if the eye were a choice fruit. In *Death Proof* too, the red shiny metal careening off into the air might be a bit of cheek that the death-proof car had sheared off. The red metal, in its aftermath of plowing straight down a woman's face, seems to cry as it hits the pavement. There's brinkmanship here: Tarantino seems to suggest, "I've held your attention and entertained you, now it's my moment for my favorite gesture and my whim."

Perhaps Tarantino achieves his control over our affective responses through several techniques. As mentioned, both of these films' quasi-musical numbers are carefully weighted and terraced so they build to a moment of climax; then he can slip in whatever he wants with the appropriate whiz-bang. Second, both sound effects and bodies are cartoonish, which make such extreme effects palatable. There are the funny Foley sounds, like "waba waba waba" or "wa wa wa wa" or "growls" or "chings," in both *Death Proof* and "House of Blue Leaves." Audiovisual relations encourage playful modes of hide-and-seek from viewers. We hear an enticing high-pitched "zvvinnng" and scan through the image to find its complement, for example, like the just-drawn vertical sword peaking from the back of the Crazy Eight pack. We see the flat blade of Thurman's weapon and then hear a high-pitched ringing tone that belongs to it. Each time the match surprises us. And then there's the music that saturates characters and determines their agency. The cool grace of the RZA's pop-disco cue informs Uma Thurman in "House of Blue Leaves," and the innocent, joyful playfulness of Dave Dee, Dozy, Beaky, Mitch & Tich's mid-sixties rock song "Hold Tight" infuses the girls in the car in *Death Proof*.

The film's sequences pose an odd equation between life, flesh, and death. Once bodies have been killed, they morph into toy mannequins. That's partly why the deaths' aftermath is less upsetting for many viewers than one might expect. In *Death Proof* the women's bodies are only stuffed mannequins—inflatable sex dolls?—thrown up into the air. In *Kill Bill*, the men's bodies spouting fountains of blood resemble chickens with their heads cut off. Their human animus has gone missing. There are also fantastical reassemblages. In *Kill Bill*, Thurman spears a leg; then at a distance a woman's body curls and spits blood—and then murmurs a funny whimper. The spears' trajectories seem telepathically extended. Violence also turns spectacular, and unpredictable, moving in ungauged, thrilling directions. We may not be surprised when Thurman refuses to sacrifice a prepubescent Crazy Eight, but we are when she throws him into a giant, red, blood-tinged pool. Slashes rip not only bodies but sheets of hanging drapery; these transform into a corpse's winding sheets marked with red-inked calligraphy.

How might these spectacular nearly unfathomable shifts between life and death be enabled by the soundtracks, which straddle genres and epochs? In *Death Proof*, the song represents the moment when "rock and roll" has become "rock" (because of the distorted guitar sounds, the British-sounding vocals, and a melodic and harmonic style that has departed from the blues and become more like power pop), but hasn't yet become "serious art," so it can still be danceable, low-key, and short. (Compare, for example, this song to mid-sixties Kinks, like "All Day and All of the Night.") This naïve, sweet liminality makes it possible for the young women to wander, and stray too far, toward death.

In *Kill Bill*, the RZA's track reflects two different musical styles: (1) mid-seventies AOR eclecticism: rock that's fully embraced fancy studio technology, a clean sound, with maximal overdubbing, drawing on soul and funk (like here the wah-wah guitar and the early drum machine); and (2) electronic dance music, or indietronic scaffolding, which governs the production practices (stratified textures featuring culturally loaded elements in a basically danceable arrangement). The music features a mixture of elements (which combine rock elements like the distorted guitar and soul/R&B elements like the wah-wah guitar, the vocal sample, and the drum fills), with particular sounds, like the scratching. The mix may enable many types of bodies and deaths, all mingled together, though also kept slightly distinct. But the most important connection is when the music stops and the sound effects start. The sound effects seem like elongated ghostly carbon imprints of the songs, as if they are the residue of earlier actions. RZA's cat-crying synth in the high register becomes the larger "Mannheim rocket" glissando that emerges from the thuds and clanks of bodies and swords in "House of Blue Leaves," and the Death Proof car's revving engine seems to desire the role of the bassline. It's as if the songs themselves had been killed and reborn, apotheosized as sound effects. Do these "rebirths" lend some hope for the characters and a continued animus?

Both scenes start from a moment of slumber. In *Kill Bill*'s "House of Blue Leaves," Uma Thurman and Lucy Liu together whisper the commercial slogan: "Silly rabbit. Trix are for kids," which puts us in a childlike, dreamy state, perhaps ready for TV cartoons. (Remember that *Death Proof* also had a cartoon allusion with the Donald Duck hood ornament.) Similarly, during their night drive all of the girls are in a sleepy mode until one of the girls becomes enthusiastic thinking about Pete Townshend and The Who. Then both scenes gain energy: the women suddenly bopping faster and faster in the car, the Crazy Eights running down the corridors, sounding like a cattle stampede. Similarly, the death-proof car growls with a ferocity greater than its visuals. Perhaps there is something of the music video in these sequences: what animates the characters is unpredictable—like in music video the figures are infected through contagion by the music. Perhaps the characters, too, are not just music video performers but cartoon characters. The border between objects and people becomes unclear and the characters undergo mutations. These actors are just as much superhuman action-film-genre agents, vigilantes, reborn kung fu masters, the dirtiest of the doers. There's a sense that the antagonists have been called for; they're the other half. Thurman says, "Is that who I think it is?" Sydney Tamiia Poitier (Jungle Julia) says "That's my boy, growl." (And the dog chariot comes over the hill, growling.) Antagonists and protagonists are fierce. They strike poses. They brace. They ask for and need one another.

Film as a Roulette Wheel. Anything Can Happen at Any Time—(500) Days of Summer

(500) Days of Summer possesses the most schematic of storylines: boy gets girl, boy loses girl, boy becomes wiser in the mechanics of love (and the film's "coda" concerns his shift from a girl named "Summer" to one named "Autumn"—he'll convert his experiences gained from this romantic go-round to the next, we assume, successful relationship). The film's special turn revolves around the fact that the days of courtship are scrambled (at the film's opening, the male narrator tells us this couple won't make it, and we'll figure out why). Like many contemporary films, *(500) Days* has only one music video number. After the protagonist Tom Hansen gets laid, about one-third into the movie at midday, he joyously walks into the street and gives high-fives to passersby. The musical-like number reflects his pleasure of such an experience—as he enters the park, people fall into dancing formation behind him and wish him well. An animated bird sits on his shoulder. Perhaps, since the music video number appears only once and is taken over by special effects, it here seems to possess magical powers (like some of the musical

numbers in the *Wizard of Oz*). Music video, with its repetitive verse-chorus structure, and its foregrounding of cycles rather than a straight drive-through, seems to help engender the vignettes' scrambling. I, for one, welcome this. Surely after this wonderful first sexual encounter, it's downhill from here; we know we're heading for a bad outcome and I don't care to follow the narrative. So after the music number, we can go anywhere. Just like in William Burroughs's *Naked Lunch*, there's a sense that the cards could be thrown up any which way. A roulette. A Nietzschean world where everything exists all at once in simultaneity. And this unusual quality of openness extends for a long while: the dates and times whirl back and forth exuding a blissful anywhere, any place. After awhile we'll be pulled back in, but in the moment, we might take this sensation seriously.

The film achieves this happy freedom through several devices. First, the film has a *mise en abyme*. Tom Hansen works at a greeting card company and, as he admits, dates and commercially induced sentiments are remixed and recycled. It really doesn't matter what comes up. And like the greeting cards, the characters are also stock. The film's an *Eternal Sunshine of the Spotless Mind* redo with the characters as stripped-down versions of the latter's Joel and Clem. (*Days of Summer* assumes it shares the same niche audience.) The scrambling also occurs in the later two-thirds of the movie where, even in Hollywood classical films, not much tends to unfold (as Kristin Thompson notes, these latter thirds are the slow dullards).[16] (500) *Days of Summer* possesses many of the features Bordwell identifies in postclassical forms. There's the sense that fate set things going, and characters are beholden to chance or contingency. People do things because that's their nature, not because they're changeable, introspective, or can be understood.[17] As mentioned, after Summer's bestowal of unhappiness— surprise—a surrogate arrives for Tom who will do just as well. I don't know about you, but I don't have much problem with this. I've enjoyed the shuffle (see Figure 2.8.).

Figure 2.8 (500) Days of Summer's single complete musical number.

Shifting Rhythms, Temporalities, and Spaces—Timur Bekmambetov's Day Watch

Why *Day Watch*? Its pleasures are not immediately apparent to many. Some students I've screened it for have said it's all over the place. But it's one of the most accelerated and "musical" films I know. It also deploys some of the most imaginative sound effects.[18]

Day Watch has a mercurial, fast-changing surface. Consider the opening. A stentorious voice intones, "Why does the wind blow . . . as if we don't exist?" alongside mournful vocalizations, which, along with the camera's drift along a dark, craggy surface, suggest epic time. The camera pierces through hanging crystal fragments in a thicker-than-air suspension: these fracture into dust (recalling the biblical injunction "dust to dust"). As the camera curvingly orbits the dark mass, its Matterhorn-like mountain reveals it to be but an over-scaled, vertical stick of chalk. Only sound helps gauge what we're experiencing: the solemn voice alludes to a timelessness; the glassy, harplike sounds describe the transubstantiation from crystal to chalk; and, as we trace an arc, the music buoys us, swaying in lullaby waves. Bang. Then. Sunlight—triumphal music, the camera fast plunges downward through kaleidoscopic patterns into an abyss; we'd been carried upward in a beautiful wafting lilt, now, suddenly and vertiginously we drop. A suspended and drifting timelessness, and a plummeting descent brings us to the profane. Cartilage, bone—then piss. A man's arm nestles inside a horse's flank. He jabs to stop the hot stream of urine—a gap— and sharp strums of a guitar set a driving rhythm. Fields of snow. Blowing, cold. Resting horses stretch into the distance. Under the nestle of the horse's flank, the man's pupil suddenly widens and his dirty finger presses through a map of glyphs into a future—past the map to what will be a fantastical fortress. His eye's pupil becomes a glyph; his finger resembles a breast. He calls, "ALWAH!" We should ride! Yet when we gaze upon the undulating fields of rippling snow before him, and listen to a soft silence, we might instead resist and relax, responding to the ocean-like waves of the billowing snow, or the buoyant feeling that accompanied our rounding of the Matterhorn/chalk mountain. Here the wind whistles and whispers to us. But again, those whip-lash changes in pace and rhythm. Men rush on horseback, looking like Persian drawings of warriors with their swords, with battle cries, and a potential for violence. The sharp strums of the guitar. The heartbeat that marks off time. Will these be forceful enough to carry us through and pierce the mythical castle only dreamed of by Tamerlane as he gazes at his map? Soldiers wait for us on turrets folded up like protruding sculpture. Most likely this fantastical multicorridored fortress will vanish like a chimera. Tamerlane, once crowded beneath his horse's haunch, with his glyph-like eye, will soon find his goal beyond, after many sonically and visually layered barriers and impedances. He seeks something even more compressed and nested—both spiritual and profane. Nestled inside a castle's dome placidly sits a gold-plated man covered with bird shit tending the precious chalk with a curved stick. To find what we seek (which we don't yet know)? The sound insinuates possibilities before we look.

As this description begins to suggest, *Day Watch*'s opening takes us through a dizzying array of spaces, and temporal epics, in search of objects and relations among figures we can't piece out (see Figure 2.9.).

Past these first 7 minutes and into *Day Watch*'s first 15, the viewer continues the hunt for something (the chalk?), through mountains, castles, and fields of snow, labyrinths and paperback books, cloistered areas, a current cityscape, a street fair, an empty alleyway, an abandoned glass building, a railway station of lost souls, and then out onto a highway—all, at last, to follow not the chalk, but an elusive high-pitched tone. What was that? Sound tells us as much about the temporal times we've elided and the barriers we're passing through as any other cue (sound precedes and follows after a breach between spaces and places, coloring these, telling us stories about them). Perhaps strengthening the role of the soundtrack, the objects we follow rhyme much like a music video's, but remain inscrutable. An old woman carries a loaf that looks like Tamerlane's leg of lamb. A pot of spaghetti upchucked by shopkeepers resembles the stones hurled off Tamerlane's castle buildings—but these had the same black eyes as the glyphs on the maps. There's an odd squeak from the protagonist's van. Is it the mosquitoes from the Gloom? The viewer is raised above the fairground; suddenly the town looks like a Chinese village with paper lanterns (reminiscent of the earlier Asiatic touches to Tamerlane's castle). Does the wind here remind one of the film's opening?

Bekmambetov, who has a background in commercials and music video, directed this first of the Russian-made Hollywood/MTV-style, CGI-driven epics, *Day Watch*, and its precursor *Night Watch*. Both films are densely allusive, with

Figure 2.9 Multitemporality: Tamerlane's vision in *Day Watch*.

echoes of Proppian folk tales, Tarkovsky and Eisenstein, European painting from Rembrandt to Kiefer, and a soundtrack shifting among punk, polka, Herrmann, Mussorgsky, and Prokofiev. The films' conceits—the melding of fantasy/sci-fi/horror/melodrama and ambiguous characters, whose roles switch between vampires and vampire hunters—make possible a sound-centeredness. Characters' eyes glow, bloodcurdling screams move objects, spaces suddenly change into a dimension called "the Gloom." The film flaunts obscure mechanisms and a general malaise. Rapid cutting among peoples, spaces, and epochs, all richly depicted, makes possible a multichronology—a sense of time simultaneously unfolding on several levels. A network of visual motifs and allegorical characters hover over and attach to sonic elements. Scholars have argued that Hong Kong's vibrant action-genre cinema comes out of a historical moment of extreme unrest. Its people, shadowed by mainland China, experience a day-to-day sense of temporal uncertainty. Russia, too, shimmers between old feudal and new neoliberal capitalist structures. *Day Watch*'s instability, born of Communism, Perestroika, the new Russian oligarchs' repressive regime, and kleptomania, along with a public increasingly aware of the costs, lends the film its bold but dreamy feel.[19]

Line and Flow—The Films of Johnnie To

David Bordwell has valorized director Johnnie To as the sole inheritor of the Asian action film tradition that extends back through John Woo to King Hu.[20] A prolific Hong Kong director, To for many years made two films a year; one in the arthouse vein and one for the general public. He's worked in all genres— from Lubitsch-like comedies to horror—but his specialty is crime films that narrow in on gangs like the Triads.

I believe I'm drawn to Johnnie To's films because they have flow and line. As our protagonist Tracy Lord says in *The Philadelphia Story*, as she cradles a sailboat, they're "yar." They don't bunch up at the beginnings or ends. They're fleet and light-footed. The film's structure, too, often feels palpable—as if we might almost feel the section's joins and large-scale shape ripple beneath the surface. Perhaps To's skills stem partly from the ways he mobilizes a vast collection of stylistic devices and moves; he seems to draw on one effect and then another freely, based on appropriateness, need, or whim, holding all else in ready reserve.

On the larger scale, the films carry a moral. They provide a model for living: experience and be within the segment, where a moment takes on power, weight, and history, but then let go. Often the films narrate the process of letting go. In *Sparrow*, the gang of pickpockets risk their health, their profession, and indeed the tools of their trade—their hands—all for a woman they know will run off with another man. In *Breaking News* the gangsters, holed-up in siege, intimately share a sumptuous meal, even though they intuit they will soon die—each alone. In *Triangle*, two posses of men chase after an antique burial vest of gold coins in a swamp at night, curated by a scarecrow and a crocodile. The vest keeps hurtling over the chest-high blades, for whom? The crocodile? (It had heard the vest's rattling.) We grasp the men's folly as they wave and shoot at one another while the bounty comes down. Stephen Teo and Charles Kronengold have drawn attention to To's facility at working with male ensembles. Fluctuating relations within these ensembles keep the film flowing forward.[21]

Of To's many techniques, my favorite is dilation and contraction of time. Some shots are very long, some are medium length, some come as a flurry: all suggest different temporalities, but keep the forward drive. In *Sparrow* the male and female love interests sit in a car and suddenly, as they draw on their lit cigarettes, we drop into slow motion—a beautiful, sensual moment—and then we're back in the regular flow of the film. In *Election* there'll be a long slow-mo of people meeting on the corner, and then suddenly a multitemporal Jacques Demy–like musical sequence, of people entering the crosswalk at different speeds cradling their umbrellas. Then it's over. In *Election* a young female prostitute jumps up and down (for the head mobster's amusement), with the camera at varying speeds and in greater close-up recording her bobbing breasts. Then there's a cut to a competing gang's men drinking tea inside the restaurant in slow-mo with a slowly circling, dollying camera echoing the sleepily turning overhead fan and the men's periodic raised toasts of cups of tea. Next, two very sharp cuts transport us across the street through the glass of a clothing shop's window to a mobster's hands abruptly fastening his red tie, as if a knife had metaphorically sliced his neck. Finally there's a wide, slow tracking shot of the aspiring soon-to-be head gangster walking home amid soft red-pink open market lights with hanging ducks, all rosy and sunset-like. The images themselves cohere as a musical sequence. They also sketch the relations among men without words.

Line is built up through a number of devices: one is the recurrent use of batons. People pass these objects from character to character (as in *Election* and *Triad*). In *Sparrow*, two men practice pickpocketing oblivious tourists to show who's best, and we follow the stolen goods as they move among the men's choreographed gestures through crowds. There's always a lot of passage in To's films—riding bicycles, running, walking, driving, big gliding overheads, cars pealing out. But perhaps To's most striking signature is shown in the beautiful formations of men deposed, often in alleyways or along streets at night— perhaps three men on the left, one or two to the right, and then two or more moving back toward the background, all canted and torqued in varied directions, so that the viewer's eye can move from figure to figure toward the street's end. The men are lean. They wear long, clear black suits. They raise their guns. They often are shot in full or half shadow. They make beautiful patterns. (See further in my Afterword.)

To balance these extended images are rich compositions in compact spaces, like a restaurant-scaled glass aquarium with five men shoved into an elevator in *Sparrow*, or two men crouched in a long elevator shaft in *Breaking News*, or an extended scene shot in a door jamb in *Throwdown*. Pickpocketing is a subject perfect for To—based on fleetness, skill, grace, and subterfuge—like judo. Within these longer sequences of motion, tableaux, or activity, there are short exchanges between people, quickly sketched, yet dense in meaning. In *Breaking News*, striving, attractive police detective Rebecca Fong and her supervisor speak in his office for a moment after a department meeting. He mentions her father not being well and things not being black and white. She says for her, things *are* black and white. Three short sentences and we now know an affair has occurred between the two. The supervisor may have awarded her the commanding role over the heist to win her back, but though she wants the job, she hews to her own codes. We're left with her sense of solidity and his winsome melancholy. In *Sparrow*, the octogenarian Mr. Fu bullies Lei, his kept young woman, to control her, yet he also takes loving care of her. He knows when he's been one-upped by younger males, however, and after a pickpocketing contest showcasing male prowess between him, his retinue, and the young upstarts, he frees her. He awards her a jade necklace and howls like a baby after she leaves.

I wouldn't be surprised if To loves Howard Hawks: both value long-shot compositions, grace among characters, and honor, work, and play. Against all this visually stripped-down line, the music courses through, spare and fleet. Often intimate, a guitar with flute and perhaps a touch of percussion, it never lapses into something more blocked or useful first, like a pop song. Music, here, is sketched in yet continues; it mirrors the image and supports the larger whole. At the close of *Sparrow* the five men, all heaped up, ride a bicycle. The lead character, Young, reaches up with his arm toward a sparrow that quickly takes flight. This line carries us past the film. When I studied painting in college, my professor would say artists often overworked the face—the painter got frozen there. Johnnie To, on the other hand, always passes through. In this way he's a model for life. Tread lightly, experience deeply, be present and keep moving.

The films I've described in this chapter reveal some of my favorite post-classical cinematic techniques. A sublime film might combine them all in an uneven surface. Music video has finally discovered how to create odd, misshapen, lumpy forms. Why can't cinema do this more often? *Adaptation, Cowboys & Aliens*, and *Don't Look Now* are examples of distorted large-scale forms. *Bourne Ultimatum* and *Sherlock Holmes*, too, are examples of speed. But I and perhaps other viewers hunger for even more intensification and more unusual forms.

A whole panoply of techniques support post-classical cinematic styles. Of the many, let me describe a few. In Steven Spielberg's *Munich*, the performers are shot as silhouettes or shadows, and one of the characters plays with little dolls that resemble the performers. This intimation of the human as form rather than identity makes it easier for a very fast film to shift among flashforwards and flashbacks and genres like the documentary, thriller, and melodrama. Many films also often use a large map or schematic diagram to help ground the story. (*Smokin' Aces* draws on a wall's illuminated map and *The A-Team* uses toys and a miniature board.) Films like *Eternal Sunshine of the Spotless Mind* and *Anna Karenina* fuse many sets and spaces. Any parameter might be intensified. Sudden moments when the past and the future falls away in a film can be moving. One of my favorite examples is from Tsui Hark's *Seven Swords* (2005), when the warriors stand together on a mountaintop and the rest of the film momentarily disappears. Nor have I discussed all of the directors and films to have broken the rules. David Lynch's *Mulholland Drive* may be the most extraordinary. There's also Wong Kar-Wai's *2046* and Todd Haynes's *I'm Not There*. Later in the book, I discuss Michel Gondry's *Eternal Sunshine of the Spotless Mind*.

Let me quickly summarize the techniques from the segments I've described. Spike Lee's *Summer of Sam* and James Merendino's *SLC Punk!* have moments when the film switches register and the viewer loses a sense of ground. The new content can't be attributed to the film's diegesis or the psychic state of some character: for a little while, the viewer is left to fend for herself. Tom Tykwer's *Run Lola Run* is an example of a database narrative, where repeated formal patterns take on greater weight than does any teleological drive. David Fincher's *Se7en* becomes as much an unfolding painting as a narrative. Postproduction touches, as much as action, direct its moral arc. Michael Bay's *Transformers* has a beguiling surface of speed, color, and line. It too resembles painting: its image seems untethered. Apart from the soundtrack, the film becomes spectacle—a moving blur of color. Quentin Tarantino's films, on the other hand, contain numbers verging more on the musical than classical Hollywood action sequences or plot exposition, even though no character necessarily sings. (Perhaps much sings around the protagonist—objects, sound effects.) These musical-like numbers' influence spreads like a contagion, making possible a heightening of the film proper. In Marc Webb's *(500) Days of Summer* almost any moment in time might come to the fore at any moment. The film encourages us to read unfolding events backward, forward, or any which way. Timur Bekmambetov's *Day Watch* contains so many heightened moments and shifts in time, space, era, and epoch that they supersede a viewer's tracking of the story. Johnny To provides a new synthesis of the intensified style, blending multiple techniques into something that creates new types of flow, movement, and time.

David Bordwell has described many features of post-classical cinema. He notes an intensified style that has changed the cinematic surface: abrupt cuts between telephoto and wide-angle lenses, shaky handheld framing, shifts in deep narrative structure. But he claims that none of this has fundamentally changed the experience or content of Hollywood cinema. His perspective derives partly from cognitivism (the belief that the brain is hardwired for particular sorts of stories) and partly from a grounding in classical film history. "Nothing comes from nothing." he notes: "Every new artistic practice revises existing practices, and often the 'unconventional' strategy simply draws on other conventions."[22] What we see now is a reworking of earlier forms and devices. But changes in some formal levels tend to deform others; music scholars have often claimed that changes at either the small or large scale can create shifts throughout the entire structure (for example Wagner's invention of the leitmotif and musical works that stretched for hours).[23] The same might be said for painting: figure/ground relations might at first seem universal, or biologically given, but many practices in and beyond the West have established other basic structures.[24] Cinema has experienced sustained, intense pressure from the other arts, and responded to many technical innovations over the past 20 years. Commercial imperatives and audience desires have shifted as well. I contend that these pressures and possibilities have changed the nature of a film. And these fundamental changes have been partly spurred by a development Bordwell talks little about: the greater prominence of *audiovisual* passages, tears in the surface, segments, blocks, and intensified musical numbers this chapter has considered. Today a film can be simultaneously available to the editor and director. They can build thickets of material, creating dense moment-to-moment audiovisual engagement that works to hold the viewer in the here and now (much like music videos do), only to move out into something more spacious and plot-driven again. In this way the viewer gains a chance to lose herself.

This chapter has described different types of audiovisual form: blocks and segments; multitemporalities; loops; musical numbers; quasi-musical numbers that integrate heightened musical behavior; sound effects and bits of music as fragments; tears in the film's surface; motivic work; and audiovisually seamless, minute changes that wash over the surface through color, texture, or sound. There may also be moments or sections that seem lumpy, and others that reflect a smoother flow and sense of line. A glance over this list shows that these modes and techniques possess musicality. When I began analyzing music video in the eighties, the form seemed to reflect features of the pop song. This surprised my interlocuters. It didn't seem at all intuitive that a clip's images might break into segments to show off verse, chorus, and bridge; that the image would try to accentuate and help us remember the song's hooks; that color might reflect timbre.

Now it all seems obvious. My guess (and hope) is that new films will become more musical. There may be a moment when we say that a film's "musical" structure is as important as its narrative, when we might consciously consider a film's small-, mid-, and large-scale form. The 2012 James Bond film *Skyfall* remains classical in many ways, but in others becomes a fragmented picaresque. It divides into musical segments much like *Moulin Rouge*. Its color palette and look shift across areas, and its visual and aural motives play across the film.[25] I hope *Skyfall* foretells new films. Or, as I've suggested, films might take devices from different cinematic practices—extreme transitions between sets as in *Anna Karenina*, another approach to lighting or performance—and forge something new. There will be more of this kind of work—there's a hunger to fill the gaps between genres and forms like YouTube, music video, commercials, narrative film, sitcom, and documentary. Bekmambetov has said we might even call this new form "musical":

> You need a story, you need a character, you need to set a scene, but these are only tools, they're not the goal. As an artist I grew up in the tradition of Russian modern art that included Malevich, Kandinsky, and other early 20th-century artists. They were witchcrafters. Their art was witchcrafting. Theirs was not a figurative art, it's abstract. And the film is the same. It's about the combination of a high-pitched sound with a flying camera—you're playing with elements and you're creating an abstract art. The story, the genre, and everything else are tools you must use because cinema is a mass cultural art. You need to be understandable, otherwise nobody will go to see your movie. But what I enjoy most is abstract. I'm playing with different styles, tones and genres, and how to combine them together to create abstract compositions. I'm kind of cheating. I'm dressing movies as a commercial product, but underneath it's just art. . . .
>
> Music is the closest art for me, because there is no story in music. It's more emotional. It speaks directly. You cannot describe it in words.[26]

In these new films we'll see sections like a pop song, movement that feels like harmony, surfaces traversed by motivic work. It'll all be there. Bring on the next wave! I like Hollywood's neoclassical turn—music-video director Mark Romanek's *Never Let Me Go* and Florian Henckel von Donnersmarck's *The Lives of Others*. But my ways of watching and feeling have been transformed by the collisions of genres and media. I'm waiting for filmmakers to catch up.

CHAPTER 3

Music Video into Post-Classical Cinema

How much has music video shaped today's intensified digital cinema? There hasn't been much scholarly discussion of this question. But the influence has been profound—perhaps more than we realize. Film sound and image have been reconfigured to their core. The soundtrack in toto has become "musicalized": sound effects and dialogue are now shaped alongside composed music into musical phrases.[1] Sound effects and other sonic features can also adopt leading roles, driving the film's teleology; or sound can mediate, enabling individual film parameters to come to the fore. The image too acquires a sense of speed and flexibility: the image's contents can seem as if they had been poured from one shot into the next. Cutting, too, can bestow an almost percussive rhythmic drive. The image in the new digital cinema often avoids a ground (the traditional camera position of the tripod flush to the horizon) because the sound wafts it along. Only by being so soundcentric can the image detach itself from a codified, shot-bound format like shot-countershot and the 30-degree and 180-degree rules. Images released by sound can be filled in by it.[2]

Only one theorist, Marco Calavita, has seriously considered how music video has shaped the new digital cinema. He argues, however, that other factors, like European art cinema, Hong Kong action films, American experimental filmmaking, and Hollywood musicals have had a stronger impact.[3] Calavita begins where I do, by acknowledging music video's importance in the critical and popular literature on film in the eighties and nineties. At that time, critics and the public described music video as the agent of a changed cinematic style: these observations first surfaced with *Flashdance* (1983) and continued, with an increasingly critical slant, moving toward outright denunciation. Writers often complained that MTV-like fast cutting was paired with thin storytelling and cheap, youth-oriented aesthetics—lowbrow humor, flashy sex or action sequences. For many critics and theorists, a decline in cinema was heralded by this "MTV style."

Calavita's historical account seems right to me, but then we part ways. According to Calavita the critics got things wrong. They chose the pejoratively tinged "MTV style," because it signaled surface effects; but this designation failed to account for the elements that initiated it. For Calavita the "MTV style" revolution didn't happen. Instead European art cinema, Hong Kong action films, and Hollywood musicals encouraged American film directors and other industry personnel to adopt a style that looked "MTV-like." I argue instead that music video was the key driver. In what follows I will place my account of these developments against Calavita's claims. I suggest that only within the hothouse of music video production, using the inexpensive and flexible medium of videotape, could a language of music video and contemporary audiovisual aesthetics come together.

Calavita and I agree that in the eighties a young filmmaking generation watched foreign cinema through film schools, late-night repertory theaters, and VHS rental houses. But how do we judge the effect this repertoire had on filmmakers? Calavita claims these screenings were formative, but I think he overstates the point. I grew up in that era and saw foreign movies in film school. These screenings were helpful but infrequent. Repertory theaters like the Nuart in Hollywood screened a narrow playlist—*If, King of Hearts, Beauty and the Beast.* Most rental houses' assortment of foreign films on VHS were limited, and checking them out and returning them was expensive and burdensome. But at this same moment music video was programmed across the cable and television spectrum, and this programming showcased a surprisingly wide array of content: on MTV and VH1 alone content changed hourly—from Yo MTV Raps (hip-hop), Headbanger's Ball (heavy metal), 120 Minutes (alternative), Amp (techno), Classic Music Video (eighties), to Breaking Music Videos. You'd see this programming in friends' houses, bars, and hotels. In the eighties almost everyone watched music video, including filmmakers. A common conversational gambit—especially as party icebreakers—was to discuss an unusual new clip, or a clip one felt sentimental about. Filmmakers who were engaged with new visual styles found music videos attractive partly because the genre provided one of the most direct ways to break into the industry—one could experiment, build a show-reel, get spotted, and land a directing gig on a feature. Making music video was also a training ground in its own right: a director could be responsible for all phases of production, including conception, casting, locations, props, shooting, and editing. You could pitch an odd treatment that no one in the record industry could unpack, head out to an obscure location, shoot a ton of footage—and no one would know what you were doing. This experience contrasted sharply from working in commercials, where the treatment was most likely written by an ad-agency person, and shooting and editing was supervised by industry reps. These reps, with storyboards, clipboards, and stopwatches in hand, entrenched within their "monitor towers," made sure you adhered to the timings the company and client had vetted.

So when Calavita writes, "It certainly makes more sense to say ... that along with the French New Wave, avant-garde filmmaking, and perhaps psychotropic drugs, nonlinear electronic editing has affected the style of Oliver Stone's films more than an attempt to ape MTV has," my response is, "Really?" I can imagine Stone on mushrooms watching music video. Consider his *Natural Born Killers*. There's surely more music video than Godard in the scene where Mickey and Mallory shoot it up in a bar. (This scene celebrates the camera's close relationship to the soundtrack.)[4]

Besides European art cinema, Calavita considers Hong Kong action films an important influence on the MTV look. And he's right that the sharp-edged kineticism of action films might be important to consider. But, for the most part, the eighties films Calavita discusses tend to be predictable in their arrangement of long shots, medium shots, and close-ups, with much of their energy deriving from a slight mismatch between shots (because shots were filmed out of sequence without strict adherence to continuity) and sharp sound punctuation (Foley). Music videos do more than that. They are exciting because one can never predict which shot will follow another, or what we'll see, moment to moment. (We can start with a long shot or a close-up and cut back to it at any moment. We can suddenly come across a dance number or a new vignette.) We also want to consider how many people were seeing Asian action adventure films in the eighties. And hadn't Asian action films already incorporated music video?[5] In the eighties music video was a worldwide phenomenon, including Asia. Asian fans viewed not only regional music videos but also videos from America and Europe. For all international film directors multiple influences need to be considered.

Here we might take a moment to consider David Bordwell's notion of "intensified continuity," even though it doesn't deal with music video directly.[6] Bordwell argues that precursors of the accelerated film style can be found all the way back to the earliest films. Bordwell cites *Grand Hotel*, for example, as more an ensemble than a narrative film. But his examples (like Calavita's) can tend to look like a handful of oddball, striking examples. The music video era, on the other hand, produced an *efflorescence*. I take seriously music video's predecessors in works by Godard (*Breathless*), King Hu (*A Touch of Zen*), Richard Lester (*Hard Day's Night*), and Nicolas Roeg (*Performance*), but I believe it was an *onslaught* of music video that mostly shaped the field.

The second part of Calavita's argument is that before MTV there were already films with pop-oriented soundtracks aimed at youth culture, like *Saturday Night Fever* (1977) and *American Graffiti* (1973). So his idea is you've got two strands—jaunty, disjunct visual styles coming in from non-Hollywood cinema, and American music-centered films emphasizing pop genres; and then technicians discovered how to put the two together. Here is where I *must* take issue with Calavita's argument. Philosophers and cultural theorists have long argued that the ways technologies are deployed and then developed within cultures tend to form local, idiosyncratic trajectories.[7] I'd argue that Calavita doesn't consider how putting music and image together might be built on knowledge embedded in a set of viewing and production practices. Music video audiences and practitioners have contributed to their own forms of learning, seeing, and hearing: as more and more music video directors became film directors, and viewers immersed themselves in the music video experience, the "MTV style" flowed into cinema.

Like many theorists Calavita doesn't fully attend to the nuances of audiovisual relations. Technicians in the field of music video tell their own stories about its history. They suggest music video has a genealogy that contributed on its own to an intensified aesthetic. Here's just one example: for the Jay-Z video "99 Problems" (2004), director Mark Romanek shot twelve hours of gorgeous Brooklyn footage, with people doing engaging activities—gospel singing, cheering on dog fights, walking the streets—coupled with striking interiors and exteriors. Romanek's favorite editor, Robert Duffy, was unavailable, so he turned to those who were considered the best in the industry. He went through three editors—no slouches—but none could produce a serviceable edit. Jay-Z, who had seen the striking raw footage, couldn't believe it. He suggested he and Romanek should stop investing any more time and money in the project and release anything. Fortunately Duffy became free and Romanek told him, "Look, I've run out of money. No one can edit this, so you're going to have to edit this for free."[8] Sure enough, Duffy produced one of the most beautifully edited videos. The lesson here is that sound and image don't *naturally* go together. Music video editors who are specialists still struggle with their craft. Duffy has a refined audiovisual aesthetic that draws on a history of viewing and making music videos.

By the middle of the eighties music video editing had become as lucrative as film editing. In the interviews I've conducted with music video directors they've told me these editors often excel because of athletic practices tied to rhythm, grace, and speed: director Marcus Nispel, for example, said his favorite editors were former drummers or practiced kung fu. Directors Kevin Kerslake and Spike Jonze, who shoot and cut their own footage, play hockey and skateboard, respectively. It's telling too that music video director Mark Pellington, who developed a unique language of shots based on the fast cutting of single still-frames, isn't the best editor for his own work. He draws on a specialist. A complementary story concerns Matt Mahurin, one of the biggest directors of the eighties and early nineties. He would cut his own work in post-production, because no other editor could assemble his shots.

Films like *The Bourne Ultimatum* and *Moulin Rouge* exhibit more than a way of putting sound and image together. Their aesthetic is not just based on collapsing two lively tracks, visual and aural, on top of one another; the films are grounded in a sensitivity to sound-image relations that derives from music video's heritage. In other words, even if you sped up Godard's image tracks, you might not know how to put them against pop songs.

There are other drivers of intensified cinema and the new audiovisual aesthetic. iPod culture could be significant. Music is now set to almost every environment—grocery shopping, mall cruising, working out at the gym, waiting in phone queues.[9] We expect a musical accompaniment that fits the rhythms of our lives and even structures our gait and our gaze. From these contexts we might have learned ways of musicalizing our experience, as if an audiovisual bubble had enveloped our daily routines. The musical, too—not necessarily the songs themselves, but rather the musical sequences' projection of dream-like experience—might have created a space for some post-classical modes, as in *Eternal Sunshine of the Spotless Mind*. Some scholars have speculated about the contributions of horror-film music and sound to the development of the new audiovisual turn.[10] Calavita and Bordwell, of course, list other factors. Among Bordwell's most significant are technological changes, like the ability to move things around fluidly in nonlinear editing programs. Videotape technologies lent new flexibility to the editing process in the eighties, but nonlinear editing offered immediate and powerful effects.[11]

Looking back at these earlier developments, one wonders what will become of short-form-audiovisual and music-video-like genres in the future. Will they colonize more and more kinds of media? Or will viewers become bored with them and move on to the next big thing? Perhaps audiovisuality is the natural state of things, held in abeyance until recently by technological limitations and obstacles to distribution. Perhaps also with globalization we desire a mode we can all share—a sort of common language—that audiovisual media can help fill. If so, audiovisuality may be here to stay.

What initially drove the audiovisual turn may be hard to determine. It might require interviews with makers and audiences, and a better archaeology of poorly catalogued media. But I have a sense we will better gauge transmedia flows in the future. With so many surveillance systems designed to track us as consumers, we might track flows of media as well. Perhaps we might start with a costuming touch or a sonic fragment (like Rihanna's "Eh-Eh-Eh" in her song "Umbrella") and with some sort of software recognition watch the ways these elements move across commercials, Facebook, music videos, films, television, and YouTube. Some new memes almost beg to be tracked—their contours are telegraphed in such bold relief, like the fast strobe-effect cutting leading up to the song's hook in "Gangnam Style." What would we learn by following these flows? I intuit they would contribute to our understanding of how we think and feel, and how ideas move. This understanding will be increasingly necessary to creating and responding to political advertising, for example.

Understanding new digital audiovisual aesthetics might require a range of approaches. Surely we might want to consider critical historical analyses by Philip Auslander, Norma Coates, Murray Forman, Amy Herzog and Holly Rogers as well as current industry studies like John Caldwell's.[12] Parameter-by-parameter and genre-by-genre analysis would also be helpful. Just focusing on color, we might turn to the research of John Belton, Alan Cameron, and J. P. Geuens; for sound recording and design, the work of Mark Katz, Mark Kerins, Melissa Ragona, Ron Sadoff, Jeff Smith, Benjamin Wright, and Bill Whittington.[13] Stronger theories of the relations among sound, text, and image (extending the work of Claudia Gorbman, Nick Cook, and others), more close readings of audiovisual works, and a commitment to interviewing industry personnel would all be helpful. Audiovisual-based genres could be better defined. Some can be finely grained. "Riot porn" (including protesting flash mobs), "war porn" (prosumer music video clips produced by military service members), and "witnessing footage" (surreptitiously captured and smuggled footage of war crimes) are different from one another, with their own unique sonic styles.[14] Music analysis in film and media departments and film analysis in music departments would support the field. Popular music as well as sound and film music studies are probably the most easily incorporated. Theo Cateforis, Charles Kronengold, and Mitchell Morris write some of the most accessible prose. There's other important work in popular music and sound studies, including analysis by Jay Beck, Walter Everett, Tim Hughes, Robert Fink, Simon Frith, Kay Kalinak, Richard Leppert, Susan Mclary, Richard Middleton, Alan Moore, John Richardson, Philip Tagg, and Robert Walser. Most needed are audiovisual studies from a cross-national perspective. To my knowledge, there is not yet a reader on world music videos as a global phenomenon or on the musical across countries. The question of how sound/image memes move through culture might require quantitative approaches, which would extend the reach of the field from the humanities into the sciences.

What will audiovisuality look like in the future? My guess is it will surprise us. I've long hungered for more labyrinthine films, with musical passages, in which the viewer can get lost. Surely there will be exciting work with apps, 3D, video-game-like configurations, and the exploration of haptics.[15] Much to my surprise, however, I've seen other configurations rising much more quickly. There's the high-low interpenetrations of Anish Kapoor and Ai Weiwei's remakes of "Gangnam Style" (surely shaped by the 2008 presidential viral media campaigns).[16] Perhaps because there's a strong documentary program at Stanford, the media objects my students bring to class are not just totally wild videos like Nicki Minaj and Cassie's "The Boys" (which are flooded with Pepto-Bismol pinks and inflated, distorted props and sets) and longplay videos, but also a new type of hyperrealist musical documentary I never thought would emerge—for example, Alma Har'el's musical number within her documentary *Bombay Beach* and her supplementary music video for Beirut's "Concubine." There's also Abteen Bagheri's video for A$AP Rocky's "Peso" and Jon Jon Augustavo's, Ryan Lewis's, and Ben Haggerty's video for Macklemore's "Thrift Shop."[17] These show how digital technologies make possible dreamlike and nearly profilmic results at the same time. I'm particularly excited by the work of Chris Milk and Vincent Morisset. Both make interactive multimedia music-video like works where, through Xbox Kinect or skype-camera interfaces, a viewer's gestures trigger sound and/or image events. These rich haptic-experiences may halt narrative teleologies in favor of the present moment, and provide dance-oriented pleasures. Surprising turns await!

CHAPTER 4

Moulin Rouge!

DELIRIOUS CINEMA

Moulin Rouge! shows the extremes of the prismatic, intensified style. My students might counter with gun-heavy films like *Lock, Stock and Two Smoking Barrels* or *Smokin' Aces* that, for them, seem more representative, but I'd claim *Moulin Rouge!* has a unique capacity to overload the viewer with sensory detail and whiplash changes. In today's films intensification occurs across all film parameters, though these films tend to emphasize distortions of classical narrative form.[1] *Moulin Rouge!* too distorts narrative—but it does so in its own radical way.[2] And few other films bring forward the kinds of *experiential* intensification emerging in both life and films: its intensity is ready for our HD home theaters, smartphones, iPads, and all the rest. *Moulin Rouge!* achieves this through an array of techniques I'll lay out. I'll also seek to convey why the film so moves me and other viewers (particularly, I think, my university students). I'll show how *Moulin Rouge!* becomes what the character Harold Zidler calls a "ravishment of the senses." At the center are three key techniques: (1) a musical (rather than traditionally narrative) form resembling a pop song's; (2) a way of holding viewers in the film's present; and (3) invocations of allegory that help draw the viewer's attention away from death. To describe these techniques, I'll first consider *Moulin Rouge!*'s narrators and places, large- to small-scale form, and then the role of the soundtrack.

A Brief Synopsis

Christian, a young, self-acknowledged naïf, comes to Paris to learn about truth, beauty, and love and to write. He's swept into the bohemian culture, and encouraged by neighbors to write the script for the Moulin Rouge's "Spectacular! Spectacular!" At the dance hall, he falls in love with Satine, the most prized and expensive courtesan. But he can't have her because she has been promised to the Duke in return for funding owner Harold Zidler's modern, electrically equipped building, which will allow her transformation into a real actress à la Sarah Bernhardt. Satine and Christian fall in love and Christian's play conveys this illicit love story in miniature, with Satine recast as a courtesan, the Duke as a maharajah, and Christian as a penniless sitar player. Satine and Christian scheme to run away together, but then Zidler reports she has consumption and will soon die. The Duke's manservant has been told to kill Christian unless Satine sleeps with the Duke. She decides to lie to Christian and say that she doesn't love him. But during the opening performance, the couple reaffirms their love, and they sing their secret love song to one another. Satine dies, but something lives on.

Multiple Narrators

In this chapter I'll consider the ways aspects of *Moulin Rouge!* support the film's three techniques (a musical form, a holding in the present, and allegory). These include multiple narrators; set design; depictions of love and romance; story; geography; form (established through terracing, foreshadowing, and processual flow); tropes; performance and improvisation; song numbers; and sound effects and scored music. Let me start with the first.

Moulin Rouge!'s prismatic qualities stem in part from its early introduction of multiple narrators and conjurors, a grand total of eleven of them. The conductor, at the film's beginning, not only directs the live show but also shadowboxes, holding his arms like a clock's; leaps like a lilting ballerina; brandishes his elbows as if braving a storm; and then hops, dances, and kicks in an attempt to bring forth the film's scenario. He plays conductor, impresario, and fan. But his authority is constrained, because the Green Fairy claims power first. She projects the film's image through the light that passes through her bottle of absinthe, thereby beckoning us into the diegesis. (Like a noisy projector, her wings make mechanical fluttering sounds.) Soon Christian and Toulouse-Lautrec appear. We might treat either as the key narrator, but who narrates whom? Christian, as a writer and as the valorous male lover in the exalted heterosexual couple, will immortalize Satine's story, we assume. But it's the dwarf Lautrec who calls Christian forth with his song, reporting that the young lover relayed the story to him. He appears in moments when the story stops (at the close of "Elephant Love Medley," for example), and with his singing begins the story anew. Near the end he appears to double as Death's emissary (along with Chocolat, the black angel), and may be the only one left in Montmartre to tell the tale. Zidler too plays narrator, as he enumerates the Moulin Rouge's growing requirements—labor, finances, and electricity. He sings, "Why must we live this way? The show must go on." In a fat suit that inflates him to two and a half times the size of the rest, he towers over the stages, peering down on his workers; his gaze extends through telescopes and peepholes. From his high vantage point he even narrates Moulin Rouge's future through the building's miniature and, like the Green Fairy, is apotheosized as a mural on the side of a tall building. Satine too has moments of meta- or extradiegetic awareness when she says, "Marie, it's these silly costumes," and "You're gonna be bad for business, I can tell."

Perhaps narration extends past characters to inanimate elements. First, the windmill quietly asserts a prescience. Responsive to the characters, it becomes grayer or redder, bigger or smaller, louder or softer. Its mechanical processes may have set everyone including Christian into motion. Humans pale under its eternal circling: when Zidler says, "Everything's going so well," he sways back and forth, making windmill arcs; late in the "Rhythm of the Night" can-can celebration, two possibly male lovers form windmill arms (perhaps signaling the world's continuance after Satine's death); Satine in her black lacy dress brings her arms up and down, calling "Whirr, whirr" as if she were the windmill (churning sexuality); the Green Fairy's vortex into the can-can rotates like the distorted arms of the windmill; and even Christian, perched on top of the elephant with arms wide, might be said to mimic the windmill's revolutions. Through sound and image the elephant too, takes on an animate force. And the music at the opening tells the film's story in miniature, as a medley: the *Sound of Music* theme scored as "romance music"; then a snippet of mysterious, swirling music; and then of energy and sex (the "Can-Can"); to return to a sense of stillness. Perhaps, too, it's only a voice that narrates, occasionally calling, "There was a boy," often in tandem with wind and breathy sounds (first presented as the camera tracks down the narrow streets of Montmartre). Or it may be the camera itself that, willful enough to claim its own trajectory, takes us through the story. Perhaps narration becomes even more diffuse: the story derives from unconscious material. Christian the writer attempts to get started with nonsensical stuff like "a narcoleptic Argentinean and a dwarf dressed as a nun," and then real characters spill forth from his dreams. A type of narration emanates also from the cries, yearnings, and fears of the denizens of Montmartre, filling up the night sky. All these potential or fragmentary narrators lend a more open quality to the film, untethering us from any fixed point of view (see figure 4.1).

Like a music video, *Moulin Rouge!*'s enigmatic ending encourages us to reassess its characters; this ending, too, against the film's body proper, inhibits us from forming clear trajectories for the characters. The Green Fairy most likely dissipates, leaving odd traces: after she leads us into the diegesis, only a few elements associated with her remain, perhaps the dangling "There Was a Boy,"

Figure 4.1 Some of *Moulin Rouge!*'s multiple narrators.

sung by an unknown voice; painted murals immortalizing her (the film does much with apotheosis); a green hue or sparkle that sweeps over the image and fades away; or she's transubstantiated into Satine herself. Christian, a healthy male likely still in his teens, might not surprise us if he wrote his novel and then fell for an average girl, became a bourgeois, and raised a family. Zidler, his company sacked once the Duke did not "get his end in," could peddle his wares in a small nightclub, with another saleable young woman as his "gosling." Satine is dead. So all that leaves is Lautrec, disabled and melancholy, to tell the tale. The story stays with Lautrec—and the windmill.

In *Moulin Rouge!* camera, music, story, and characters all contribute to the film's unfolding; none is powerful enough to claim the lead, and all seem open and multivalent. These materials also accrue in an unusual way. Gestures, sound effects, textures, colors, and props form an amalgam and move in concert to establish a shape, as if the film were ebbing and flowing like music. With intensified, accelerated films—including also Michel Gondry's *Eternal Sunshine* and Timur Bekmambetov's *Day Watch*—our attention must be fleet to keep up with a constantly changing present: as with music and music video, we are released into waves of activity, and we must go along for the ride.

Moulin Rouge! holds us in its "now," rather than letting us stray to its future, in part by organizing audiovisual relations like an archipelago. The film presents a kaleidoscopic assortment of viewpoints against music's tightly woven lattice. A perspective can emerge, recede, and return again, and we can connect all of its appearances. I heard that "Penny Lane" calliope melody and here it is, surprisingly, again. "I remember," I might think and wonder. I hear "Diamond Dogs," "Lady Marmalade," or "Diamonds Are a Girl's Best Friend," and suddenly some patina of David Bowie, Patti LaBelle, or Marilyn Monroe colors the characters and settings before me: "Where was I when I first heard these tunes and how do they pertain to this moment?" Such a mysteriously rich form! Perhaps *Moulin Rouge!*'s exceptional qualities are a culmination of the intensified and accelerated style. Emphasizing stylistic markers that have been increasingly infiltrating cinematic discourse, this film arrives at a moment near supersaturation.[3]

Design and Love

Stanley Cavell notes that the romantic couples in comedies of remarriage
tend to exist in gorgeously spun, finely articulated worlds.[4] This seems true
not only for comedies but also for all great romances—Howard Hawks's
Bringing Up Baby, Jean Renoir's *Rules of the Game*, and Mani Ratnam's *Dil Se*,
for example. In *Bringing Up Baby*, Susan's wild pursuits find the perfect
match in leopards, stolen cars, and zany characters, all unfolding in a *Midsummer Night's Dream* forest. The couples' charades in *Rules of the Game* fit
the elaborate fox-hunts, soirées, and hide-and-seek games in a country
manor. *Dil Se*'s high stakes—a terrorist and her lover who seeks to disarm
her—reverberates against the barren cliffs of Kashmir. Satine is dying, but
it's a world of velvet and absinthe. Within the whirlwind, the couples stand
gazing toward one another.

The beauty (and pain) of the now is supported by the "ravishment of the
senses." In *Moulin Rouge!* the arabesque designs create another nonnarrative
impetus—tendril, beading, odalisque painting, bit of tassel. We also might
follow color as its own discrete trajectory: the green of absinthe; the Green
Fairy; Zidler's evil green flush. The same is true of Christian's purple at his
writing desk that may finally bloom into Satine's red satin dress and his coat's red
lining in the "Elephant Love" medley. Color has its own animus. For example, as
the camera approaches the sign over Christian's window, it blooms redder.

Moulin Rouge! repeats audiovisual materials to increase sensual density.
The dots on Christian's lederhosen rhyme with those on Satine's trapeze—
dots that will be picked up by the floor's fallen white petals that finally turn red,
signaling Satine's death. The Busby Berkeley cluster of revelers in the Moulin
Rouge courtyard rhyme with the rotating wedding cake of dancers who support Satine's "Rhythm of the Night" costume changes. The circles expand into
larger set-pieces: the lazy Susan–like spinning "Like a Virgin" number, and the
"Can-Can," where the camera dollies left while performers in serpentine spirals
whirl to the right.

Geography

I'd love to have a mental map of the Moulin Rouge, its city and surrounds: the
twisting passageways into Montmartre and Zidler's establishment, the station
whence Christian's train arrives—even where to get a good meal in town, and
where the wealthy patrons and service workers live—but I can't construct one.
Much obscures the landscape—the overhead camera sweeps past me, but

too far from the street's details; the storybook buildings cloak their scale; the two-street views that are taken also conflict (one traversal through the town reveals vibrancy, another dissolution—which belongs to the present, past, or future?). The broken paths make it unclear how spaces connect to each other. What trail does Satine make from the prostitutes' changing rooms to the boudoir in the elephant's head?[5]

Moulin Rouge!'s geography might be laid out like this: it's a fairly straight shot from the Eiffel Tower, on to the monster-headed entrance of Montmartre, and then to one of Christian's garret windows. Then there's a sharp about-face to the front of the Moulin Rouge, which has a windmill in the center with the Duke's tower to one side. Then comes a courtyard with the elephant slightly to the left, and Moulin Rouge's main dancehall. Like the windmill, the elephant shifts location and scale. This architectural nexus and the city's larger topography prove unstable. We assume Christian has only one window in his garret (because light streams in from one side), but we discover there are two. From the mouth of Montmartre, the camera throws several obstacles in our path, so we can't place the windmill in relation to Christian's garret. The Green Fairy's path into the can-can revelry moves through the Moulin Rouge courtyard's entrance, not the exterior that faces Christian's window. (So from Christian's window, her descent might be around and into the compound, not straight down.) *Moulin Rouge!*'s decentered, twisting qualities begin in a fantastic layout of Paris.

But then *Moulin Rouge!* may be less about actual locations than poetic cartography (perhaps like Christopher Nolan's *Inception*). The basement or ground is the place of mechanical energy and wanton carnality, the train, the city of sin, the can-can dancing. Second and third stories are about writing plays, seduction, falling in love. Levels four and five, on rooftops and in the sky above, are out of time. The dwarf's singing of "There Was a Boy"; Christian's performance of "The Hills Are Alive"; the Green Fairy's chorus-lines; the Astaire and Rogers–like number in the clouds ("Your Song"); and the "Elephant Love Medley" are places of euphoria, orgasm, so out of time as to exist forever—apotheosis. The psychic distance between sky and ground is wide, and since we don't fully understand the music's intentions, these shifts remain mysterious. Shifts occur from higher to lower (do contrapuntal paths unfold between balconies or inside the theater?). How we move among levels is also obscure: through a hole cut into a ceiling, through a Hitchcockian time-warp funnel that bulges and shrinks and then pours into several funhouse-mirrored doors, from the ceiling on a trapeze (where did Satine begin?), on hats flying into the city's night sky, and over the city as an illuminated and transfigured landscape triggered by Christian's singing.

There's also much play with doubles and miniatures creating further disorienting effects. For example, a miniature Matterhorn placard accompanies the Green Fairy's flirtations during the drafting of *Spectacular Spectacular*'s script. The gargantuan elephant becomes an enormous miniature (impossibly on the same scale as the Eiffel Tower) in the "Your Song" number. In relation to such dreamy geography, the "elephant brain" boudoir may be the film's center—a place of timeless memory.

Story

What of *Moulin Rouge!* as a story? I must admit I'm not so happy with its rough outlines, but perhaps I don't really care. I'm smitten by the film's first half (and often stay there), but less fond of its second, with its lingering close-ups. From her first appearance until the "Elephant Love Medley," Satine projects both her desire to be an actress and her interest in love. For me, this trajectory makes her heroic. A touchstone, Michael Powell's *The Red Shoes*, provides a related meditation on a woman's wants and ambitions, but while *The Red Shoes* has its protagonist choose art over romance, *Moulin Rouge!* opts for romance. Once Satine becomes interested in Christian, her world seems to narrow to only him. The film's argument that art (here, acting) can be used in the service of true love doesn't resonate much, at least for me. What if the film could keep both ambition and love in play, to show off other facets of Satine's ambivalence? The days between Satine's abandonment of Christian and her final performance at the Moulin Rouge are left unexplained. Viewers must calculate the gains and losses of her choices and might wonder if Satine has done so too. She has only one week to live. Will she be able to fulfill her dreams with Christian? (I agree with Zidler that she can't tell Christian about the Duke's plan to kill him, but *couldn't* she successfully run away with him?) Satine must think: "So little time—but I can save the people I've worked with." Satine sleeps with the Duke. In a subtle, brief shot, the Duke's cameo, against barren trees and blue-gray rain (like the opening of David Lean's *Oliver Twist*), taunts her with a stern gaze. We then see her from a high angle overlooking the courtyard as she crosses from his castle tower, the back of her white dress ripped. She has sickened and will die. The Duke's blue-gray world radiates outward, threatening the film's ending: the final Bollywood number is saturated with a deep, grim blue, and Satine's skin gleams with a grim pallor. But how is the heroine's death made bearable? Perhaps some aspect of her seems to survive even beyond Christian's story. Her faint resembles other dancers' swoons, and we remember her as the Green Fairy—like Tinkerbell, Satine can be kept alive.

Form

Moulin Rouge! first insulates us from and then brings us to Satine's tragic end. Does the film fascinate us, holding death at bay as Scheherazade does by telling her king a thousand-and-one stories? I mentioned Baz Luhrmann's three most powerful techniques: (1) holding us in the moment or the now, (2) binding us to a musical form that resembles a pop song, and (3) wrapping us in allegory, thereby giving us hope that the inevitable can be transcended.

So first—the film's radical form, its musicality. How does the film's form support the breaking of such bad news? Simplicity. We're told Christian will fall in love with Satine, who will die. The film's opening also signals many times that Satine is already dead. Knowing we're heading for heartbreak helps us to stay in the moment; we don't want or need to know the future. The movie's villains are also comical, for the most part. Zidler and the Duke possess little of the malevolence of *The Red Shoes'* Lermontov, for example. And with such carefully rendered, lush audiovisual materials, the viewer may wish to stay in the here and now, to move through passages of extreme compression or elongation, without attending to the future.

Moulin Rouge! is a distorted pearl. The first half is deliriously accelerated and the second half unreels slowly, with lingering close-ups and three or four large-scale musical numbers. At the film's midpoint, the "Elephant Love Medley" reaches an almost complete sense of here-and-now stasis. "We can be heroes!" assert the couple, and there is something so believable and hopeful about this. They have "stopped time, if just for one day."[6]

Musical sections also hold us in the present. Almost all of the numbers unpredictably open out. They run much longer than their expected course, often through a new turn or unexpected jolt that spirals out into another musical segment. Off-balance because we can't gauge the section's close, we must attend to the immediate past and future. The emergency rehearsal of "Spectacular! Spectacular!" in Satine's bedroom, for example, with a collectively enacted catalogue of potential participants and effects (elephants, courtesans, acrobats, sitar player, and electricity), is so madcap it could work as a finale. But then the Duke asks one more question: "How might this end?" Then and there. Full stop. Materialized in an instant, a mini-stage-play unfolds with curtain calls, costume changes, and ad-hoc props. During the first night's debauchery at the Moulin Rouge, the sexy can-can dancers' performance trumps what we've seen in cinema: the women's skirts jousting suggest something between a battle cry and a mating ritual. Their ruffled skirts make shebang swooshes, transferring the camera's whip-pan effects from the realm of the visual into the aural. We keep watching, partly because there's the intimation we might see some genitalia (possibly of a hermaphrodite—note the curtained imagery with Zidler directing us into the Moulin Rouge). And though our stamina may be waning, Zidler flips an advertisement on wooden placards and everyone must shift into double-time. Satine's descent from the trapeze engenders a long string of segments: a mélange of "Diamonds Are a Girl's Best Friend," Gloria Estefan's salsa-inflected "Rhythm of the Night," and Bowie's "Diamond Dogs" as closer. The bohemian revolutionaries cap the creation of their new script with Christian's first glass of burning absinthe. Good show. But then multiple green fairies flange out in the sky, and the New Bohemians sing on a window ledge as the Green Fairy traces words in a sparkling font that projects its own tune. Christian and Satine head for the sky in the "Your Song" and "Elephant Love Medley" numbers. Both numbers are as rich and elaborate as anything in musicals. But these two numbers keep going as we head back into the elephant's head. The "Elephant Love Medley" includes not only "We could be heroes, forever and ever" (that's plenty for me) but also "I will always love you." Here the couple's spinning evokes the ultimate image of love (as in Hitchcock's *Vertigo*), spiral on spiral, behind which twirls a star-emblazoned background. Perhaps I'm devoted to *Moulin Rouge!* because, after periods of frenetic activity, I come across a patch that suggests what it feels like to be in love (see figure 4.2).[7]

David Bordwell has claimed that today's films remain classical and their defining features are comprised of a five-act structure with a character who pursues goals and becomes changed by the film's end. But films like *Moulin Rouge!* suggest we need the five-act frame only as a mechanism for structuring cinema's expansive consumption of time: the turning points of some acts can be submerged or subverted to the point of irrelevance. Other forms can be superimposed upon the five-act structure, creating a shimmering or prismatic effect. And why can't films take sojourns, stepping off and following other more musical designs—the sonata, the rondo, the ritornello—before they return to the traditional form? With *Moulin Rouge!* we might want to think of the first half as a pop song. Three large numbers, "Your Song," the "Elephant Love Medley," and the "Can-Can," can be grouped together as choruses. The emergency rehearsal of "Spectacular! Spectacular!" and the multiples of the Green Fairy dancing in the sky could be pre-choruses. The New Bohemians' writing

Figure 4.2   Moulin Rouge! suggests what it feels like to be in love.

of the script, Satine's nearly dying and then changing dresses, and Satine's seduction of Christian and the Duke work as verses, with their more quotidian
material. If we experience *Moulin Rouge!* as a pop song, Luhrmann's careful
phrasing of material takes on greater weight.

During the "Elephant Love Medley," when Christian and Satine sing on the
elephant's back, the past seems filled by hills and valleys too steep to turn back
to; the future lays little claim on us. How is this possible? Until this point there
have been few narrative markers. *Moulin Rouge!*'s narrative thrust is gently terraced or cross-cut so we don't notice large plot-turns. From the beginning
Christian and Satine keep re-enchanting one another and re-falling in love. The
Duke reappears, suggesting, "I will change the course," or "I will control things,"
but someone thwarts him. In the midst, there's much business. Allusions to
Satine's death are peppered throughout: the vertiginous, dreamlike lead into
the "Can-Can" sequence; Satine descending on her trapeze; Christian's allusion
to her death and an accompanying frozen black-and-white still of Satine.

Musicality: Flow, Phrase-Shapes, and Contrast

How is *Moulin Rouge!* like music? First, *Moulin Rouge!* modulates music, sound
effects, camera movement and editing, actors' dispositions, lighting, sets,
props and other elements to create a sense of continuity and processual flow.
Continuity is created partly through foreshadowing and repetition, and flow is
partly established by the ways we are led on through the characters' and the
camera's interlocking gestures. The blurry, druggy, and plentiful sexuality in
the can-can scene, for example, has been foreshadowed by prostitutes leaning
against the buildings of Montmartre's side streets as well as the Green Fairy's
sparkly, wiggling buttocks. Before the "Elephant Love Medley," "Your Song"
preps us for the more absorbed romantic couple. Flow is established through
the ways the camera leads us through the tunnel-like and winding paths of
the Moulin Rouge. Performers point or move in concerted lines and, through
editing, gradually rise up to the top of the frame and then come back down.
Dialogue, too, is passed among characters: one finishes another's thought, or
another utters a notion shared by all, like the Duke's "It's a little bit funny, this
feeling inside." Thus we're handed over from moment to moment.[8]

Second, within these currents that establish a basic flow, material coalesces
into larger and smaller phrase-like shapes. Closings of phrases for sections
may be the easiest to identify. One large phrase ends just after Christian narrates, "The woman I loved is dead," and we hear the whip of a skirt closing off
possibilities. Other endings: Satine sputters, "A writer?" and the nondiegetic
music gets suddenly pulled as if a tone-arm had been ripped across a record.

In some closing sections, the lurid color suddenly turns gray, as if to clear the palette (for example, after Zidler signs the deed to the Moulin Rouge, an overhead shot shows color has leached from the courtyard). A character gazing out a window or Satine's fall from her trapeze lends some stillness too. Beginnings are more razzle-dazzle—the jazzy bugle boys singing as Christian waits for Satine at the head of the elephant, or the raucous crowd-noises and singing that opens the "Can-Can" section. Nested within these larger shapes, several elements work to create terracing or builds. Mayhem often intensifies and when the frenetic activity is brought to a pitch, a singing voice cuts through the texture. Examples include Christian's singing the *Sound of Music*'s "The Hills Are Alive"; his cry, "Cause you can-can all night aah!" in the midst of the can-can's "Teen Spirit" section; and his interjection of "My Gift Is My Song" to Satine's seductions in her boudoir. Within these terracing forms, we have even shorter, nested phrases. A brief phrase might end when suddenly the soundtrack thins and a character's softly spoken words like "Yes, yes" or a breath come forward. Shapes for briefer nested phrases are also closed through Satine's swoons, and Zidler's calls of "Everything's going so well," as his voice drops in pitch and his body droops. Elements create a sense of flow and are shaped into phrases at the small and large scales.

Third, like sections in a pop song, materials in *Moulin Rouge!* can be sharply juxtaposed. These hard oppositions work through nested structures—mid-scale shapes that are mirrored at the micro- and large-scale levels. At the mid-level, sharp changes occur when Satine rolls around on the floor calling "Yes, yes!" and Christian responds with the more chivalrous "Your Song." The stillness of Satine's descent on the trapeze contrasts with the raucousness of the can-can's numbers. Luhrmann sharply contrasts large sections too. For example, while the New Bohemians write the theme song "The Hills Are Alive," the scene is infused with zaniness, one of the most maligned of performance modes. As Sianne Ngai describes it, the zany consists of attempting to manage too many tasks and doing them poorly.[9] I'd claim we watch the zany for a moment because she might provide an unusual and useful approach to the world—she's following her own beat—but we most often turn away quickly. Zaniness is embarrassing: Lucille Ball trying to leave the home and gain a career; Wile E. Coyote vs. the Road Runner; Crazy Eddie selling appliances in TV commercials. All of these goofballs may be loved, but they also evoke a sense of repulsion. As Ngai points out, there are a range of zany types (one of the most malevolent is Heath Ledger's Joker from *Batman*). But the New Bohemians, as one of the most benign examples, *transcend* the zany, making good on it, and inventing, through collective action, the new production—"Spectacular Spectacular." Next *Moulin Rouge!* rapidly switches, and what a switch! It's not immediately apparent in the euphoria and decadence, but peeling paint, mold, the stench of struggle and strife, and performers' faces riven with desperation and fear are all part of the "Can-Can" sequence. Zany but triumphant, euphoric but desperate. By being adjacent, the two scenes' affective modes seem to contaminate one another, creating a new affective color.[10]

Dramatic change can also be strikingly local. Many quick turns of emotion (what scriptwriters call "beats") keep us in the here and now. As Satine readies herself for her first boudoir meeting with the Duke, her handmaiden stitches her up, and she dreams of being the great Sarah Bernhardt (sad and nostalgic). We then shift quickly through her handmaiden's encouragement (nefarious); Zidler's entrance, with a query about his strawberry (threatening); her squeal (submissive); Satine's and her handmaid's about-face (humorous); Satine showing off her dress (dazzling); Zidler singing "Everything's going so well" (melancholy); and Christian standing with his hat behind his back while chorines sing (sexy, taut, nervous). In another example of a fast emotional pivot, Christian calls, "India! It's set in India!" (hysterically) and then switches suddenly to, "The most beautiful courtesan" (clear, still, and direct).

Moulin Rouge! also holds us in the moment with characters' faces. It takes a moment to read a face in close-up, as if we're witnessing the dawning of an aspect. Then suddenly the face seems clearly etched, sharply telegraphing its emotive content. Christian is sheepish but desirous; Satine is flirtatious but puzzled; the Duke is curious but stunned. A countershot invokes a similar dynamic, with a new affective disposition. In order to understand the response of one character to another we must ford two adjacent shots and the edit between them. Perhaps characters feel things more quickly, directly, independently, and strongly than we do. In this way they seem bigger than ordinary people— allegorical, even—and hence worthy of emulation.

Large-scale formal design helps Luhrmann establish *Moulin Rouge!*'s sectional differentiations. Christian's attic, where "Spectacular Spectacular" takes place, is a fun house with angles askew; shots of figures either too large and close or too small and at a distance; walls and ceilings that balloon out mysteriously; and window views painted not much differently from the enormous placard for *The Sound of Music*'s Swiss Alps. The "Can-Can" sequence, on the other hand, has many cubbyholes, mysteriously opening and closing mirrored doors, and swirls upon swirls.

The dramatic use of shape contributes to contrast and continuity, and provides a means to structure large sections—particularly through the use of lines, clusters, and circles. The film's opening might be said to emphasize verticals, either jagged or straight (like the train and the passages through Montmartre streets). Spirals organize the Children of the Revolution's drafting of the script, the "Can-Can" sequence, and Satine's fall from her trapeze. The big musical numbers in the second half also emphasize spirals. But some sections return to an orientation toward line, like the phallic joke of the "Spectacular Spectac-ular" cardboard cutout of a tower, carried like a missile on its side by extras as we head toward the balcony's long passageways where Satine and Christian steal kisses. Up and down we go too, from basement to rooftop and back. These runs support the final promenades along the center aisle in preparation for the new Moulin Rouge theater's final performance of "Spectacular Spectacular." (The most striking preparatory marches are Christian's in "Roxanne"; and first Zidler and then Satine's in "The Show Must Go On," each performer heading off in isolation.) Earlier spirals prepare for the Bohemians' advance in a massive semicircle in the closing "Freedom, Truth, and Love" (see figure 4.3).

Tropes

Such an intricate, multileveled formal design may make it possible for sexual metaphors, symbols, and odd behaviors to run free. *Moulin Rouge!* is a large audiovisual lyric poem. We'll pass through a world of sorrow by a River Styx (Paris's Seine). We'll also ford an enormous body of water (England to France), travel by train, and pass through the threatening open mouth of the Montmar-tre Bridge, past a priest. Paris is littered with memories, and while Christian weeps, a church bell rings and an infant cries. Perhaps as consolation for Sat-ine's inevitable death, the film draws toward wanton sex. One might say we're in the "no" of the unconscious where there is no time. Christian's typewriter spins around like a slashing blade into an "eye" of a woman's skirts (echoing Bunuel's *Un Chien Andalou*). We come toward a curtain and Zidler's head pops up like an erection, followed by (labial) pantaloons. Next a sea of skirts and panties upend us. When we begin the "Can-Can" sequence, types stream in: clowns, mutes, 1940s bankers, 1980s Wall Street types.

During the "Can-Can" sequence, Satine is allegorized through a number of images. Red roses, money, hankies, and canes uncannily appear in clusters and then disappear around her. A nervous "familiar" in black and white stripes, almost out of *Nosferatu*, hovers nearby. An allegorical Satine serves here to hold us in the moment. She stops time. A clown wearing a star will frame her head to crown her. The diamond heart she's awarded seems like a cutout of her elephant-heart window. Together, multitiered, these form a *mise en abyme*.

Figure 4.3 Simple forms—circles and lines—lend *Moulin Rouge!* structure.

While Christian will always have upright wine bottles or tapered long candlesticks beside him, suggesting potency, Satine will appear later against a backdrop of undulating women mimicking her poses—often Indian statuary making beautiful snaking S-curves. In the "Can-Can" sequence we can discover gay figures with their own love stories, apart from the main heteronormative one. (Perhaps we might follow these instead—most touchingly, to a later four-handed piano duet.) After much business and confusion—even the film's editor seems overcome—everyone is forced into a stutter by the image, suddenly glitched, torqued, and run in reverse. Satine then becomes a feathered bird brought to Christian through billowing smoke (like his train arriving into Paris) and crowned by a star. The scene builds to a close. The squirting of hats through the roof of the Moulin Rouge into the city's night sky (touch of pink) and circular lake suggests a woman's genitals and orgasm.

Satine is dying (or perhaps already dead and ghostly), but in the "Can-Can" sequence we might not care. She's first presented as a black-and-white photo, as if she's already a memory. Reverb accompanying this photo suggests a tomblike space. When she descends on her swing (with clipped wings as if she can't fly), her skin has the pallor of a corpse. She's a hardened diamond. She falls as if to her death into the arms of a black man, who is rendered as an angel of death. A gong sounds. Robin Woods's analysis of Hitchcock's *Vertigo* claims the film's power stems from its varied tempi: the flower petals (fast), the people (moderate), the redwoods (slow), the ocean (slower still). *Moulin Rouge!* works similarly, with flower petals too, as well as turning shiny skirts and glittery baubles (fast), dancing performers (moderate), Satine's consumption and death (slow), the elephant (slower still), and the gong (slower still). The latter points to our own moments of stillness and silence. Allegorical imagery works as a timeless iconic language, as images that must be read. These slow the film down. We often see figures behind Satine representing her—and her dreams—like the photographs of the great Sarah Bernhardt. There are also murals and paintings on walls, and decorative touches on stalls and chairs of a woman (Satine?) on horseback, but also a woman spread-eagled either upright or upside down, pinned to the windmill's sails (for example, in Zidler's office), and a windmill and a laughing moon. All these seem out of time, harbingers of eternity.

Characters, Performance, and Improvisation

In contrast to the slow processes of allegory, the film's physicality creates a giddy immediacy. Some of *Moulin Rouge!*'s charm stems from its overspilling joy and excitement. Much of the action feels improvisatory, with characters willingly sharing lines, flexibly shifting roles, and working toward building community. The bohemian revolutionaries toss words back and forth for one another and then make space for Christian breaking into song. "Spectacular! Spectacular!" is an on-the-spot, virtuoso creation constructed collaboratively. For the "Can-Can," Zidler leads the crowd out the door, into the rain, and back inside again, where they shift to double-time. When he sings, "On and on, the show must go on," all of his workers almost telepathically share the same dreary sentiment, singing as they labor. When Satine falls from her trapeze, Zidler creatively finds a way to make good on it: "You've frightened her away." When Satine can't make her meeting with the Duke, Zidler suddenly invents "she's confessing her sins" and gladly wraps himself in a tablecloth, holding breasts of aspic, a happy substitute for the Duke. And together, Christian and Satine discover the means to swap bits of songs and then share a duet. This instant inventiveness and openness to improvisation helps keep us within the moment.

The Couple's Budding Relationship

Character development is most often shown through musical means. *Moulin Rouge!*'s plot turns are often signaled by words that hover like zeppelins ("she's dying"; "the Duke"), but they don't do much narrative work. The "Elephant Love Medley" presents Christian as a worthy lover for Satine, though when he first arrived in Paris he described himself as a naïf. In retrospect we might sense that each musical number contributes to his maturation. In "Your Song" he gains greater powers of fealty, empathy, and care. In the first rehearsal of "Spectacular! Spectacular!" he develops the art of collaboration. In his first meeting with the bohemian revolutionaries, he claims a sense of childhood, and in the "Can-Can" sequence, he gathers sexual knowledge. Satine's character development is more elusive. As an actress, she's a prismatic figure. Her presentation of self shifts as volubly as the music and shows us an array of types. In the "Can-Can" sequence, the lighting and low-angled camera give her face a cartoonish look (note the flared nostrils). In the bedroom farce, she resembles a wind-up doll. But before "Your Song" she shifts quickly to the kind of lady a medieval troubadour might wish to sing for. When she changes costumes with Zidler, we see she can be "bright and bubbly" or a "smoldering temptress," but she most wants to be a real actress. The sudden glimpses of sorrow, as when she responds by singing, "We can't do that," against Christian's "We can be heroes," are when we know her as someone who can be enabled or loved. Does *Moulin Rouge!* possess features of a thirties Hollywood remarriage story? Christian and Satine make a history for one another, educate one another, and find ways of amusing one another. Looking over the film's first half, we can see long arcs where one character comes to the fore and leads the other, and then allows the roles to reverse, much like a pair of figure skaters. (It's worth taking seriously the moment when Satine and Christian cross sides before they head out from the head of the elephant in "Your Song.") Satine says this directly at one point when she claims, "I'll take care of it, Lautrec."

Music

What animates all of this? I would claim that not the actors, but the soundtrack is where real intimacy lies. Many signs of the body are there: groans, sighs, whispers, shrieks. *Moulin Rouge!*'s division into two parts is partly accomplished through the soundtrack. The first half is primarily composed of disparate musical excerpts strung together, the glue made up of a roar of the wind and whispering of voices, the beating of fairy wings, crowd-noises, rustling skirts, cheers, and string arrangements. This sonic continuity is punctuated in the "Can-Can" sequence by dramatic foley effects—like a dropped silver platter that sounds like a cymbal, or a glove that squeaks like a water pistol. Sound effects become even more surreal in Satine's boudoir when the sounds of Zidler's feet resemble the trotting of tiny ponies (most likely realized by a foley artist pattering fingers on a desk), and Satine pulls the Duke's legs out and in with the twang of a jew's harp. Speech is also sung, contributing to a shared musicality. When Audrey says, "Now where in heaven's name are we going to find someone to read the role of the young, sensitive Swiss poet goatherder?" a trumpet "wah-wah-wah" melody follows her descending vocal line. *Moulin Rouge!*'s second half becomes more traditional, with simple accompaniments of a tinkling, descending piano, an oboe, strings, flute: sweet stuff. (Audrey's wish—could we please just have a bit of decorative piano—comes true.) The reality principle has taken over.

In *Moulin Rouge!* the songs help narrate the story. We know Christian falls in love with Satine when he sings "Your Song." The Duke also falls in love with Satine when she sings "Your Song" (a light suddenly sparkles in his eyes), and we also know that the moment she sings the song, she, too, sings herself into love. *Moulin Rouge!*'s colorful whirlwind is fueled by so many different elements, from the city's twisting cartography, the intoxicating power of absinthe, offers of plentiful and wanton sex, piles of red velvet and brocade, and recurring defiant-youth-oriented music like "Teen Spirit" and "Lady Marmalade."

Moulin Rouge!'s first half is particularly winsome. As mentioned, the music and the soundtrack are comprised of a mélange of sources, each with its own particular ties to space, place, and time. In Christian's garret, some Beatles-style materials resound. But what does mid-sixties London have to do with *Moulin*

Rouge!'s denizens? The "Can-Can" sequence showcases "Lady Marmalade" (70s mixed-race bluesy sexuality) against "Diamonds Are a Girl's Best Friend" (50s male conservatism); "Teen Spirit" (90s teenage male angst) puts us in a different subject position than David Bowie's "Diamond Dogs" (70s androgyny, hipper and wiser). Sonic sources draw us back and forward in time and space and trigger associations to race, class, gender, sexuality, and age. When we hear Christian's loony-tunes music during the drafting of "Spectacular! Spectacular!," does this suggest a return to Christian's childhood or a counter to the forth-coming lascivious "Can-Can" sequence?

The soundtrack can traverse history more freely than the image. When Christian stands at the elephant boudoir's heart-shaped window waiting for Satine, chorines sing, reminding us of another era (World War II), when women lined up to pump up their men. During Satine's oversexed wind-up doll performance with both Christian and the Duke, classical chestnuts—lowbrow, old fogeyish, and remote—suggest Molière's farces. Does this music suggest that despite the setting's lushness and sexiness, true love has not yet arrived? And when Christian speak-sings, his voice is often supported by a pop song arrangement, like "All You Need Is Love"—lush strings fill in as accom-paniment. But when Zidler or the Duke sings these words, nothing happens.[11]

As I've suggested, music in *Moulin Rouge!* has its own codes that circulate in their own networks. If music can live on, reappearing with its own teleology, suddenly, emerging without any provocation, can't Satine live on too? Here are a few examples. Exiting Christian's bedroom after our first hit of absinthe, we hear a few measures of a calliope as if from the Beatles' "Strawberry Fields For-ever." Soon we'll be taken down into a hallucinogenic place: Zidler's ballroom and the "Can-Can" dance sequence. For now, the music might signal youth and innocence, and we might also hear the high trumpets in the Green Fairy's number in the sky as an homage to "Penny Lane." The Beatles references will eventually return in the "Elephant Love Medley"—Christian sings "All You Need Is Love"—but that's nearly an hour away, with a completely different context. We first hear Satine's death motif as Christian weeps by the window: "The woman I love is dead." At the end of the "Diamonds Are a Girl's Best Friend" number, as Satine is carried upward on her trapeze swing, a brash chord progression moves inexorably forward, as she sings haltingly, "Diamonds are a girl's best. . . ." In the gap, her pitched sigh attempts to complete the song but fails, and this death motif returns, creating harmonic closure, but not com-pleting the melody. Neither the stillness of a gong-stroke nor the onrushing trumpets can save her.[12]

Instead, triumphant, "Diamonds Are a Girl's Best Friend" returns *again* at the close of the "Elephant Love Medley" ("You're going to be bad for business—I can tell"). Perhaps the "Can-Can" sequence's gong also intermedially returns at the end of the "Elephant Love Medley," now transubstantiated into a costuming touch. Here Lautrec wears a kimono, reminding us of slower processes and 19th-century associations with the East. These materials—the death motif, "Diamonds Are a Girl's Best Friend," and the gong—will seal Satine's death at the film's end.

"Elephant Love Medley"

For me, the sequence that can best hold us in the now is "Elephant Love Medley." I close with this to help convey the film's unusual senses of time. When Christian and Satine sing while perched on the elephant's back, the past seems filled up by hills and valleys too steep to turn back upon; the future lays little claim on us. We're in a short saddle of now. Narrative drive stops. This nowness, an absorption in where we are, seems to exceed that of other musicals. How is this achieved? Satine wears a shiny red-satin cinched dress— the color of desire—and we need little else. The linking of song titles is fragile— Satine misses the first riposte. Christian sings "all you need is love"—and she, with her own rhymes of "a girl has got to eat," "she'll end up on the street," says, a half-step off, "love is just a game," instead of Christian's lyrics, "love is all you need." We hover, wary of the missed beat. Still, this process is not narrative, but more an assembly or a catalogue, one item linked to another. There's a fear that Satine or Christian will fall off the elephant, and the risk also keeps us in the moment. Myths about the world created on the backs of animals help this moment expand into allegory. So too that the couple might be on top of a wedding cake or helm of a ship (like the *Titanic*). We watch to see if the tentative courtship can continue, if one expression negates or picks up on the last. We're enchanted by the ways shorter phrases expand into longer ones as the singing progresses, and each singer shares a turn; first, sharing the musical style of the other, but with different orchestration (Christian has strings, "Just one night," but then Satine responds with an English horn, "There's no way 'cause you can't pay"). A solid rhythm arrangement and fuller orchestration (strings, brass, chorus) then fill in. Satine and Christian share the lyrics to the same song, with the blessings of the timpani and strings, finally to sing together, heroes forever and ever, stopping time, just for one day.

CHAPTER 5

Music Video, Songs, Sound

ETERNAL SUNSHINE OF THE SPOTLESS MIND

Since the early 1990s critics have been complaining that films look like music videos, and indeed close study of this "low art" can help to explain contemporary film. The new visual elements (relying on close shots, wide-ranging camera movements, and rapid editing) have long been central to the music video genre because they illuminate musical form.[1] Free-ranging camera movements like dollying, handheld, reframing, and crane shots reflect music's flowing, processual nature; blocks of image highlight song structure; intense colorization illuminates features like a song's harmony, sectional divisions, and timbre; visual motifs speak to musical ones; and editing and editing-like effects such as strobing, flash frames, and superimpositions not only show off the song's rhythmic strata but also function to switch among elements (narrative, dance, lyrics, hooks), letting none take the upper hand. Music videos foreground unpredictable teleology and ambiguous endings.

Why does this aesthetic appear in the cinema now? Economics, production practices, and technological developments all contribute. David Bordwell argues that technologies are the most crucial: for example, Avid editing, where, "images are but colorful rectangles sharing a flat space"; Pro Tools and Logic with their multiple tracks and zoom functions; digital intermediary, which allows visual areas to be clustered in groups, and connections to be made both across time and instantaneously with the soundtrack.[2] Surround sound and better compression algorithms similarly place sound materials as points in space, or seamlessly meld them into immersive environments. My argument extends Bordwell's to claim the aesthetic includes not just camera and editing, but all parameters—acting, lighting, performance, sound effects, and musical materials. Everything becomes heightened, set off, voluble. The films' forms distort as well, from the local to the large scale. I call this new stylistic configuration "intensified audiovisual aesthetics."

It is beyond this essay's scope to ascertain music video's influence in relation to technology, or the ways it worked with other shaping forces.[3] Suffice to
say that today many film directors break into features not by graduating from
film school with a strong showreel, apprenticing in the industry, or writing
scripts but through making music videos. Directors like David Fincher, Spike
Jonze, and Hype Williams worked in music video for a long time before making
the shift.[4] They acknowledge that music video provided them with unusual
training. Fincher calls music videos a kind of "sandbox" where he could try
anything; he never learned traditional filmmaking, nor does he want to.
Responding to the constraints of the genre, music video directors often turn to
a song's structure to generate the image.

Such untraditional schooling may have helped foster new ways of knowing
music, image, and sound. In this context Michel Gondry makes a good case-
study as a music video director who became a film director, thanks to his preeminence in his original medium. The *New York Times* has called him "the
most sought after video director in the world" and his work was among the first
to be distributed on Palm Pictures' music video compilation DVDs. His
training as a drummer and extensive experience in animation seem to have
attuned him particularly sensitively to changes in popular music. At the same
time, as a filmmaker he brings a particularly powerful sensibility to the cinema. Without diminishing scriptwriter Charlie Kaufman's importance to the
film, we can see that Gondry's contribution to *Eternal Sunshine of the Spotless
Mind* (2004), for example, goes much deeper than what is typical for Hollywood directors. If my approach here has an auteurist flavor, it is because Gondry played a major role in the mise en scène, the sound design, the development
of the script, the comportment of the characters, the creation of visual schemes,
the control of location, and the establishment of rhythmic flow; in addition,
the film is suffused with his personal motifs and favorite techniques. This itself
reflects the practices of music video. Music video directors wield control over
every phase of production: the making of storyboards, casting extras, selecting
props, shooting, editing, and many processes normally considered purely mechanical in other genres. It should not surprise us that *Eternal Sunshine*'s star,
Jim Carrey, calls the director "Cecil B. Gondry."

In examining this film in depth, this essay has two sections. In the first I
discuss a number of visual details and call attention to their "worked" quality,
paying special attention to the film's varied and densely layered soundtrack,
separately and in its close relation to the imagetrack. I will argue that Gondry's
engagement with music and other elements of the soundtrack, and his ways of
mixing old and new technologies, work to create a form capable of holding
many points of view. In the second section I focus on the ways in which Gondry extends traditional and contemporary Hollywood filmmaking processes;

deploys sound and image to ground local shifts in color, exposure, film stock, and additional postproduction techniques; and foregrounds process and flow, color and texture, the use of tableaux and rhythmic effects. *Eternal Sunshine* is structured as a lattice of sound-image connections. Although the film can be understood to take place largely inside one character's head, its multiple points of view are not governed by a single, overarching perspective; often its separate strands do not even meet one another. This latticework allows for surprising connections, however, and thus for a strangely moving cinematic experience. For better or worse, films like *Eternal Sunshine* tell a truth about how we experience people and ordinary life in a late-modern cultural context.

To give a brief synopsis of the film: Joel (Jim Carrey) and Clem (Kate Winslet) have problems that are due in part to their unproductive conversation.[5] The film unfolds as a series of flashbacks, making the chronology of events uncertain, but by the film's midpoint its plot outlines become clearer: Clem has broken off their relationship and, with the help of a company called Lacuna, had all her memories of Joel erased. Joel, in response, undergoes the same procedure. Lacuna's staff visit Joel's apartment to assist in the memory-erasing process. Joel, unconscious but still able to hear some things in the environment, may be moved by their romantic entanglements. Halfway through the process he relives some memories of Clem and refuses to give her up. When Mary, Lacuna's receptionist, discovers she has undergone the memory-erasing procedure to forget a relationship with Dr. Mierzwiak, Lacuna's chief physician, she informs all of the company's patients that they have had the procedure. Joel and Clem meet again in the film's present, presumably spurred by memory traces to return to the site of their first encounter. They decide to begin the relationship again.

Though *Eternal Sunshine* is strongly shaped by music video aesthetics, it also works within a Hollywood context by borrowing some conventional cinematic techniques. At the broadest level, Kaufman's script adheres to Hollywood screenplay form.[6] The first traditional plot point occurs before the film begins, when Clem erases Joel. Joel's response to Clem, to erase her, constitutes the second turn. A strong midpoint happens when Joel commits to keeping his memories. The fourth takes place when Mary informs clients of Lacuna's practices, and the fifth when Joel and Clem decide to stay together. The film also has strong Oedipal pulls and an unyielding, pressing deadline (erasure by dawn).[7] But within this clear narrative framework, much is opaque. The film's baffling opening, for example, leaves viewers with little sense of forward motion. *Eternal Sunshine*'s first half is based more on process than teleology: we follow a device that erases one memory after another and the machinations of a brain as it shuffles through material.[8] As with music video, it is difficult to gauge where we are going; the viewer just has to go with the flow.

Much of the film's context supports a looser structure: masturbation, medical procedures, fantasies, memories, dreaming, as well as fluctuating and altered states brought about by drugs and rapidly shifting charged emotions.

Music video imagery, though it can have narrative elements, is often processually structured, which better reflects a song's own movement and keeps our focus on the music. Music videos often center on a single or a few processes. (Here I define *process* simply as the act of carrying on or going on, a series of actions, changes, or functions bringing about a result.) Such projects can seem arbitrary, as one activity might as well have been picked as another. In addition, a sustained treatment of an activity might come unexpectedly, and its duration may be unusually prolonged or drastically abbreviated, cut short by images of the band performing. The video's main project may be dispersed across a number of the song's sections. When footage of this material reappears, it bears an uncanny sense of return. Sections of *Eternal Sunshine* can be seen to work in precisely this way, especially in the extensive cross-cutting among Stan and Mary's love affair, Patrick and Clem's courtship, and Joel's memories. (This is partly because we are unsure where we are picking up or leaving off.) Each serial representation of memories possesses a new visual-aural scheme and a particular way of rendering the experience of memory.[9] Upon reflection we can see that *Eternal Sunshine* "follows the traditional romantic model, with the usual descent into the underworld in pursuit of a great prize followed by re-ascents—in this film, psychological rebirths or epiphanies."[10] But the viewer is often unaware of or confused by this quest, in no small part because Joel is too passive and depressed to stand as a volitional character.

At the local level the film has a striking kinship with music video. Gondry's music videos demonstrate that he can handle many visual and aural motifs; these individual motifs together create threads that subsequently work in counterpoint. The best example from Gondry's video work might be Daft Punk's "Around the World," in which each of several character-types—mummies, women in bathing suits, old-school hip-hop figures with double heads, spacemen—become linked to a particular musical line. As with many of his videos, *Eternal Sunshine* organizes its material in this way: a motif is introduced and extended by repetitions and other processes, such as looping. These threads work differently than do motifs in most films. A typical narrative film might feature between five and seven motifs (a music video likewise). *Eternal Sunshine*, deploying music video's techniques on a feature film's scale, has over thirty.[11] Each one of these motifs, as it reappears, moves from being imperceptible to occupying the foreground and back, then crosses into other threads and makes surprising connections. Meaning accrues and gets released unpredictably. Here are six examples:

1. Forty-two examples of blurred, composite, and ambiguous faces appear dispersed across the film. These images pop up unexpectedly, suggesting that Joel's cathexis to Clem is arbitrary. The compromised integrity of the human face—within the genre of romantic film—begins to undermine the naturalness or rightness of heterosexual coupling.

2. An airplane thread suggests childhood and memory, work and leisure, loss of the world and death. Here, an early image of a hanging ornament with birds (a type of biplane) may link to the crashed airplane near the film's end. Clothing—baby Joel's airplane-patterned pajamas and Clem's black lace, fiery Barnes & Noble dress (foreshadowed by a framed photo of a plane in descent with a red-tinged postcard tucked into a corner at the house of the couple's friends Carey and Rob)—help to suggest the couple are tied to the plane that will go down. Joel watches this plane's flight at a picnic and sees it wrecked through a rear car window. A variety of musics against the plane's appearance further load the image's semiosis (see Figure 5.1.).

3. The film's several montage sections reassert many threads quickly. Several brief references become subliminal here: images of alcohol appear twenty-three times. During Joel's second visit to Mierzwiak's office, a Tsingtao bottle appears for only two frames. Montage sections also function as switch points whereby material within threads can cross media, from text to image to music. We frequently see tape recorders and other old recording devices (as well as recorded media such as VHS tapes and audiocassettes). In one montage sequence we suddenly hear the lone words "tape recorder."[12] Conversely, crossing from sound to image, we hear an out-of-tune piano before we finally notice upright pianos in the film's middle and closing montages.

4. Some of the visual material is delicately worked, while other imagery is handled more broadly, to create cycles of recurring material. American flags appear several times: once with the elephants.[13] Joel mentions that Clem creates the illusion that "she can take you to another galaxy." A poster near Joel's bed depicts a meteor piercing the earth's atmosphere, about to jam

Figure 5.1 −6 of the 14 images that make up the string of airplanes.

into a man's head. Joel wears a galaxy sweater when he and Clem witness the elephant parade. Panties, on the other hand, are worked so thoroughly that they become material. (I like the unattractive, out-of-focus pair hanging behind Patrick and Clem before they visit the frozen Charles River.)

5. The skeleton motif comes in various guises: Joel's sketches of Clem (as Greek myth and childhood story); a life-sized stuffed doll wrapped around a smaller Groucho Marx figure; red-outs during Joel's memory-erasure; a miniature skull on a clock, which becomes a doppelganger for Clem; a potato doll. On the lighter side, the skeletons resemble Mexican posada figures, which might seem life-affirming but also lead to faux suicides (note the suffocations and black and red lines around Joel's and Clem's necks). Suffocation scenes are sometimes staged with superimposed lamps: lamps and whiteouts become linked to the skeleton motif (see Figure 5.2.).

6. The spot motif, most commonly seen on Joel's temple, one time as a pox on his face, another as patterning on curtains, carries over into dialogue when Mary, off-frame, screams, "It's a birthmark." An almost imperceptible detail follows: a spot painted on the ceiling.[14] Perhaps here is a secret in the film.

Figure 5.2 –15 of the 42 images that comprise the string of faces.

Does the film's hovering between spots and blanks suggest an oscillation between guilt and nothingness?[15] Or perhaps this is just a decoy, pure decoration—we do not know. Even more confounding, we have black spots throughout the film, then the viewer may notice a surfeit of carefully placed red spots as well. What do these marks mean? Perhaps these *red* (as opposed to black) spots form a trail for the viewer to hold on to as the film progresses. Visual motifs in *Eternal Sunshine* remain small and malleable, as are the swatches of music and bits of text we tend to remember. Gondry seems to be moved by the ideal of reducing dialogue, music, sound, and image to their smallest possible units, which can then interchange with one another—an ideal of erasing the differences between media.

It is hard to ascertain fully which kinds of work these motifs accomplish. Each creates part of a set and, as it comes forward and recedes, helps form a thread crossing the film. These threads overlap and interpenetrate, suggesting contagion, something that is common in music video.[16] For example, the biplane ornament hanging in Joel's bedroom window contains two glass birds. It could therefore be said to work as an image of the couple as well as a link in the descending plane thread. Joel's friend Rob puts together a birdcage using a hammer. As a young boy Joel mutilates a dead bird with a hammer (while another bird cries before flying away). The music in the opening scene (with the biplane ornament) suggests the workaday, with its sluggish, out-of-tune irregularity (and odd structure of five-measure phrases); the childhood scene's music, on the other hand, is highly nostalgic, scored for strings with a rinky-dink piano reiterating a single "lost" pitch in the high register. Is there a connection here between labor, love, loneliness, childhood, and the loss of the chance for Joel and Clem to have a family?

Many motifs seem archetypically evocative, like faces, skeletons, and lamps. But many are also placed in unusual structures and are not typical motifs to begin with: often they seem both highly emotionally charged and personal to Gondry. The open form and disrupted, ambiguous imagery of the film creates a space for Gondry to import imagery he has developed in music video: a group of boys, one of whom wears a colander on his head; a person in a dentist's chair on a busy street; or a couple in a bed on the beach in falling snow. These images belong to music video's high emotional intensity. Because music is rich in affect, music video imagery tends to have a moment-by-moment semiotic wallop unparalleled in film. This imagery, in combination with its speed and flow, creates a sense of compression and disappearance. *Eternal Sunshine*'s repetitive focus on lost items, fetish objects, and fragments—stolen panties and *Bartlett's Quotations*, Clem's frequent rejoinder "remember me"—is an attempt to stop the flow, to grasp something permanent in a moving form.

A kind of flow reminiscent of popular music is achieved in the film through both musical and visual devices. Some musical cues continue across several scenes, like Joel's waking up during his train ride to Montauk; glissandos also rise and fall and musical cues modulate rapidly up or down. Visually, moving imagery—cars, dollies, and characters' well-drawn gestures—and abrupt cutting all keep things progressing. Tour-de-force set pieces highlighting movement include Joel's drive, his walk to his living room, the swallowing of his medicine and rolling on a gurney; a bad memory in which the camera spins around the room as Mierzwiak explains, "I'm in you"; the film's last montage sequence, experienced from the back seat of a moving car. Even dialogue and concrete sound prompt us to move forward. Words pass rapidly among sources, from voices Joel hears in his head, to those spoken in the live environment and those emitted from the telephone. Room-tone shifts in pitch and timbre during a scene's course, an event that rarely occurs in real life but contributes to flow.

Repetition both structures the film and relates to Gondry's stylistic preoccupations. With a mathematical mind as well as a childlike playfulness, Gondry loves circular forms. We can see this in his video for the Chemical Brothers' "Star Guitar," in which the terrain seen out of a train window begins to loop and multiply. Pop songs and videos generally use repetitions and loops more extensively than do narrative films, but in Gondry's pieces, each time we return to the same, it feels like a new turn.[17] *Eternal Sunshine* presents repetitions and variations reinforced by multiples and loops within scenes. Three Joels appear simultaneously during Wozniak's first mapping of Joel's memories, for example; the sound of a record scratching, which reappears throughout the film, further cues us that we are stuck in repeat. Several musical motifs reiterate insistently. A four-note motif (high-low-high-low) is phrased with a breath in the middle, suggesting a loop within a loop and repetitive labor. A five-note, sometimes six-note pizzicato figure runs across the film; its promiscuity suggests obsessive repetition. In this film it is mostly the music that tells us that we are cycling.

The film resembles music video at higher structural levels. It divides into segments that work as inset music videos, each organized by unique visual and aural principles. The film's opening, in which Joel takes the train to Montauk and returns with Clem, is held together by cartoon music and reverberant ghostly environmental sounds; the color scheme emphasizes milky blues and whites. The title sequence, with lurid peacock tones as virulent as those in *Taxi Driver* (Martin Scorsese, 1976), is accompanied by indie/alternative and orchestral night music. A drive back from the train station matches more flatly tinted dark imagery and nearly inaudible snatches of saccharine pop tunes. Rather than narrative teleology coming to the fore, the disjunctiveness of these sections is highlighted through formal features based on similarity and difference.

In this way, *Eternal Sunshine*'s segmentation departs from Hollywood norms as several set-pieces take on the same weight as plot points. Joel passes through the eye/drain, is birthed through a tiger blanket (while grasping for a memory), nearly suffocates in Clem's hands, and faces off against a Medusan image of Clem during Mierzwiak's first memory-mapping. Four times the soundtrack approaches closure as it moves from the tonic in its first inversion to its more stable root position. Here Joel swallows Mierzwiak's memory-erasing pills, runs away from Clem at the Laskins' summer home, suffers Mierzwiak's machine's last memory deletion, and, at the film's end, nearly loses Clem as she walks out the door.

Several other processes help suppress narrative and create a sense of musicality. Clem's changing hair color suggests a cycle like the seasons. Joel becomes both younger and older as the film unfolds. (The process of becoming more youthful includes Clem's encouraging "Slidy Slidy," a tangerine-centric hide-and-seek game of "Duck ruck ruck," and roughhousing on the bed.) In *Eternal Sunshine*, becoming younger and ageing are retrograde processes. In addition, several audiovisual parameters, such as movement in the frame, camerawork, and sound effects, pull large parts of the film toward moments of culmination and deceleration: here images and sound gradually accrue into a visual and aural "whiteout" before liquidating into a corresponding aural diminuendo and a fade to black. On the supplementary DVD material, Gondry's focus stays with topics like light and snow: he is interested in changes of weather. Patterns like this play against the film's plot points, adding a new layer of information and complicating *Eternal Sunshine*'s structure.

I have described a formal structure based on cycles and nested patterns (plot points, moments of acceleration and deceleration, inset music video sections, loops, repetitions, strings of motifs) and little narrative drive. Let me describe one way that the soundtrack seizes the foreground. A cluster of five sounds—a keyboard tremolo, a midrange beep, a record scratch, a low-pitched clarinet motif, and an electronic noise that sounds like crumbling—help to cue us that a memory has crystallized, started to degrade, and then become erased. But the order of these sounds is often reversed or interchanged with other diegetic sounds like a doorbell ringing or the output of an inkjet printer. When we are within a memory, much of its meaning remains ambiguous, including its beginning and end, and its relation to other memories. The most definitive markers for how to phrase visual material seems lodged in the soundtrack, but this information demands exegesis. Patterns of diegetic material—fax machines, phone lines, the banging of a hammer—also group together like the memory-erasure cluster, making all sound worthy of focused attention.

Music video's semiotically indeterminate images can draw listeners' attention to an audio track that's open to interpretation. In *Eternal Sunshine* several kinds of visual distortion—off-balance framing; periodically out of focus, handheld, speeded-up, slowed-down, or out-of-synch camerawork; strangely color-processed and markedly over- and underexposed footage—work to lend an ambiguity to shots and the edits between them. Take, for example, color-processing and exposure: *Eternal Sunshine's* color shifts from one shot to the next as well as across shots. Among the most highly prized technicians in the music video industry, color timers are known to tweak each shot individually, so that shots can be made to reflect musical changes; they will also often play the music alongside the image to more finely calibrate the color. Changing colors draw attention to texture, surface, and materiality. Rapid shifts also require that the viewer resituate herself: visual gaps encourage viewers to find meaning where they can and one source close at hand is the soundtrack. With regard to exposure, both blacks and whites in *Eternal Sunshine* are pushed until they lose their detail, a phenomenological impossibility except perhaps in the moment when the human eye's iris expands or contracts and fails to register a scene. Out-of-focus, unbalanced images; speeded-up and slowed-down footage; and ex-pressionistic color-timing and digital intermediary, as well as jump cuts, possess a similar ambiguity that sound can help the viewer resolve. Images, music, and sounds hold together through shape, movement, color, texture, and expressivity.

Before discussing the soundtrack, let me comment on the film's acting, which helps mediate the film's prismatic effects. In *Eternal Sunshine*, figures often move in freer ways—seemingly less constrained by the limits of gravity and physics—than do actors in classic Hollywood. (One might equate these performers with restless zoo animals: leopards pacing or monkeys ricocheting off trees.) Music video directors are accustomed to working with dancers and performers who speak through their bodies, who possess a hypermobility. Gondry mines what James Naremore calls the "visceral side of acting," where skin flushes, tears swell, sweat pours, and breathing becomes labored.[18] Bodily processes, too, are exploited for their musicality, as both sound and gesture. It is not insignificant that Gondry chose a physical comedian as his lead actor, and I have two theories that might explain this. First, music video is short, lacks dialogue, and must showcase the singer, underscore the lyrics, and high-light musical material. In a way it returns us to the silent era, particularly to a form of typage used by filmmakers such as Eisenstein. Music video directors have to find shots that possess signs of human emotion powerful enough for the images to project over the music; but the performers, while usually pol-ished and self-assured, are not actorly. Second, music videos do not present classical performances because they lack cause/effect and action/reaction re-lationships, except in the most fanciful ways. My interviews with music video directors suggest they have a fascination with, and desire for control over, cin-ematic elements that are unavailable in music video.

Against the showy star performances, we also have other representations: Clem as a stalker, an ominous and mysterious figure depicted as a background, a dying and dead body, a doll, an embossed surface on a coffee cup, photographs. This range of depiction—from star performer, background figure, to person rendered as inanimate object—is a music video conceit, useful for the ways in which it reveals pop music's structure.[19]

Sound holds the film's secrets. An early cue is when Stan, beginning a memory map of Joel's brain, slams the first personal item onto the steel tray. A plastic snowglobe (a quote from *Citizen Kane*—the city within is Boston) charms, but it is the closely miked sound bouquet of Clem's laughter, whoopee-cushion squeaks, and a music-box that floods the viewer. Clem's orange sweatshirt draws Joel to her, but it is her singing that takes him back to childhood: "oh, my darlin'," sings Clementine, then Joel sings this as he tries to comfort himself as a toddler, and his mother sings it to him as she bathes him in the sink. The film is depicted as a quest, and it is the music that cues us to its turns. Downward glissandi lead us into the first memory of Clem leaving as Joel chases her past shop windows. "Michael, row your boat ashore" triggers Joel's access to childhood. Glissandi also take us to the first moments of toddlerhood. In a subtle intertextual reference, the cue that accompanies Joel while he swallows his memory-erasing medication is the same as for the production company logo that appears in the title credits ("FOCUS," with the "O" out of focus, no less). Even before Joel consumes the pill, we are cued to forget and remember.

The preeminence of the soundtrack may be partly due to Gondry's background as a musician: a semiprofessional drummer, he marks beats and creates graphic scores reminiscent of 1960s experimental music. Devices to move the soundtrack into the foreground include a kind of frequent, frank play with the roles of diegesis and between diegetic and nondiegetic sources. The music stops and starts, unprovoked, when Joel and Clem reunite on the train. Often the music unexpectedly shifts genres, such as during the opening credits, when a tape tossed from a car window hits the pavement. This "music video moment" suggests that recorded music (represented diegetically as a cassette) possesses a mysterious authority. Sounds are also foregrounded by being untethered or pushed away from their sources. Near the opening of the film, Joel stands alone before a beachfront property and a distant voice that resembles Clem's calls, "David." We learn much later that the empty house's owners are named David and Ruth Laskin, but this does not explain why we should hear Clem say David's name. A record scratch often sounds in the film, but we never quite know why. Yes, it seems to mark a wiped memory, but why has that sound been chosen to do so and why does it appear in so many guises? These isolated, sphinx-like elements seem to possess a secret about the film: if we could unlock their mystery, we might understand the story.

The collages of environmental sounds are so beautifully built up that they become musical. Partly these sounds call attention to themselves by being wrong for their spaces; partly an isolated sound or two, brought to the fore, become so interesting that they function as an environment's melody or its musical hook.[20] In the Barnes & Noble store, the voices belong more to an airport than a bookshop, and the lights going off sound like timpani. Breathing, a 60-cycle hum, cymbals, and a "whoosh" accompany Joel's passing-out under medication. The diner where Clem and Joel first meet is accompanied by crickets chirping (though crickets would not whir in a diner at midday), and the coffee machine sounds like a wild bird. Its registral spread and melodic content can be heard as setting up some of the film's key musical themes: the long glissandi and a high-pitched, quickly articulated melodic line that sounds like speeded-up audiotape, sometimes performed on instruments, sometimes electronically.

Bursts of cacophony—crashing, bumping into things, dropping objects, general mayhem—also contribute to the sound score. These noises not only advance the film's themes of lack of control and loss of memory but also work to create a rich sonic texture. As a drummer, Gondry might have a strong relation to sonic materiality. Many moments in the soundtrack suggest that people and things are linked at a subsurface level: characters silently drum; the sounds appear elsewhere.

Much of *Eternal Sunshine*'s dialogue is close-miked voiceover, which draws attention to the soundtrack. More than in most films, close-miking here magnifies whispers, murmurs, breathing, sighs, and intimate features of a voice's grain. Traditionally in Hollywood film, camera placement can vary tremendously while mic placement does not, so that audio levels stay consistent. Once we attend to changing audio levels, we are taken out of the film's diegesis. *Eternal Sunshine* constantly plays with miking, moving it nearer or farther. Words will pop out of the sound texture or move toward inaudibility, rising and falling rapidly. Voices are heavily processed and distorted. We hear an unusually volatile mix of live dialogue, recorded at the filming, and looped dialogue, recorded later in the sound studio. These are often spliced together within the same sentence. Music, image, and dialogue become equally musical.

The film's dialogue consistently emphasizes sing-song, hooky effects like assonance or rhyme.[21] "ClemenTEEN, the tangeREEN." "Two blue ruins." "Duck, ruck, ruck." Phrases are often said twice, thus encouraging variation. Repetition addresses problems of memory; it helps to ground the flow of information when material comes too fast; but even more importantly, as in a pop song, when words are uttered twice, their materiality—their pitch and timbre—comes forward. Potions, potions I said." "I want to have a baby. I want to have a baby." "What should we do? What should we do?" "Half-baked, no half-baked." "Slidy

slidy slidy." "Female, female?" "I didn't make the plane crash. I didn't make the plane crash." Repeated words are also sung, and by more than one speaker, which makes no real-world sense. Both Clem and Mierzwiak call out, "Pa-a-a-trick, ba-a-a-a-by boy." The dialogue crosses over into and describes the music. When Joel says, "Osidius, swoop and cross. Osidius, swoop and cross," he's performing a rhythm of short-short-short-long which is a primary musical motive of the film. Patrick's singing in the van—"mane-sher-sherr" (Stan tells him to shut up)— takes us back to the Lata Mangeshkar song we hear in Clem's apartment. Again, this is nonsensical as Patrick was not there. The film contains much singing and some piano-playing. Stan and Patrick's line "Showtime at the Apollo" suggests in a different way that this film is a musical event.

As with environmental sounds and dialogue, the scored music often vies for attention and diverges from traditional film practices. Joel's and Clem's first encounter, on a train, differs so much from conventional narrative approaches that the viewer may have trouble engaging with the story. In a way this musical cue constitutes traditional dramatic scoring, using orchestral instruments like clarinet and bassoon, but it continually stops and starts. Moreover this music contends with diegetic sounds: the clarinet converses with the train's squeaky wheels and Clem sniffing her nasal decongestant, while the bassoon answers Joel's chuckles. This editorializing draws even greater attention toward the soundtrack.[22] While it is strange for an intimate train sequence to receive such orchestral scoring, other sequences are scored with an opposite aesthetic. In scenes with Patrick we often hear cheesy synthesizer sounds panned artificially hard, so that string sounds are on one side, woodwind sounds on the other. The film also often interweaves *diegetic sound* overscored with *nondiegetic music*, as when the young Joel bangs out a four/four on a dead bird and an out-of-tune piano and strings fill in the accompaniment, thus making the boundary between music and sound more fluid. Gondry seems to want his materials to run free and intermingle.

Eternal Sunshine draws on the history of film-scoring techniques. Leitmotifs describe character: when Clem sleeps in Joel's car after their romantic encounter on the Charles River, a graceful flute-line accompanies her. Similarly, when Joel and Clem meet in her apartment, a recording of Hindi film music switches between male and female vocalists, suggesting star-crossed lovers.[23] We hear aural close-ups, as Michel Chion might describe them, such as the chugging of a fax machine.[24] *Eternal Sunshine*'s score contains a refrain: workaday music and schoolchildren's voices frame the film's beginning and end; children's voices also prep for the middle—Joel's return to childhood. The film's postmodern deployment of modernist, popular, and ethnic music, orchestral and electronic sources, sound collages and unusual arrangements gives the score a contemporary feel.

The film's musical score *is* remarkably heterogeneous: Bollywood, New Orleans jazz, Stockhausen, Penderecki, Hindemith, expressionism, Bernard Herrmann, Tom Waits, punk, alternative and closer-to-mainstream pop, vaudeville, early American folk tunes, opera, Warner Bros. cartoon music, carousel or circus music, night music, classical divertimenti, Strauss, barroom tunes, Henry Mancini, Martin Denny, and children's songs are all represented—music that, once popular, has now receded from the musical lexicon. This use of heirloom music underscores what is lost in the process of forgetting. Unexplored ways of feeling and knowing are locked into these musical styles. The film's composer, Jon Brion, also makes some clever instrumental arrangements—a string quartet, mellotron, a plunky guitar, and record skips, for instance, make up one of the film's cues. What these unusual sounds communicate in their new contexts calls for decryption. It is almost as if, to underscore the film's themes, the soundtrack becomes its own dislocated memory. The image correspondingly deforms in response to the music. Regarding a shot of Clem and Joel on the frozen Charles River, for example, Gondry says that a puzzling stream of lights in the background was only added once he'd heard the cue Brion had composed for the scene, and that he added it with the specific idea of enriching the music.

A close mapping of the film's musical structure would prove daunting: many of the musical cues are short and tonally undefined; and the record scratches, animal calls, 60-cycle hum, computer clicks, and so on have pitch and rhythmic content. The vast assortment of musical styles interspersed with concrete sounds slow the narrative flow. Nevertheless, we can discern one or two broad themes that work dialectically.

Much of the music, such as modernist classical, Indian film music, or eighteenth-century divertimenti, might be foreign to Hollywood audiences. The most intimate scenes in the movie—elephants on parade, a night drive with montaged images replaying out the back window, Clem and Joel wrestling in the snow—are accompanied by stripped-down, delicately arranged folk music that is both diatonic and acoustic, such as an out-of-tune piano, strummed guitar, or a small string ensemble. It seems that the more modernist and ethnic styles form an outside, while the delicate, simple, and folksy music forms the characters' private emotional core. This more intimate music is paired with material associated with memory, heterosexuality, and family. But, even though these more intimate musical cues threaten to become the score's dominant thread, they are partly countered by the prominence of the drumming motif, which obtains a greater degree of continuity and is worked through in a concerted way.

Joel frequently drums his fingers—a condition endemic among drummers. As a little boy he also drums while gazing out the window into the rain. His friend Rob hammers away on a birdhouse while his girlfriend exclaims, "Rob, give it a rest!" Later, kids smash a dead bird with a hammer. Clem's apartment radiator continually clicks, adding a new rhythmic stratum to Mangeshkar's song. Bongos are conspicuously placed on a counter in Joel's apartment. The cue accompanying the kitchen scene of Joel's childhood contains a fast, pizzicato rhythmic figure in addition to traces of 1970s pop/Muzak, and the sound for the picnic scene of Joel's first contact with Clem consists solely of bongos against the drone of the red airplane. The drumming in this scene—a key one in Joel and Clem's relationship—seems to be the culmination of the previous drumming allusions and exemplifies drumming's special role in the film. This is not just due to known facts about the director's background, but also because these musical swatches are long while the visual motifs are short. The film emphasizes natural sounds and the accidental sounds of ageing technology, and presents drumming as second nature: these sources are understood as emotionally and conceptually more important than gestures that bear the signs of intention.

What I have described is an extreme fragmentation of the music and image, but *Eternal Sunshine* succeeds in its Hollywood context by drawing on a number of key cultural texts, most prominently the plot of *Vertigo*. As with Hitchcock's 1958 film, we start by attempting to resolve the secret of an unknown woman, and through that pursuit we discover facets of her persona. The betrayal, the stalking in strange locations, the shifting hair color, the dumbing-down of the woman, the grave, the desire for a fully lived moment with the beloved—"I have you now," "I am exactly where I want to be"—the sense of loss, all recall *Vertigo*. And like Hitchcock's Scottie, Joel is reduced to a childlike catatonic state.[25] Much of the footage in *Eternal Sunshine* might be seen as an expansion of Scottie's dream, in which we move through the detritus of Joel's brain.

When Clem first appears on the train, she looks like something out of Dr. Seuss or *Alice in Wonderland*, with wristwarmers, floppy round handbag, and the goings in and out of rabbit-hutch-like doorways. This imagery helps to take Joel back to childhood.

Eternal Sunshine also bears traces of Greek myth. The film's labyrinthine structure, with its compound spaces and loops, harks back to the story of the Minotaur (a truck might stand in for the Minotaur). Clem, as a skeleton in the boat, recalls *The Owl and the Pussycat*, but also Charon, the ferryman who takes us to Hades. Clem's changing hair color and disappearances and reappearances allude to Persephone, and Joel's following her and forgetting his past recalls the myth of Orpheus. The couple discusses the constellations of Orion and the Pleiades.[26]

Eternal Sunshine presents familiar themes, imagery, and narrative devices in the context of new media. The first noticeably post-produced effect—a car falling through the sky to crash in a vacant lot—is preceded by a subtle detail: a shot through Lacuna's van revealing the street, canted sideways. As Joel chases Clem past shop windows, space becomes strange and prismatic. Super-imposed lamps and signs disappear and reappear. The streets perpendicular to this one are exact mirror images of each other. It is a De Chirico effect, but it is also a direct description of contemporary filmmaking practices—a director and editor at an Avid viewer and browser windows watching images flipped on their X-axis, while they fantasize about phantom memory sounds and images whipping by.[27]

As in much music video, *Eternal Sunshine*'s constellation of perspectives remains unresolved.[28] In music videos, visual motifs can attach themselves to different musical materials—a bass line, a rhythmic motive, an odd timbral effect—and not annihilate or even influence one another. They can be truly multiperspectival, simultaneously holding conflicting and contradictory evidence.[29] Music videos can also present things in part, as a type of music-image cryptogram or koan; it is up to the viewer to piece these together.[30]

As in a music video, many things are rendered with loving detail in *Eternal Sunshine*, such as props, colors and locations, yet we do not know what Joel's job is, who Joel's father is, or anything about Clem's parents. The film feels like a Cavellian remarriage comedy, yet many of the indices that work to define this genre—the status of the woman's parents, productive conversations, and the move to a green world—are lacking. It also possesses traits of melodrama, most particularly through overly close familial relations and constricted spaces. We cannot get much of a handle on Clem, whether she is real or colored by Joel's desires, whether she is a rescuing angel or a cuckolding bitch. Might Joel suffer from a mild case of mental illness? His sketches and moods certainly suggest so. The status of the key struggle between the couple—whether Clem practices infidelity or not—is unresolved. Is Clem an alcoholic? What is the relationship between key sites, such as Joel's bed, the Charles River, and the beach at Montauk? Does Joel try to get back to Clem because he loves her, to resolve his Oedipal desires for his mother, or because another male, Patrick, is moving in on his turf? When are we in a dream or in a real memory? How does the "real" Clem know to revisit Montauk once Joel and Clem have had their memories erased?

I have claimed that *Eternal Sunshine* has an atypical form. While a classic Hollywood film might possess three or four primary themes, *Eternal Sunshine* has ten: (1) work; (2) time; (3) faces and cathexis; (4) childhood; (5) Clem's constructed persona; (6) the integrity of Clem and Joel as a couple; (7) synoptic connections among people, epitomized by imagery of vortices; (8) the boundaries between culture, nature, and the other; (9) the similarities among mind, machines, and music; and (10) memory and knowledge. Rather than a narrative, these strands function as if they were woven into a music video: material residing within each theme exists apart from material in other themes. When crossing among materials occurs, the effects can be subtle, working on principles of shared influence or contagion. No single theme supersedes or annihilates another. I will briefly describe each of them below.

1. *Eternal Sunshine* is a Hollywood creation insofar as it posits that our life's solutions can be most readily found through successful heterosexuality. While the film does not commit to a socially progressive agenda, it presents a harsh portrait of labor. The psychological stress and tedium of low-wage work wears on Clem: she reports she is a "book slave"; her job at Barnes & Noble leaves her "pretty tired, pretty bored." She faces her customers vacantly and vents frustration with nonfunctioning office equipment. Her lack of center comes through when she claims (we never learn quite how seriously) that she "applies her personality as a paste" and is "anxious about not filling every moment." If Clem's solution to alienation is freneticism, Joel's is passivity. His work is so undefining it does not even warrant a description in the film, and, as he says of his life, it's "a blank" (two years of missing diary entries do not faze him). Lacuna's "skilled technicians" Stan and Patrick (whom Gondry and Kaufman liken to incompetent Kinko's workers) remain disengaged, their hostility toward clients showing when Stan suggests, "let's not roach the guy" before they raid the drinks cabinet. Stan seems a particularly exploited wage-slave: although he pulls day shifts and all-nighters he still does not seem to be earning a decent income. Small-scale sabotage is *Eternal Sunshine*'s low-paid workers' one respite: necking behind the computer at Barnes & Noble, partying while your client lies unconscious in bed, stealing a client's panties, quirky uses of leisure time (like making potato dolls, night picnics on ice), and breaking into a rich couple's beachfront property. It is clear these minor acts of resistance come up against rigorously enforced boundaries: Joel claims to have contracted food poisoning to skip a day of work, and Stan fabricates an illness for Patrick; one exuberant outburst of "Yay!" elicits a dressing-down from the boss. But against this bleak depiction of work, questions of time and interpersonal relations are rarely addressed.[31]

2. Perhaps *Eternal Sunshine*'s true theme, and its sense of sadness, derives from the fact that its characters cannot experience time positively. (The film could be said to exhibit the problem of a promise of a pleasure deferred, as each scene moves graspingly onto the next.) Joel's neighbor underscores the problem when he counsels Joel not to "wind up at Mickey D's. McRomance.'" Time spent poorly gets passed on to viewers: when Joel takes Clem's hand and says, "I feel I'm exactly where I want to be," she's immediately snatched away.[32]

3. The film's largely apolitical but still critical reading of contemporary society runs alongside another thread.[33] The series of blurred, hybrid, or ambiguous faces suggests our object choices are arbitrary. We do not love a person, but rather cathect onto some aspect or feature of him or her. On the other hand, the film depicts Joel and Clem as "made for one another."

4. Many moments are psychologically "deep," though in clichéd ways: the images of Joel sucking his thumb while curled up on the floor; or Joel, in a reenactment of the Little Hans story, playing the fort-da game with a yo-yo under a kitchen table. Clem is more than a woman, she is Thanatos for Joel. The skeletal imagery that is tied to her, the feigned suicides and games of suffocation the couple play, point to a desire for death. Perhaps Clem becomes a figment of Joel's imagination, transformed into a kind of Beatrice who leads him through his unconscious. Her angelic-bitchy traits seem impossibly encapsulated within a single character.[34]

5. The future does not look hopeful for the couple. Clem is most likely an alcoholic, and the film takes pains to show her drinking heavily day and night. Joel's drawings of her as Vampire/Harpy can be understood as his rage about this. Alcohol and infidelity are often coterminous, and Clem's extroverted, sexually loose personality makes us wonder about what she really does. She says she feels bored, restless, and trapped. Joel is figured as depressive, and a sequence of his sketches (shown as flash frames) plays out a suicide. Neither is he a good partner: stuck in repetitive, hostile behavior, he says things sure to enrage Clem and, though we do not see it, we get the sense that these conversations are repeated.

6. Progress, for Joel and Clem, seems to lie in developing a tolerance for what each finds difficult in the other and trying to talk to one another, though this talk turns out to consist of lines they have said before. Against this bleak picture we have a lot of Hollywood happy fluff: running around in the snow, using chopsticks as if they were elephants' trunks, rolling in and out of bed. Yet one moment may carry more weight. In long shot, we see Clem laughing, pushing Joel down on the ice and telling him, "It won't crack or break." The ice can be taken as a metaphor for the relationship's solidity.[35] The discussion of the constellations, shot from overhead as the couple seems to float on a sheet of ice, also suggests the characters' and filmmakers' hunger for apotheosis.

7. The film presents one potentially valuable suggestion about the politics of how we are linked to one another. When Joel tries to extricate himself from Clem, much of his life's fabric comes undone. The film suggests this through imagery of vortices: Joel and Clem are yanked down a drain, and Joel suffocates at the other end; Joel crawls through a quasi–birth canal composed of bed linen and then winds up "on the other side" on a sheet of

ice—at this point, a fitting metaphor for nothingness. Joel, as an Orpheus who ventures into the unconscious, risks much. He loses the memory of his most beloved childhood object-choice, his Huckleberry Hound doll. We note at the same time, though, that his memories are presented as if they are everyone's—incredibly ordinary.

8. The film contains no speaking roles for people of color. Instead, kitsch objects suggest a hunger for a richer, less "white" life: Clem's use of phrases like "Vamanos, señor!" folk-art potato dolls, posada day skeletons, Chinese meals, and Bollywood film music. The bric-a-brac filling the frame also suggests a relation between art and nature: here, art is created out of a fear of separation from, and desire to return to, nature. Filigree, plants, and ornamental clothing (often featuring butterflies or flowers) that surround especially Clem suggest a link to the natural world. So too do the heaps of woolens and fur in which the couple are often bundled up. The frequent return to liminal spaces—such as a frozen lake's edge with cars in the distance, a snowy seaside with a bed on the shore, a little boy gazing out at the rain through a window, houses taken back by the sea—help to underscore the boundary between civilization and the wilderness. Gondry grew up on the border between a forest and a Versailles suburb, and questions of nature come to the fore. *Eternal Sunshine*'s depictions of animals reflect this fraught relation between people and the natural world. Carrie and Rob's dog gets shooed away without the chance to say its piece. A bird calls, and we might wonder whether the bird in the children's wagon is its mate.[36] Animal calls woven throughout the soundtrack suggest that the claims of nature are one of the film's secrets.

9. It is unclear how *Eternal Sunshine*'s mechanisms work. Joel's unreeling mind and a predatory erasure machine are clearly engaged in a struggle. From this, however, we cannot infer why a search through Joel's youth has been abandoned in favor of the last memories of Clem (his mind's free association, a sensing that time is up?). Nor do we know whence came the sudden spur to imagine Clem's made-up goodbye, nor why Joel's mind recreates Clem as a guide rather than a vindictive bitch. (What mechanism causes our dream content sometimes to shame or terrify us, and sometimes to comfort or encourage us?) Whatever narrative pressures have accrued, the film's final third becomes profoundly anti-narrative. As we experience Joel's free associations and fantasies, we have the sense of looking directly into another's mind. Machines and minds (in their repetitious feedback loops and sometime associative detours) may resemble music. Is music linked to the unconscious?

10. One might argue that *Eternal Sunshine* offers some common wisdom: we cannot predict the actions of people we love, grasp what it is we love about

them, know all parts of our psyche, or alter the past, so we will make mistakes. But perhaps (according to such a reading) we *can* choose to affirm this part of our condition. In *Eternal Sunshine* Joel neither knows what part of him loves Clem, nor can he prevent her from destroying their relationship. Near the film's end, Joel plays the tape of his rant about Clem (an eloquent illustration of the ways our unconscious selves emerge regardless of attempts at self-control). Joel cannot undo his negative responses to Clem's desire for a family or a more present companion. Even while destroying his brain, Joel cannot break free from his memories: as the Lacuna process takes hold, he cannot control each memory's arrival or its effect on him. Nevertheless, as *Eternal Sunshine* progresses, Joel appears to gain acceptance of life's predicament: he smiles winsomely as Clem scolds him during a meal at a Chinese restaurant and as she steals a piece of chicken off his plate during a beach picnic (the film's most generous gestures are tied to food).

However, the film complicates these commonplaces through technique, contradictory statements, and narrative structure. The dazzling array of flashbacks, flash-forwards, disparate music-video-like scenes, and inset narratives isolate Joel's moments of self-awareness and blindness. Just as *Eternal Sunshine* presents two incommensurabilities about relationships—either our love-object is destined for us or it is arbitrary—it presents three incommensurabilities in the realm of knowledge. Joel accrues an authentic wisdom: the kind many report attaining through meditation, prayer, psychotherapy, ageing, AA groups, or hard knocks. Joel gathers partial knowledge through the effects of sci-fi procedures: the memory traces emerging from his consciousness and the cassette tape Joel and Clem now have, which will help them reflect on past modes of relating. Joel gains no knowledge at all: at the film's end Joel and Clem must begin again. Are these repetitions or repetitions with turns?[37] Is this a Hollywood ending or a trope on one? The film's enigmatic ending and the film's multiple, incommensurable perspectives belong to the structural devices of music video: they nudge the viewer to watch the video again. Thus one senses the creaking mechanisms of the film's structure. In its oscillating incompleteness, the film's constellation of possibilities about self-knowledge, history, and memory take on no greater importance than the other threads. The viewer is again plunged into the texture of the film. *Eternal Sunshine* is truly prismatic. One cannot catch its true meaning.

As in a music video, in *Eternal Sunshine* things refuse to add up. The fine web of connections is so densely interlaced with musical materials that it is difficult to know how anything works. What we can say is that music videos and this film accomplish different things and create different effects than do classical Hollywood films. People here are depicted as fragmented, patchwork constructions, but because people's lives are made up of the same cultural materials they are at the same time interconnected. This hints at the possibility of solidarity, or even a kind of sympathy—a sense that people listening to one another can establish the coordination normally possible through collective musical activity. But personal relations are shown as finally mysterious. All that remains, one may feel, is a kind of pure *affect*—the charge or valence of emotions that seem to exceed their stimuli.

Eternal Sunshine's characters are less than coherent. They may thus less resemble traditional Hollywood characters than real-life acquaintances in late modernity, particularly as such acquaintances begin to fade in memory. Memory can render people as fragmented and incomplete; memories of people may also coalesce into something colorless or split into polar opposites. Meanwhile musicians in ensembles can produce texts that suggest a model state of receptive coordination. Auteurist music-video directors like Mark Romanek and Hype Williams produce images that exist in so graceful a relation to the music that their visual lines become part of the music; the directors become session musicians. Similarly the actors in *Eternal Sunshine* are intertwined in the deepest of ways, even though many of the most important connections involve an absence: Joel confronts Patrick, who appears as a head without a face; he sketches Clem as a skeleton in a tableau; Mary, Clem, and Joel bond over an exchanged cassette tape. Such a high degree of heterogeneous interconnection is rare in feature films, but it represents an ideal of music and music video.

Nicholas Cook claims that once music-image relations form, meaning becomes volatile and unstable.[38] In *Eternal Sunshine*, elements like a child's plane, a hammer, and a lamp take on a strange animus. *Eternal Sunshine* contains many moments when the soundtrack seems to hold the answer, when it drives the image. I have spoken to a good number of people who report loving the film yet needing to watch it again. They feel they have not grasped it. What does it mean when mainstream culture produces illegible sounds and objects?

Music videos, like *Eternal Sunshine*, embody certain kinds of experience: intensity, condensation, transience. Music disappears from us while we are listening. Similarly, the semiotically overloaded imagery, in its relation to the music, comes so fast that we cannot fully experience it. The temporal distortions in *Eternal Sunshine* are bewildering: the film contains five layers of flash-forwards and flashbacks in the first 20 minutes. *Eternal Sunshine*'s sense of time is often ambiguous, in part, because we cannot fully ascertain a memory's status. But music video too deals with jumbled and indeterminate time, simply in the fact that the image might be projecting forward while the song's lyrics, harmony, or arrangement points to the past.

Both music video and music-video-influenced films rely on montage sequences—the music video directors' speciality. While a narrative film might have one or two such sequences, *Eternal Sunshine* has five. The role and importance of montage also shift in this film. Perhaps *Eternal Sunshine*'s most powerful moment comes during its final montage sequence, in which Joel remembers first meeting Clem. Here we have a liminal case: both montage and narrative. How strange for a montage sequence to be the most memorable and touching moment of the film, to carry the film's main theme.

Why is this sequence so affecting? The image streams from right to left, while most films favor a left-to-right motion. The darkness and passing lights of a night drive elicit a state of melancholy reflection. Joel's looking out of the back window past sand and airplanes onto a projected tableau suggests a screen onto childhood. Overlit happy images of the couple, spliced in as subliminal frames against images of friends carrying files like office drones, elicit a sense of loss. Something that appears to be a sledge rests on a pile of bric-a-brac, a "Rosebud" image. The out-of-tune piano reiterates pitches in the upper register, hinting that something has gone missing or has been forgotten. But these details fail to capture the power of the sequence. At some level we are left with just affect and the mystery of music-image relations.

One might wish to decry this new "glance aesthetics," which destroys the Bazinian "world of looking." But this aesthetic springs from somewhere—from music video's attempt to speak to popular music, to showcase its form, to make image musical. This new visual style, based on musicality, dislocation, free-association, flux, color, and texture, leaves us with a sense of sometimes being grounded in, sometimes hovering over, our bodies. These musical films may yet help us learn something about ourselves.

CHAPTER 6

Reciprocity, Bollywood, and Music Video

MANI RATNAM'S *DIL SE* AND *YUVA*

This short chapter makes a first attempt to understand the phenomenon of especially moving three- to eight-minute segments that possess a heightened audiovisual musicality. While I define this musicality broadly, I've been driven to this project partly by Bollywood musical sequences from the last 20 years. Not an expert in the subject, I'd still like to include some insights gleaned from periods of enthusiastic viewing. Hindi cinema is vast. It's the largest film industry in the world, and it diverges from other cinemas in many ways.[1] Long traditions in theater, painting, dance, and other art forms have shaped Bollywood's style. The cinema has also been influenced by British colonialists; censors banned certain types of sexual display and others became unpopular, including, until recently, kissing. In the last 20 years, both with the global diaspora of Indian populations and the opening of global markets, Bollywood has become increasingly hybrid.[2] With the country's over 500 different languages, and a need to forge a nation out of many different populations, one primary cinematic style known as "masala" emerged, which attempted to appeal to almost everyone, including the young and the old, urban cinemagoers and those in rural areas. The style incorporated many modes—comedy, fighting, romance—and especially musical numbers.

Bollywood cinematic techniques have complex histories. One of my favorite explanations for the development of its trademark supersaturated colors is this: Cinema was brought to farmers on mobile-cinema trucks, with screens hoisted on site. Supersaturated colors were required to project under such conditions and the look stuck. Playback performance (the practice of dubbing one actor's voice with another actor's body) became a norm after a happy accident with one of the earliest attempts to incorporate sound. When an actor performed, but was unable to sing, someone else filled in behind a screen.[3] It became the norm.

Many Bollywood musical sequences, including more I'll discuss, do two things simultaneously: they retain traditional Hindi cinematic features (connected with music, dance, theater, painting, and so on), and they also incorporate the hyperde-tailed aesthetics of today's music-video and popular-music production practices. This chapter focuses on two clips ("Fanaa" and "Anjaana Anjaani") from Mani Rat-nam's *Yuva* (2003), with music by A. R. Rahman. I'll read these clips in light of their intercultural connections. But first it's worth considering some typical fea-tures of Bollywood music-image sequences that *don't* appear in contemporary American music video: (1) images of euphoria; (2) the importance of line and certain kinds of movement; (3) particular kinds of places and spaces; (4) a sense of high stakes; (5) the importance of duets and lip sync; and (6) the grammar of framing, camera movement, and editing.

Euphoria

Mainstream, commercial American music videos present heightened affective states, but tend not to be able to sustain them. They're designed so that viewers will come to learn the attractive features of a song and then buy the recording. To encourage repeated viewings, they tend toward visual overload and con-ceptual or narrative complications. Feelings of bliss don't always result from this sensorial barrage. One reason the sweet, jubilant naiveté of Hindi cinema may not appear in Western musical multimedia may be because American cul-ture lacks the requisite structures of experience. India's long traditions of the-ater, painting, dance, music, and art provide the contours with which to achieve this state. Their very traditionalism may provide comfort in the face of encroaching modernism, as claimed by M. Madhava Prasad.[4]

Line and Movement

Indian song has stressed melody and rhythm over harmony: winding melodic lines and rhythms built on long cycles. What I call "music video aesthetics" and David Bordwell calls the "new intensified continuity" tends to gum up the works when the image and soundtrack are conjoined, because the moment at hand becomes isolated and pressured. Bollywood music-image sequences can both draw upon intensified continuity to bring forth individual musical details and also hold true to the long, sinuous lines.

Some of the most lovely Bollywood gestures, like raising one's hands over-head, don't appear in American music videos because they might seem disingen-uous. In Ratnam's "Anjaana Anjaani," a couple play air guitar and drums with an unabashedness that would be disallowed in American music video. While Bol-lywood choreographers and filmmakers don't have access to the forms of sexual display that isolate body parts in the frame, they can make use of extremely delicate hand and neck movements, derived from Indian classical dance, that rarely appear in American music videos. As the couple sing under the red umbrella in "Anjaana Anjaani," the finely articulated hand movements point to the Indian practice of solfège in which hand signals illustrate scale-degrees (see figure 6.1).

Places and Spaces

In "Fanaa" the circular, patterned dance floor and the lattice- and column-shaped polyurethane light structures might derive from the ornamental floor markings, pillars and walls that appear in earlier Hindi courtesan films like *Mughal-e-Azam* (1950) (see figures 6.2 and 6.3.).

Figure 6.1 "Anjaana Anjaani": the couple's delicate gestures help articulate the song's musical features.

Figure 6.2 Depictions of space in early Hindi courtesan films like *Mughal-e-Azam*.

Figure 6.3 *Yuva*'s nightclub setting references locations like *Mughal-e-Azam*'s.

"Anjaana Anjaani" presents expansive shots of the ocean, a twist on the wide-open images of nature that appear so frequently in Hindi musical sequences. (These images of nature surely reflect a cultural imaginary, but might they also reflect formal features of the songs, like the emphasis on expansive, melismatic line? See *Barsaat* [1949].) Anna Morcom connects the imagery of wide open spaces to euphoria and love (wide open spaces are actually rare in India).[5]

Fabric

Hindi song sequences present a rich iconography of clothing—the sari flutters and billows, obscures and reveals body parts, wraps around and entwines lovers. It also extends performers' wave-like, rounded gestures and the movement of a woman's flowing hair. In motion, the colorful, shimmering, semitranslucent, undulating qualities of the fabric seem to pick up musical features like timbre, rhythm, and melodic contour. Western culture has no clothing so richly coded, so amenable to extending the body, and perhaps none that tends so strongly toward musicality (see Figure 6.4.).

High Stakes

There's a sense of *commitment* in Bollywood song sequences. Jyotika Virdi and others have pointed to the ways that cinema provides the ideology that knits together a nation divided across language, ethnicity, caste, and religion.[6] Song sequences are especially crucial to bridge divisions created through different languages. A second reason for the intensity: for men and women both, romance and marriage is particularly fraught because family is so central and divorce so rare, particularly in rural communities. The moment of the lovers' first meeting, or the event of their wedding, are rarely casual occurrences. One senses the liminality of these moments. In "Fanaa," a group of men and a group of women bring the couple together. In "Anjaana Anjaani," there's a good bit of adolescent joshing, slapping, dunking, and yelling in one another's ears.

Figure 6.4 Early uses of the sari and a woman's long, flowing hair toward musical ends.

Within Hindi cinema's melodramatic mode such moments work in sharp contrast to the later solemn meetings on the wedding divan.

Duets

Many Hindi pop songs are written as duets. American pop songs tend to be solo. The U.S. music industry often adopts the wearisome practice of performers' and band members' constant, nonstop mugging for the cameras. In Hindi musical sequences the characters often focus on one another rather than us. Prasad claims that Hindi cinema isn't based on a western visual system of scopophilic voyeurism but rather on the darsanic gaze.[7] Through an intermediary the viewer looks at the god and the god gazes back. Indian cinema avoids the private. Kissing is taboo; sexual display is public and readable. The wet sari trope appears in "Anjaana Anjaani." The public nature of Hindi cinema may give us more room to enter the mise en scène and draw out our own details from an array of visual and musical motifs.

Lip Sync

India's cinematic practice of lip-syncing creates hybridized figures who appear to possess superhuman properties. In "Anjaana Anjaani," Kareena Kapoor's voluptuous body fails to match playback singer Sunitha Sarathy's breathy voice. This amalgamation of sounds, gestures, and physique contains a greater range of feminine modes than a single person might embody. At the same time, playback singing makes it seem as if the singing voice has the power to animate the figure. The voice moves the flesh. This can help to explain the dreamy, transfixed expressions that often cross actors' faces in close-up.

Camera and Editing

Overheads, shooting through two columns or an archway, and dollying along the diagonal bias past a phalanx of dancers moving in contrary motion all appear in "Fanaa." (An earlier example of dancers moving in contrary motion to the dollying camera occurs in *Barsaat* [1949]). Abrupt cuts between disparate locations—a town, green fields, mountains, and snow—may work formally to connect with the music's long lines. A clever turn on this tradition occurs in "Anjaana Anjaani" when the camera cuts from the beach to a red field, which we later discover is the underside of an umbrella.

A comparison of Ratnam's *Roja* (1992) and *Yuva* (2003) suggests music video aesthetics have shaped his work, a fact many critics have noticed. Western influences are even more striking in A. R. Rahman's music. "Fanaa" and "Anjaana Anjaani" contain features of traditional Indian film songwriting and arrangement, already long influenced by Western musical styles. Yet they also more directly incorporate the contemporary four-on-the-floor bass-drum pattern and layered synth textures of euro house, American lounge jazz of the 60s, and bass lines rooted in 70s soul. While these are Hindi film song numbers, they're also consumed separately, like American music videos.[8] As with contemporary music video (and departing from earlier music-image practices such as the Hollywood musical) the viewer is encouraged to chart an audiovisual path through the wealth of detail that "Fanaa" and "Anjaana Anjaani" contain. This might demand repeated viewings and listenings. Once the viewer grasps these lines, she is "tuned up" and can keep pace with the changing affective states.

"Fanaa": First Section

The melody of "Fanaa" has a floating, open feel, especially in relation to the bass. Besides the bass line, the rest of the rhythm tracks are light and smooth and, along with the synth pad, also seem suspended. The video's blue wash may reduce intensity, but the flood of light emanating from the walls, ceiling, and floor; the variable-speed footage of moving bodies and torsos with only rare shots of feet; and the preponderance of intervals of an open fifth in the midrange and doubled octave in the bass create the sense that the people inhabit some zero-gravity medium.

Ratnam specializes in long lines that surge into the distance, or swooping camera movements that wrap around the figures. The hook line "Fanaa" can seem to waft past the handsome, paired bouncers and head for the circular light with its curlicue tail. Already we're within detail: the graphics on a T-shirt echo the patterning of the reflected walls of light; the red-and-white clothing of a departing club member will become a visual motif (red shifts between rose and pink as it passes through clothing, props, and lights). Once inside the club, faux drugs drift by, and an odd sound effect seems to trigger the camera to speed up. Here, already, is variation. In the tunnel-like entryway, the snare pattern seems to speed up a woman's movements. The whirring sound, too, accelerates the image. Is Kareena Kapoor our object of desire or should we keep moving? Some of the variable-speed footage connects with the song's rhythmic strata as do frequently panned and/or phlanged "whirring" sound effects; the tripartite phrasing of the camera movement relates to the repeatedly echoed "Fanaa." When the camera sweeps up and down from the balcony to the floor as it passes punctuating activity (for example, a breakdancer's thrown-up legs, an embracing couple in a cage, a woman passed across dancers' shoulders), we may not yet guess that this might reflect the aggressive, dramatic contours of the synth bass line; perhaps such an awareness snaps into place as the music makes a "shhh" and we dolly past a phalanx of men.

Next Section

A bass ascends gradually in broken thirds. We, too, rise in stages to the top of a stacked spire of turning circles. There is a moment of macho-ness and a clearing for it. A phalanx of men demonstratively punch out the lyrics' syllables. Here, "Fanaa" gathers speed by playing upon gender anxieties. Male gestures are strong and angular. Men call out "Fanaa" and women respond more prissily, "oh, oh." But relations become more complex. As the sequence progresses, women take on harder, firmer gestures. More fill in the phalanxes dominated by men, and sing within the chorus, suggesting a claim for power and authority. There are multiple presentations of the voice, sung and shouted; processed in the high register; fragmented or echoed; appearing as "party voices." This multiplicity might give the sense of more flexible identities. The plucked string instrument (perhaps a thumbi) we hear in the high register is also no surprise.[9] It emerges from tiny, isolated ornamental fragments in the upper register near the beginning of the song. Though men get the dominant beats in the measure (they stomp on the ones and threes), the aggregate of women have their own social world. On the circular spire they bring themselves into a communal state of ecstasy, an explosive whiteness.

The Next Section

A. R. Rahman uses a low, breathy, spoken woman's voice in other songs to suggest an enchantress. The flash of a forearm tattoo and red beaded earrings strengthens this association. As she leans over the man the woman's voice and body begins to turn a large-scale mechanism where eventually bodies are rotated slow and heavy, like the arms of windmills.

Last Section

Does the similarly placed patch of red suggest a move toward greater intensity? Phalanxes of dancers rush along the diagonal axis toward the camera. In the midst of the run, men use their hands to measure distances between pitches, a frequent trope in Mani Ratnam's song sequences. Here attention is drawn to both large and local scales. Phalanxes begin to move in semicircles in contrary motion to the camera: the male and female phalanxes bring the charmed couple together.

"Fanaa" presents no coherent space a viewer can map out. Almost every part of the set that the camera gazes at is different. Dancers in the background pick out subtle rhythms that complement what's happening in the song's foreground.

"Anjaana Anjaani"

"Fanaa" and "Anjaana Anjaani" may be paired (the water-like theme and red and blue color scheme binds them both). Ratnam's aesthetic often seems rooted in late 80s videos, a period when video imagery tended to strongly underscore songs' sectional divisions. To highlight the chorus's grandeur, in "Anjaana Anjaani" tiny human figures are engulfed by the ocean's vastness. The verses are filled with a kind of everyday wonderfulness. A lounge-jazz-inflected bridge happens while Kareena Kapoor gets washed over by breaking waves. The pre-chorus (or "mini-break") expands outward and, similarly, a crane pulls up and away from the couple as they sing under a red umbrella. Here there's a tension concerning which medium—music or image—is more capable of extension and expansion, a theme of this video. The music in the introduction hovers, and correspondingly, locked in a state of suspension as if it were eternity, Kareena Kapoor and Vivek Oberoi playfully swat at one another in slow motion. The song's arrangement was most likely scored for this environment. There are synth sounds of waves and thunder, and the voice becomes more nasal as the camera dips above and below the waterline, reflecting the way that water muffles sound.

The visual track too draws from Western materials: visually "Fanaa" and "Anjaana Anjaani" look like an American pop dance-music video and a Chanel commercial, respectively, while the two clips' music contains more identifiable contemporary and traditional materials. (For example, "Fanaa" clearly draws on trance's wavelike builds, yet there's also the aforementioned thumbi section.) Some effects seem nearly indescribable and unplaceable for me, and I tend to identify these with traditional Indian artistic practices. Mostly, these are bound to a sense of pleasure I can't quite define.

YOUTUBE

CHAPTER 7

YouTube Aesthetics

Because YouTube is vast and uncharted, this chapter makes no claims of comprehensiveness. The number of clips streamed on YouTube stretches to the sublime—1.2 billion videos a day, enough for every person on the planet with Internet to watch a clip each day.[1] This chapter provides close readings of popular YouTube videos with the aim of identifying broader generic features. Little scholarship exists on the topic, so we'll need to do our best. Part of what separates YouTube from other media are the clips' brevity and the ways they're often encountered through exchange with others. A clip's interest derives from its associations with colleagues, family, friends, and contexts within communities. Clips can get forwarded because there's an intensity of affect that can't be assimilated; humorous or biting, the clips might be diffused by a friend, associate, or colleague.

I like to think of YouTube as a whoopee cushion. Sometimes the mad rants and drivel in YouTube comments exist for a reason: other people get excited too. I worry we're infecting one another with potentially unsavory feelings and behaviors. If my work were only on YouTube, I'd aim to disentangle myself and develop a more authorial tone, but I'm multitasking here, engaging simultaneously with several media. The most expedient approach has been to immerse and respond in kind. So here we go under the veil, or across the interface, as Alex Galloway might say.[2]

"Badgers" is a typical YouTube clip in a popular genre.[3] For me, it's one of the best exemplars of YouTube, even though it has an unusual past and a forward-looking future (more on this in a second). My students found it for me. The constraints of "Badgers" are simple. Suddenly, behind an animated pastoral image of grass, a tree, and one knoll, a badger pops up, and then more and more, alongside a mounting chant of "badger, badger, badger." A mushroom appears (with a song "mushroom, mushroom"), and then a snake ("It's a snake"). Then we start over again (see figure 7.1).

I'd argue that the "Badgers" song's aesthetic effects hold us in a state of suspension, as if we were caught in the beam of a low-voltage Taser. It also excites primitive brain-alarm systems: some Neanderthal self sees badgers as a potential

Figure 7.1 "The Badger Song": YouTube aesthetics.

foe. Badgers look cute and beckoning with their outstretched arms, yet they're regimented and pop up suddenly—a badger army gathers (even if they're doing calisthenics). Mushrooms are risky as well—their poison looms. And of course snakes.

But besides the threatening or ominous signs of badgers, some are more friendly. The "Badgers" song replicates the kind of cognitive play that toddlers enjoy—the disappearance and appearance of objects. Perhaps tracking the constancy of objects might be too simple for an adult, but there are enough badgers that one really needs to pay attention. The swelling and terraced calls of "madger" holds one in a state of ruffled alarm. There's also camp—some German dude singing "Shnake! Ooh!" High above the low conga-like drumming is a wheezy metallic sound, an artifact of the low-fi recording. Camera and movement within the frame set up a looming response and then release. Badgers pop, mushrooms lurch, and then, as a laughing snake rolls to the right, the background glides left. This creates a comforting pattern of hop-hop-hop-slide.

Musically "Badgers" is surprisingly rich. The tune shifts between major and minor. The mushrooms build intensity on the upbeat of three; the snake comes in on four. The badger clip's encouragement of viewer participation may help explain its popularity. Seeing a gesture of popping up and raising hands may elicit a similar response from us. A student told me that in high-school hallways he would pass friends who would suddenly call out, "Badger badger badger!" and flail their arms up and down. The "Badgers" song is also fun to do when you've been drinking too much with friends. One person grabs a sleeping bag; another puts a napkin on his head. You're off and running. We may sense that we're one badger in a larger community of them—rising up is our big chance to take part in the event. Does "Badgers" speak for YouTube in general? Each one of us makes a proclamation with our uploaded video clip and hopes all will respond in sympathy. Also, its buzzy affect—barely tolerable—fits with so many modes of labor and recreation.

I think everyone should always have a few YouTube clips in their backpocket. One might want to share them with friends, at a cocktail party, or around the water cooler at work. More important, a few favorite YouTube clips gives one a center against such a vast, changing media landscape. Some clips might be ennobling and others may provide guilty pleasures. I have to admit that, long-term, I've always loved "Theremin Cat" and "In My Language," and felt hurt that my students are so blasé about them.[4] YouTube demands a raising of the stakes: one clip is never enough. The YouTube effect may be most powerful if the next clip is crasser, bigger, or more ridiculous than the previous. So pulling from my pocket, and upping past "Badgers," we might consider "The Gummy Bear Song" that boasts 316 million hits, which I can't seem to wrap my head around. Perhaps it's just the perfect thing for parents to give to their 3- to 6-year-olds and the kids have been watching it repetitively (like 100 times apiece). Nevertheless, in case there are a couple of adults watching it too, let me provide a reading.

"The Gummy Bear Song" is a novelty dance/pop song in homage to Gummibär, a German brand of bear-shaped candy.[5] It features the green Gummy Bear singing "I'm a Gummy Bear" and dancing or hopping to a Polka "oom-pah" accompaniment through a variety of settings. Like "Badger" and "Crazy Frog-Axel F," its main features are an obnoxious repetition of lyrics and catchy melodies.[6] "The Gummy Bear Song" feels like it has a hundred ways of singing the lyrics, "Oh, I'm a Gummy Bear." All of the choruses' and verses' words are taken up by this phrase, alongside variants (yummy, tummy, funny, lucky, chummy . . . bear). There's one exception: "movin' its groovin' jammin,'" and, in the break, "boing day ba duty party." It's not much different from "Crazy Frog-Axel F." One verse goes "Ring ding dingdingding ding / Ring ding dingdingbembembem / Ring ding dingdingding ding / Ring ding dingding baa baa." (I hope I'm not running into copyright infringement here.)

"The Gummy Bear Song"'s visuals combine production techniques, switching from old-fashioned, soft 60s-style animation, to the newer, harder, Pixar-like CGI. The clip is intermedial, moving between comic-book spaces to jarring 3-D attempts to pierce the viewer's fourth wall. Sometimes Gummy Bear has an odd halo for no apparent reason. Gummy Bear's materiality is uncertain. Does its flesh wiggle, is it hard or soft? How fast can its body go, and in what ways? As Gummy Bear hops up and down we can't quite figure out its nature. It turns around and shows us its butt-crack and then wiggles its buttocks, which should give us a lot of information (very flexible!), but we're not sure! There's etched-in furriness on the hard plastic face that makes little sense. (A bear, why not the rest of its body?) The voice is heavily Auto-Tuned, rendering Gummy Bear even more opaque. Music-video aesthetics help ground the clip to some extent. Two-thirds of the way in, the bear starts playing the tuba, which helps explain the soundtrack's flatulent sounds. He then starts bouncing on a big exercise ball, which makes endearing "glom, glom, glom, pop" sounds. When the song's harmony modulates upward, Gummy Bear ricochets into the stars. We have a better, if not completely certain, sense of the environs and our over-"bear"-ing protagonist through audiovisual relations.

I

Scholars have attempted to map YouTube, but they only provide a glimmer of what YouTube entails and how it works. Alex Juhasz calls it a space for crass commercialism and further reification of mainstream media. For her, YouTube fails to build communities.[7] Michael Wetsch and Henry Jenkins, on the other hand, claim that YouTube fosters community and acts as an agent for self-expression: the site makes possible new identities, sexualities, and modes of interaction.[8] Virginia Heffernan could be considered a connoisseur who classifies clips as high-art, indie, quirky, and "the outsider."[9] These authors, I feel, have been the best at describing YouTube's landscape. Since YouTube remains open territory, it may be useful to begin mapping its aesthetic features. I'd claim salient attributes include (1) pulse and reiteration; (2) graphic values; (3) a sense of scale that matches the medium; (4) irreality and weightlessness (what I'll call the "digital swerve"); (5) reanimation; (6) unusual causal relations; (7) intermediality and transmediality; and (8) sardonic humor and parody. Any clip may embody some of these features, though not all. Sometimes a YouTube clip can seem to possess many of the elements commonly present in music video, though in a YouTube clip these can appear even more distorted and strange.

PULSE AND REITERATION

The most prevalent prosumer YouTube aesthetic is insistent reiteration. (Forms include AAAAAAAAAAAAAAAA, and variants like AAABAAAB-CAAAA.) Many YouTube genres take up an obsessive pulse. Crazy or overly anthropomorphized animals, such as in "The Sneezing Baby Panda," "Gizmo Flushes," and others, show animals acting repetitively in videos sometimes punctuated by a sudden departure from the pattern.[10] The homemade documentaries with personal testimonials linked one after another often lead to something even more repetitive: people make compilation clips with the best smiling faces or the funniest falls out of chairs. Software tutorials—for example, how to do things in Photoshop—suggest each repetitive new touch (a new color, border, scale) is near-identical to the last. Millions of "one-trick pony" clips based on stop-motion or single frames also saturate YouTube. In YouTube's early days, Noah Kalina took a photo of himself every day for six years and then collated the material.[11] In another clip, arty college kids paint, repaint, and then repaint a room again. A new LEGO animation, this time featuring differently colored dots on their block-like surfaces, achieves a slight turn on all other LEGO videos. Athletic clips of accidents are megapopular. Skateboarders tumble off walkways, sides of buildings, canted ramps, and side rails. We can count on the rise and the plop. Mashups are built up through videos sliced together, anywhere from two clips to hundreds. Clips start forming a regular progression. A march-like obsession and equal opportunity take hold.

Of course, not all of YouTube is stuck in a loop. For one thing, corporate materials can flaunt striking classical and alternate forms. The trailers for Quentin Tarantino's *Grindhouse* and Wes Anderson's *Darjeeling Limited* on YouTube are cinema in mini forms—chock-a-block with drama and wielded tightly together through a narrative arc. Though sometimes the ways my students watch whole movies on YouTube when they're feeling too busy or financially strapped to rent the video for an assignment—clip 1, clip 2, clip 3, clip 4—also recreates You-Tube's reiterative feel. Old-school music videos circulating heavily on YouTube look fabulous. (They blow away contemporary ones, though no one could ever imagine shooting such grand creations today. Money and labor would vaporize on the postage-stamp-sized venue—yet why not go for a widescreen extravaganza shrunk to a shadow of itself, if viewers like it, and it carries greater weight than current music videos?)

And of course operas, experimental art forms, and university lectures are legally available for downloading on YouTube, although their view counts are low. I'd still claim reiteration reigns supreme on YouTube, and within each genre, distinct features linked to repetition are foregrounded. The mashup on the one hand sometimes seems to possess a struggle in search of an epiphany, a yearning for freedom, for salvation. In a music video like "Chocolate Rain," on the other hand, the repetitive keyboard pad, the over-and-over return to the lyrics "Chocolate Rain," and singer Tay Zonday's recurrent dip to the side (as the clip says, "I step away from the mic because . . .") are surely repetitive, but repetition becomes a virtuosic experience because the viewer engages in multiple streams of patterning as she rejudges time and space. Here, the Philip Glass minimalist synth pad reiterates; the higher-pitched, more buzzy, timbrally differentiated "rain-like" articulations clock in on another cycle; the head turns adopt a slower periodicity; the faint, vertical stripes on the set's wallpaper suggest another gridded, spatial-temporal dimension.

Many recent straight-ahead music videos have also been taken over by an insistent pulse. "El Sonidito" is one of the most marked examples that celebrates a repeating one (one pitch over and again)—others include "Chacarron Macarron" and "Sunday Afternoon."[12] Not only the image but also the music accompanying these videos strips down to the near minimal. The numbing low-grade stimulus induces a feeling of being stoned or under hypnosis. Reiteration in political viral web media occurs in clips like "APT Obama Obama," where Obama's name is sung over and over again. "Barack O'bollywood," an homage to Bollywood, reiterates the word "acha" as the imagery disperses into kaleidoscopic replication.

Why would reiteration become so central to YouTube clips? There's a surprisingly wide range of reasons including aesthetics, production practices, prosumers' level of training, contemporary technology, and sociocultural contexts. One key factor is YouTube's production practices, most particularly, prosumers' do-it-yourself aesthetics. Fans with no training want to make something. With favorite materials—things to be deformed and reconfigured anew—they start projects but they may not know how to put materials together. Cultural forms like the pop song are well-honed products that have been studied and taught. In contrast, today's makers eschew these constructs, jumping in instead with their editing software and getting going. In the midst of alternating their materials, a realization dawns near the two-minute mark that they'd prefer to make something resembling a pop song and they peter out. Professional makers with more training may pick up on the style, even if it's primitive, because it seems like the next big thing. Such processes seep in, sometimes on a subterranean level, transforming culture on a global scale.

Reiteration also suits our time—YouTube clips project what we are and where we may be heading. The pace and demands of business and leisure time have been accelerating and the number of inputs continue to proliferate. Experiences are based on quick, overlapping hookups: the email to which we must respond, the cell-phone text message calling for an answer, the tweet that demands immediate attention, the voice of the person next to you, the song coming up on the iPod, the slot you occupy in the queue for the IVR phone bank. A fast pulse helps put it all on one gridded timeline. In addition, as a shot of repetition, YouTube can also work like a tonic. Jammed into that space for a minute, locked into a fast, repetitive, jackhammer mode, the web surfer, suddenly released back into the everyday media sphere, experiences wide open spaces.

Competition among media also encourages obsessive repetition. YouTube's response to the hyperintensified, CGI-laden, blockbuster-seeking, new digital cinema and to video games may reveal a sharp competitiveness. The nagging quality may not only pull viewers away from other YouTube clips and more distant websites but also away from all external screens. Though more intuitively grasped than understood, all clips may bear the knowledge that they reside within a conversation with a million others. The only way to pierce is to deploy something that grips—an audiovisual earworm, a slick, fast, robust meme. One reiterative approach is psychedelia (like Cyriak's work). These clips may provide a low-fi, low-cost, mind-twisting, blockbuster-like intensity in miniature.[13]

Reiteration has an aesthetic function as well. The marks surrounding the YouTube clip and the frames strewn across the computer monitor can create a sense of baroque obsessiveness. YouTube links must respond to everything on the page: all the tiny graphs and signs repetitively laid out, and everything else on the monitor's screen. Together these establish a cluttered field from within which the clip seizes attention.

The types of work we're doing support clips that foreground repetition. Typing away at the computer has a "11111" pulse, as does following link after link after link. The clips mimic back these rhythms to us. We can set ourselves to the 1 + 1 + 1 rhythm. The clickity-clicks we make match the website clips' speed.

But perhaps we should not be surprised by so much reiteration. The feature may have always been attractive to us biologically, yet never before could it be so easily achieved. Young children love it, as do many adults. As a Girl Scout I loved repetitive songs—"Ninety-Nine Bottles of Beer on the Wall," a song that subtracted a number with each refrain (98, then 97), until we'd sung our way down to one. But perhaps the repetition of today has a particular valence. Repetition in a media-saturated environment has been ongoing since the 50s, as musicologist Robert Fink has argued.[14] Supermarkets with nearly identical products lined up in rows produce a numb, slightly stunned state. But today is different. All spaces seem like they're nearly or fully taken—a Rubik's Cube. Where can something slot in? Perhaps all one can do is turn over a slot. Hence, today's repetition is about a search for a term that must find its place in the web's landscape, the small bit that will lock into a place against recurring others.

Put another way, we might say the reiterative one represents the contemporary configuration of the individual Internet citizen in relation to the larger whole. Each one of us at the computer faces out into the web. We occupy a slot. One's aware of the pressure of proximate neighbors in the virtual cubicles linked straight or swerved at angles to mine. As each web user uploads a clip, a bouquet-like blip of pixels, she broadcasts a miniature digital signal, radiating out as a single voice alongside a million other monads. These self-assertive blooms start seeming like they've all been done before, though now with a slightly different turn (a new efflorescence). YouTube's repetition is an attempt to deal with the unfathomable depth and breadth of YouTube—it's sublime. The mind seizes up as it tries to reflect upon it. (Here, a YouTube clip is a microcosm of the whole.) When all the clips are parodied, YouTube will reach a state of near entropy. The parodies will make it seem like the game's nearly over, reminding us, similarly, of how entropy will seize up the universe.

Reiteration also has to do with late capitalism and the consumption compulsion. When the megapopular lead singer in YouTube's "Shoes," dressed in drag, sings "Shoes" in the most affectless style possible, over and over, s/he suggests that repetition is tied to the impulse to buy, buy, consume, consume, *must* enjoy, *must* enjoy, start over. Yet as Deleuze would argue, with the Darwinian turn can come a slight difference. YouTube clips can mysteriously trip themselves into another place—sometimes darker. In "Shoes" we start from a suburban family zoned out on couches as if they're on ludes, to finally a frenzied rave. Perhaps only the reiterating word "shoes" has raised the family's level of delirium.

Repetition may reflect sociocultural changes. Howard Hawks's 30s screwball comedies were popular in an era when the popular press and other sociocultural forces encouraged couples to become helpmates and friends. Today's repetition may help anchor us in enormous sociocultural disruptions as we switch jobs, become unmoored from friends and family, and compete against factory robots and global labor. Similarly, childhood memories like those of coping with a steady stream of legal and biological parents may have a chance to be ameliorated. Clips like Dan Deacon & Liam Lynch's "Drinking Out of Cups" seem to suggest that a moment might be dislodged and held.[15] If we control repetition we can insulate ourselves a little from outside forces. These last forms of repetition are often accompanied with lost objects and surrealism (see figure 7.2).[16]

Drug culture may play a role too. The new drugs like Adderall, Ritalin, and Focalin help us exceed at repetitive, slightly odious tasks. The repetition of one syncs with it. Arguing for the importance of drugs might seem odd, but there's been much scholarship about the ways drugs help shape a historical moment.[17] Think of LSD and the psychedelic sixties, heroin and bebop, rave and ecstasy. Other factors, of course, are at play as well (what youth culture is up to, for example).

YouTube may be the new digital cinema's shadowy twin. Both can possess a sharp, quickly reiterating pulse. The hyperstylized *Bourne Ultimatum* features reiterative articulation. The jagged editing and sharp shifts in camera movement—zooming, drifting, jerking, and then reframing again—as well as performers' physical articulations, such as a hand stretched forward, a head turned, or an eye blinked, establish a rapid pulse. Once hewn to this rhythm there seems little way to deviate far from it. We can pass through patches with a bit more nervous activity or less, but reiteration, at some level, seems nearly ever-present.

But perhaps this emphasis on repetition (and its frequently accompanying surrealism) is only a temporary condition. It's there because we feel we don't

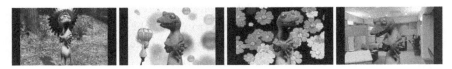

Figure 7.2 Dan Deacon's "Drinking Out of Cups": desirable, free-floating sonic and visual fragments.

have control over the web. Soon more powerful search engines will make better use of social networking (Facebook is trying to optimize searches through friendship profiles, for example) as well as more effectively tag sound, image, and moving media. It won't be so necessary to find a basic pulse, tie ourselves in, or drug ourselves out.

SCALE AND GRAPHIC VALUES

YouTube's aesthetic values include bold graphic design and well-judged scale. This may be related to the medium and its mode of delivery—a clip's limited length, its level of resolution, the forms of attention it encourages. Poorly lit, small environments shot and uploaded with low resolution may tend toward fuzziness; in response, makers, viewers, and consumers may seek stronger audiovisual definition. YouTube clips must often garner attention in a competitive environment; many that struggle to gain legibility, go bold.

What makes a successful YouTube clip? If we can imagine the forms traced as a cartoon—crudely outlined and colored in very simply—and it still speaks, my bet is it has a better shot at success. "The Sneezing Baby Panda," "Haha Baby" and "Evolution of Dance" would all make catchy cartoons. Of course these already have had cartoon remakes but they lack the same charm (and view counts), perhaps because their shape, color, movement, and proportion don't fall into exactly the right ratios. "Best of YouTube" clip homages, with celebrity medleys like Weezer's music video "Pork and Beans" or South Park's cartoon skit, seemingly convey little of what's magical, charismatic, or wonderful about the top-ranked YouTube clips.[18] Some of the most popular clips' particularity must be locked in the ways these figures reside exactly where they are within their flat, miniature cubicles. One wonders whether there's some majestic Darwinian phenomenon going on. Millions of baby clips. Millions of clips of little boys in the backseat going to the dentist. Why does one emerge?

YouTube clips tend to feature simplistic and evocative representations of the body and shape—either as face, body part, or body whole. Clearly legible objects trigger rich affective responses, and help quickly give the performer a pseudo-context (chairs, cups). Contrasting textures—the shiny and the dull; the smooth, brittle and rough—also help clips come forward. Color schemes differ from television: color on YouTube distributes around unified tones, the blues in "Laughing Baby," the muted greens in "Numa Numa"; or showcase the luridly pastel, or monochromatic; but whatever the color scheme, there is less room for the widely various, free, or ad-hoc. Space contracts. While long-form media take us in and out of corridors, alleys, countrysides, and intimate spaces, YouTube sticks to single frontal views. (The differences in art and design between CD covers and album covers mirrors YouTube clips in relation to television. Both YouTube clips and CD covers tend to project reduced, tele-scoped information.)

Not only graphic values but scale counts too. Today we watch media on a va-riety of different screens and audio-playback setups—everything from home theaters to cell phones. Do YouTube clips have a sweet spot—the right visual scale and resolution and audio fidelity? Or is it sweet *spots*? (A clip might nestle into some optimum set points—the tiny, the monumental, and the in-between.) When I saw *The Watchmen* trailer in the theater, I almost fell out of my chair; it was so beautiful. On YouTube and my PC desktop, however, it looks like nothing. The images are meant to engulf or embrace. Widespread metallic human figu-rines' arms, monumental bird wings, arcs of electricity are meant to spread past me tip to tip. We want max shake-my-bones-and-flesh sound too. Gordon Clark's *24 Hours Psycho* plays all right, I think, on a screen covering an entire wall at MoMA (the Museum of Modern Art in New York City). I also don't mind *Psycho* projected from a DVD onto a smallish screen in a classroom. Yet I don't want to watch it on a tiny television or laptop. "Leave Britney Alone" is right on a thumbnail window mixed in with everything else on my computer monitor. YouTube clips' pleasure may stem from the illusion of conjuring up the per-formers. There may be some sadism here. I enjoy watching YouTube performers because I have the pleasure of *stopping* them. "Fred" is fun on a dinky scale, not on a film's widescreen, because he creates the illusion that he's a mosquito beg-ging to be quashed. So is the little boy in the backseat or that baby panda. Not that I would but I *could* rub them out.

DIGITAL SWERVE

This parameter may be both harder to describe and make a claim for. I'd like to say relations between image and music on YouTube show us that both modal-ities exist in a state of lightness or ungroundedness—they're infused with what I like to call the "digital swerve." Let me explain. When I started working on this project, I concurred with David Bordwell that the new global aesthetic colonizing today's moving media forms could best be described through in-tensified continuity—a style partly defined by camera technique (prowling, moving, handheld)—as well as shifting lens lengths and rapid editing. Accord-ing to Bordwell, technology is the key driver in the new heightened audiovi-sual aesthetic: software like digital intermediary, Avid editing, Pro Tools and such make a painterly, capture-based aesthetic possible. Bordwell also sug-gests (and I followed suit) that not only technology but also users' practices have shaped the new style—for example, the embrace of the remote control and DVD extras made possible more disjunctive editing and fragmented sto-rytelling. Solutions to earlier production problems—like the roving cameras deployed for 70s on-location shoots to cover superstars (like Marlon Brando) who were available on set for only one day—also contributed to cinema's changing look and sound. For the new style I thought music video's influence deserved at least as much credit. It had been watched studiously by so many viewers (people forget that at one time the latest music video was a go-to topic of conversation), and had been the means by which so many directors honed their craft, embracing it as an alternative low-entry art school, the conduit through which they'd build the portfolios that landed them film contracts.

But recently I've thought differently. The digital itself produces an intensified audiovisual aesthetic—with both buzziness and weightlessness. Celluloid is very different from digital capture and storage. As Lev Manovich argues, film possesses some properties that belong to the digital: the single frames (all 1s), the film projector's beam of light as it flashes on and off (0, 1s), and celluloid's succession (more 0s and 1s).[19] Andre Bazin, however, argued strongly for celluloid's analog component. It functions as a mask of the world, an analog, a replica; light falling on the randomly placed silver halides leave a mark or trace, something *directly* from the world remains on the film.[20] Extending Bazin's argument, Laura Mulvey claims that film possesses contradictory pulls that shadow our own biological processes.[21] One of cinema's aspects is teleologically driven, an Eros. The motoric film projector (and the camera as it records) drives forward, it purrs. The frame's constant passaging, filled with changing configurations that press forward and away, resembles our own life-drives for power, sex, reproduction. Cinema's motoric nature is also why we see so often literalized trains, cars, people running, people walking. Yet half of the film is comprised of stillness—a black, a darkness that occurs in the transition from frame to frame. Cinema itself, replicating so many of our beloved narrative forms, has a teleological drive—just as much toward Eros and power as toward a death-drive, a willingness to embrace cessation.

The digital possesses different properties, as David Rodowick argues.[22] The digital is a transcriptive, rather than an analog, process. Think first of a grid, a fine tic-tac-toe lattice, and within each block resides a pixel that flips on and off within its slot. The grid remains constant even as the pixels switch. Our experience is that of the grid's continuous burn, and the weightless fluctuations of pixels blinking on and off. The electronic light continually oscillates, appearing and vanishing, yet never completely rests. One way to give life to this digital weightlessness is through phantasmagorically embodying it, making it musical. The digital music in tandem with the digital image creates a monstrous hybrid automaton. This phantasm is literalized in *Hellboy 2*: here the Green Monster that terrorizes the city, once shot down, becomes flowers' spores and green goo rolling and drifting away—nothing but dreams and nearly substanceless puff and stuff. Similarly, *Hellboy 2*'s clunky robots crumble like wet meringues as soon as the switch is flipped off. In *The Day the Earth Stood Still* (2008) the globe and locusts seem comprised of gossamer. In *Transformers: Revenge of the Fallen*, metal machine monsters melt into ball bearings or turn into filament-dust. In *Speed Racer* cars careening into each other sometimes go right through another as if they were ghosts. The digital images' swerve or momentum calls for a shadow schema, a filling in. As Jonathan Sterne claims, the soundtrack is digital as well—we might say we have digital on digital—but perceptually the soundtrack provides a more continuous function, more closely aligned to our analog experiences. (Digital sound samples from both the top and the bottom of the wave form create a stronger illusion of continuity.)[23]

I'm not arguing sound *always* affects more embodiment than does image. Which media asserts more presence is based not only on its mode of presentation but also on its level of resolution. To date the digital image tends toward the colder, more inhospitable in the partnership between sound and image; in the collaboration, sound does the heavy lifting of making it real. It's not always this way: today we watch on multiple platforms, moving fluidly among IMAX theaters, HD home systems, TV computer monitors functioning as television circuits, and lower-res cell phones and iPods. Occasionally the sound becomes more schematic (try to watch a DVD on an airplane with your multi-thousand-dollar laptop and off-the-shelf iPod earphones). Yet overall it has become the soundtrack and its image: the heightened audiovisual aesthetic is sound-driven. Reiteration put in play either in the sound or image sutures the music and the image together, it nails it down. The "Badgers" song's aesthetic derives from its jackhammer pulse and buzzy timbres. It reflects and is true to the medium itself.

REANIMATION AND DEATH

In a postindustrial era as nearly all forms of media are converted into digital substitutes, and one experiences an expanding shift from the real into simulation, I'd claim a deathly taint creeps into the mix. Jason Stanyek and Ben Pickett in their forthcoming book *Digital Recreations: The Intermundane* consider the ways new technologies make possible the reanimation of older media so that, for example, an older deceased film star like Gene Kelly dances in the rain to techno music in a Mac commercial, and the now-dead Nat King Cole sings a duet with his still-living daughter in a music video. I maintain a parallel track to their work, finding examples on YouTube that focus not on the dead, but the nearly dead. For example, the band Journey dropped their lead singer Steve Perry when he became ill. (Perry asked his fellow members to wait until his health improved.) The record company and band held a global YouTube contest to replace him and found singer Arnel Pineda. Pineda's singing is so good, he's almost a new and improved Perry—all the phrasing, all the nuance, but a younger voice and body. Now that employers can draw from a global pool of workers, it feels as if anything or anybody can be imitated; a replacement copy with even better-shaped contours can be slotted in. The replica improves on the original and the original becomes more inanimate. That Pineda was discovered in the Philippines might elicit anxiety and racist sentiments for Journey fans.

Another example is that YouTube is full of the nearly dead. The prosumer YouTube clip "Charleston Style" takes footage of African American dancers doing the Charleston in the 40s and subtly alters their movements, like puppets, so they now dance to the recent Daft Punk song "Around the World." This clip almost certainly was inspired by the "Around The World" music video directed by Michel Gondry.[24] "Charleston Style" could be thought of as riffing on the Gondry video, but the Charleston remix uses the real memory, not the screen memory, of people of color. It now seems clearer that Gondry's robots and skeletons reflect a desire to hold on to some fragment of black culture and make it dance, but his bodies have become deracinated, lost of history and autonomy.

CAUSAL RELATIONS

Music video can raise questions of cause and effect, foregrounding relations so ambiguous that the music seems to be the engine mobilizing people, objects, and environments.[25] YouTube clips raise questions of cause and effect even more sharply—however one sometimes wonders if this is the primary hook energizing the clip. A quick glance bears this out. In "The Sneezing Baby Panda," did we know a panda could sneeze? And so hard that it would blow away both mother and baby? What animates that dancer in "Evolution of Dance"? Mexican jumping beans? Perhaps some wiry worms wiggling inside him, or mysterious powers rippling throughout his limbs? Why would the little boy in the car's backseat be so punch drunk, as if a parent had possibly malevolently slipped him a mickey?[26] One might argue that many media in their infancy focused on mysterious relations of cause and effect.[27] Since YouTube is just getting started, its development might trace its sibling's, the cinema's, first steps, which began with a "cinema of attractions"; here, a fascination with the basic mechanics of things like Lumière's earliest film strips with a train coming into town; Edison's "Fred Ott's sneeze"; Méliès's figures popping in and out alongside puffs of smoke.[28] Music video first featured male musicians who terrorized women alongside awkward animation that made things appear and disappear (like The Cars' "You Might Think"). In truth, YouTube's strangeness might have to do with the fact that we are experiencing its first iterations.

Political YouTube videos emphasizing mysterious causality include the Rickrolled series.[29] The multiple iterations of Rick Astley's 1987 music video hit "Never Gonna Give You Up" became one of the most intertextual, its popularity perhaps second only to "Yes We Can." A fan took the original song, stripped out Astley's voice, and edited in snippets from Obama's filmed speeches. Remarkably, Obama had spoken every word contained in Astley's lyrics at some point, and Obama's words merged with the backing tracks of the song directly, without any noticeable alterations in Auto-Tune. In the most causally obscure of the series, "John McCain Gets BarackRoll'd," Obama flashes up on an enormous screen behind McCain, as the elderly candidate gives a speech from the podium at the Republican convention. At some level one wonders how Obama became so musical. What gave him the right to appear here? Is the audience aware of what's going on? Who made and endorses this clip? A second example, "Obama and McCain—Dance Off!," features the heads of the candidates grafted onto younger bodies who breakdance. It's not clear whose body belongs to whom, how that body moves, what the performers think of the music, or where the clip's going to go (see figure 7.3).[30]

There are multiple reasons why obscure causal relations are central to YouTube aesthetics. David Rodowick provides one.[31] Our experiences of screens have changed with the computer's multiple windows we can activate, click through, resize, move, and hide. In video games, too, we enact spatial transformations of the environment within the frame. Our gestures transform coordinates as we surf through the web and participate in the game experience; these might, through contagion, be transferred to YouTube. Though we cannot truly modify the inner workings of a clip, the most popular YouTube clips seem intensely bound up with powerful, obscure causal relations. Though we can't, we have the illusion that we might, through one click, control the internal workings of these clips. And at some metalevel, we still, of course, can stop the show.

"Chocolate Rain" is a music video that emphasizes causal relations and fits the scale of YouTube. In this video, singer Tay Zonday leans back from the mic.[32] Zonday must have found this gesture so baffled viewers that he needed to add a clunky kyron-text-generated disclaimer: "I step away because. . . ." A mystery remains, however, concerning the song's strange sources, especially since the recording equipment remains offscreen. (Imagine if we saw Zonday at the mixing

Figure 7.3 "Barack O' bollywood," "John McCain gets Barack-rolled," and "Obama and McCain—Dance off!" spoofs provide insightful criticism of the candidates.

board. How much allure would that have?) Zonday's mature voice emanating from a young person's body adds to the enigma. And the screen's yellow tint? Does it speak with the lyrics? Does "Chocolate Rain" become golden? Occasional synth attacks in the upper register might suggest the beginning of falling rain. Where's the rain? Shouldn't it be there? The lyrics have an apocalyptic bent—perhaps Zonday is an emissary from the future. We feel pressure to listen. Repressed fantasies might be evoked as well. As it points to the future, the video mines a historical sense. "Chocolate Rain" is powerful because it elicits so many responses—awe, disdain, envy, affection. Of course, there is an audiovisually oriented political version—"Obama Sings Chocolate Rain."[33]

Another clip to consider: can a cat really flush a toilet? In "Gizmo Flushes" perhaps there's a secret mechanism set to go off after each of Gizmo's circular runs. And why does the cat want or need to do the revolutions? Does the cat exert strange powers over the owners? Have the owners somehow tricked the cat? Do they know when they are supposed to provide commentary; are they on cue just like the cat?

"BallsCrash" has the everyday boredom followed by a sudden twist. Just like many other YouTube clips, there is a lull followed by a sudden confusing action that creates disarray. In "BallsCrash," father and daughter loll on the bed, while a mother videotapes from a distance. Suddenly the soon-to-be toddler, who has been kicking periodically, stretches her leg out further and drives the heel of her foot down into her father's groin. How will the father react? He doubles over, obviously in pain, but we can't determine how much. And what does the baby think of this?[34]

Many of the figures in YouTube's top videos have a touch of remoteness to them. The baby in "Haha Baby" as well as panda in "The Sneezing Baby Panda" sit on a Dutch angle, facing toward yet also away from us. The two boys in "Charlie Bit My Finger" are pushed back, protectively swaddled in blankets. In "Leave Britney Alone" Chris Crocker's face becomes a mask. (He resembles the famous theater's smiling and frowning faces.) "The Asian Backstreet Boys" (one of my favorite clips) has an ambiguous figure in the background typing away. "Numa Numa" resides very low in the frame. Obese, his features sag downward, succumbing to the weight of gravity even as he joyously raises his plump arms. Why do these dispositions work? Is it that we, as viewers, want to participate, to do some work? Is it that we find pleasure in seeking out these characters to claim them as our own?

CONDENSATION

YouTube clips that have garnered over a million hits tend to elicit deeply Freudian wishes and desires. YouTube is full of hostile puns, jokes, and returns to childhood. In "Numa Numa" a subtle allusion to Humpty Dumpty unfolds.

Gary Brolsma's singing karaoke alongside a high, male, but feminine-sounding falsetto pushes the clip's affect into a state of delirium. His facial gestures are so quick and malleable he becomes a Disney animation. (Watch: he's good with choreography for the camera, judiciously moving back from and toward the camera's lens in relation to the music. He's expert at navigating the small space he's been given. But he might topple or slide down from the screen.) The fact that the clip conjures forth childhood fantasies, along with more adult anxieties concerning control and sexual desire, and that we sense we can click away from the clip and remove his audience, makes it overwhelmingly attractive.

"Gangnam Style" may be one of the best for dirty little jokes.[35] The clip's theme starts kicking in with recreational riverboats, designed as big ducks with their perky tails rising up from the river. Throughout the clip many pretty girls appear; soon we'll cut to a woman's moving buttocks, as she does aerobics from a crouched position while Psy bends over her silently screaming, in awe or due to overstimulation. Earlier he had been sitting on a bench, and then bang!—two men seemingly explode from his butt. Psy's love interest shows up on the subway, wearing black, shiny short-shorts and an orange mini-apron ducktail. (Our attention is quickly drawn to her apron-tail because her hair is also dyed black and orange.) Psy will emerge from the smooth surface of a standing pool of water, head up, perhaps with a desire to subtend both the ducks and the girls. He'll next reemerge, to strengthen this point, with head and toe pointed up. The horses in their stalls, with their heads bobbing up and down, and the dancers' wrists, mimicking the horses, support the subtending. Uncap that thing! The clip's concerted about its derrière humor. A too-long green shirt-tail (like an alligator tail) dangles from the pelvic thrusting "horse rider" of Psy in the elevator; the rider's coat-tail so long it tickles Psy's back. Psy turns sideways with his hand cupped like a little duck tail. The singer seemingly has an overaccentuated bulge on the toilet (the illusion created through dark shadows in the toilet water). Earlier, a large piece of newspaper had flown up to cover his crotch in the white-mush blizzard inside the horsey corral. Oh well, that's the front end, but front ends may mean the same as backends in this polymorphously perverse clip. "Gangnam Style" takes liberties. We begin with the female love interest wielding a paddle! (The racket has a cartoon of Psy's face on it.) Psy emphatically retorts through strong wrist gestures, calling "Gangnam style." Perhaps we have a happy *Taming of the Shrew* or *Kiss Me Kate* story. At the end, Psy's paramour's lacy coral dress shortens up.

Gangnam Style is so engaging for many reasons. It riffs on and pokes fun at the history of music video style (for example, the tracking shot of the performer strutting down an aisle toward the camera; the group dance). It suggests a unique place and community—the Gangnam district in Seoul. It has a wonderful dance (the horsey dance, as infectious as earlier hits like Soulja Boy's dance, and The

Macarena). The song is crammed with catchy hooks—"Gangnam Style...whoop whoop whoop," and these sonic hooks seem to help trigger the visual upendings described above.

Like "Gangnam Style," most popular YouTube clips often have a bit of ribald body-humor, even a bit of sadism. "David After Dentist" and all of those drugged-up, post-doctor-visit people (many with extremely high view counts) are examples, but we can find cruelty in almost all the most popular clips. Mishka the dog doesn't look very happy to be singing "I love you." The mother kitty taking away the kitten is a little scary in "Mama Cat Comes to Rescue Her Little Kitten." "Charlie Bit My Finger" and "BallsCrash" show real pain. I think even Keenan Cahill in his lipsync performance of Katy Perry's "Teenage Dream" looks a little miserable. His expression shifts between elation and grimaces.[36]

INTERMEDIALITY

YouTube is loquacious. Intertextuality and hybridization occur across platforms, among users, and within clips. Here's one example about the ways YouTube exists in a conversation with other media. In a Hulu commercial now on YouTube, Alec Baldwin admonishes viewers that television turns brains to mush (he passes scientists working on brains in vats and human subjects already devolved into propped-up couch-potato tableaus). Of course, here, we have multiple layers of intermedia rivalry—a film star trashing television in favor of web broadcasting, which now appears apart from its original source. The clip reflects Thomas Frank's arguments about mass contemporary culture—no longer is there any outside space beyond advertising. Corporations have internalized all forms of discontent and dissent and they'll pimp it back to us with a wink. Alec Baldwin states that aliens have come to warp our mind and force us to watch the Internet while some green tentacles start to wrap around him. Here he riffs on the cultural critique that advertisers seek to capture and transform us into good consumers. He and a scientist exchange a maniacal laugh. A few days later, Yahoo posts the world's most annoying laugh ever. Is this a link? Was one clip a response to another or is this a synchronic event? The laugh is one of the most perfect memes. The small fragment pierces like a doubly punched mosquito's buzz and sting. Hulu and YouTube talk about themselves and try to consume "the Other."

YouTube links talk to one another—they make a turn on previous iterations. Today's audiovisually based culture tends to coalesce around contested aural and visual signs rather than extended text—during the presidential election 2008 on YouTube there was strong interest in Edwards's haircut, Palin's dress or moose kill. When the Right didn't get its desired mileage from Reverend Wright's "Chickens Have Come to Roost" speech, Fox News fans started distributing clips insinuating that Michelle and Barack Obama had engaged in a terrorist fist-bump. The Left responded speedily, with an attempt to shift our culture's understanding of the fist-bump from the globally threatening to the pacific—a cool "how are ya?" Audio and visual signifiers then erupted, as long chains of responses, across Twitter, blogs, YouTube, et al.

Similarly when Obama's book *Dreams from My Father* appeared as a book on tape, viral web media remixes mashing up Obama's street-style cursing quickly followed. Soon appeared "The Whitest Kids" doing a sendup with Abraham Lincoln's street-cred "homey" epithets before he's assassinated at Ford's Theater.[37] The sound and visual bytes slid in and out of the web, sometimes crystallizing into an icon, and then circulating back. That so many actors, sportscasters, and celebrities have been mashed up, from Christian Bale to Kanye, turns Obama into more of an average Joe.

Dense conversation and intermediality can happen internally within clips too. On YouTube this happens less frequently than one might expect because sophisticated production skills and a strong sense of art and music history are often needed to pull it off. Nevertheless, internal cross-mediality suggests where media and cinema might be going. Trailers are some of the best examples here: consider the trailer for the film *The Spirit*. (Note: Remashed trailers and film scenes are some of the most popular content on YouTube.)

The Spirit trailer is a segment Alfred Hitchcock might have dreamed of if today's technologies were available to him. The director often quipped that film was like life with the boring bits cut out: he wanted to play audiences like an orchestra, propelling them along the paths of his moods. *The Spirit* achieves a similar control over its audience through hyperstylization. Ferried across a series of affective flashpoints, viewers traverse media. An animated line comes into focus and the sound before the drawing helps us identify it as a heart monitor's flatline. The music and animated line swell and generate a tree turning into birds taking flight. An audiovisual whoosh streams across the frame. We follow it as it becomes a figure leaping off a building. The words "Silken Floss" impress themselves on the frame—the inky blacks, firehouse reds, and strongly bolded text suggest S & M. The movement across medial surfaces makes it seem as if *we're* a hot potato, as if we were a stone skipping across a lake. Intermediality can create an experience in which we shift our attention so rapidly among media—text, sound, animation, CGI, live action, music—that our experience is of only touching surfaces, never ground (see figure 7.4).

Trailers are a great form of cross-mediality, especially blockbuster films' trailers. *The Transformers* trailer keeps us busy. We hear a sound, our attention turns toward it, something leaps across the frame, we follow it, then another sound fills in what we heard. But our attention is already elsewhere. Trailers of

Figure 7.4 The Spirit trailer: mobile, affective flashpoints.

this sort, including the one for *Miami Vice,* often become full-fledged music videos toward the end. (They tend to open with enigmatic sounds of machine noises, heartbeats, or suggestions of drumming, and two-thirds in, work themselves into pop songs.) These are small, worth watching again, and more satisfying than the movie. Perhaps because YouTube is short and often made by prosumers without advanced skills, cross-mediality is not the most emphasized of techniques. But I'd argue it may be the wave of the future. "Barack O'bollywood" and the opening of LL Cool J's video "Mr. President (ft. Wyclef Jean)" showcase this style.[38]

Mashups form a subset of the new intermediality. They may not be as formally rich as the above examples but they have their own delights. Often based on pure alternation or swapping in and out with some regularity, and only working the indices of sound and picture, in a mashup the edited shots and sounds of a performer can hang as fragments. As materials sweep past, the musical hook or image lingers like a pungent smell. If you needed to pare down and carry forward a reduced- or animal-like presence of your beloved performer, this would be it. Often one medium retains its liveliness—a song lyric, the body moving, a musical hook, and the other freezes in mechanical repetitions. The live bit pulls apart from a wash of other material pressing through. Any moment can teeter toward something revelatory or lost.[39] A mashup can be unpredictable. On YouTube there are thousands of such swaps including ones for the pop songs of the year as well as for the 2008 campaign.

In some cases the aesthetics of reiterative clips achieves a kind of striation. "Barack O'bollywood" presents a fast reiterative pulse. It also possesses a number of "audiovisual hooks" that appear with regularity.[40] Each recurrence of an audiovisual hook connects with previous occurrences. Against the reiterative pulse, these hooks can be experienced as chains—points linked together as they fall into predictable patterns. In "Barack O'bollywood," whenever an elephant or a bulky silhouette of a figure appears, we hear a low trumpeting sound. (The frame empties out, the visual material sits low in the frame, and the aural tessitura is low too.) Every time we see an animated cutout of a belly dancer, we hear a high-pitched "ch-ch-ch." When we see Obama's head, we might hear a voice in the middle register calling out "acha-acha-acha" as Obama's mouth opens and closes. When watching "Barack O'bollywood" we may start looking toward parts of the frame at certain instances in search of objects accompanied by sounds. We experience our attention as striated, moving horizontally across a video that has established a rapid beat.

PARODY AND THE SARDONIC RESPONSE

A key feature of YouTube is the sardonic response. Any overly gushy work is ripe for a remix—from Bruno Ganz acting out Hitler's breakdown over the loss of his Xbox game to "Eric Clapton Shreds." *Moulin Rouge!*'s sped-up goofy scenes could be seen as a response to such YouTubelicious moments. The scenes are so aware of their own daffiness that one could never take a swing at them. The truly sentimental-bashing prescient was *Mystery Science Theater 3000*. Who would have known that the little puppets would usher in a stylistic revolution?

Parody and the sardonic response occur partly because technology makes it possible; adding a second layer that circumvents, undercuts, or makes ridiculous the original object is one of the easiest things to do. In the anonymity of the web, YouTube makers are in search of a ground—your sarcastic take immediately places you in relation to a select group of viewers as well as the producers and fans of the original material. Your parody, now tied to original content, piggy-backs on an already accrued attention.[41] Sarcasm also pierces us. Anything that pushes against social norms tends to grab attention. Some of YouTube's new, peculiar forms of brute-comedic aesthetics are surely generational. My students describe some things that they find extremely funny—absurdist, hostile—that leave me baffled.[42] Some of the more aggressive forms of YouTube sexuality I find a bit hard to take, but it's easy to see how they work within a larger cultural and economic milieu. With contemporary subjectivities now fractured rather than whole, it seems my students can adopt the alienated roles needed to participate in these rough-and-tumble practices, and then switch back into more traditional, humanistic-based stances.

II

Before I describe some forms of engagement with YouTube, let me provide a close description of several clips that exhibit some of the aesthetic features I've just detailed. These clips are well designed for YouTube—they would work poorly on television or in the cinema.

In "Haha Baby" the father's provocations to laugh sound like ringing chimes, conjuring associations with toys like a rolling plastic ball on a stick and a toy xylophone. The child's uproarious laughter has an uncanny quality: full-throated, both animal- and adult-like. Perhaps there's a man inside that baby suit. Every parental call elicits rapt attention, and then we can see, emerging in real time, the full-fledged rejoinder. Yet at the same time, there is a lingering shadow. Is the child laughing for and by himself? Even more unsettling: is the laugh mechanical? He's the dream Tickle Me Elmo doll—wait and it goes. Or is it that the child and father aim for the perfect duet? The baby is so round he resembles a china doll. (What will he be like when he gets older?) There's a patch of blue in the back, some on his shirt, plus his round blue eyes, so at least the color scheme is unified; the lighting has the morality of one of Vermeer's domestic interiors. The circle on his shirt suggests the button that triggers his laugh. Best though is the call-and-response itself. Listen to the clip without picture—the two, together, make one enchained melody (see figure 7.5).

YouTube's top clips include pratfalls, parodies, skits, recent music videos, and odd assortments of things. Curiously, one old music video was on the all-time popular list for a large part of spring 2009: "Barbie Girl" by Aqua. A beloved tape when it came out in 1997, it didn't crack MTV's annual top ten.[43] Why did "Barbie Girl" become popular again? Was it that Barbie turned 50 and the public experienced an overwhelming wave of nostalgia for her? Or was its popularity driven by a Mattel promotional scheme in which employees have been asked to perform as YouTube drones and click the Barbie link over and over, just as Warner Bros. spurred prepubescent girls to become viral Avril Lavigne–bots and watch her video "Girlfriend," while they instant messaged, talked on cell phones, did their homework, and surfed the web? But I'd argue that the "Barbie Girl" clip has something special in its own right (unlike "Girlfriend" with its trashy premise of girls who undermine one another over a boy). The clip's small format and highly compressed digital transfer suddenly make Aqua's real figures doll-like (as if these hybrid phantasms can truly achieve the dreams of today's CGI).[44] Aqua's video has a double edge—it's infused with the same nostalgia you'd project onto your old toys, but it's also a threatening other. The music, gestures, outfits, and sets are all slightly out of joint; we no longer know how to read them.

It's odd that "The Evolution of Dance" became a hit. I wonder if viewers respond to it as a toy one perches on a desk or window sill at work, those jiggling

Figure 7.5 "Haha Baby": a Vermeer-like pictorialism.

dolls with a trace of the uncanny. Perhaps it's like the grinder's monkey at the Mardi Gras—a quick, glancing amusement for passersby. Thinking about the video's image for a moment reveals how unlikely it is. Contrary to everything we've learned about dance from Fred Astaire and Gene Kelly, you can't see the dancer's *feet*. There's some degree of visual interest even before the dance starts. The stage cants both up and down. Crescents flow up and down from the ceiling (evoking half-moon light); the dancer's ring of balding hair triples the semicircles. The white stripes on the faded jeans and the T-shirt's red logo "Crush" help telegraph the figure; even if the body were to be erased we might interpret these graphic marks as a body moving in space. The dancer's objects—water bottle and hat—perched invitingly on a stool, seem to call for his attention. The dancer's opening move, an Elvis Presley imitation, does little to impress us: only in the transition to the next pop allusion is there a jolt. The dancer is a chameleon—first tubby around the belly, middle-aged and balding; suddenly hip and suavely masculinist; young; gay; female; black or whatever. He's willing to take on any identity. He performs "Baby Got Back," Sir Mixalot's ode to big butts, with equanimous relish, shaking his posterior as if he were part of a chorine's lineup. He can also be Michael Jackson's "Billie Jean"—cool and remote; he can do conservative country square dancing, embracing a dumbfounded silliness, and then circle back again to the dorky Bangles "Walk Like an Egyptian." Some of his moves are sloppy and bungled (for kung-fu fighting he teeters back and forth), but for "Staying Alive" and "Billie Jean" it's pure YouTube aesthetics—effortless, seamless, stripped to bare essentials, pure gesture and thought. Have these professional and awkwardly amateur stretches been planned, or do they emerge in real time? The movement through the joins among dance numbers is expressive and canny, but it seems to emerge spontaneously. Part of the pleasure is guessing what the next song will be, what kind of gestures he will make, and how he will move to them. Is he quicker than us? (See figure 7.6.)

Some clips achieve a kind of intense beauty. A colleague sent me a clip of an Israeli animation titled "Pop Goes the Weasel."[45] The theme is cloyingly sentimental: in an empty apartment, among the last set of moving boxes stacked up in the center of the floor, one package sprints free and, in the strange world of animation, decides to unwrap itself. Out wiggles a music box that presents someone's history through photos, letters, and such. These scraps of paper and tchotchkes break loose and reanimate the house before returning to their intended places as packed

Figure 7.6 "Evolution of Dance": Judson Laipply strikes a pose.

contents. Beneath the clip's trajectory, the materials the music box provide describe *mankind's* historical progression through media.[46] The childhood drawings resemble cave paintings; the first text, the printing press; music clips remind us of bootleg cassettes; images are thrown up on the walls and then cluster to form continents, the Internet. One person's childhood memories become encapsulated within the history of communication. This makes sense, because for now there's a developmental homology: we're used to working first with rudimentary materials—crayon drawings, print—and then the computer, though this, of course, is changing fast. (Children now start out on the computer and adults draw with crayons in restaurants.)

III

YouTube is a polysemic, heterogeneous phenomenon. It speaks differently depending on how and with whom you experience it. In what streams of social networks bearing clips do you belong? How are you using a clip at work and for leisure? In this section I'll describe what it might feel like to participate in a network (like Facebook) as a prosumer, as a lone individual, and as a scholar.

KINSHIP NETWORKING

On the one hand, YouTube provides intense media experiences. Several friends say they need never go to the cinema. Sometimes a clip sent by a friend or colleague produces a moment of intimacy, as if we were in a conversation and one of us had suddenly turned the witty phrase that concretized gathering experience. The three-minute clip swells in the light of our shared feeling. The clip's cleverness helps it merge into our paths of dialogue and mutuality.

YouTube also provides an extremely satisfying experience for me as a teacher. Students post YouTube videos on BlackBoard. I watch and distribute them to colleagues worldwide. Associates and friends email back, and I report on this correspondence to my students, who sometimes give me clips to send back. Never before has information flowed so fluidly among students and scholars. My course is no longer point to mass, it's peer to peer.

PROSUMER

The quality of my students' video work shocks me. It's often as good as what professionals produce, but on greatly reduced budgets. My students have grown up making things and they've already logged the hundreds of hours of practice needed to do good video production—and not only that, they've done it often through ad-hoc means, such as shooting on cell-phone cameras, boot-legging rock concerts, and playing around with the free software like Garage Band and iMovie that comes bundled with their computers. My guess is that with so many skilled young media-makers and so much distributed content, it will be near impossible to make a living directing, shooting, or editing.

YouTube can possess a communal, egalitarian feel. Is it different from ham radio, DIY podcasts, or self-published blogs? Video clips can sometimes create a sense of a false polis (because we never do link up and engage in an extended dialogue). But YouTube experiences also are saturated with associations I have with the people who sent them to me. And why not analyze my students' work as much as any other clip on YouTube? Their clips receive a significant number of hits—1,000-plus for a remix of a Daft Punk song—and they seem as much a part of the zeitgeist as anything.

THE INDIVIDUAL VIEWER

But as a solitary viewer, apart from friends and colleagues, my experiences differ. Here YouTube offers me the experience of the *flaneur* wandering through low-rent districts, shadowy drug dens, and public urinals. How can it be that 1,257,000 have seen this clip, but now, while I'm with it, I feel I'm engaged in my own private peepshow? I assume no one else is here. Only the ghostly mark-ings of the Kilroys, the weird graffiti ravings below the audiovisual clip, unraveling at their own pace. Mine is the inverse projected fantasy of television: with a TV experience, almost everyone wants a communal simultaneity. On YouTube I imagine a game of telephone. Someone whispers into my ear, then another. I speak in hushed terms into the next. It's almost as if I were sitting in a seat, just warmed, that I pass over to the next viewer. Since the graffiti responses share no quarter with me, with only a trace (a cookie, some web-spying memory), I take my leave.

And I wonder, who are the people who post on YouTube and what are their archives like? YouTube resembles the budget hunter's dress shop Filene's Basement. People go through, ransack, and move sales items in and out. Lots of "30 to 60 percent off" signs. In the corners things get raggedy. And there is no map to do archaeological work on YouTube. The top-10and top-100 lists I find through Google searches are crap. Through Pitchfork music video I find something I like through a fluke. How to start an archive? I imagine mini-networks of viewers unknown to us in the YouTube universe; these link as an underground system. No one sees it and suddenly it goes viral, erupting into the whole system.

Virginia Heffernan notes that everything is muddy, torn, underwater on YouTube, a lost Atlantis.[47] All of that empty data that no one watches makes me anxious. It doesn't bother me that blogged data float around never to be read. But those orphaned audiovisual clips haunt me. Is it because they're mini-homunculuses in need of attention? I imagine all of the web clips turning around in their cells like tadpoles in small paper cups.[48] And is all of that data, which must be stored on chips, poisonous in its mercury? When reactivated, do the links themselves demand additional energy? That all of these clips sup-posedly sit in an anonymous warehouse, football field in size, cooled in little boxes, seems incomprehensible.

YouTube also causes me trepidation. I dream I return and YouTube's nearly wiped clean—the site's a mini-apocalypse. Fans have moved on to the new and better—YouTube becomes an abandoned city. Where's Gizmo the flushing cat now?[49] Even if I were to have downloaded these clips, they can't be shared that easily. There may be a YouTube underground but how would I lead my less tech-savvy and more law-abiding colleagues and readers to it? A new era: how many times have the American public hungered after and peddled contra-band—liquor, pornography, prostitution, illicit drugs, firecrackers, bootleg concert recordings, pirated DVDs—but *YouTube clips?*[50] The anxiety I experi-ence with YouTube is not so different from many other modern fears and irri-tants. Will I keep my job? Am I up for a fight with Comcast? Has Diebold rigged the election?

Sometimes I also experience agitation. Scholars tend to experience a liveli-ness when they engage with a world, regardless of its content—wrestlers, prostitutes—partly because of the pleasures of asking questions and building a topography. But I've already steeped myself in the middle- to lowbrow. As a music video scholar I've watched my share of clips that left little mark on me, from Bobby Brown to Bon Jovi. If I extend my world to hamsters with pop-corn, I'll fry some brain synapses.[51] Will spending time here yield clarity or answers? Most of the materials I look at are sophomoric, *literally*—without a way to drill down into YouTube (there are few guides beyond the top 50) I channel my students' tastes. When I ask my students where they found their links they look at me baffled. "From friends." "Where did *they* find it?" And the trail goes cold. In addition, there are not yet funding streams for YouTube studies nor much of a community of scholars for me to collaborate with.

Here's an example of odd scholarship. While wandering around YouTube I came across a clip called "I Sit on You." A few days later it struck me as impor-tant. The video's conceit is simple and perhaps sadly endearingly: a mid-dle-aged man sits on peoples' laps who, from what we can tell, didn't ask him to be there. It might be the most inane of ideas, but one wants to give permission to a paunchy middle-aged man to participate. I'd like to go back and watch the clip again but what are the search terms? "I Sit on You?" There's no sensible method here.[52]

As a scholar I've also developed strange skills, such as practicing the art of the 40-second watch. With a film, I might devote 15 minutes of attentive watching before I turn away to do something else—but 40 seconds?

YouTube and Google have not been helpful here. I've written to them, introducing myself as a professor who teaches YouTube aesthetics, but no response. Without answers, I've been left to my own stories and imaginative devices. Some grouchy staffperson *must* have decided that viewers only get to see the top 50 clips of all time and then buried the search function to the next ones in the series. Is YouTube the world's largest archive without a librarian? And does Google have the right to keep information about the archive private?[53] Why can't we sometimes be free of the advertising? YouTube is very profitable now. I remember when there was no advertising and the site felt owned by users.

YouTube may have vast social effects, but how will we grasp them when its content is elusive and so many other media impinge on our lives? An example: YouTube's practice of placing an ad at the bottom of the clip and at the right-hand corner of a page is worrisome. It's a higher rate of advertisement than one might see on television and there's almost no border between ad and content. Will my eye develop the Benjaminian carapace? I've trained myself not to drift below the frame and to avoid the right-hand side as well, to unsee. (Especially the markings below seem treacherous—a graffiti-filled danger-zone, a cesspool to drop into.) Will these blotted-out areas influence actions in other aspects of my life—a delayed response to cars coming at me from behind or in the right-hand lane? Have young people learned restricted saccadic rhythms? Restricted eye traces compounded with other practices of narrowed, focused, and distracted attention involving new media—speaking on cell phones, text messaging—could be risky. Highway travel becomes perilous to one's health. Is YouTube encouraging drive-by living?

IV

PERSONAL EXPERIENCES—CLOSE READINGS

The YouTube clips that have remained with me are often tied to guilty pleasures. More often than not, the butt of the joke is on humans or animals who refuse to play their proper parts. I'm not sure I'm responding with empathy. Some of its pleasure come from embarrassment and fear. I'm teaching a large Intro to New Media class. A student in the back flashes a cell phone. I'm sure someone on the web has turned me into a squirrel. "I Am That Name" and "Theremin Kitty" are two of my most favorite tapes. I try to get my students excited about them. They don't really. I feel crushed. Since YouTube is partly about personal responses to other clips and communities, let me share a few of my own.

In the spring of 2008 I was new to YouTube. A colleague had directed me to Morning Masume, a manufactured girl group from Japan. I hunted down the group and found a mashup of one of their music videos recut to Earth, Wind and Fire's "September." Tears started welling up. The Japanese girls, dressed in Catholic-school-like uniforms, strutting down the catwalk together as an empowered ensemble, alongside Earth, Wind and Fire's lush '70s soul song, spoke about bliss and lost moments. The music hinted at some time that was right, a moment of ecstasy close by in the past (one season), and the girls with their gestures were unquestionably it, but they were also inaccessible to me because they were preserved in a new context—a mashup. It reminded me of my own not-fully-appreciated youth. This for me was a rare find—precious. Then I noticed that the commentary was off—punky guys aggressively mouthing off about girls as jailbait, worth serving real time for. A day or two later when I went back to watch it, it was gone. Would some reader find it for me?

One of my most intense YouTube experiences: I'm reading a Virginia Heffernan article on YouTube. She's enlisted experimental film and video artists to comment on their favorite clips. I'm reading the prose and following the links. I come across one that takes me to a frame filled with black and white quadrants. There's a woman's voiceover (probably viewing the security footage) hysterically responding to a parent. On the grainy black-and-white video screens, I can see, in long shot, two men throwing into the air what looks like a small, black square, back and forth, and explosive fire going off. Every time there's fire, kids break and bolt under the tables. Actually, partly because of the quadrants, it's kind of elegant. I'm watching it in a half-sleepy, half-heightened fashion. Then I realize it's the Columbine shootings: the actual footage. I try to tell friends about my viewing experience, but no one will go and view the link. I feel marked. A few months later a student in my large lecture course of 150 students rather matter-of-factly posts on Blackboard that she has seen the link, but I'm sure the others don't know what she's writing about. There doesn't seem to be an appropriate way to respond. The student's and my path never cross.

An odd experience: I screened an excerpt from Jack Smith's "Flaming Creatures" to my upper division class and I feel great about it. There's an opportunity and I screen it again for an introductory large lecture-based class with 150 students, and my jaw drops. In the upper-left-hand corner is a man holding his penis and shaking it vigorously back and forth. I suck in my breath. A student calls out "Jesus." I don't have tenure. I teach at a conservative university in a red state and it's the day we're doing student evaluations. Then I realize I'm okay. Students can't determine whether the main protagonist, dressed in a wedding gown, is a boy or a girl; blindsided, they never get much past the center of the frame. Thank goodness for fuzzy, degraded, ultracompressed footage. I never could have seen this on the postage-stamp-sized YouTube viewspace on my computer screen.[54]

I wonder if the live, anonymous, participatory, relatively unregulated nature of YouTube provides its thrill. Perhaps I will see something that, for better or worse, will mark me.

POSSIBLE FUTURES

Jacques Atalli argues that music forecasts coming future trends. Minimalism (like Philip Glass and John Ashley) and hip-hop (from Public Enemy to Kanye West), with their driving propulsive rhythms and rhyming schemes, might have foreshadowed YouTube's embrace of finite moments of now, each tantalizingly suggestive of the observable, each carrying a germ potential to break loose. I'm curious about the history of styles on YouTube. What will happen to the practices of repetition in the future? Will they become faster and more furious? What will people make parodies and collages of?

There's no way to know because YouTube provides no access to YouTube. Their own curatorial materials (clips being watched today, recommended clips) become unsearchable after that day has passed. I have no sense of how quickly YouTube is changing and in what ways. I can report one thing. It happened right before my eyes. The first YouTube clips I saw projected an awkward vulnerability. The "Asian Backstreet Boys" is one of the most intimate and celebratory YouTube clips.[55] In the spring of 2008, people developed a hardened mask—the showman, the huckster, the shyster. By the spring of 2009, prosumer clips had reached a level of professionalism—almost glossy and perfectly tuned to the constraints of YouTube. Where will it go from here? It would be wonderful if scholars could chart a history of YouTube clips—what stylistic trends and ways of putting material together have there been?

I think we're back to where we began. We can't see the edges of YouTube; the site is in a continual state of flux. My description here mainly illuminates own my path. William Rothman asks us to acknowledge that some of our best moments happen at the cinema.[56] I can't say that about YouTube—more I would say that what I've experienced I remember as peaks or intensities. I wonder if others feel it similarly.

CHAPTER 8

Audiovisual Change

VIRAL WEB MEDIA AND THE OBAMA CAMPAIGN

I received a 2009 "Season's Greetings" video clip from Barack Obama. Did you? After I clicked on the link, I saw the Organizing for America staff wave to me, and then Obama smiling warmly, perhaps conspiratorially, as he signed a card with my name. I had the option of forwarding it. (The president would sign a card for any recipient.) While highly partisan clips tend to circulate in "echo chambers" of like-minded web users, less partisan ones can cross the political divide. I might have sent this gentle greeting card to my Republican friends. But before I hit "forward," I noticed something. Like many YouTube clips, this one not only had wit and originality; it was also highly intertextual. That folksy Spanish guitar music took me back to "Yes We Can," but now it was jazzier. Obama's smile and signature reminded me of the moveon.org clip sent by 12 million people in the last forty-eight hours of the 2008 election. In it, McCain, Bush, and a woman with an arthritic hip who stood in line for hours to vote alternately thanked and cursed me for failing to cast the decisive vote, thereby electing McCain president; my name was emblazoned across various surfaces.[1] I voted of course, and it was nice, a year later, to be remembered.

Viral web media constitutes a new form, and scholarship is only beginning to assess its use and impact. Adding to the small but growing research in this area,[2] this essay turns back to the last presidential election, the first time many Americans participated online in the political process, in order to convey the range of materials on the web, to track how they were shared, and to provide analyses of some of the most influential audiovisually based web media clips that circulated, including will.i.am's "Yes We Can," John Legend's "Green Light," the "Obama-Rick Roll-ed" music videos, and the presidential debates posted on YouTube.

Though there are no metrics yet for gauging the influence of audiovisually based web media, we do know that people today view more media content online than on television. During the 2008 election, 88 percent of all voters went online for political information. People watched nearly 1 billion clips of political content.[3] Audiovisually rich political clips were forwarded via Facebook (Obama had 2.5 million subscribers), nested in blogs, marked as "favorites" on YouTube, and both created for and downloaded from the My Barack Obama website (MyBo). It is widely acknowledged that Obama won the election, at least in part, due to his MyBo site and his appeal to youth. According to Scott Thomas, chief designer of the Obama campaign, Obama emphasized that "if we get people more involved in the process then it opens up politics for the people."[4] At MyBo, you could download materials to host a block party, discover how to register and vote in your county, access political positions and talking points, log phone-bank calls, buy T-shirts, watch day-by-day campaign coverage, upload your own video clips for others to view, blog, donate, and track your level of participation. Obama's team included 50 videographers who posted several clips daily. Music-video-like clips folded seamlessly into the MyBo experience, often reaching desired constituencies directly.[5]

This chapter comprises two parts. The first contextualizes music video and other audiovisually rich viral media, discussing their socioeconomic pressures, changed generic borders, ethical valence, political relevance, and aesthetic features. In the second part I analyze a variety of audiovisual clips. In 2008 these clips, often bound together dialogically or through strings of allusions, created a dense mediascape. Reviewing this mediascape critically may help us prepare for upcoming elections. Furthermore, public discussion about an array of subjects like gay marriage, "socialism," the economic downturn, and health care is increasingly being articulated through music-video-like clips. We don't usually know who funds, produces, and distributes these clips, so we can't challenge them directly. The close readings aim to provide analytic tools in support of new-media literacy.

First let me provide some context. As with many of today's more traditional media—newspapers, mainstream popular music, and television—commercial music video's present and future are uncertain. On the one hand, the genre may be recovering from its lowest ebb. Collapsing budgets due to illegal file-sharing and the waning power of record companies, a diminished presence on cable television, and the near extinction of a lush, densely articulated style because it plays poorly on the web all bode ill for the future of the form. Many leading professionals have fled the field; those who remain tend to avoid filming on location, instead opting to shoot in-house with green screen. Poorly paid animators then produce backgrounds through inexpensive software. On the other hand, new digital cameras and inexpensive software make it possible not just for professionals but also for amateurs to produce engaging content, potentially democratizing the practice of producing music videos.

Similarly, music video's generic borders may be expanding. In the eighties and nineties people seemed to know what a music video was: a pop song set with memorable imagery, paid for by a record company to promote the song or musicians, and screened on cable. Now, however, with YouTube's cornucopia of clips, and new digital cinema's musical segments, boundaries have blurred. Commonsense definitions of "music video" no longer hold, but no other term has taken its place. In one YouTube-hosted series, for example, newscasters with their voices processed through Auto-Tune software "sing" their stories accompanied by tracks built in Fruity Loops, an inexpensive music production program. While some elements of these clips suggest a prior understanding of music video, others don't, and the experience leans close to watching news footage with a musical twist.[6] Music videos have always blended genres, incorporated other media, and adopted experimental techniques, but now clear indicators of production, reception, and intent often go missing. Without another term to take its place, I'll describe short clips with lively audiovisual soundtracks and rich audiovisual relations as "music videos," their progeny, or their siblings.

Music Video, African American Experience, and Entrainment

How might we broaden our sense of music video's ethical dimensions? Consider the genre's connection with the persistence of American racism. Twenty-five years ago, MTV programmers were behind the curve when they refused to play videos by African American artists, like Michael Jackson's "Billie Jean." Since then, music videos have advanced despicable images of militarized, criminalized, hypersexualized, overcommodified performers of color, at the same time that remarkable videos by African American performers, directors, and producers have also been important.[7] Without neglecting its racist history, I would argue that music video actually served as a progressive force in the last election cycle, operating—like racism itself—both consciously and unconsciously. Racism remains woven into the American experience: even today, African American college graduates have a much harder time finding jobs than European Americans, even if they've come from our country's most elite schools.[8] Studies show that American adults exhibit physical signs of stress and anxiety upon an encounter with another ethnicity; the results are most marked between whites and blacks.[9] But recent research also suggests that racist responses can be overcome, especially when participants share a common dilemma and goals.[10] Certainly, elections spur the infusion of common dilemmas and goals across the public sphere.

Leading up to the 2008 presidential election, the music and music video industries acted progressively, pulling out all the stops, broadcasting a range of clips that helped us rethink race, class, gender, and political processes. One could see these possibilities in videos by Beyoncé, Kanye West, Alicia Keys, Kid Rock, Linkin Park, Ludacris, and Jack White.[11] Older videos with similar claims reappeared as well.[12] Exhortations from popular music publications to "get out the vote" were equally impressive, and many performers were openly excited before and jubilant after Obama's win.[13] During the campaign, Barack Obama spoke often about his connection to popular music. About hip-hop he said, "I am troubled sometimes by the misogyny and materialism of a lot of rap lyrics. But I think the genius of the art form has shifted the culture and helped to desegregate music."[14]

As Obama indicates, the hypersexualized images in music video suggest that the genre is not inherently progressive. On the other hand, closer attention to audiovisual relations does show that pop songs and music videos are more generous than we might think. Musical performance aims to build a rapport between performers and listeners, and it also serves to solidify communities rather than exclude participants. Psychologists and neuroscientists claim participants experience this process through entrainment: "The alignment . . . of bodily features with some recurrent features in the environment. Music, bodily movement, or any recurrent rhythmic pattern can be something we entrain to."[15] Music videos take viewers through physical states, moods, and emotions in relation to people, objects, spaces, and environments with which they might not readily find themselves engaged. If viewers take up the song's call, they won't distance themselves, and they will come upon relations and modes of being that they wouldn't normally encounter. This intimacy can be carried into daily life. I will argue that five elements of music video create forms of identification we can relate to entertainment (and this process of entrainment helps to explain music video's seductiveness and ideological power). These five elements are: the music; the moving, charismatic body; the body as it unfolds in a complicated, pressured space; the camera's assertiveness; and narrativity and realism.

First, the music: Popular music can show us the contours, the ebb and flow, of our emotions. As Suzanne Langer argued long ago, a song allows us to track the movement of sentiment.[16] A tune isn't feeling per se, but it bears the shape of feeling. We might describe this more simply with a neurological model: when we listen to music, some part of our brain matches the shape of music's arc, or pattern, through the brain's mirror cells. But music doesn't pin itself to actual objects in the world. So when I'm listening to music, I have feelings but their attachments can be vague. Music video can direct these sentiments.[17]

Second, the charismatic body: Watching music video with a moving, charismatic body, I might experience changeable sentiment, kinesthetic expansion and contraction, a dynamic sense of embodiment; I might then project these experiences onto the filmed body.[18] A productive way to visualize how this might work would be to consider George Mather's animated studies, in which a viewer projects figures and comportment onto a filmed series of moving dots.[19] With music video, I throw my understanding of the bound and then unbound muscles throughout my body, as well as the music I hear, onto the filmed body. Through the process of entrainment, a link forms between my body, the performer's body, and the music coursing through both. Bernard Herrmann proposed a simpler model: film music seeks out attributes in the image.[20] In a music video the best candidate for accepting these attributes is the charismatic performer. So I paste the music onto the figure and follow its trajectory. So far so good—this process operates in the musical and with film music as well. Fred Astaire and Ginger Rogers enable this process. The music video camera, with its intense hovering over the body, produces the same effect, only more profoundly.

Third, the body within a complex space: Music video's bodies can exist in changeable, complicated spaces. Closely locked in, tethered to the performer's body, a viewer must navigate through rapid editing, changing speeds, and shifting scales. She can't stray far because if she does and an edit happens, she may jump into empty space; she may lose the video's thread. In music video, the visual imagery and unfolding music link and unlink, instant by instant. To participate, a viewer can't dawdle. All elements in music video become what I call "gridded" or, put another way, rhythmicized.[21] The body is taken up by musical elements like a reiterating pulse within the film's frame. Rudolf Arnheim might argue that the distances between the space and the moving body also become measured—quantized.[22] The unfolding space, the body, and the music all have contours that one is encouraged to try to follow and to keep pace with. The body is moving. The space is moving. The music is moving. One can feel threaded through and along with it. This kinesthetic interpolation, driven by the music, a body's schema, a directed camera as well as unfolding space, remains more profound, insistent, and consistent than the kinesthetic interpolation realized through many other media. If a musical or visual trope comes upon a viewer quickly and the performing body is jerked, the viewer too feels pulled. If the performer's body slows down, one tries to meet it.

Fourth, the camera's assertiveness: In the last five to ten years, music video has become increasingly sophisticated in its cinematic address, mirroring numerous developments in narrative cinema. For example, Warren Buckland describes the ways Steven Spielberg's camera in *Minority Report* (2002) tracks a character, frequently encircling him/her as well as suddenly interposing characters within the field of view so that the viewer has the illusion of being placed within a semicircular or nearly 360-degree unfolding space filled with self-directed agents.[23] This creates intense character identification. Music video has adopted these modes of address as well.

Fifth, narrativity and realism: The musical most often bows out from real-time narrative once the song takes over. Even when the performers break into dance in real spaces, props can become, as Jane Feuer points out, dancing partners; it's now "time out."[24] In music video, both a real world and a heightened, phantasmagoric audiovisual world can exist all at once.[25] If a musician draws a sword from a stone, this performer becomes heroic for being able to handle real-time lived space as well as the heightened audiovisual world. Even the most way-out videos can demand that musicians inhabit their spaces in engaged, intimate modes.

In Beyoncé's music video "If I Were a Boy," the singer performs as both a policeman and his female lover (see figure 8.1). She sings about male privilege ("If I Were a Boy I'd . . .") and, because this is a music video, shifts easily between roles as the song continues. The camera interpellates me in such a way that, at times, I stand alongside Beyoncé as a friend, mirror-image, or witness. As the camera follows Beyoncé down the stairs, my subject-position might be the singer, her boyfriend, or the objective observer. I'm also the third policeman in the squad car. From inside the vehicle Beyoncé performs finely articulated gestures like wrist flicks and head turns that, while not synced with the music, reiterate gestures already seen in the video. As I watch Beyoncé, I'm encouraged to realign the video's present moment of unfolding to earlier experiences and to make connections among them. So I'm constantly threaded through multiple subjectivities as I follow the music. Called upon to participate in this working-class, mixed-race community, I feel I could be a member of the group.[26]

In sum, as we'll see in the next section, music videos work to interpellate us—engaging us physically as well as prodding us intellectually. They create forms of identification with ideas, values, subjectivities, and bodies.

Figure 8.1 "If I Were a Boy" experiences forms of identification tied to the genre.

The Power of Viral Web Media

Will.i.am's "Yes We Can" has been seen as the most influential political video of the 2008 presidential election—it won both an Emmy and a Webby Award and has been viewed over 26 million times.[27] The story behind "Yes We Can" is familiar to many fans. In response to Barack Obama's speech acknowledging a loss in the New Hampshire primary, will.i.am composed the "Yes We Can" song in two days, incorporating large portions of Obama's voice from that speech. After soliciting a few directors, he reached Jesse Dylan, Bob Dylan's son (whose motto is "Remain open to possibility"), who said yes. The video was shot with $10,000 and Dylan's Red Digital Cinema camera. On the first day of shooting, John Legend, Scarlett Johansson, and will.i.am were shot; all the other actors and musicians were shot on the second day. Fashion photographer Herb Ritts's cinematographer Rolf Kestermann, who is admired by Dylan for a "nothing but essentials," classically beautiful look, shot the video. Short of time, performers were taped only for the segments in which they appear but, according to Dylan, will.i.am had a complete scheme for the video in his head. After 10 hours of editing, the video was uploaded to YouTube. It was the first time a political clip went "very viral."[28] (By contrast, the Republican Party's official music video, John Rich's "Raising McCain," had been viewed by only about 200,000 people at the time this book went to press.)[29]

The images in the video derive from two sources—television footage of Obama speaking after the New Hampshire primary, and star performers shot against a plain black background (like Kate Walsh, star of *Grey's Anatomy*, and Nicole Scherzinger, singer from the Pussycat Dolls). Nearly everyone appears in medium close-up and frequently as part of diptychs and triptychs. Text graphics ("Yes We Can" and "Vote") occur sparingly. As part of an aesthetic trend—performance against an amorphous background shot with minimal resources—"Yes We Can" recalls other music videos and television public service announcements like Bono's "One Campaign."[30]

As with many music videos, the incompleteness of the images in relation to their musical context and the video's whole can spark a viewer's interest, thereby encouraging repeat viewing: Why would Scarlett Johansson be the one recording with an old-fashioned microphone? What is suggested when John Legend raises his arms? Who plays which instruments, and why?

The song's arrangement might also pique a listener's interest: the acoustic steel-string guitar stands out as the primary instrument, and both song and video draw on its stylistic and sociocultural associations with folk music and the singer/songwriter ethos. The guitar provides a ground for the wider variety of vocal parts. We hear many kinds of vocal address, both spoken and sung; these possess different cultural and stylistic resonances, including blues, folk, R&B, country, and pop. "Yes We Can" showcases a range of vocal performance: breathy and full; in registers from low to high; plain and ornamented, syllabic and melismatic settings of the words, or ad-libbed vocalizations; overlapping, separate, or in unison. Roughly half of the performers seem to take their cues from Obama's speech, working earnestly to match his speed, while the other half take theirs from the music, suggesting a more relaxed response. will.i.am is able to navigate both modes. The singing voice in the highest register draws our attention; Legend's voice is the first to do so. The phrase "I want change" seems to break free from the rest of the song. These words are not part of Obama's speech, and their first-person singular stands in contrast to the "we" of "Yes We Can." Even here, within the song itself, we might consider one of the questions Obama's speech raises: What is the relation between the individual and the collective?

How might a series of medium close-ups of performers against a neutral background be so affecting when accompanied by a pop song? To answer this I'll provide a close reading of "Yes We Can" through consideration of parameters like lyrics and large-scale form. Such an approach might assist analysis of other media whose power seems elusive (like billboards or commercials).

Large-Scale Form

Patterns begin and end, overlap, and sweep across "Yes We Can," and the video presents a clear shape. Strong emotional hooks are subtly reinforced: for example, a bright streak courses down the frame's center. This light is created through the blonde hair, pale skin, and white clothing of Johansson, and again via actress Amber Valetta holding her son, evoking the figure of Madonna and child.[31] Christian mixed-race imagery foreshadows this ending, suggesting something more interesting or hopeful: John Legend's raised arms and Valetta's Madonna-like pose suggestively allude to the New Testament, and Obama's/Legend's doubled reference to Martin Luther King as "king on the mountaintop" adds additional resonance.

David Bordwell argues that narrative forms tend to present a changed state of characters who move from poor to better fortune or vice versa.[32] The opening shots of "Yes We Can" reveal distressed performers: will.i.am seems to have misplaced something, Johansson looks unhappy, actor Bryan Greenberg scowls, and Obama listens solemnly. But as the video unfolds, the performers become more lively. Obama smiles on the beat; toward the video's close, performers excitedly knee-dip; in the last few shots, will.i.am seems to find what he was looking for—the words "hope" and "vote"—and Johansson smiles beamingly. Laura Mulvey claims films commonly begin with a state of disruption and close with intimations of death and rebirth.[33] Death is evoked toward the end of the video by a shot of Canadian singer-songwriter Esthero, who has a skeleton's head tattooed on her forearm and who has brought her fist down to point toward the camera; the Madonna-like Valetta (pregnant and disposed like a Raphael painting), by contrast, points to the coming of a new life (see figure 8.2).

Other finely hewn devices contribute to the video's shape. "Yes We Can" emerges out of three short and one longer syllables, "it-was-the-*creed*," and a declarative statement that precipitates an ongoing process; these both echo the opening of Genesis ("in-the-be-*gin*ning)." Its unfoldings include the triadic images of the mother, child, and father; savior, lord, and spirit; the split-screen triptychs; the three solo instruments; and so on. The in-unison opening expands as one voice drops low and another enters above, suggesting branching, fecundity. Next, the two male voices return to unison and a third male voice falls in line, as if in march formation. As the video progresses, voices continue to aggregate, suggesting coalescing forces.

The video emphasizes "builds," or "swells," in the image, music, and Obama's oratory. We witness figures rising in the frame, turning toward the camera, or filling in the frame, and we hear rising melodic contours and a thickening arrangement while Obama's subdued delivery moves to a more pressured mode of oratory. These swells find moments of audiovisual sync, but they are also self-directed. As such, they convey the video's message: if we contribute, we'll reach the goal.

A rounded A-B-A structure is established elsewhere as well. Moving in from the video's outer edges, Greenberg's severe glare is matched near the close by a happier expression. Kareem Abdul-Jabbar and Common are shot from about the same scale. In the song's opening, the word "creed" is nasally articulated. At the video's close, the nasal timbre returns, brought back through an inner voice we might identify as country.

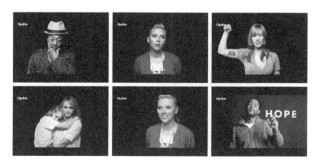

Figure 8.2 "Yes We Can": a shift from uncertainty to greater stability, and allusions to birth, death, and Christian imagery.

The singer's twang connects to Johnathon Schaech's T-shirt, Esthero's pirate's wink, and the scruffiness of a guitar-wielding Fred Goldring (the executive producer of the video). These features recall a historically significant working-class expressiveness.[34]

Placement of the figures within the video's space creates form. During the eighties, hip-hop videos' band members and extras would form a bell or arch, and the center would become the privileged space. In this video, the singers form an arch around the center. Obama takes the center but he also stands aside. (Does this suggest a listening subject?) The video's momentary turn toward the minor mode is paired with a black screen and emptiness.

Incorporating a speech into a song presents unusual compositional demands. In "Yes We Can," the divisions between chorus, verse, and bridge are not as clear as in most pop songs. The moments with clapping, singing, the repeated hook line "Yes we can," and crowd sounds suggest a chorus, while sections with more lyrical variation work like verses. Fragments of verse, chorus, and bridge material appear in nontraditional sections. For example, the chorus's hook line "Yes we can" occurs in the verse, making the boundary between verse and chorus less firm. A music video's form tends to be shaped by song sections. "Yes We Can" breaks into the following:

> Verse One: "Yes We Can" begins with a history lesson: the ratification of the Constitution, slaves and abolitionists blazing a trail toward freedom, immigrants striking out for distant shores, pioneers pushing westward. One might imagine University of Chicago law professor Obama lecturing by way of a historical narrative.
>
> Chorus One: News passes from person to person. A verse fragment appears, "yes we can to opportunity," as part of the chorus.
>
> Verse Two: Adam Rodríguez raises his arm and calls out, "Sí se puede," and the song and video intimate that community organizing begins. We might imagine a march. Masses begin crystallizing, and then a quiet statement is spoken by two people: "Nothing can stand in the way of millions." will.i.am returns as a familiar, grounding figure.[35]
>
> Chorus Two (partial): John Legend and several women start singing more demonstratively ("I want change . . . they will only call out louder"). The calls for change follow refrains of "Yes we can." Bridge: Obama states, "We have been told we cannot do this." He seems to be in conversation with participants. The section suggests a pause. A bit of material from the chorus appears.
>
> Verse Three: Recounting shared obstacles ("The hopes of the little girl . . . are the same as the dreams of the boy") helps participants seek common goals. Out-chorus: Herbie Hancock enters on the piano and performers take up the cause.

Figure 8.3 Costumes in "Yes We Can" suggest an American past.

Shot for broadcast television, Obama's speech features bright lighting and sharp focus. "Yes We Can" encourages us to focus on the candidate by contrasting his footage with the studio performances, which were taped with softer, more diffused lighting and the Red digital video camera that is designed to approach the look of film.

Spanning a sweep of 20th-century dress, the video's clothing and accessories, through associations with class, role, and social station, provide dramatic interest and formal definition (see figure 8.3). will.i.am's shirt suggests a military officer's uniform (it sports epaulets and a small pin). Later, Taryn Manning wears a necklace of stars, against which the lyrics "from sea to shining sea," and the subsequent shot of Legend's arms stretched wide, suggest the U.S. flag sweeping across our country. Herbie Hancock enlarges on these values as he shifts side to side at the piano. Eric Christian Olsen's fleece bears an insignia resembling a Scandinavian flag; we see a vintage T-shirt; a South Asian–style shirt collar; a Kennedy-ish sweater; a porkpie hat; a Great Gatsby–style cap. Women's dress is also carefully assembled: a smock from the Dust Bowl era; an eighties leather jacket (urban or lesbian); an African American woman wearing a headband (a fifties proper school girl); an ethnically undetermined woman in a gospel dress. Two-thirds of the way into the video, fabrics and hair become more lush and sensual—a greater intimacy. There's also quirky play with T-shirt design. Several African American men wear T-shirts printed with the head of Duke Ellington. Near the video's close, suddenly one turns toward us from the center of the frame wearing a similar T-shirt but with Obama's head. Might we equate Obama's musicality with Ellington's?

Cross-Modality, Gesture, and Periodicity

With limited resources, music videos often provoke narrative interest through gesture. The downward gazes of will.i.am and Johansson suggest a tentative start. Contours, both visual and musical, engage us; in the opening, will.i.am's

and Scarlett Johansson's up- and down-turning gazes help draw our attention
to the guitar's most strongly projected pitches' rise and fall.[36] Common leans
his head in and out in one of the first few shots, inviting us into the video. Soon
performers nod emphatically. Nodding works cross-culturally as a means of
entraining participatory subjects; here nodding sutures viewers to the video.
By the video's close, Herbie Hancock's oscillating back and forth, Common's
swaying toward us, and Johansson's and other's knee-dips combine to suggest
a shared excitement. It takes several closing vocal flourishes unrelated to the
song's thematic materials, a process composer Arnold Schoenberg would call
"liquidation," to disperse this enthusiasm.[37]

Within the minimalist palette of "Yes We Can," small gestures carry weight.
Our gazes seek out those of the performers, and the subtle play among blinks,
vocal phrasing, strummed guitar, and editing create intimacy between performers and viewers. Two-thirds of the way into the video, after a long series of
shots without blinks, both a guitarist and a singer perform with their eyes
closed—a period of contrast and respite. Soon this singer will perform with
her eyes partly closed, and then Herbie Hancock will wear partially tinted sunglasses. At the video's close, the performers gaze encouragingly at us again. We
too now see freshly.

"Yes We Can" draws on what George Lakoff describes as "cross-modal meanings."[38] Performers stand sturdily, even those who sway a little. This physical
stance can be translated into a linguistic equivalent: the performers are rooted in
the earth (they are the salt of the earth). Camera movement and performers'
swaying occur most frequently during long vowels and suggest desire. "I *want*
change. The *moon*." On "*Yes we can*," performers stand the most upright, suggesting *this* is the *ground*. In the music, the accompanying guitar first articulates the
root or lowest third of the chord before strumming through the rest of the pitches.
Again, what is communicated is a fundament, a foundation. Music theorist Justin London argues that nested periodicities—slower and faster rhythmic strata
periodically lining up—are one of the most powerful means to entrainment.[39] In
"Yes We Can" we note that (1) Obama and the studio performers sync regularly
on syllables (*creed*, *writ*-ten and *docu*-ments); (2) Obama's longer declarative sentences establish broad emphases, and the core speaking/singing voices underscore these sentences; (3) visual and rhythmic patterns flow in waves on phrases
like "destiny of a nation"; (4) the image oscillates between figures gently swaying
and subtle camera movements that reframe them; (5) the woman singer's presentation of "oh" carries us past refrains of "Yes we can," creating a longer phrase; (6)
together the split-screen triptychs, harmonic rhythm, and editing produce the
illusion of performers progressing from screen left to screen right. This forward
motion suggests we'll arrive at a landmark: "yes we *can*."

Musical Features

In "Yes We Can" (and many other music videos) the placement of performers in the frame, across a series of shots, can suggest visual contours. These contours can correspond to a song's melodic contours.[40] In the first verse, through a series of both visual and aural terraces, we make our way to the phrases' and the frame's high point. (Here Obama's forehead rises out of the frame and he declaims "justice and equality.") In shot 13, the guitar player's strummed chords are *wrong* (he plays G major to C major when the audio track presents E minor to B minor); but the out-of-sync chords as played carry us visually upward toward this rising close of the verse. The figures in the second chorus that remain high in the frame suggest we've crossed a distance; we've crested one plateau. From the bridge through to the out-chorus, the image showcases a long, gentle sweep up, and then down, and then up again, helping us experience the video's close as one composed of wavelike contours.

While Common's gentle opening nudges lead us into the video, his splayed fingers also lead us out. Common here helps count out a three-against what was before an emphatic four-note pulse. His gestures suggest that if we can count three against four, we will be able to find another time, a new way of coordinating with one another, a rhythm different from how we have lived in America. Becoming educated musically, learning complex syncopated rhythms against a straight 4/4, is thus linked to learning the language of social justice. The American public's growing familiarity with African American rhythms coincides with social change. For example, late forties and fifties rhythm and blues (R&B) helped shift rhythmic emphasis from beats one and three to beats two and four; this emphasis started to become second nature for many younger white listeners at the same time that the civil rights movement was beginning to gather steam. Listen closely. The clapping suggests a 6/8 pattern, while the chanting of "Yes we can" is 4/4. Compared to where we began, we have become virtuoso musicians.

The video showcases many types of vocal address—speaking and singing, numbers and groups of voices, and types of performative vocal practices, from call and response to choruses, as well as a range of singing styles. Languages include Spanish and Hebrew, and there's speaking that's first taken up by the singing voice and then later by an instrument (Obama—John Legend—the violin; Johansson—Nicole Scherzinger of the Pussycat Dolls—the piano). Complementing the voices filling in, the guitar comes in on one speaker and floods across to the other, suggesting expanding participation and space. By the end there have been images of three different European American men playing the guitar, again suggesting amassing forces. Suddenly, at the final out-chorus, projected forward in the mix, the performers' speaking and singing (in the lowest and highest registers) help pull us to the video's close.

The song's basic harmony consists of four root-position chords. Its chord progression (I–V/vi–vi–IV9 [dominant ninth chord]—or G major, B major, E minor, C major9 [dominant ninth chord]) feels like it undulates rather than "progresses," though, because it doesn't present the V or dominant chord (here D major) that would create a strong drive back to the tonic. It's richer than the standard I–IV–V–I for two further reasons: (1) The second chord enlivens the harmony with a secondary dominant (V/vi) that's resolved with the third chord (vi) (a momentary tonicization of E minor). (2) As strummed, the fourth chord (IV9 [dominant ninth chord]), composed of the notes C–E–G–D), first sounds the C (suggesting the subdominant). But when the ninth of the chord (D) rings, this fifth-scale degree "fights" with the other pitches, as if reaching for the dominant harmony the chord progression lacks. Singers reinforce this, often projecting G–D. This "shimmering" C major—G major suggests two worlds or perspectives (perhaps even that we can gracefully coexist in a complex America). A short bridge provides contrast as it shifts between G major and C minor: this oscillation recontextualizes the tonic chord (G major), turning it into the dominant of C minor (see figure 8.4).

The harmony bears a kinship to both historical and contemporary pieces.[41] Listeners' associations with "Guardame las Vacas" (a Spanish medieval folk song); Pachelbel's "Canon in D"; Peter, Paul & Mary's "Puff the Magic Dragon"; and the Beatles' "Let It Be" may lend the music a sense of historical depth. When heard repeatedly it becomes clear that the harmony for "Yes We Can" and its sibling pieces have a familiar disposition—something humble, hopeful, but perhaps also under the weather. The song's mixture of sentiments may derive from its oscillation between major and minor chords, or its hovering between two tonal centers. For a moment, the song's tonicization of C major suggests a moment of both conciliation and transition. In the video, we see the performers working with and pushing past the harmony; they thus gain a sense of agency.

Varied techniques add nuance to the arrangement's focus on the acoustic guitar, like partially dampening, fully strumming, or arpeggiating chords. Playing the guitar first with fingertips and then fingernails suggests a move from intimacy to something more public. Similarly, moving from the guitar's medium-low register to its lowest, and later emphasizing the high E and B

Figure 8.4 Harmony in "Yes We Can."

strings, suggests a reach upward. The guitar performs forms of address such as a march and then a heartbeat; the entrances of additional instruments like a second guitar, a violin, and a piano extend the song's pattern.

As noted earlier, music, speech, and image "build" or "swell." The vocal phrases often bridge across the four-bar cycling harmony. This creates a propulsiveness that, along with added voices, more strongly rhythmic performances, and a rising melodic contour, might suggest gathering forces. The presentation of the title phrase is driven home through repetition. But it is equally important that the frequency of the repetitions increases dramatically: "Yes we can" appears once at the end of the first phrase, twice at the end of the second phrase, and many times in the chorus's beginning. In the image, three swells appear before the first chorus's close. First, figures gradually turn and face the camera; next, gestures become more heightened; and third, additional figures fill the frame. The music, text, and image reach a simultaneous peak at the chorus's end when the red-headed singer Esthero sings "oh." This conjunction, now, a long distance from the opening, suggests that the struggle is half won.

In "Yes We Can" words, sounds, and gestures concretize the song's message. Examples of clear, one-to-one mappings occur when John Legend starts singing on the word "sung"; when voices of the crowd correspond to "call"; when the first appearance of the lyrics "women who reached" is sung by women; and when at "pause" the guitar strums a single chord and then waits, then shifts at "warned" as a heartbeat is tapped out on the guitar. Other mapping moments occur when the violin enters on the word "dissonant" and John Legend in relation to "unlikely" shakes his hand "no"; when women croon as if "crying" for change; when will.i.am fidgets at "told we cannot do this"; and when at "three words" he demonstratively lifts three fingers.

At other times, lyrics are expressed more obliquely. John Legend sings "the moon" in his upper register, with a sweeping legato, as he sways. Obama articulates "justice and equality" crisply and rhythmically, his gestures' definitiveness suggesting the moral values of commitment, equanimity, and insight. And perhaps, when we hear the line "the boy who learns on the streets of LA," we may imagine Common, seen wearing a street jacket and shot from afar, as a former child of the inner city. Letters from the graphics for "change" also appear regularly in pairs, suggesting marching; voices trade entrances as if getting the word out.

One shared thread of materials crosses from voice to gesture to text. A European American female sings "oh" on the end of a third beat. Legend then sings something close to "hope," as if the "oh" has transformed and become crystallized into a palpable object; later he seems to reach up and grab the high-pitched word. Soon Nicole Scherzinger places her hand (gloved for emphasis) on her heart as if to catch and embrace it. In the final shots, Legend and will.i.am again look up as if the words had fallen from the top of the frame, Legend's hand also traces from top to bottom, as if the words came from God above; the red text suggests a second chance to eat of the fruit of the Tree of Knowledge.

Additional gestures are often shared and passed from performer to performer. These gestures work to establish the sense of a relay: in the video's first third, John Legend preaches, listens to Obama, and then spreads his arms as if telegraphing the message. Later, Shoshannah Stern, gesturing in sign language, demonstrates an obstacle (deafness) that can be overcome; and on the words "not as divided," a man gestures as if taking on the obstacles of the woman who signs. A second thread mixed low within the song's arrangement—a softly called "Sí se puede"—foreshadows the soon-to-appear, foregrounded call. Adam Rodríguez raises his arm as he shouts Cesar Chavez's rallying cry—an acknowledgment of the historical inspiration for Obama's catchphrase—and "hope" is sung by several performers. The intervals between performers calling out these words become briefer, suggesting the coming together of forces that hope can make possible. Printed text suggests the same; the rhythmic, accelerated cutting suggests a crescendo. At the end of the video, faces appear on almost every single word of "Yes We Can," suggesting a communal pledge to participate.

Race, Gender, Sexuality, and the Medium

Much of the first verse, on the history of the United States, is performed by men, though in truth, women participated in the nation's expansion: they were homesteaders who braved an "unforgiving wilderness" and immigrants who "struck out from distant shores." They were also slaves and fought hard in the abolitionist movement. Formal interest arises when gendered or ethnic voices are segregated and then combined, but leaving out women's voices from America's first struggles is problematic. Although the video works hard to reflect ethnicity in generous ways, "Yes We Can" could better reflect a wider range of sexual orientation.[42] Further, Kareem Abdul-Jabbar (born 1947) and Herbie Hancock (born 1940) are the only older people. At the piano, Hancock adopts the position of elder statesman.

One might argue that the video primarily appeals to European Americans, but the fact that Obama, will.i.am, and other performers like Common and Herbie Hancock don't identify as white suggests that the appeal is complex. The song's chord progression, type of guitar, rhythm, and strumming suggest singer-songwriters raced as white.[43] We also see a white couple but no other images of family across other ethnicities. Obama appears in the company of mixed-race studio performers once (two women), though the race, gender, and generation mixing suggested by the split screens of Obama's political rally and the performers in a performing studio suggest that spatiotemporal differences are not so large. The image of equipoise between a young European and an African American male, and the word "hope," that call forth the absent Obama, are what we are striving for.[44] As a structural signpost, two males appear again, this time both African American, as witnesses or sentinels who usher in the swelling out-chorus.

In 2008 there was a groundswell of citizen videos, many of which foregrounded lively or musical soundtracks. Might "Yes We Can" have inspired people—of all races, genders, and sexual orientations—to participate? Possessing features both simple and complex, the video offers several points of entry. Its "Yes we can" slogan and clear visuals fit YouTube's schematic aesthetics and low resolution. A listener can also easily follow the strummed guitar, 4/4 rhythm, and regularly changing harmony. On the other hand, the video calls for thought and reflection. The relations among performers are enigmatic and complex. As Obama narrates one history of America, the black-and-white televised images hark back to Martin Luther King's "I Have a Dream" speech. The folk guitar, chanting, and song's harmony also recall earlier struggles around race, sex, and class. The clip's unusual song form, phrasing, and rich tapestry of singing and speaking suggest depth. A viewer might wonder: "Is this the story I know? Where do I belong in this narrative?" As previously described, various performers attempt to convey parts of Obama's speech—some haltingly. Passing of gestures among one another, and presenting them to us, as well as the nodding and "Yes we cans" may nudge us to participate too. A supporter might reply with a clip like "Obama Is Irish" or "Oui, On Peut," a zydeco rendition of "Yes We Can."[45]

The clip's online distribution also encourages participation. In miniature, the video's performers may carry more weight than they would on television—the technological magic that brings them to us feels palpable. We may also experience greater agency with viral media, because a click allows us to seek out the video's performers, who address us directly—one more click or turn away from the monitor would break a fragile bond. As we forward the link to those in our affinity groups, our sense of connection branches outward.[46]

Remakes—Remixes—Mashups—Intertextuality— Obama—McCain—Rickrolled

There were hundreds of remakes of "Yes We Can," from clips showcasing single, fixed shots of hands on the piano keyboard so others might pick up the tune, to young children singing a cappella on school stages, to a global remix

where people around the world sing out the text. Some parodies could be considered offensive: a *MADtv* (Fox, 1995–2009) version substitutes a fictional-
ized Kim Jong-Il for Obama,[47] and there's also a blackface minstrel version.
One version I much admire features a college dance class in Virginia. The camera's tripod is tilted at an angle, the lighting is low, everything is out of focus,
and the bodies and faces are hard to pick out, yet perhaps because this may
only be a rehearsal and the dancers seem focused on responding to one another,
the video projects great intimacy.[48]

Some of the most popular clips participated in the "rickrolled" meme.[49] A
fan took the original video from Rick Astley's 1987 hit "Never Gonna Give You
Up" and overlaid snippets from Obama's filmed speeches. Remarkably, Obama
had spoken every one of Astley's song lyrics at some point, and Obama's words
merged with Astley's singing and the backing tracks of the song, without any
noticeable alterations in Auto-Tune. The remix revealed much about the candidate's musical persona—it seemed to suggest that every which way you sliced
him, Obama still possessed an unwavering commitment that sprung from his
core. As the lyrics suggested, "he was never going to give [us] up, never going
to let [us] down, never going to hurt [us]." A musical Obama paired with Astley's singing communicated other meanings as well: Astley was a white singer
with a deep baritone voice, and his song's arrangement fit well within the African American traditions of R&B. Obama, like Astley himself, straddled black
and white music and performance; like many pop performers, Obama could
work within and speak to a racial plurality.

On YouTube, rickrolling someone is a prank—you send a friend a link on a
topic in which she or he might be interested. Contrary to expectations, when the
receiver clicks on the link, Astley's music video appears—your friend has been
"rickrolled." By mid-campaign, getting rickrolled often meant being sent to the
Obama remix rather than Astley's video. Soon, even McCain got "Obama-rickrolled." In a clip showing him at his own convention, every time he paused at the
podium, behind him the Obama remix of "Never Gonna Let You Down" was projected. While Obama seemingly possessed alacrity, intelligence, and musical grace,
McCain's pauses appeared to reflect slow thinking or a failure to seize the moment.
He and his supporters appeared stiff and dumbfounded (see figure 8.5).[50]

The rickrolled clips exploited a feature of the mashup: an element—either
sound or image—can be taken out of context and stripped bare. Placed alongside foreign material, previously unrevealed meanings come to the fore, but a
knowledge linked to the original fragment still also projects forward, perhaps in
a purer form—as a kernel of truth, an essence preserved even as it has been
recast. In the case of the Obama-rickrolled clip, we discover Obama may have
greater affinities with the affluent 1980s than we might originally have expected,
and that he's amenable to new contexts, including black-white relationships.

Figure 8.5 A viral phenomenon: McCain gets rickrolled (Hugh Atkin, 2008).

His commitment comes forward as well. The McCain clip's own language—a two-dimensional flat-screen presentation of Obama, and a more three-dimensional McCain at the podium—ultimately upstages McCain himself. We now suspect that he and his constituency share both rigidity and fragility. McCain also has something we always noticed, a woodenness, perhaps due to his ideological background, war experiences, or age. In mashups and many audiovisual spoofs that import music or imagery into other contexts, the new meanings that come forward almost always function as overstatements. During this election, Obama was said to project laudable qualities in audiovisual contexts, while Clinton and McCain looked increasingly ridiculous.[51]

"GREEN LIGHT"—JOHN LEGEND FEATURING ANDRE 3000

"Yes We Can" is a key text in the 2008 election campaign, but the most moving video clip for me, and one that resides more firmly inside the music video genre, is "Green Light."[52] Songwriter John Legend calls it "a party song," but I would argue that "Green Light" was much more than that. Though viewers who watched and forwarded the clip may not have consciously identified "Green Light" as political during the election, the video, widely viewed both on the Internet and on television, caught and commented on the zeitgeist. Though purportedly taking place at a party, the video is overdetermined with a wide variety of sonic and visual references to the history of African American artistic practices. As someone who spoke at colleges, gave interviews across the country, made web testimonials, and sang at the Democratic National Convention, Legend can be considered one of Obama's lead surrogates. Although the lyrics "Give me the green light" and "I'm ready to go right now" could be seen as an invitation to socialize, they might also be heard as a call for change.[53] (It has been argued that consciousness-raising songs like the Impressions' "People Get Ready" claimed new rights without directly articulating a political stance.)[54] Helping white viewers feel comfortable within a largely

African American setting may also have been important for Obama's campaign. Studies show whites and blacks do not fraternize a lot, except under particular conditions.[55] The video works hard to make viewers feel part of the event. Bodies turn and gesture toward us, beckoning us to participate. In addition, never before in the music video genre's history have mainstream videos so concertedly used European Americans as ornaments; the obverse is more common.[56] Thomas Elsaesser might claim the video's many moments of cross-racial mimicry attempt to perform rather than represent impossible relations inextricably intertwined with, dependent on, and doubly occupied by the other.[57] These tropes demonstrate how quickly music video picks up thoughts, anxieties, and fantasies swirling in the culture—crystallizing them into images and sounds.

Today's audiovisually based culture tends to coalesce around contested aural and visual signs rather than verbal or printed ones—Edwards's haircut, Palin's dress or moose kill. In 2008 one contested icon was the fist-bump, and "Green Light" helped shift its meaning in a progressive direction. When the Right didn't get its desired mileage from Reverend Wright's "Chickens Have Come to Roost" speech, Fox News insinuated that Michelle and Barack Obama had engaged in a terrorist fist-bump. The Left responded speedily with a chain of aural and visual signs to recuperate our culture's understanding of the fist-bump: it was cool, not aggressive. Here's the string of signifiers as they unfolded: Obama's fist-bump with Michelle Obama at a town hall meeting; Fox News' insinuation of a terrorist jab; Media Matters' mass emailed rapid rejoinder of still images of athletes fist-bumping one another; Jon Stewart and Stephen Colbert's dress-up parody (Colbert playing Michelle Obama); the New Yorker cartoon cover (fist-bump integrated among other signs the Right has used to promote racism); John Legend's viral music video "Green Light" (with partiers fist-bumping); the Miller Lite Super Bowl commercial, with beer drinkers and businessmen confusedly fist-bumping and slapping one another; a "Bump" application for iPhone; and a year later The Root calling for a national fist-bump day.[58] "Green Light" helped define what a fist-bump could mean.

Sprinkled throughout "Green Light" is iconography associated with race. There are practices associated with black culture, like fist-bumping and the passing around of Roscoe's waffles and fried chicken. The video also includes Afrocentric imagery such as a Kara Walker–like painting of antebellum silhouettes, and an image of Stevie Wonder which hangs on the wall.[59] Perhaps signaling a connection between the space's foreground and its background, at one moment in the video a dancer in a red dress mimes the Walker imagery (her gestures and outfit might be read as tribalized). As the video builds momentum, the imagery seems to shift: a bulldog; Andre 3000's reference to "piglet"; the dancer wearing a red dress; the Busby Berkeley–styled white dancers used as ornamentation for the partygoers (see figure 8.6). The video also complicates race relations in an optimistic manner by becoming more racially inclusive as it unfolds.

The music's impact delivers from many sources. The drum machines suggest physical attributes, thereby eliciting a call to the body. Accents on beats two and four sound like handclaps, and an unsteady pulse in the lower register suggests a heartbeat.[60] The song also draws on culturally understood tropes, both historical and current. The vocals that run up and down (suggesting transcendent "oooohs") recall the more expansive moments in 1970s groups like Earth, Wind & Fire.[61] The synthesizer glissandi also recall seventies disco, and the harpsichord suggests class. The harpsichord becomes funkier as the song progresses, which brings it more into the orbit of the clavinet (an electric clavichord popularized in the seventies by Stevie Wonder and others). "Green Light" crosses racially identified contemporary popular genres. The tempo is unusually fast for R&B (about 156 beats per minute); this and the basic beat pattern connect the song with two-step garage, an electronic dance music genre popular mostly in U.K. clubs (which would have a different sort of crowd and be a very different setting from where this video takes place). The fast tempo also forces a kind of precision out of the vocalists, especially Andre 3000. The two high notes in falsetto (at the ends of consecutive phrases) form a long line that moves very slowly and deliberately; lyrical and sweeping, this line contrasts with the fast tempo—implying a different experience of time. The downbeat in popular music can be understood as wielding authority over the rest of the measure. John Legend strongly articulates the first beat of the 4/4 meter when he says, "I'm *ready* to go right now," while pointing emphatically, but he also steps back, sliding from beat two to beat four. (One thinks here about "Yes We Can," which also plays with Barack Obama shown on beat one and then stepping aside, thereby performing the role of a listening subject.)

Figure 8.6 "Green Light": do music, performer, or director provoke the move to a new spatiotemporal world?

"Green Light"'s closing images of the party's day-after show revelers strewn on couches, floors, and inflated lounge chairs in the pool, upside down like inverted crosses, here the opposite of the right-side-up crosses in "Yes We Can"—a healthy high made low. The really wiped-out partiers are the European Americans. Does that mean that they, not the African Americans, don't know how to maintain control? Or is it simply that what went on was so wild they passed out?[62] In any case, in "Green Light," as in so many music videos, effects and causes become mysterious, multiply attributable, and then music steps into the breach as a force of dynamism—both music and the music video take on greater authority.[63]

JOHN LEGEND AND WILL.I.AM PERFORM "YES WE CAN" AT THE DEMOCRATIC NATIONAL CONVENTION

The Obama campaign had a close, long-standing relationship with music video. Speaking to one largely African American crowd in Raleigh, North Carolina, at the height of the Jeremiah Wright controversy, Obama brushed his right shoulder with his right hand, and the crowds cheered, recognizing the allusion to a 2003 Jay-Z song entitled "Dirt Off Your Shoulder."[64] Similarly, the opening of the Democratic National Convention reenacted the will.i.am "Yes We Can" video.[65] The iconography here is worth unpacking: a trumpet line rings out as an allusion to mariachi. The video's setup is restaged for the convention to include a European American woman who signs and a European American man who plays the guitar. Then John Legend and will.i.am step out. Legend wears a fieldworker's kerchief around his neck (an echo of Rodríguez calling out "Sí, se puede" in "Yes We Can") and the same bourgeois suit that he wore in "Green Light." Legend and will.i.am stand in tennis shoes (a visual representation of the original video's focus on "grounding"). Behind them sings an "international choir," which recalls "Yes We Can"'s ethnic inclusiveness. A monumental screen projects the "Yes We Can" video in the background, once again encouraging us to hear Obama's cadences as musical.[66] Girding the screen are Greek columns. Obama's campaign branding was sophisticated. The "O" logo with its rising sun and fields (a new day) and America's red, white, and blue serve as ground for four subthemes: (1) "The campaign brand" (MyBo's homepage with the familiar Obama-blue gradient, Web 2.0, wet-floor look); (2) "Instant vintage" (a retro feel like the campaign's famous Shepard Fairey poster); (3) "Presidential" (an emblem evocative of the official presidential seal); and (4) "Supporters" (the friendly, fat, sans-serif typeface that adorned buttons and signs). The convention's iconography presented all of these subthemes while "Yes We Can" underscored themes two, three, and four.

TARGETED DEMOGRAPHICS AND POPULIST
CLIPS ON YOUTUBE

It is difficult to characterize all audiovisually based viral web media of the campaign. YouTube's archives are vast and without curatorial supervision. During the campaign, it was often hard to tell whether clips had been produced by political parties, the music industry, or prosumers.[67] Speaking off the record, Democratic National Committee (DNC) staff told me that clips targeted at individual communities were perceived as effective. One example was "Barack O'bollywood," a Bollywood remix blending Bollywood and psychedelia, highlighting a new mercurial aesthetic that foregrounds reiteration. (The words "acha acha acha acha" ring over and over, and the cartoonish imagery is prismatically replicated like a kaleidoscope, with one quiet moment when Obama resembles a still drawn from a Satyajit Ray film.) A DNC-produced mariachi clip was a blunder: the music did not belong to the targeted community but rather one from another region; viewers noticed the difference. "American Prayer," featuring Joan Baez and Dave Stewart alongside Martin Luther King, aimed to engage an older demographic. The clip is suffused with an anxiety that Obama might be assassinated.[68] Of the hundreds of clips produced by fans, "Barack Obama is IRISH!" and "Obama Obama" were especially effective, particularly the latter, with its catchy Obama chant sounding more like an Australian didgeridoo than an homage to a West African tune. (This clip took off with dj and dance-music communities.)[69]

Populist anti-McCain clips were playfully aggressive about McCain's possible cognitive deficits.[70] "John He Is," a remake of "Yes We Can," showed someone hyperventilating into a paper bag while McCain sang "bomb bomb bomb Iran" in a Beach Boys style. *Saturday Night Live*, and other late-night comedy/news shows ran much content that then circulated on YouTube. Stephen Colbert hosted a "Make McCain Interesting" campaign in which prosumers could insert their own footage behind McCain speaking about rising health-care costs. One contestant recast McCain as a character within Madonna's music video "Vogue," speaking as if on autopilot, completely unaware of the gay men doing pirouettes around him (see figure 8.7). Another subbed him in as a rubbery, faltering character on *Star Trek*, one whom Bones can't assist and only the Gorn alien chooses to vote for.[71] Another mashup worthy of mention, "Getting to Know You," shows McCain repeatedly eyeing Palin's calves furtively while anxiously turning his wedding ring, accompanied by a Marni Nixon song from *The King and I*.[72] Besides reiteration, parody and sarcasm are part of YouTube's aesthetics. A remake or a reworking is easy to do, and there are few limits on irreverent, contentious, or bellicose behavior. Yet not everything readily lends itself to parody. Most anti-Obama clips featured a stand-in or a still frame of Obama—as a moving image he proved too charismatic (see figure 8.7).[73]

Obama—young, hip, mixed-race—seemed to be able to assimilate any musical style, whether salsa, Bollywood, rap, folk, or heavy metal. Almost nothing stuck for Clinton or McCain. (Both chose audiovisual clips that looked vapid, milquetoast, or hostile.)[74] Voters might have almost felt that McCain's and Clinton's more limited connections to American popular culture made them less qualified to represent today's American public.

THE THIRD PRESIDENTIAL DEBATE ON YOUTUBE

The third presidential debate, as presented on YouTube, contains features similar to music video.[75] The clips are chopped into bite-sized segments. The viewed window is split and small, creating a gridded space and also, because it's split screen, a temporal ambiguity.[76] How far are candidates Obama and McCain from something one knows from real time? What kinds of time gaps and distances might exist between them? A viewer who had participated with the web might see the candidates through the prism of audiovisual material encountered before. Perhaps they resemble not individual candidates, but one fantastical hybrid animal sewn down the center like Dr. Doolittle's two-headed llamas.[77] The thin revolving line set between them, and the rolling scroll below, ripple and move, forming rhythmic patterns. While Obama's lyrical flow may feel more palpable because of the flag's stars' undulating riverlike flow beneath him, McCain gets the short, jabby gestures of the brittle, popping-in-and-then-disappearing CBS logo. In this kind of musicalized space, a viewer might respond more quickly to Obama's mellifluousness. His voice and gestures telegraph intelligence and thought. McCain holds the fastest tempi with his nervous, four-times-the-average eyeblinks.[78]

Figure 8.7 McCain Vogues—Director Wayne Simbro responds to Colbert's "Make McCain Interesting" challenge.

It also becomes clear that Obama's gestures and body provide a home, a person one can "entrain to," as opposed to the inhospitable McCain. David McNeill's work on hand gestures and body movement shows the ways they reflect thinking. (For example, hand gestures come before sentences and convey aspects of thought in embodied form.)[79] Even watched silently, Obama's clarity and depth of knowledge come forward. McCain's fearfulness and defensiveness are palpable.

THE FUTURE OF CAMPAIGN-ORIENTED VIRAL MUSIC VIDEO

Studies show that Americans are shifting away from being a text-based culture.[80] In a globally audiovisual communication culture, as Virginia Heffernan has said, "the only authentic response to a YouTube video is another YouTube video."[81] Perhaps the decline of literacy and the rise of an audiovisual culture need not frighten us—a few Yahoo homepage headlines, trips to Snopes.com (a myth-debunking site), *SNL* skits, Facebook links, and music videos may tell us a great deal. A call may arise for a democratic, audiovisually based culture in which citizens have skills for reading sounds and images—like the ability to grasp the aims of producers and the cultural histories of a video's sources and a way to engage in *participatory* audiovisual politics.[82] This could form the "next chapter of the great American story."[83]

Yet old stories about what being "American" means also persist, as we were reminded when S. Joseph Wurzelbacher, or "Joe the Plumber," a Republican surrogate deployed to argue that the Democrats would unfairly tax small businesses, quipped that Obama was almost as good as Sammy Davis Jr.[84] Here he may be asking us to recall the grace Davis projected, but I think he rather intended the comment disparagingly, as a throwback to old patterns in American race relations. I'd like to think that a more friendly reference by Tina Fey, in one of her *Saturday Night Live* skits, with Sarah Palin as guest, may have carried more force. Performing as Palin, she claimed during a mock press conference, "What can I do? McCain sounds like a garbage truck, while Obama has the voice of angels."[85] Music video may have helped us to hear it that way.

POSTSCRIPT

Presidential election 2012 was not the same. There didn't seem to be as much interesting or exciting viral video. A few clips have really stayed with me. Rosie Perez pondered what it might be like for Mitt Romney to have a vagina; Romney met surreptitiously with wealthy donors and disavowed the 47 percent;

and he sang "America the Beautiful" over abandoned American factories and offshore tax havens in the Cayman islands. But the campaigns seemed to get especially nasty with a utilitarian "whatever it takes to win." I lived in California, a state already slated to one party, so no one bothered much to campaign where I was. The Obama campaign got gritty, micro-targeting potential voters through data mining. Email would be sent to you based on perceived affiliation (if I went to a church, I'd get a more "spiritual" email message). The Democrats decided that foot soldiers and door-to-door campaigning were most effective. Much activity moved over to Twitter. I and many experienced amusement over Anne Romney's comment of "You people" and "Eastwooding." But for many of my friends and me, 2012 was not as joyous as 2008. In 2008, regardless of your party affiliation, so many participants wanted their voices heard. I hope for an efflorescence of participation again.

CHAPTER 9

Reconfiguring Music Video

BEYONCÉ'S "VIDEO PHONE"

Today not much is left of the music video industry. Profits have fallen, budgets have been slashed, and fewer videos are being made. Videos today can look like they're aping devices of the 80s, as if what we saw then wasn't reflective of musical styles or a zeitgeist but rather economics.[1] While it has always been difficult to make a living directing music video, now even the top directors tend to say, "I'm going on vacation—I'm going to direct a music video" because they don't get paid for what they do.[2]

I'm hopeful, however. Artists and technicians within other genres and media are laboring under similar constraints. (From 2008 to 2013 the *New York Times* dramatically cut staff and shut down foreign bureaus, but the company still plans for an uptick.)[3] Music video has always been mutable. I think it will survive this transition. Perhaps also, this moment presents an opportunity. If we listen carefully and attend patiently, we'll learn new things about the possibilities of the form.

I've claimed that music video is strange and getting stranger.[4] Perusing the Internet produces unusual experiences: as we come across videos set adrift between election news clips, exhortations about how to keep your mate sexually engaged, and the newest fad diets, or click among streams of text, snapshots, and other YouTube links, music videos can now become the anchor rather than the source of discontinuity. Has the form of music video become the supertext? Music video's elongations and instances of condensation, its alternating thickets and wide-open spaces, map onto the web's larger structures. Do the web's simultaneous windows and jumpy advertising also shape music video aesthetics? On a webpage, music videos compete with lurid pop-up ads and other scrolling devices. So why do the song and image project further than they ever did? The videos themselves still want to claim a liberatory otherness: "I kissed a girl and I liked it."[5]

Does music video's true home now reside elsewhere—in the film trailer, the mashup, the wedding video, the visual arts flash project, the DIY (do it yourself) aesthetic? Does this mean the genre has new means of realizing itself? We might first ask what music video is today. Older definitions don't seem to work. In the 80s and 90s people knew what a music video was—a song set to memorable imagery, paid for by the record company to promote the song or musicians, and screened on cable. Now, however, with YouTube's cornucopia of clips, DIY aesthetics, and the new digital cinema's musical segments, the boundaries have been blurred. In "Auto-Tune the News," newscasters with their voices processed through Auto-Tune "sing" their stories accompanied by tracks built in Fruity Loops, an inexpensive music-production program.[6] While some production touches suggest prior understanding of the music video, others don't, as the experience leans close to watching news footage with a musical twist. Music videos have always blended genres, incorporated other media, and adopted experimental techniques, but now indicators of production, reception, and intent go missing. While commonsense definitions of "music video" no longer hold, no other term has taken its place. I'll often describe short clips with lively audiovisual soundtracks and rich audiovisual relations as "music videos" or their siblings.

Given the number and variety of clips on YouTube, it's hard to draw a border between what is and isn't a music video. Clips I would once have considered as belonging primarily to another genre, perhaps because they appeal to different constituencies or foreground different techniques, now seem to belong firmly within the music video canon. Two examples: "The Gummy Bear Song" and "The Duck Song" most resemble children's cartoons.[7] Yet many music videos today use just as inexpensive and schematic animation, because it's easy to do and projects well on the web (Kanye West's music video "Heartless" with its simple, block-like forms, achieved via the rotoscoping animation technique, seems to reference these). "The Duck Song," a somewhat sophisticated tune with more than a wink at *Sesame Street*, is performed by an adult singer-songwriter on the guitar. Who am I to say this is a children's cartoon? My students listen to "The Duck Song" as much as anything else, and singer-songwriter Bryant Oden also sells his tune on the Internet.[8] The clip "Haha Baby" can be experienced as a music video—the father's and child's laugh becomes a singable melody.[9] The husky dog "Mishka" also has her own song when she sings to her owners "I love you." (It sounds like "I wuv ooh.") Short-form clips with striking musical accompaniment, like "Kung Fu Baby" and "Dramatic Chipmunk," strike me as music videos, even more so than "The Duck Song."[10] "Evolution of Dance" and "Charlie Bit My Finger"[11] at first glance seem outside of the genre, but once they've been remixed through Fruity Loops, they begin to work like music videos.[12]

In this chapter, I won't be able to define all the generic features of today's music video, but I'll make a first foray in that direction, arguing that many audiovisually oriented clips on YouTube now reflect an aesthetic different from those of earlier genres on television or cable. We can begin to understand today's music video if we consider some of the aesthetic features that define YouTube: (1) pulse, reiteration, and other forms of musicality; (2) irreality and weightlessness (tied to low-resolution and the digital); (3) scale and graphic values; (4) unusual causal relations; (5) variability and intertextuality; (6) humor and parody; (7) volubility and condensation; and (8); formal replication of the web. I'll apply these YouTube-oriented features to a music video most viewers would identify as traditionally belonging to the genre (here, a performance set against a prerecorded song, released by a major record company, and designed to draw attention to the song and sell it). My case study will be the recent video by Hype Williams for Beyoncé and Lady Gaga's song "Video Phone," shot in October 2009.

But before I consider "Video Phone," let me take a moment to ask how we might think about YouTube.[13] Music video is making a strong global comeback because of the new platform. The number of clips on the site stretches to the sublime—YouTube streams 1.2 billion videos a day, enough for every person on the planet with Internet to watch a clip each day.[14] As the site's number-one streamed content, music video consumption is dramatically up. It's the perfect form to quickly set the pulse of our daily lives, as well as to grab a moment's respite while websurfing or engaging in repetitive work. Music video clips on YouTube might help us gain the pulse of today's world: perhaps in our heteroglot but connected environment, these clips will help global citizens discover a shared rhythm. The eruptions of enthusiasm for Psy's "Gangnam Style," Carly Rae Jepsen's "Call Me Maybe," and "The Harlem Shake" suggest so.[15] YouTube and music video raise many questions, more than this chapter can address. There are new modes of attention, forms of cross-cultural exchange and ideological content; there have been shifts among industry personnel, amateur media-makers, and audiences; and many have had to deal with shrinking budgets, bandwidth, and screen-size.[16]

Several scholars have offered ways to consider YouTube, but an overarching description of the platform is still lacking. Alex Juhasz claims that YouTube fails to build communities. For her, YouTube is a space of commercialism and further reification of mainstream media.[17] Michael Wetsch and Henry Jenkins, on the other hand, celebrate the ways the site makes possible new identities, sexualities, and modes of interaction. They claim YouTube fosters community and acts as an agent for self-expression.[18] Julie Russo documents remix culture, especially in gendered and gay communities,[19] while David Gurney has written about YouTube humor.[20] I seek to locate aesthetic and formal principles present in many YouTube clips that have also infiltrated music video.

In these next sections I'll first consider an individual feature of YouTube (like reiteration and pulse) and provide some examples. Then I'll consider this feature in light of Beyoncé and Lady Gaga's "Video Phone." (Any YouTube or music video clip may embody a number of these features, though not all.)[21] Recent music videos and YouTube clips today feel like open territory; often these features can appear distorted and strange. As we'll see, this is strikingly so for Hype Williams's video for "Video Phone" by Beyoncé and Lady Gaga.

1) Reiteration and Pulse

YouTube's most prominent aesthetic seems to be insistent reiteration.[22] Forms include 1+1+1+1 or AAAAAAAAAAAAAAAAAAB. There are the goofy or overly anthropomorphized animals who repetitively circle around or chew their food like "Gizmo Flushes" or "The Sneezing Baby Panda." Suddenly at the clip's close the animal might perform an action that departs from its previous activities through a slight, but surprising turn.[23] All of the vlogs and homemade family documentaries of events seem to lead to more repetitive compilation clips: falls out of chairs, the prettiest smile. Mashups seem to compress the phenomenon even more, splicing together clip after clip until it takes on a pulse.[24] Straight-ahead music videos have taken on an insistent pulse, too, like "El Sonidito" or "Sunday Afternoon."[25]

We might consider any parameter in light of repetition, including movement within the frame, color, editing, and so on. You Tube lyrics might be one of the most insistent features. "The New Llama Song!!!!!," for example, has an attenuated vocabulary and a very strong earworm. A lot of text is rapidly delivered and hard to make out, though it's accompanied by subtitles; then an emphatic "llama, llama, duck" returns. In "Two Talking Cats: Two in One," garrulous kitties simply meow back and forth to one another. Even in "Derrida Bears" (also known as "Reading and Time: a dialectic between academic expectation and academic frustration") the bright language of academe becomes stripped down to the simple message of "You must do it!" and "I refuse to." The four-letter words become more and more frequent, finally becoming the only viable option.[26]

Much of YouTube's content—talk shows and cooking shows—looks like what once appeared on television. But something feels different, perhaps related to the image-quality, scale, duration, or YouTube's conversation with other media on the site. I feel more strongly a sense of articulation and pulse with YouTube clips than I do with television. A voice intoning "Today I'm going to talk about . . ." or "Now I'm going to move the cursor . . ." on YouTube remind me of the days before and after this assertion, as well as of the gestures that preceded and might follow. Perhaps a different species, but exhibiting a similar phenomenon, the YouTube clips with people talking quickly and rapid editing calls attention to the punctuation of the cut and the initial onsets of the voice.

The quintessential YouTube clips, the user-created engagements with babies and animals, most often last less than 50 seconds. In these the subject participates in some self-contained activity that rises and falls. Then, as we draw to a close, "wham!": something unexpected occurs as an explosive event (the panda sneezes, the raccoon steals the rug). The new turn calls into question the rhythms of everything that has appeared before.

Reiteration is predominant in today's media for many reasons including aesthetics, production practices, prosumers' level of training, contemporary technology, and sociocultural contexts. Perhaps most influential are the pace and demands of business and leisure time, which have been accelerating. Today's rhythms of work and leisure could be considered as comprised of overlapping patterns: the emails, the cell-phone texts, the tweets, the person speaking next to us, the canned music streaming through an ear as we wait in a phone queue. YouTube clips provide rhythms we can activate and control. Sometimes they may go faster or slower than those swirling around us, but within the multiple streams that we participate in, we have the possibility to dip in and out of them. YouTube clips can move at an extremely fast pace. Once we've experienced such a compressed sense of time we may feel recharged and ready to enter what we perceive as a more slowly moving real world.

Competition among media also encourages obsessive repetition. YouTube's response to the hyperintensified CGI-laden blockbuster-seeking new digital cinema and to video games may be to insist even more strenuously on its importance. The nagging quality may not only pull viewers away from other YouTube clips and more distant websites but also away from all external screens.[27] Reiteration has an aesthetic function as well. Beyond the YouTube clip's borders, and bracketed within the monitor's frame, marks and objects of odd sizes and colors litter the visual field. A regular, aggressive pulse suggested by a YouTube clip helps normalize and organize this disorderly activity.

Reiteration has also to do with consumption compulsion. When the mega popular YouTube "Shoes"'s lead singer, dressed in drag, sings "Shoes" in the most affectless style possible, over and over, s/he suggests that repetition is tied to the impulse to buy, buy, consume, consume, start over.[28] Yet as Gilles Deleuze would argue, with the Darwinian turn can come a slight difference.[29]

The production practices of YouTube—including the DIY aesthetic—exert a strong influence. Fans with no training want to make something. With favorite materials, today's makers jump in with their editing software and get going. Near the two-minute mark, they may realize that they've locked themselves into a pattern without much form, but they're stuck—AAAAAA, or ABABABABAB. Professional makers with more training may pick up on this style, because it seems like the next big thing. Such processes spread like a contagion, transforming culture on a global scale.

As I've suggested, the most-viewed content on YouTube—professional music videos—are riven with repetition. They do this in part by foregrounding songs, which create repetition through rhythm, chord progressions, repeating sections, and recurring melodic, timbral, and other hook-like material.[30] Other YouTube clips may organize themselves around this content. Almost all amateur viral videos seem stuck in a loop too. Orange in "The Annoying Orange" says, "I want hey hey. I'm orange. I'm apple. Hey orange. Hey apple. Hey Hey orange." "Nyan Cat [original]" foregrounds a two-bar ditty that repeats with slight variation, and a low-res dot-matrix drawing of a cat that continually speeds through the frame's center. While the feline's body remains inert, except for a single periodic hitch, its feet cycle around and around, generating a rainbow trail against a grayish-blue background and a few points signifying snowflakes. "Gangnam Style," rated as YouTube's most viewed clip, and a professionally produced music video, has a "wahp, wahp, wahp" that threatens to become stuck in permanent repeat. The many amateur versions of "The Harlem Shake" foreground an "earworm" sonic fragment too, seemingly taking a cue from "Gangnam Style." After counting a repetitive "Hey," "Hey," "Hey, hey, hey, hey," "The Harlem Shake" switches into a looser and freer section, as if it has been restructured like a devolution. But if we attend carefully we'll notice that this second, post-transformation section is looped too, and the loop only stops once the audio track runs down.[31]

THE CASE STUDY—BEYONCÉ AND LADY GAGA'S "VIDEO PHONE"

Pop music has always employed techniques of reiteration. But something is different now. Many bloggers and journalists have noted that Beyoncé's most recent songs contain earworms—"Single Ladies (Put a Ring on It)" seems to get lodged in people's brains and won't let go.[32] The words "Video Phone" can sound like an excerpt to a lyric from "Single Ladies." Perhaps simple phrases like "put a ring on it" and "call me on the phone" repeated over and over, embedded in an over-dubbed chorus of real and synthesized voices, help drive the sound into the brain (the sounds both ring and reverberate and suggest calls for action). In these videos, Beyoncé's hips circling around and around alongside the musical hook reinforces the pattern. Other sources of repetition: Lady Gaga's songs are highly identifiable, and form a sound world of their own; since we return to Gaga's performance throughout the song, her professional, highly polished approach, as it returns, may reinforce a sense of repetition. The "Video Phone" song proper also contains much repetition. (In the upper registers, a synthesizer patch spends most of its time cycling among a few pitches, for example.)

Many elements in "Video Phone"'s imagery feature reiteration. The opening, strobing overlays as a *Reservoir Dogs*-like bevy of men and Beyoncé strut past lonely warehouses (see figure 9.1a), suggest instability. Once the video starts proper, the first series of Beyoncé's multiplying are formed through two types of visual imagery: (1) echoed grayed-out heads filling out the left- and right-hand sides of the frame (as if they were scroll bars for videogames), with these gray heads beginning to multiply; and (2) Beyoncé's dancing in the center of the frame with echoed, streaming images trailing after her. Together these suggest an infinite regress. Cameramen with their camera heads also begin to reproduce (see figures 9.1b and 9.1c). Beyoncé and Gaga, as women lined up in chairs, become exchangeable, rotatable. Visually this video suggests 80s music video aesthetics, with its constant deployment of different dresses, setups, and color backgrounds. (The videos for Whitney Houston's "I Wanna Dance with Somebody," directed in 1985 by Brian Grant, and for Neneh Cherry's "Buffalo Stance," directed in 1989 by John Maybury, are touchstones.) But this video seems more adept and concerted in its effects. The setups feel reiterative. Though there is some cross-bleeding, the basic pattern is one after another in a series, with the series becoming more important than teleological drive. But here the reiteration is able to carry us into new realms. More is at stake: sex for profit, pleasure, acceptance, power, or war.

On YouTube, repetition is often combined with boredom and tedium. Repetition, of course, can also be paired with a kind of jacked-up, unrelenting excitement, like the songs of Katy Perry, but "Video Phone" is a case of the former. The finger snaps are desultory, often lagging behind the beat. The synthesizer patch in the upper register conveys ennui, and the exotic melody in the mid-range sounds like an inexpensive 8-bit Casio sound from the mid 80s—thin and tinny. The drums in the rhythm section seem cheap—sometimes sounding like banging on trash-can lids, and sometimes like tapping on heavy plastic. This arrangement does not suggest money or luxury—there are no live strings, for example. "Watch me on your video phone" sounds like a corporate slogan we're consigned to hear over and over.

Figure 9.1a–c Video Phone's mashup aesthetics: the image points to *Reservoir Dogs* and the soundtrack to Sergio Leone's spaghetti Westerns. "Video Phone"'s sense of repetition is established through digital trails and multiplying cameramen.

2) Digital Swerve—Irreality and Weightlessness

It has often been claimed that analog and digital media have different properties, and that celluloid, videotape, and digital media possess important distinctions. Though celluloid film shares some features with the digital—the single frames (all 1's), the film projector's beam of light as it flashes on and off (0, 1's), and the strip's succession (more 0's and 1's)—it departs through a more immediate connection with the world.[33] For André Bazin film functions as a mask of the world, an analog, a replica; light falling on the randomly placed silver halides leave a mark or trace, something *directly* from the world remains on the film.[34] Film also possesses contradictory pulls that shadow our own biological processes. As Laura Mulvey argues, the motoric projector and the frame's constant passaging resembles our own life drives for power, sex, reproduction.[35] Half of the film is comprised of stillness—a black, a darkness that occurs in the transition from frame to frame, marking it as thanatos, a death drive.

According to David Rodowick, the digital departs from film aesthetics, because it's a transcriptive rather than an analog process.[36] Digital technologies employ a grid that remains constant as pixels switch on and off. The electronic light constantly oscillates, appearing and vanishing, yet never completely rests. I'd claim that digital music, a phantom representation in its own right, in tandem with the digital image creates a monstrously hybrid automaton. As Jonathan Sterne argues, the soundtrack is digital as well but perceptually the soundtrack provides a more continuous function.[37] In *The Day the Earth Stood Still* (2008, Scott Derrickson), the globe and locusts seem gossamer-like. In *Transformers: Revenge of the Fallen* (2009, Michael Bay), metal machine monsters melt into ball bearings or turn into filament-dust. In *Speed Racer* (2008, Andy and Lana Wachowski), cars careening into each other sometimes go right through another as if they were ghosts. At these moments the soundtrack is particularly blustery. The digital images' swerve or momentum calls for a shadow schema, a filling in.

Often YouTube's physics are odd. V-loggers hover near the monitor screen intuiting that if they stray too far away from it, they might drift off. Kitties and baby goats leap and fly. Only the newborns remain grounded. Parkour acrobats take flying leaps from building to building. "Supersonic Freefall" (Felix Baumgartner's drop from 128,000 feet to the earth) was one of YouTube's exciting events, and NASA has a YouTube music video of an astronaut in space. Why is this? This is not your normal television. Is it the low-res quality? The small frame? The short length? The distance between the private view and a global reach to all planetary viewers? A stylistic mode that arose out of competition, or a common language that's infected all clips as they converse with one another? The Gummy Bear YouTube clip might deserve its 322,220,239 hits: the bear's materiality is compellingly uncertain, switching unpredictably from watercolor to CGI.[38]

BEYONCÉ AND LADY GAGA'S "VIDEO PHONE"

A lo-res aesthetic hovers over the video. The grayed-out images of Beyoncé's head against the more luridly colored ones remind us that we might be, or ought to be, watching on a video phone. Flickering images in the video's opening as well as its first verse (here the lyrics state: "cologne in the air") destabilize the video. The materials of "Video Phone"—plastic, lycra, and tiger prints—seem cheap, as do the more working-class, Walmart, mass-marketed colors. These visual touches raise questions about whether we can receive pleasure from mainstream, commercial products. Props and costumes might look tossed together; the blue hooded mask and pink jacket suggest an irreality. Beyoncé's occasional harder chest thrusts, hip bumps, and knee bends seem like an attempt to lock the video down, to stop it from floating free.

Even as "Video Phone" celebrates the ephemeral, transitory, disposable, shiny, and new, it harks back to earlier technologies and eras. At 2:18, we hear the sounds of an antiquated film camera's or projector's ticking chatter of claw and unspooling sprocket holes. The older imagery of Josephine Baker and Bettie Page pull us back to an era of peep shows, and Lady Gaga sings old fashioned phrases like "hubba hubba" and "I'll be your Gene, you'll be my Brando." We hear brass horns from a big band. Can we place the clip's costumes in relation (Josephine Baker, Barbarella, and Bettie Page)? Where should we place ourselves in the media swirl? We don't know.

3) Scale and Graphic Values

YouTube's aesthetic values include bold or strongly projected graphic design and well-judged scale. This may be related to the medium and its mode of delivery— a clip's limited length, its level of resolution, and the forms of attention it encourages. Small environments with low-quality audiovisuals may encourage makers, viewers, and consumers to seek stronger definition. YouTube clips must often garner attention in a competitive environment; many struggle to gain legibility.

What makes a successful YouTube clip? If we can imagine the forms traced as a cartoon and it still speaks, my bet is it has a better shot at success. "The Sneezing Baby Panda," "Haha Baby," and "Evolution of Dance" would all make popular cartoons. YouTube clips tend to feature simplistic and evocative representations of the body and shape—either as face, body part, or body whole. Clearly legible objects trigger rich affective responses, and they help to quickly give the performer a pseudo-context chairs, cups). Contrasting textures—the shiny and the dull; the smooth, brittle, and rough—also help clips come forward. Color schemes differ from television. There might be an array of unified tones, or these clips might also be luridly pastel or monochrome, but whatever the color scheme there is less room for the widely various, free, or ad-hoc. Space contracts. While long-form media take us in and out of corridors, alleys, countrysides, and intimate spaces, YouTube sticks to single frontal views.

YouTube clips have many ways of responding to the small format. In "The Gummy Bear Song" the bear squeezes into the frame, then hops around a lot, all the way from the far distance to the extreme foreground. On the other hand, "Nyan Cat" is just a flat, line-drawn cartoon. The flying aerodynamic kitty gracefully streams across the middle of the frame forever. Neither of these would look quite right on a television screen. Sometimes low-res YouTube clips seem even more valuable for their beat-up look. But the image within the frame is usually a big head, with some ornamental décor toward the back (a hanging T-shirt, a special throw-blanket on the bed). Mishka, the talking dog, looks large and golden, neatly centered on the bed. The five articulated musicians around the guitar in Walk of the Earth's cover of "Somebody That I Used to Know" become one large hyper-beast. Many of the most popular YouTube clips, like "Gangnam Style," present their beginnings and endings with a cartoon drawing, as if to acknowledge YouTube's low bandwidth and small format.[39]

BEYONCÉ AND LADY GAGA'S "VIDEO PHONE"

Since the early 90s, one strand in Hype Williams's oeuvre has been minimalist. He's often worked with simple set-ups such as a few performers before a blank cyclorama. Nevertheless, his earlier videos were different: the men and women came up to and backed away from the lens; figures in the background established a dense interplay with those in the foreground. The Beyoncé video is all frontal—all direct address. The video seems to be a primer on how to do frontality. (You can pan up the body. Place two heads on the side. Shoot a composition with three-quarters of the body. Use a close-up on the eyes. Create a tableau of three figures, and so on.) Details are blunt: chairs, guns, a large bull's-eye. Costuming works emblematically to trigger fast associations—all details perform work (Beyoncé's red pumps have little bows on them—Gaga's yellow pumps don't). Yet subtlety is also important, at least on one register. The shapes of shadows shift from shot to shot—circular, ribbed and curved, boxy, or sweeping down from the top of the frame.

4) Causal Relations

Music video can raise questions of cause and effect, foregrounding relations so ambiguous that the music seems to be the engine mobilizing people, objects, and environments.[40] In "The Sneezing Baby Panda," did we know a panda could sneeze? And so hard that it would blow away both moth[...] mates that dancer in "Evolution of Dance"? Mexican jumpi[...] the little boy in the car's backseat be so punch-drunk, as if a p[...] malevolently slipped him a mickey?

David Rodowick provides a reason for the emphasis on caus[...] Our experiences of screens have changed with the computer's multiple[...] we can activate, click through, resize, move, and hide. In video games, [...] enact spatial transformations of the environment within the frame. The way[...] gestures transform spatial coordinates as we surf through the web, and partic[...] pate in the game experience, might, through contagion, be transferred to You-Tube. Though we cannot truly modify the inner workings of a clip, the top all-time YouTube clips seem intensely bound up with powerful, obscure causal relations that are in play. We have the illusion that we might control these clips at a meta-level.

The scale of YouTube clips contributes to our sense of power. Many clips have small dimensions that create an illusion of our authority over annoying or overly dependent characters (we can snub them out in an instant). Chris Cocker of "Leave Britney Alone," Fred Figglehorn of "Fred Loses His Meds," and Gary Brolsma of "Numa Numa" may be tolerable in miniature, but they'd be unbearable on television.[42] The clips wouldn't have as much charm if they were closer to our size. A second, contradictory impulse: YouTube clips can also seem as perfect as Persian miniatures. Every figure and detail of the landscape can be exquisitely proportioned, and all within the frame can take on a doll-like quality. Perhaps Beyoncé and Lady Gaga's "Video Phone" projects both aesthetics: the miniature's perfection, and the viewer's desire to wield control.

The glitch has become another odd mode of causality. We might call it the meme of today. The glitch has so supersaturated media that definitions have become vague. I'll define "glitch" here simply as a surprise, such that the viewer wonders whether there's a technical error. Usually glitches are short-lived and resolve themselves quickly, but they don't have to. Glitches often appear as a noisy image, or a stutter in the editing, but possibilities are open. The glitch relates to cause and effect because the viewer wonders if he or she or possibly someone should be called upon to do something (where's the technician?). What's engendered this? The glitch is potent, because it's easily replicable and rapidly transmitted. It may mean something to viewers—perhaps the possibility of a time out, or a new way to imagine the world. In "The Harlem Shake," all of a sudden something may have seized the broadcast and flipped it: we have a new scape. Is it the lone performer, dancing more and more actively as he seemingly revs himself up, or the music, as it's building intensity, that blows a fuse? This is pure music-video aesthetics. Music video confuses cause and context. In "The Harlem Shake" did the music cause a sudden transposition of crowds so that

irm? This clip may be one of the best ways
ɔs informs the present. Its sudden switch
music videos and thinking about them.
with causes and effects.

\)EO PHONE"

)ut power: "Can you handle this?" or
er, or is she playing us? Is she on our
\)eyoncé, as experienced on YouTube
...₅ than if she were on cable TV? (Madonna's
__ and "Open Your Heart," both directed by Jean-Baptiste Mon-
dino in 1995 and 1986, respectively, have nothing on this.)[43] Inexplicably sometimes the guns go off and sometimes they don't. We hear sounds that suggest
orgasm, but can't be sure. What are the triggers that push Beyoncé into what
feels like a sexual state? What does she want? Does she need us at all? What if we
could randomly access this music video? Would we have a better experience?

And is Beyoncé more of a top or a bottom? She appears to have power here.
Chewing gum, she's the bored, jaded sex-worker. But we can't quite gauge her
actions—if she wants to, she might walk away. Gaga's relation to Beyoncé is
unclear. Are they colleagues sharing a medley or competitors for fame, money,
or sexual favors? (Gaga may be performing too hard to chew gum.) Perhaps
most uncanny are the soundtrack's voices. We hear women's moans throughout,
but it's not always clear to whom they belong. Are the multiples of Beyoncé
engaged in their own pleasure? Is it Lady Gaga, Beyoncé, or backing-track singers
who moan increasingly as the song progresses? What is the status of the childlike
robo-voice saying, "You wanna video me?"

5) Variability and Intertextuality

On all fronts YouTube is loquacious. Avid YouTube users are familiar with the
endless riffs on popular clips (these often overwhelm the original, making it
near-impossible to locate a sought-after clip). Intertextuality and hybridization occur across platforms, among users, and within clips in almost every
domain. YouTube's promiscuous mingling, for example, functions internally
within a clip, fracturing its contents even more than music video ever did.
Here, while music video often showcased a moment-by-moment shifting aesthetic, YouTube cranks the volubility up a notch. One musical genre on You-
Tube simply multiplies: performance occurs within multiple frames within
the clip, or a figure is multiply duplicated ("Enter Kazoo Man: Metallica Enter

Sandman" and "Michael Jackson Medley" are good examples).[44] I predict we'll see these layering practices proliferating.

We can look to film trailers for variability and intertextuality as well. The film trailer for *The Spirit* (2008, Frank Miller) possesses key features of the new audiovisual aesthetics. Hyper-stylized, it follows a series of affective flashpoints, nimbly crossing media. *The Spirit* projects a type of intermediality so mercurial that our attention flits speedily among media, only touching surfaces, never ground. An animated line comes into focus and the sound before the drawing helps us identify it as a heart monitor's flatline. Something streams with a whoosh across the frame. We follow it as it becomes a figure leaping off a building. The words "Silken Floss" impress themselves on the frame. We might feel as if we were like a stone skipping across the water. The movement across medial surfaces makes it seem as if *we're* the hot potato.

Mashups also form a subset of the new intermediality. In a mashup, the edited shots and sounds of a performer can hang as fragments. Other materials sweep past, but the musical hook or image lingers like a pungent smell. If you needed to pare down and carry forward a distilled, perhaps animal-like presence of your beloved performer, this would be it. Often one medium seems to retain its liveliness—either in the music or the image—while the other materials freeze in mechanical repetitions. The live bit pulls apart from a wash of other material pressing through. Any moment can teeter toward something revelatory or lost.

We might extend the idea of a mashup into new territory: a mashup might be a new combination of things we've already seen. These clips' charm depends on their novelty. In Lindsey Stirling's "Crystalize," a pretty gamine dances while playing her violin to a dubstep arrangement. Well, we might have seen that, but not in the midst of a glacial labyrinth comprised of ice-canyon walls, monoliths, and caves. The clip becomes a sort of wild fusion of an eco-nature documentary, "The Ice Capades," "America's Got Talent," and other things. We've also seen several people working together to play a single instrument, but never as finely coordinated as Walk off the Earth's cover of Gotye's "Somebody That I Used to Know." Remixes and mashups of the most popular YouTube clips, such as skateboarders and kitties, are familiar, but YouTube celebrities sharing screen-time in a professional music video would be novel. "YouTube 2012" is as professionally produced as "Gangnam Style," and it gets kicked off by Psy breaking Walk off the Earth's guitar. "YouTube 2012" has become one of the most popular clips on YouTube.[45]

BEYONCÉ AND LADY GAGA'S "VIDEO PHONE"

Mashups too may have influenced "Video Phone." One of YouTube's most popular mashups, "Tick Toxic," features rapid cutting between Gwen Stefani and Britney Spears, each shot first establishing and then giving ground to the second performer.[46]

The clip's rapid change in mood or tone may have been picked up by "Video Phone," with an alternation between Gaga and Beyoncé. (Gaga is on record stating that she didn't want to be dress-up Gaga. She wanted to be a second B.)

As mentioned, variability and intertextuality occurs across all fronts, sociocul-turally as well as within the clip. "Video Phone" takes place within many forms of conversation. This is the first video Hype Williams made with Beyoncé after the 2009 Grammy Awards, when Kanye West interrupted Taylor Swift's acceptance speech for "Best Female Video of the Year" by shouting that Beyoncé had one of the best videos of all time. Hype Williams may have felt a special pressure to stand by Beyoncé and make the "mother" of all videos, extending the range of people and places she might represent. At the same time as "Video Phone," Lady Gaga's "Paparazzi" and "Bad Romance" were in play. The immensely popular Gaga/Beyoncé "Telephone" soon followed, with a promise to serialize these events.[47] In "Telephone," we might imagine Gaga's serving prison time for all of her "bad" deeds, like sex trading with Beyoncé in "Video Phone"; poisoning her lover in "Paparazzi"; or selling herself and then killing her trick in "Bad Romance." (As Beyoncé in "Telephone" notes, she's "been a bad, bad girl.") Similarly Tyrese may be poisoned in "Telephone" for responding inappropriately to "Video Phone"'s women. "Video Phone" and "Telephone" share many aesthetics including a sonic low eight-bit rate; collaborative or competitive dancing; and a visual and aural stuttering and breaking up of sound and visual imagery. "Video Phone" is just as intertextual as "Telephone."[48]

6) Humor and Parody

Parody permeates the web. DIYers embrace this compositional strategy because it's so easy to implement. You take the commercial or the television skit and you redo it: you can restage it or remix it—easy approaches include intercutting two or more clips and adding or deleting layers. In the anonymity of the web, You-Tube makers are in search of a ground—your sarcastic take immediately places you in relation to a select group of viewers as well as the producers and fans of the original material. Your parody, now tied to original content, piggybacks on an already-accrued attention.[49] Sarcasm also pierces us. Anything that pushes against social norms tends to grab attention.

BEYONCÉ AND LADY GAGA'S "VIDEO PHONE"

Since any clip might be parodied, remixed, or just made to look foolish, many YouTube clips adopt a knowing stance. "Video Phone" works this way. You might attempt a campy remake with college-bound males, but the video has already anticipated that. It's already envisioned all the permutations. Already, there are spoofs and parodies of "Video Phone" on the web. It's something two or more boys or girls can do in their bedrooms. Props are easy to make. Do you have some sheets and several pairs of tights? Everyone's got a water gun or can pick one up at the local five-and-dime. "Telephone"'s funny gowns made of unhemmed swatches of cloth pay homage to this.

7) Volubility and Condensation

YouTube clips that have garnered over a million hits may elicit aggressive wishes and unconscious taboo desires in the deepest Freudian sense. In "Numa Numa," a subtle allusion to Humpty Dumpty is going on. Gary Brolsma's singing karaoke alongside a high, male but feminine-sounding falsetto pushes what's unfolding into a state of delirium. His facial gestures are so quick and malleable he becomes a Disney animation. The clip conjures forth childhood fantasies of play and innocence, along with more adult anxieties concerning control and sexual desire. Brolsma's someone we might have ridiculed as kids, but he's also very attractive in his own way.

YouTube is full of puns, jokes, and returns to childhood. Sanctioned and illicit stories can exist simultaneously. New digital technologies enable media to hover between multiple meanings—threads can be kept active throughout the clip or film, appearing and submerging as their presence becomes more and less important. In Lady Gaga and Jonas Åkerlund's "Paparazzi," Gaga is either a woman who's been wronged, and who fights to make a comeback, or a cold-hearted calculating murderess who deserves to be placed behind bars, but there's no way to tell. In *Life of Pi*, digital environments and fine use of post–production color enable both a spiritual, religious story and a Machiavellian, tooth-and-claw, Darwinian one. For a viewer, this shimmer creates a Wittgenstein duck-rabbit effect.

The YouTube clip "MeTube: August sings Carmen 'Habanera'" touches on so many styles and genres that it could be called a "postmodern retro-digital Germanopunk crypto-geriatric Eurotrash parody."[50] Socially sanctioned and disallowed behavior shimmer in the clip, failing to resolve. In "Habanera" August sings along with an old cassette tape recording of opera singer Maria Callas, while his mother tools around serving milk and cookies. The setting is a run-down British flat, with old peeling, floral wallpaper, a kitchen table, and a piano, and the images look like low-res, old-school television footage. Either August's singing; a robot (which has morphed out of August's tape recorder and now has his head in it); one or two musicians who have suddenly shown up, sat down, and started playing in the background (one wears full leather regalia); a repetitive glitch and sudden color processing; or the music enable surprising turns.

The drab, desaturated grey-beige living room shifts to a more deeply saturated color-scape of a nightclub, with pockets of deep, brilliant red that fail to resolve. Highbrow musical salons and disco infernos (mom dances too) shuttle by, and August dresses up as Carmen and a trovador. At the clip's conclusion we're snagged back to the original abject apartment, but the wonderful dreamscapes or potentially real rehearsal still hover. As is often true for music video, we don't know what's causing what. Perhaps a man's love for Maria Callas has engendered this fantasia, but it just as easily could be the robot's doing, or the background musicians who want to hang out at the house, or the mother, or the technology, or—most likely—the music. It's YouTube, music video, and a TV serial drama. It's high and low. August and Carmen's glitch enables a progressive image, facilitating gay culture in the heart of the family.

BEYONCÉ AND LADY GAGA'S "VIDEO PHONE"

To give a sense of the ways condensation works in "Video Phone," let me provide a more extended analysis of the clip, focusing on the social issues and psychic material called forth. Music video has always worked with condensation and a plurality of meaning, but "Video Phone" seems like a departure from the past, with its reduced materials yet complex signifiers. If we take seriously the video's multitude of visual and aural signs, Hype Williams, Beyoncé, and Lady Gaga seem remarkably expansive, willing to take over vast swaths of global and national discourse. The clip shimmers between meanings. One of two trajectories for "Video Phone" could be read as less progressive, while another one could be more. The music video's allure stems from its ability to hold these multiple perspectives simultaneously.

A first trajectory: In "Video Phone" Beyoncé becomes our new Bettie Page, our all-around American pinup girl for the troops in Afghanistan and Iraq (see figure 9.2a). Does her power and beauty transsubstantiate our guilt over torture? Cameramen shoot her buttocks, and then she threatens men who are hooded and bound (see figure 9.2b). We take the pictures on our cell phone. Yet her roles as B-girl and shy pinup along with the semiotics of her costume—an oversized T-shirt embossed with an alien's head drawn in Third World colors, sporting the word "peace," a jaunty beret, and both male and female gender-symbol earrings—provide a more hopeful second trajectory (see figure 9.2c). The video's color palette—moving through a trajectory from red and black to deep pink, blue and gray, pastel colors of baby pink, blue, and yellow to Third World (possibly Jamaican) colors of orange, green, red, and black, as well as the rising sun emblem of World War II Japan, point to a transnational, Third World, perhaps more politically progressive and inclusive politics.

Figure 9.2a–c "Video Phone"'s complex signification. Does the imagery suggest fashion-driven signposts or a narrative?

A history of popular culture and performance, including African American culture, is also encapsulated. Beyoncé's first dance is a direct homage to Josephine Baker. Beyoncé's movements, long waving braid, and flared miniskirt are a few references (one might be tempted to expand the exotic elements, adding drumbeats and palm trees). Howard Hawks's film *Gentlemen Prefer Blondes* (1953) is also referenced through Beyoncé's and Gaga's costumes of long satin gloves and dress, the performers' carefully choreographed work with chairs, and Beyoncé's readjusting of her breasts and bra. Many odd elements that might seem like loose ends appear too—early-80s album covers by Roxy Music and The Residents; 1980s big-shouldered military-style fashion; the work of Robert Mapplethorpe and Kenneth Anger; femme fatales like Yvonne De Carlo; films like *Reservoir Dogs* (1992), *Barbarella* (1968), and the *007* series; and an homage to women participating in more male working-class pursuits such as welding, motorcycle riding, and driving big cars. Can all of these varied images of pop culture, sexuality, and global power be put into a meaningful relation?

"Video Phone" gains cohesion through its suggestion of an arc of desire culminating in orgasm. Music video directors have become more skilled at suggesting such an arc: Francis Lawrence's video for Lady Gaga, entitled "Bad Romance" (2009), similarly, suggests a wide range of types of pleasures, all within five minutes. "Video Phone"'s closing shots perhaps allude to Luis Buñuel's opening for *Un Chien Andalou* (1929) with its slash through the eye. Both a gun in "Video Phone," and a knife in *Un Chien Andalou*, suggest penetration.

"Video Phone" could be seen as gay identified. Beyoncé and Lady Gaga are divas loved by both the gay community and young women (many in the gay community were very excited that Gaga might have been transgendered; Lady Gaga has later denied this.)[51] Beyoncé's big T-shirt (see figure 9.2c) might comment on Jamaica's homophobia: embossed with an alien wearing both male and female gender-symboled earrings, it might speak in code about present-day international gay rights: for example, from 2009 until 2013, a law has been circulating in Uganda's courts and legislature to put homosexuals in prison. Those convicted of "aggravated" gay activity or having AIDS can be executed. The American right is supporting this.[52]

Some of music video's power stems from the fact that they are open to so many readings both mainstream and resistant. For pornographer Paul Morris, who offers a queer, posthuman interpretation, "Video Phone" is all about Beyoncé's chewing gum and Lady Gaga's genitals.[53] He notes Gaga can be imagined as a very white small male/tranny utterly outdone by Beyoncé (the word "tranny" can be used in many contexts, here it is a male-to-female transsexual or transgender person). The camera guys are white; the shirtless/headless men are black (except for at minute 1:46, where the male might be black, Latino, or white). The blue hoods (see figures 9.2a and 9.2b) add a softcore terrorism/torture reference, sexualized as blue/boyhood. The bound boy at minute 1:46 (see figure 9.2b) is wearing a blue/male hood, pink/fem jacket, and no shirt. His legs are spread, suggesting strength, confidence, and male genitalia. The halo around him and the blue background suggest blamelessness and anonymous identity. This moment (vulnerable, anonymous masked white male, legs spread, torso bound) refers to the crux of the video. Halfway into the clip, Lady Gaga spreads her/his legs to "prove" to the camera the crucial absence of male genitalia. The lyric "You like what you see?" really means "Do you like what you don't see?"

The video's lyrics contain puns and innuendos. "You wanna video me" parallels "you wanna use me" or "you wanna fuck me" or "you wanna own me." Since this clip concerns video phones, the "can you handle it" suggests "can you masturbate to me," or can you handle the absence.[54] The absence in Beyoncé is her vagina (her lack of a penis); for many gay-identified viewers, the absence in Gaga is the effort to remove or deny male genitalia. An intimation that the video considers sexual difference comes early. At the opening, Beyoncé sings "uh-uh," or "no," while wearing a bandit mask and leading her male posse (Kill Bill [2003/2004] and Reservoir Dogs references: her "no" takes on lethal force with the soundtrack's reference to Ennio Morricone's scores for spaghetti Westerns (see figure 9.1a). After the slow dissolve to Beyoncé's eyes, we see a nervous camera-headed man straightening his tie who might embody our subject position—we too might feel nervous when Beyoncé directly asks us: "Shorty, what's your name?"

I've claimed that music video is a heterogeneous medium, with many simultaneous, equally engaging events.[55] With music video, we must chart our own paths through music and image to find meaning. Music videos also ask us to watch them repeatedly. Lacking in narrative devices and text, and with a shortened form, they rely on reduced materials to convey drama. On the web, with low-resolution and stripped budgets, directors find that their resources for engaging attention may become even more attenuated. In "Video Phone," Hype Williams foregrounds one of the most minimalist of materials—color—through several means, including raced bodies. Departing from standard industry practice, he does not balance Beyoncé's skin tone across the video, sometimes going for very deep, rich hues, sometimes a more lightly-complected, Lena Horne look. These changes often correspond to the song's rises and falls.[56] Beyoncé's irises sometimes shift to deep brown or black, and in the pinup section they are a grayish blue. Perhaps to foreshadow the turn to a more European American pinup look, in the clip's *Reservoir Dogs* spaghetti Western intro, one of the African American men in Beyoncé's posse is trailed by a strobing halo of curly blonde hair.[57] One might judge here that our imaginary for what constitutes American beauty hovers white: we are haunted by a model that is a white Anglo-Saxon Protestant.

Yet on a second register, Williams argues differently about color. After an opening in sexualized, hyper-aggressive reds and blacks, the video turns neutral white and black, and then shifts to deeper blues and pinks. Easter-egg, pastel colors sweep in (particularly with Lady Gaga), which suggest innocence and femininity. In the pinup section, gemstone-like rich emeralds and darker gray turquoises appear. Beyoncé posing as a Bettie Page–like pinup strokes her machine gun up and down, and the shaft is a deep violet purple—a color of tumescence, of sexual excitement. If we keep our attention directed to the hues of her gun, we will eventually be carried along with a densely saturated blue and green that can lead us through surrounding fiery oranges, reds, yellows, and magentas. This blue and green possesses special resonance for filmmakers. The two hues share little in common with skin tones so they can be used in matte backgrounds to key out unwanted parts of the frame (such as in the weatherman's blue-screen). For directors, chromakey blue and green have a special, race-neutral value. Following the video's changes of color, rather than its representations of people, is a way I like to experience it.

A viewer can also follow the music. The song supports the image's dense web of signification. The music is unsettling and exotic.[58] Are there menacing elements at the periphery? The Morricone opening features a G-Phrygian ostinato (B♭, G, A♭, G), and a mysterious, dark figure that hovers over the song like a cloud. The upper register ostinato's unsettling quality derives partly because it appears on the offbeats, with its highest pitch on the offbeat of beat two. When Beyoncé states, "Shorty, what's your name?" we suddenly shift to a happier Mixolydian mode in E♭ (a scale with a major 3rd and a flat 7th), yet the Phrygian ostinato still remains. (Beyoncé will sing more of the Mixolydian scale's pitches at "cologne in the air.") Both Mixolydian and Phrygian are somewhat exotic. The Mixolydian occasionally turns to the flat side and, at one point (when Lady Gaga asks "Can you handle it?"), both the flat 3rd and the major 3rd occur simultaneously. In the rhythm track the more muffled drum hits sound like an irregular heartbeat (belonging to us or to the bound man?). However exotic, the song contains redundancies, so small changes seem big. The showbizzy horns where Beyoncé and Lady Gaga dance, and the overdubbed women's voices completing a major triad ("take a cameo"), register as key events.

A subtle intermedial device also supports the video's languorous mood. A thread is established through aporias and slight disjunctures. This line begins at the clip's opening, as one member of Beyoncé's posse is shadowed by a halo of blonde hair (0:30). Soon (1:49) Beyoncé's movements are edited to fall off the beat (a rare occurrence for music video's dancers). The "ahh" (simulating the sound of an arrow released from a bow's quiver) when Beyoncé sings "Video Phone" (3:55) rings out after reaching its target; here, an arrow pierces a man pinned to a large bull's eye (3:27), but the sound and image are temporally displaced. Plastic guns go off, but their fire appears at unpredictable times. Then skin-tone is not balanced for consistency.

Against this broken line, there are circular shapes: Beyoncé's swirling hips; the circles of light projected on the floor and against the backdrop; and Beyoncé's and Lady Gaga's circular pacing from the foreground to the background. The music, too, with its reiterating synthesizer in the upper register creates a sense of circling. The pattern culminates when Beyoncé stands strongly in the foreground and Lady Gaga, with her back to us, runs her hand from the base of her neck up over her head toward her forehead as the vocal line inexorably rises (4:30); the patterns of line and circle coalesce here, but are pushed to the background—this moment seems sexually heightened. Hype Williams has worked with blue-screen for a long time, especially once music video budgets dropped. He may have wanted to run an experiment. What would be the aesthetic requirements for valent, somewhat unresolved, inscrutable imagery? Through this process he may have lit on a new, interesting effect: we've not yet seen so many parameters so subtly mismatched to form a structural process and establish a mood.

8) Mirroring the Internet, Eliciting Participation

Successful YouTube clips attempt to embody, depict, and participate in the network. The self-similarity of reiteration makes it possible for videos to sync up with others, creating a more frictionless path through the web's nodes and links. Each clip should excite, but also elicit an urge to continue on through YouTube. "Haha Baby," "Charlie Bit My Finger," "Evolution of Dance," "Chocolate Rain," and "The Sneezing Baby Panda" put people in a rhythm as well as in an excitable state that carries them forward. Like a wind-up toy, a web user needs to keep moving through the web to diffuse energy and affect. A second point: viewers and uploaders tend to experience the web in isolation, as monads (each person with a computer peers into and attempts to draw information out of the network). Clips like will.i.am's "Yes We

Can,"⁵⁹ "Haha Baby," "Charlie Bit My Finger" and "The Sneezing Baby Panda" are directed to solo viewers. Last, YouTube clips aim to connect with one another and the world. Viewers and content seem to project a dream of the construction of a total media library. YouTube's range of clips, with their trailing panoply of video blogs, all spanning the healthcare crisis, religion, and the latest pop concert, are concerned with getting linked up. Parodies on high-ranking clips and how-tos on the most banal topics—like modes of washing kitchen utensils, including more than one spoon (and then remakes of that)—reveal a wish to fill in all the chinks.

BEYONCÉ AND LADY GAGA'S "VIDEO PHONE"

The frontal images and images of infinite regress in "Video Phone" both speak to the viewer and suggest diverging paths that all lead into the network. The dancing camera-headed men underscore the gathering images, which can be relayed out into the web. The clip's sexual excitement, against its intimations of boredom, may create enough anxiety and drive to keep viewers streaming through at a regular pace, continuing through to other web links. In response to YouTube's encyclopedic drive, this video's catalogue of women performers could be an attempt to retain and organize an array of visual imagery. "Video Phone" also reflects the hunger for people and clips that can be seen, heard, discussed, and played out. Is "Video Phone" a comment on the last presidential election and today's politics? It might reflect American culture's darker side that a campaign video like "Yes We Can" failed to address—what's been left out and put aside, in "Video Phone," seems found and brought near. One might feel ambivalent about the Abu-Ghraib type of imagery—photographing torture shouldn't be sexualized or made desirable. Nevertheless, many contemporary films depict torture (*Star Trek* [2009], *The Bourne Ultimatum* [2007], *Slumdog Millionaire* [2008], *Zero Dark Thirty* [2012]). It's part of our history and our psyche. Can these images be put in relation with sexuality, gender, and nationalist movements?

9) Politics, Music Video, and YouTube's Evolving Discourse

The politics of "Video Phone" may seem objectionable to many. It can make viewers anxious, as the YouTube commentary shows.⁶⁰ Consciously or unconsciously, viewers know African American women have fewer choices of image than do European American women. In the past, as Steve Shaviro points out, once they've aligned themselves with what's understood as the raunchy or the tawdry, they may be less able to move to more traditionally valorized subject positions (as Madonna has been able to do somewhat successfully). Beyoncé's videos have tended to be sexy but also classy—Beyoncé's older videos share little with "Video Phone"'s clashing models of good and bad sexuality. A woman may be allowed to take pleasure from bondage, but she shouldn't then be the around-the-way B-girl or pinup for our boys overseas. She might move up from peep show artist to lounge performer to an even more redeemed state in a field of nearly-pure-whiteness, but she shouldn't turn it around again by becoming a B-girl and a pinup, and then vulnerably approach orgasm while at the same time performing the role of a bored sex-worker and military trainer. But in order for clips to register on YouTube, such clashes with our cultural categories may become increasingly more common. Maybe such a range of modes is freeing and this is positive. Sexuality, humor, violence, and prissiness are often conflated on YouTube. On the site, repetition with jarring discontinuity holds viewers.[61]

"Video Phone" reflects the moment it was produced and released. Suddenly freed from the censors in MTV's Standards and Practices Division, many directors experienced great excitement. Until then, their work had been heavily constrained. MTV limited imagery of drugs, violence, and sex, based on the claims that very young viewers were watching, and parents and advertisers would feel anxious about such content. Now on the web, directors were free! Videos like "Paparazzi," "Telephone," and "Video Phone" celebrated the new possibilities, and one way they did so was through the frisson of collaging all kinds of things together. I, who'd been watching music video for 20-plus years, found clips like "Paparazzi" and "Video Phone" shocking. Now, as more time has unfolded, the videos look less radical to me, but at the time, I honestly felt a bit adrift.

Today "Video Phone" makes more sense to me. Its visual and sonic boredom and ennui might be said to reflect an acknowledgment that some part of civil life has been hollowed out, and that the only possibilities that remain are consumerist culture. As Mark Fisher notes, it's easier to imagine the end of the world than to imagine the end of capitalism.[62] This lack of horizon creates a deadened affect. Yet at the same time, one experiences excitement. What beautiful, talented performers! And what engaging music! This is really something to listen to and to watch. Hence the song and video hover between the two affective modes. Now that time has passed, I can adopt new stories with the clip. Perhaps I might take seriously Beyoncé's opening image as masked leader of a posse, and Gaga and Beyoncé posed against one another, holding their guns upright. Beyoncé could be the new James Bond, an apt heroine for *Skyfall*, *I Spy*, or *Mission Impossible*. Her different stances, postures, and attitudes reflect the changeable roles she's adopted on her mission. As the video unfolds she takes a moment to relay these to me. The video moves past the more possibly troublesome imagery of bondage to a global bent, focusing on Third World cultures. Perhaps she's really gone rogue! She's no longer affiliated with capitalist oppressors like the United Kingdom. She's part of the resistance. The lyrics are just postures too. I much enjoy watching it this way, though I'm still taken aback with the last images of slashing the eye, as if her other selves were suddenly rent apart. (Gaga's eyes are bifurcated too, in the overlaid close-ups of her.) And I want to be suspicious about my desire to unify the imagery. Does sewing things up like this remove some of the clip's radical edge? Am I comfortable with someone who is African American as long as I can place her in any role, including a James Bond heroine? But when things fail to add up, when the subject positions are unknown and various, do I feel more anxiety? How would I feel about "Telephone" if Gaga or Madonna were the heroine? But I do like to take up the masked opening image and imagine Beyoncé as Batman or the Lone Ranger. Gaga can be Tonto or Robin.

We may want to valorize what "Video Phone" does with representations of gender and sexuality. Both Hype Williams and Beyoncé have made a range of work, much of it very progressive.[63] As I argue in chapter 8, Beyoncé's "If I Were a Boy" presents new images of gender and community, and Hype Williams, too, has made cutting-edge work for stars like Missy Elliott and Taral Hicks. As long as makers and viewers critically engage with a variety of media, including those with positive representations, why not grant these artists the space to make a clip like "Video Phone"? Hype Williams rarely works with white artists; this may be the first time he's worked with an African American and European American female star in the same clip. His engagement with gay culture and aesthetics may suggest a different subject-position than that of other directors. "Video Phone" might be an opportunity to assemble loved icons, gathered from a history of looking at media. Williams's response to the song is appropriate: alienation, jadedness, and ennui belong to the song proper. Williams can make clips with great tenderness, pathos, humility, or uplift.[64]

I can't predict where music video and YouTube will go. Many genres exhibit a cycle of birth and death and relatively short runs. Who would have thought music video, after its recent low points, would come back with such ferocity? Neither am I claiming that this chapter's description encompasses all of YouTube. The site's corpus is unfathomable, stretching from documentaries, to university lectures, to clips on opera. Nor do all contemporary music videos share these aesthetics. If bandwidth, screen size, and budgets increase, music video may return to a more classical mode.[65] Given music video's uncertain future, it's a good idea to keep an eye and an ear on Hype Williams and Beyoncé. Few artists have been able to straddle large media shifts. Think of film's transition from the silents to the talkies, or changes due to television. Hype Williams, more than any other director, has flourished as music videos have moved from cable to YouTube. Beyoncé too has been able to maintain her artistic and star status in a newly digitized, connected age. These are artists to follow.

MUSIC VIDEO

CHAPTER 10

Music Video's Second Aesthetic?

How different is a Lady Gaga video from one by A Flock of Seagulls? MTV's first broadcast happened in 1981. Music video has since undergone shifts in technologies and platforms, periods of intense cross-pollination with other media, financial booms and busts, and changing levels of audience engagement. While music videos hit a low point in the 00s as budgets dried up, they have reemerged as a key driver of popular culture.[1] Music video's moment of resurgence resembles MTV's first moment: there seems to be a question of what music video can do and where it fits.

What does it mean to look back on this 30-year history? A comparison of the beginnings and the present might show vast differences in performance style, formal conceits, editing, depictions of space, and the showcasing of new technologies—or it might not. Might we track the changes from 1979 to 2012? Should we follow the arrivals of new technologies or the migrations to new venues and platforms—from low-res video production in the eighties, to high-gloss 35-millimeter in the nineties, to flexible digital technologies in the 2000s; from BET, MTV, and late-night TV to YouTube, Vimeo, and Vevo? We might instead follow the cycles of maturation (in genres like rap and metal), auteurs' interests and influence, and the ways audiences participate with music video. Or we might track the image's response to pop music's changing production practices and vice versa, or the larger cultural turn toward the audiovisual.

Such a project would be too ambitious for a single chapter. Instead, I treat a narrower topic, provide a frame, and focus on some videos from today and from the eighties. Looking back to the eighties and comparing them with the present moment makes sense: new technologies and changing platforms have shaped video-making in both moments. A variety of styles, genres, tropes, and treatments of space mark both the eighties and today. This chapter aims to provide a sense of whether the genre has become savvier and more open to experimentation or more ossified, and what this 30-year history might add up to.

What is a music video? At one time we knew, but no longer; part of the change has to do with media contexts. In the eighties and nineties, music videos were primarily seen on a few satellite services—like MTV, BET, or VH1—or in a countdown on broadcast television late at night, and it was difficult for record companies to get their clips on the air. To make the MTV rotation, clips were first vetted by a board of ten, then had to clear the Standards and Practices division. Consciously or unconsciously, directors and artists tailored their work for these committees. Standards and Practices was an especially difficult hurdle, seemingly wielding as much power as the Hays Office in the 50s. Directors and musicians could never predict which constraints would be enforced. For example, no alcohol or product placement was supposed to appear on MTV (unless you were Guns N' Roses). Some forms of smooching and T&A were okay, others not.[2] Most submissions to the station never aired, and those that did possessed a high degree of uniformity, probably resulting from the cat-and-mouse games between censors and directors. Today music video clips are dispersed across a number of commercial web sites (Vevo, Hulu, Launch, MTV, Pitchfork), as well as YouTube. There is little vetting of clips. Except for concerns about copyright violations (a constant struggle), prosumers feel free to upload a range of material that confounds genres. For example, many clips with full-frontal nudity remain up even though YouTube viewers can flag them.[3]

We used to define music video as a product of the record company in which images are put to a recorded pop song in order to sell the song. None of this definition holds any more. On YouTube, individuals as much as record companies post music video clips, and many prosumers have no hope of selling anything.[4] The image can be taken from a variety of sources and a song recorded afterward; a clip might look like a music video, but the music might be neither prior nor preeminent. In addition, the song might not be a pop song but something similar (ambient, electronic) or very different (jazz or opera).[5] Clips can range from 10 seconds to several hours; no longer is there a predictable four- to five-minute format.[6] All sorts of interruptions can occur (an insertion of a trailer clip or someone talking), and material from other genres may infiltrate (commercials, sportscasts). Music videos appear in new and unexpected media, interactive games, and iPhone apps.[7] A dizzying array of user-based content ranges from vidding and remixes to mashups. It still makes sense to call all these "music videos."[8]

We might thus define music video, simply and perhaps too broadly, as a relation of sound and image that we recognize as such. YouTube especially makes it hard to draw a line between what is a music video and not. We might keep all of the attributes that once made up music video hovering like a shadowy constellation, calling on them to help us read the new clips. We might also strengthen the definition to include the requirement that the images seem engaged with showing off the soundtrack to some extent. But even adding this corollary provides little assistance. Music, sound, and image can be so tightly interwoven in some segments of contemporary film that we might see them as music video sequences; once these appear on YouTube they can seem indistinguishable from other clips. In large segments of today's films, too, the soundtrack may be more striking than the image. Conversely, on YouTube some sleepy music videos have such a passive soundtrack that there's almost nothing to show off, but these clips are nothing if not music videos.[9]

At the same time that we define music video inclusively and expansively, we may wish to restrict the focus. In the 30 years of music video, various sorts of "canon" have emerged. We can see why it is useful to flag some musicians' and directors' bodies of work, as well as particular historical moments. It is hard to be rigorous about what exactly is within this genre, and what is an outlier. Wittgenstein's idea that genres are made up of family resemblances might prove helpful here. For example, games can share a number of features, but not all; they can be related but very different (chess and hopscotch are both games, for example). This may also hold true for music video and music-video-like aesthetics.

Recent studies have embraced analytic methods that better encompass this larger body of materials and more deeply consider what music videos were then and what they are now. Nicholas Cook has defined three types of interaction between music and images: complement, conformance, and contrast. The first shows off or brings to light; the second matches or replicates; and the last differs or works against. He also notes that one medium can fill in the gap of another's. Michel Chion's concept of added value, wherein the image seems to absorb or take on the attributes of the music, as well as the notion of empathetic and anempathetic relations, can also apply to music video. Claudia Gorbman's model, holding that music seeks out attributes in the image, is another helpful approach. There is also my own, which considers the ways sound and image reflect individual parameters such as narrative, teleological drive, harmony, timbre, rhythm, and so forth.[10]

But a broader picture of music video may require a new model. Since music videos place song and image in a relation of copresence, I suggest that we consider them as partners: we might sit them on the couch and imagine them in couples therapy. As analysts, we might consider each spouse in turn. What kinds of behavior does this persona exhibit, what attitudes, dispositions, traits, and ways of functioning? In what ways is each able to listen to or shoulder the requests of the other? Are there examples of pushing and shoving, stifling, or mutual admiration? Asking each to articulate needs in classic therapeutic language is not too farfetched: "when you do this, I feel this," or "if you do this,

I will be better able to do this." We can assume there are issues of dominance and subservience, passivity and aggression. In music-image relations, one medium often seems to be pushing the other to do something, acting as the driver. Each suffers from not being able to show all it has. If only it had a different partner! Some new entity or quality emerges from the couple's relationship, and we respond more to that quality than to either individual in the pair. This aspect is surely contingent and constructed, but it feels so densely colored. Similarly, we may think of the music-image relationship as a new hyperbeing.[11]

Two short examples will show how audiovisual relations in music video might be structured this way. Sigur Rós and Floria Sigismondi's clip "Untitled" presents itself immediately as stoic, abject, and vulnerable. The song and imagery show some overlapping traits: the visual track suggests the schoolchildren are charming, tender, oppressed, and innocent. The music is also sympathetic to these children's circumstances, but it is witnessing: it's not going to step in and help them. (This stance is literalized when at one moment a teacher's hand runs down a child's head of hair, but both adult and child remain unresponsive to the other. Music takes no note here, simply coursing on.) Establishing the unresponsiveness between sound and image early in the clip is important. Later the children go out in gas masks to play in a dark, burnt-out, postapocalyptic wasteland where blackened dust falls like snow (see figure 10.1).

Lady Gaga's "Born This Way" and Kanye West's "Power," on the other hand, project a superfluidity of emotion: energy flows from the music and image together. These two videos, both alone in relationship with their music and image, and together as dynamic multimedia clips, feel like good corporate entities. Each stares side by side like two contenders in a beauty pageant. Both feature the star placed at the center of an outwardly expanding vortex.[12]

Asking what the music and image are saying to one another, how they act as players and performers, can reveal a music video's persuasiveness or allure. "Born This Way" and "Power" suggest that the first imperative is cultural work rather than fine musical or formal relations. Music video's main goal here may be simply to pull us out of the recession and sync us up with one another. And why shouldn't music video step into the breach? I argue elsewhere that if we can get coordinated around a hook (a syllable like "Ga," a visual stutter, a "beep beep beep" buzzy tone, or a simple image like that of a kiss), perhaps we'll be

Figure 10.1 "Untitled": the soundtrack witnesses but fails to intervene.

attuned enough to address corporate domination and environmental disaster. According to Siegfried Kracauer, Busby Berkeley's musicals with lines of chorines helped keep capitalism going.[13] Why not music video today?

Let us begin a comparison of eighties videos with present-day ones, focusing in both periods on videos produced by the large record labels. I adopt a parametric approach, considering elements like form, color, editing, technology, and performance. (In a few cases—editing, performance—I'll add a brief historical overview.) The chapter ends with a return to the wider definition of music video and my suggestion of an *interpersonal* method for understanding music-image relations to help compare the two historical moments.

It is my hope that an interpersonal method will help us assess this history of heterogeneous audiovisual materials. Music video is hard to evaluate. The genre possesses an odd particularity, comprised of intangibles that have analogs to pop music like syncopation, rubato, articulation, and grain; it's fragile.[14] I will float the claim that many eighties videos possess more charm, allure, or power than their contemporaries today, not only because a community cared about them, and the work was so novel, but because the audiovisual relations were special. In eighties videos, directors were trying to discover how to get the new technology of videotape to catch up with the song. This effort is literalized in a video like A-Ha's "Take on Me," where the rotoscoped (animated) hand reaches up to the (live-action) woman as the lead singer sings "up." Similarly there is something fragile and earned about the intimacy of U2's "With or Without You" and George Michael's "Father Figure" (see figure 10.2). Both videos are haunted, as the performers and supporting characters press forward through hazy diffusion, stoically aiming to make a connection that may not happen. This lost-versus-found relation is endearing: it may remind us of our own fraught relations and our desires for what might be. Today's attempts, such as Beyoncé's "1 + 1," a supercharged, hypersexualized video ("make love to me as the war rages"—even the lyrics are jacked up), present a different aesthetic compared to U2's "With or Without You."[15] ("1 + 1" is mercurial and tightly synced.) Perhaps the eighties were a fortuitous moment when our knowledge of technology, culture, music, and image produced some special tension or frisson. But then again, today's moment has its own special newness. Directors are struggling with surprising limitations and possibilities. While budgets have been drastically curtailed, new technologies enable all kinds of

Figure 10.2 George Michael's "Father Figure" and U2's "With or Without You" strive to make contact.

new configurations. Changes in methods of pop songwriting along with new audio and video recording and producing technologies may free music videos from the classic, strongly demarcated verse-chorus alternation, making possible a new emphasis on shifting intensities and textures.[16] Learning how to enact these new modes is exciting for practitioners. Many have been in the industry a long time, sometimes working in film when music video budgets were low, but coming back for love of the genre. Their knowledge informs this generation of clips.

Audiovisual Relations in the Eighties and Today

TECHNOLOGY

Do technologies call attention to themselves now more than in the past? Mathias Korsgaard celebrates the recent foregrounding of visual effects like the video trail, kaleidoscope, stamped multiples, and sinusoidal designs. He claims these digital technologies show off music's plurality.[17] But one could argue that similar effects occur just as frequently in eighties videos, like David Byrne's "Once in a Lifetime," Prince's "When Doves Cry," and Queen's "Bohemian Rhapsody" (see figure 10.3). It is true that the technological devices in these videos are not quite as riveting or hallucinogenic as today's. There is something a bit more insistent in recent clips—friskier. But perhaps this is occurring now because MTV cast a conservative shadow, and the wider number of venues, from YouTube to Vevo, has loosened things up a bit. Another question concerns the history and the incorporation of technologies in music video. Why do some become popular at certain points and not others? It has been noted that new visual technologies often appear first in music video. (Examples include the snorkel cam in Steve Winwood's "Roll with It" and the Quantel in Cutting Crew's "I Just Died in Your Arms Tonight.")[18]

Right now kaleidoscopes are popular, for example, in Selena Gomez's "Naturally," Beyoncé's "1 + 1," and Gnarls Barkley's "Crazy." Perhaps they match today's musical materials, or they are nostalgic, or they pick up some

Figure 10.3 Early experiments with technology: Talking Heads' "Once in a Lifetime," Queen's "Bohemian Rhapsody," and Prince's "When Doves Cry."

musical feature that has recently become popular. The trails and kaleido-scopes might also project well on cell phones. Back in the eighties, the frame was frequently fractured into quadrants or blocks (as in Michael Jackson's "Billie Jean"). Today that is a familiar effect, but in the eighties it was tremendously exciting.[19]

This makes sense: music videos were higher profile then, but had lower costs and fewer aesthetic constraints. Today, with so many media forms and venues, innovations may appear elsewhere first. Not all visual effects have been useful for music video. Michael Jackson's "Black or White" was the first to employ morphing, for example, but it did so only during the song's break. Then the device nearly vanished from use. Perhaps morphing is so engaging that it draws attention away from the music; it's also relatively continuous and seamless, so may provide a poor complement to musical transformations. Bullet time, on the other hand, has remained popular (appearing, for example, in Lady Gaga's "Bad Romance"). This technique may be engaging because it makes music's time strange.[20]

In the eighties, technological gizmos were often used to foreground a song's form. Multiples might quickly carry us from a sparser verse into a thickened chorus. (One device favored then was using multiple instruments wedged into the frame's edges, such as The Police's "Every Breath You Take.") Perhaps directors have discovered how to produce strong audiovisual relations through many parameters, most strikingly through the use of color. So today's technologies do not need to do as much work. (Note the kaleidoscopes in Beyoncé's "One Plus One"; though they are musical, they seem to appear more for their local charm than as a means to assert large-scale structure.)

Can technologies help change our understanding of space and time? The trails in today's OK Go's "WTF?" and the pixilation in Kanye West's "Welcome to Heartbreak" help to suggest a Bergsonian present: we are aware that the present is like a saddle, with the past streaming behind us and the future yet to arrive. But I would argue that David Bowie's 1980 "Ashes to Ashes," with its image solarization, seems to do an even better job of this (see figure 10.4). Surely these devices respond in part to the pop song's arrangement, lyrics, and their relation to the image-scape.[21]

We may also track subtle flows of artistry and influence. In the spring of 2011, there were numerous 1,000-hit alternative (noncommercial) videos that

Figure 10.4 Kanye West's "Welcome to Heartbreak" and David Bowie's "Ashes to Ashes." Were the 80s technologically friskier than today?

foregrounded technological gimmicks. Suddenly by the summer's end, it seemed mainstream directors had capitalized on them. (Such a fast turn! How can we guess where music video will be a year from now?) Handmade, low-cost devices and techniques have always appeared alongside their more expensive siblings, often with equally striking results. In the eighties when directors were using the Quantel box to produce prism effects, others were holding beveled mirrors before the camera to produce kaleidoscopic patterns. Today, Michel Gondry has made low-tech his stylistic signature. And other music video directors on small budgets find alternatives: without fancy software like After Effects (which can produce prisms in the background), directors simply paste Xeroxed sheets of paper on the wall (such as Azis's "Bulgaria +18 [Tits and Penis]").[22] The role of the technological gimmick differs between large-budget mainstream clips and alt-independent siblings. For mainstream clips, digitally distorted effects tend to be narrativized and the performer's body and face remain legible. For example, kaleidoscopes and mirroring in Linkin Park's "Iridescent" are naturalized by a Gothic landscape that seems out of Lang's *Metropolis*. Similarly, Selena Gomez's "Naturally" has multiples, but it also harks back to Busby Berkeley's art deco look. Gomez looks dressed up for the prom, and the mirroring might suggest the fancy hotel where she and her boyfriend first paint the town.[23]

In what ways are today's visual schemes, with their sinusoidal waves, meant to complement the digitally enabled, buzzy soundtrack? Perhaps we cannot discern how much the digital image is driven by its technological context, and how much it is responding to musical features, like qualities of tempo, rhythm, and timbre.[24] We might note that the weightlessness of the sinusoidal and the buzzy has a long history: music videos have long used light shows and visual micro-articulations, and these may help to disarticulate objects and performers from their settings. Today we might consider Radiohead's "House of Cards" or OK Go's "WTF?," but earlier films and videos like Erasure's "A Little Respect" and Michael Jackson's "Rock with You" also became weightless.[25] The similarity among these examples—changing colored light—suggests that highlighting shifting musical features like timbre and time passing is more relevant than showcasing technological advances.

From another perspective, however, these showy technological effects just work aggressively. Not musicality, but rather visual or aural novelty, may be what catches a viewer's attention. (Or do these technologies work like musical hooks drawing her into the music?) Technological gimmicks, or showboating, can highlight the question of what kinds of images go with what kinds of music. Perhaps sync only needs to be good enough, and then music and image can each independently go about its business.

COLOR AND DIGITAL INTERMEDIATE

In the eighties and nineties, music video was a hotbed of color experimentation, even though directors could not change each pixel's color through digital intermediate (DI). Even before the 1994 Gatorade commercial,[26] elements in the frame were cordoned off and given lurid color; rotoscoping also gave the image fine detail through hand-tinted, frame-by-frame animation (e.g., The Outfield's "Since You've Been Gone" and INXS's "What You Need").[27] Telecine could amp up a color across the image and directors would shoot to exploit this. For example, it was common to see very bluish diaphanous cloth from drapery and orange tints from fire or candlelight in eighties and nineties videos (e.g., David Fincher and George Michael's "Freedom," or Bonnie Tyler's "Total Eclipse of the Heart"). With DI, however, color management provides a much wider range and more detailed possibilities for shading. Music video today is loudly proclaiming its capacity for hypercontrol in many ways. Think of all the videos that proclaim, "We have color!" In the Coldplay video "Every Teardrop Is a Waterfall," buckets of paint are spray-painted onto the characters, the background walls, and tenement buildings' facades; the lead singer then comes forward wearing a deeply purple T-shirt. Painting on walls has always been a music video trope, but in the Coldplay video it occurs on so many different planes—even on a virtually configured epoxy sheet placed in front of the camera. There are also new videos that foreground party drinks. Every plastic cup is separated out and given a different shade, as if the drinks had become elixirs, and then everything suddenly turns black-lit and fluorescent. Colors in videos also seem to be conversing about the latest fashions, as if trends were quickly streaming by, and some videos might miss the boat. Recently some wan-looking yellows, pinks, and greens have appeared, one suspects because others flaunt the same hue. Colorist David Hussey claims that few practitioners today want to work with magenta, because it reminds viewers of the eighties. I've seen it creep slightly back in, by way of a hot pink (see Dave Meyers and Rihanna's "Where Have You Been" and recent T-Mobile ads).

The control of color opens up many new possibilities. Music video now can go very dark, as dark as the darkest night, and then suddenly become sharply lit (like David Guetta's video featuring Ludacris and Taio Cruz's "Little Bad Girl"). Varied types of footage can be more readily combined, as in Katy Perry's "E.T.," which blends Super 8–like footage with digital projections onto blue screen. Streaks of light and color can also be added to the frame, complicating and enriching it, suggesting that the music and the people have been touched by sonic waves, God's touch, or aliens—we never know.[28]

DI can serve as a focal point or pivot. Directors put a lot of time into what Jonas Åkerlund calls "beauty work," retouching the star in post-production (Åkerlund likes to digitally enhance a performer's mouth so that it opens wider, for example). Directors often change the color of the eye's iris from shot to shot. In Gaga's "Judas," her eye color turns from green to blue. Åkerlund's videos take much care with expressive fingernail polish (notice the black with white stripes, the circled silver, and the American flags—like in "Telephone"). Imagine you have modified the star's iris and fingernails. From there you can start turning her into pure color: consider Mika's "We Are Golden," Lady Gaga and Beyoncé's "Telephone," Madonna's "Ray of Light," and Britney Spears's "Hold It Against Me."[29]

In mainstream music videos, color is usually thematized (painting on buildings, drinking from cups); even when color serves as a backdrop (as in Hype Williams's clips), it cannot just be free. Independent videos sometimes suggest that it can. Color's historical trajectory in music video overlaps with and diverges from its treatment in cinema. Eighties video seemed to be predominantly scaped in blue, whereas in the nineties videos were golden and red. These colors were independent of cultural fashions. The popularity of these colors may have been tied to timbre and production practices. Colors were certainly tied to race, genre, and gender.[30] Color provides new possibilities in terms of experience, culture, and ideology. Floria Sigismondi, tired of all the silver and gray cars, decides to imagine her technofuture world tinted with feminine gold, pink, and lavender in Katy Perry's "E.T." But first Perry flies down in a uterine, hibiscus, purple-blue-fuchsia world. Such painterly effects can make us feel that, like Perry, we too are in utero.[31]

MATERIALITY AND MICRORHYTHMS

Fine, changeable, and tangible things of the world—dust, water, smoke, and clouds—may be more insistently depicted today because digital cameras have become so adept at capturing detail. As Chion notes, visual microrhythms function well within audiovisually rich media, because they resemble musical processes.[32] As sound waves decay, they exhibit granular detail (through an oscilloscope, one can see these sound waves breaking into fractal patterns). Today these help show off features in pop songs. Producers arranging for low bit-rates choose musical objects sharply differentiated through timbre—for example, buzzy versus smooth. Grain and its absence then come to the fore: music video directors often respond to these production choices by picking highly differentiated visual detail.[33] Of course, earlier music video directors also foregrounded such effects. One of the best music videos of the eighties, U2's "With or Without You," worked with delicate projections of shadows of tree branches and water. But consider Adele's 2011 "Rolling in the Deep," with the dust motes that surround her and the water glasses on the floor that shimmy their contents as the music marks the beat. Each element is marked off so clearly it is almost as if we were examining the video's detail through a magnifying glass.[34]

With digital intermediate, smoke and clouds can become performers. Beyoncé's "Best Thing I Never Had" contains little performance, except that she sings in her bra and underwear (okay, maybe that's a lot) and then slowly gets into a wedding dress. But behind her there's a lot of business. The sky sometimes shifts color slowly, sometimes very quickly, so that the clouds themselves maintain our interest. Clouds have long been foregrounded in music video; as in Herb Ritts's video for Chris Isaak, "Wicked Games." But today, a finer grain of control allows clouds to come to the fore for much greater lengths of time. David Fincher claimed for film that the first thing viewers track is light, the play of light and shadow. With music video we track the play of light and shadow against sound.[35]

RHYTHMIC SUBTLETY

Rhythmic subtlety in the eighties was often difficult to create: clips were mostly edited on video, some without timecode (e.g., found footage). Frame counts were inaccurate; even with timecode, an editor would suffer a one- or two-frame slip.[36] A sequence of tight, brief edits might take forever. Forms of rhythmic articulation seen today were nearly impossible to achieve then. While I've only seen a few recent examples that really strike me as both virtuosic and unachievable by earlier technologies, they point to what the future might yield. Ke$ha and Taio's "Take a Dirty Picture of Me," for example, foregrounds a sense of speed-ramping, of acceleration and deceleration, as a sports car revs against passing telephone poles and mountains, and the music also whip-pans between accelerando and diminuendo. The clip suggests a new experience of frenetic tautness. Consider Åkerlund and Pink's "Sober." The shot lengths and the editing are surprising and exact; nothing this precise existed before. It took not only the advent of the digital but also a few years of practice to change the way shot lengths worked in music video.[37]

SHOTS AND EDITING

Have shots and editing in music video become more sophisticated or better able to reflect musical features? I begin here with a few historically situated styles that point to larger stylistic shifts. As mentioned, in the eighties, figures moved and suddenly froze as still frames, or were suddenly startled by hard edits as if through electric shocks. The big, boomy synth sucked up the frequency range; sounds weren't quite assimilated into pop-song writing (or much else).[38] Director Matt Mahurin's strange gaps from shot to shot often seemed like nonsequiturs: What are the images saying to one another, and the viewer? In the late eighties Mark Pellington discovered how to project a series of staccato-shots composed of two to three frames, alongside incorporated bits of text with strong graphic values (see figure 10.5). Marcus Nispel created "dolly within dolly" moves in which the camera's motion constantly circled. Tarsem Singh made videos with a lot of leader and flash-frames, raising the question of what counts as an edit. In the early nineties Hype Williams used a wide-angle lens and strange sets to distort the characters into loveable, super-hero cartoon-types. Videos for hip-hop artists like Biggie Smalls showcased a relaxed style, wherein the long shots' edits would fall off the beats and one couldn't predict where they would land. In the 2000s Floria Sigismondi employed edgy, hard edits, attenuating narrative drive. Later Alan Ferguson established an all-over technique wherein every single musical element might be picked up within the frame.[39]

Some types of framing and editing we see today could not have been done in the eighties. Jonas Åkerlund likes to use an extreme wide-angle shot of the setting and then cut quickly to an extreme close-up. Without digital cameras and new postproduction techniques, I doubt this shift would make much sense. He may also cut three or four fast shots around the face at well-judged off-angles. These are hard to see; viewers likely don't register them as a cubist realization, but just experience deeper immersion with a character.

Framing too has changed. A musically saturated culture (iPods every-where), a long period of the public shooting with cell phones (so visual lit-eracy has risen), lighter cameras, and a history of music video practices have all contributed to an image no longer framed four-square, flush along a hori-zon on a tripod. In music video today one can see much freer framing, as in Melina Matsoukas and Rihanna's "Rude Boy." Here off-kilter shapes come into the frame from all sides. Layers build up and we're not sure where they will stop. And then while all this is going on, a beautiful moment arrives.

Figure 10.5 Pearl Jam's "Jeremy": Mark Pellington's discovery of how to incorporate single flash frames.

Instead of following Rihanna's gorgeous moves, the instruments, or the engaging Warholian graphics of grenades and pineapples, my eye drifts to a slow black stain seeping slowly from the top of the frame. Contrast "Rude Boy" with INXS's "What You Need." Too four-square! Though "What You Need" looks contemporary—animation has long contributed to the most vanguard music videos—the camera's framing and the way images build toward the chorus reflect an earlier period (see figure 10.6).[40]

Some of today's videos flaunt off-angled and elongated forms on the bias streaking past the lens, like Skrillex's "First of the Year." Cars skidding and horses galloping (sometimes together in the same clip) often suggest both multitemporality and freedom.

NARRATIVE AND LARGE-SCALE FORMS

I have described visual elements such as color, microrhythms, and editing before narrative, because these are the things that come to the fore today and feel like a shift from the eighties. But narratives have changed too: they have become more subtly worked and therefore more transparent, allowing surface detail to come forward.

Though most videos today, both indie and mainstream, seem to hew to familiar forms, a handful of examples suggest other possibilities. Lady Gaga and Beyoncé's "Telephone" is a remarkable one.[41] While Hitchcock once quipped that film was life with all the boring bits cut out, "Telephone" feels like a feature with all of *its* boring bits cut out. One senses a complete film residing behind the clip. We can find ways of explaining why we have only now come across this new formal conceit. Like Michael Jackson's "Thriller" and Åkerlund's "Paparazzi," "Telephone" has a substantial introduction. (Satellite services like MTV didn't approve of long beginnings, and screening "Thriller" took much arm-twisting.) "Telephone" presents one long segment of narrative exposition and a medley-like number from a musical, with tiny bits of interlocking business between. There is also something about the video's suggestion of time, the characters, and their offscreen behavior that's new and striking: we sense they're constantly up to important business, shenanigans we've most likely missed and even right now do not quite grasp. "Telephone"'s heightened storytelling is enabled by the end of censorship.

Figure 10.6 INXS's "What You Need": a heavily rotoscoped music video looks modern, though its framing is more four-square than Rihanna's "Rude Boy."

Stakes are high—poisonings, murder, and sexual betrayal. The songs them-selves might make narrative more possible. "Telephone" is more cellular and fragmented than the average pop song, facilitating more interrupted mo-ments in the images' unfolding. With these short segments and interrup-tions, the work stretches like an archipelago and only in retrospect seems peculiar. Why is Lady Gaga wearing that leopard print and shimmying in front of the Jeep at night? Is she the limousine driver? And why is Beyoncé wearing that Sergeant Pepper military dress in her hotel room, hopping up and down all by herself as if she were a windup doll, while behind her we catch glimpses of kitschy Louis XIV furniture and painted cinderblock walls? And let's not ignore the over-the-top stuff of Gaga's hair in rollers fashioned from coke cans, and sunglasses made of lit cigarettes. The prison block is really a gay dance hall; "telephone for Lady Gaga" rings out. The harp in the soundtrack is very sweet, and its return may enable Gaga and Beyoncé's final getaway (the women and the credits outstrip the story). Ear-lier music videos like Madonna and David Fincher's "Bad Girl" or his and Aerosmith's "Janie's Got a Gun" also are constructed through musical but segment-oriented narratives.[42] Romanek's videos were often set as tableaux that implied worlds behind the videos. Åkerlund's videos suggest a synthesis of these approaches.

Floria Sigismondi's "E.T." also has a density of causes that seems to exceed what we normally experience in a music video. Is it Kanye West, the Wall-E doll, Katy Perry, the deer, or the CD that enables the sci-fi creatures to have sex and repopulate? The chain of Proppian helper agents is never made clear but the narrative still feels sensible.[43] In a different way, Laurieann Gibson and Lady Gaga's "You and I" may present a wider range of characters than traditional music videos. In her 1987 book *Rocking around the Clock*, Ann Kaplan identified a "Madonna 1" and "Madonna 2" in Madonna's "Papa Don't Preach." The pro-tagonist vacillates between two forms of identity that never integrate: a Jean Seberg good-girl, working-class type and a vamp.[44] But the range of Gaga types in "You and I" is much broader. The clip explores transgendered identity (again, freedom from censorship may have made more representations possible) in a richer way than we have seen before. Gaga is a fashionista, Addams Family Morticia, mermaid, girl next door, male James Dean, horror monster (flash-frame), dancing troll-like doll, wood sprite, bride, and fairy queen.

Some directors have become savvier about how to construct character in music video. Directors I have interviewed have stated that returning to music videos after directing feature films has helped them develop character. Tech-nology helps, as does a whole history of music video. In Francis Lawrence's "Bad Romance," both the large-scale changes—Lady Gaga as sheik, prostitute, and revenge artist—and the many fine shifts as well (including a kewpie doll and a French chanteuse) are richer than in any eighties video I can recall.[45] Digital intermediate plays a role too: you really need to know you can easily shift from those whites to hot red, with the reptilian green in between.

PERFORMANCE

In *Experiencing Music Video* I note what might be considered bad acting for the camera. Sometimes eighties musicians seem as if they have been shot with an elephant tranquilizer; they move woodenly through space until forced to a halt by a freeze-frame.[46] Such mannequin-like deportment may have occurred because performers hadn't yet figured out music video's language, or there may be something in the music itself; those big enormous synth sounds have sucked up most of the frequency range once filled by rich instrumental arrangements.[47] The new sounds may have overwhelmed performers' bodies. Stasis also represented a turn away from seventies disco: dancing was no longer cool.[48] Maybe the stance was just a haughty, chic pose that now looks a bit too obvious. But at the same time, eighties videos possess some of the best performance moments in music video history. Since there was often not much going on but the camera and the barren set, the body had to carry weight, unlike now, when a performer knows that a flurry of post-production business may appear suddenly behind her and might alter her expressions in post.[49] Eighties videos convey an intimacy and vulnerability that is forever lost; its sweetness may resemble the beginnings of film, as when Robert Flaherty's actor Nanook smiles for the camera. Look at some Tears for Fears videos or the Pet Shop Boys: such charged but ambivalent sincerity! A high point in the history of music video performance might include Sinead O'Connor's "Nothing Compares 2U," with her solo face and shaved monkish head, floating against a black background. Hype Williams's extreme wide-angle shots, with foregrounded performers mugging against cartoonish scapes, often gave a sense of the performers as blowup dolls (see figure 10.7). Francis Lawrence and Justin Timberlake's "Cry Me a River" marked the first time I felt that music video performance might project the same amount of intimacy and realism as cinema.[50] In retrospect, however, that

Figure 10.7 Three examples of performer's expressions: The Pet Shop Boys' "West End Girls," Sinead O'Connor's "Nothing Compares 2U," and Busta Rhymes's "Gimme Some More."

was an unusual video. Today so much is built around the character that it can seem as if less acting and dancing is unfolding.

Music videos have their own ways of working with a star performer and supporting figures, as I argue in *Experiencing Music Video*.[51] Perhaps directors have become more savvy about ways of working with characters who have no dialogue and appear only briefly on camera. Consider the stone-faced man wearing a single black eye-patch, who appears as an interstitial cutaway in Ph.D.'s "Little Susie's on the Up," in relation to the dead women and other assorted characters in Lady Gaga's "Paparazzi." The latter better integrate into the video and carry much more narrative weight.[52]

Today music-video image fractures into the smallest bits. In the digital era the face often bifurcates: eyes versus mouth, each heading off in different directions. Performers have found that eyes particularly must hail and capture the camera, but the mouth still needs to carry the text (as in Nicole Scherzinger's "Poison").[53] The hyperfocus on the face is complemented by today's musical arrangement, lyrics, and production. One thing that has changed is an intense focus on the processing of the voice and the ways it is brought forward—the voice might be chorused, faded in and out, auto-tuned, or shadowed by other timbres created through plugins. (Listen to the kind of fine work done in Katy Perry and Kanye West's "E.T.")

Dancing is worth tracking as well. Early hip-hop videos, like those with Chaka Khan, display a kind of freedom. When it first appeared in music videos, break-dancing seemed fresh and alive. In the eighties and nineties, performers often moved in sync in what felt like robotic simulacrum, and that practice continues today. Jonathan Dayton, Valerie Faris, and Steve Winwood's "Higher Love" in the eighties, with its stylized dance moves in gypsy costumes, was the music video that captured my attention and has kept me watching all along.[54] Today, Beyoncé's "Countdown" has lovely dancing in it, too (borrowed from experimental choreographer Anne Teresa De Keersmaeker).

SETTINGS

I have claimed that images wafted along or buoyed against a soundtrack are musical.[55] In music video, the origins of such levitation are uncertain, lending more authority to the song. But music videos also at some point tend to "touch ground," to reveal the floor or the earth. The ways music videos depict figures within space can reflect technical acumen, musical style, or fashion. For example, one typical eighties scenario showcased a night scene at a smoky bar, shot from overhead, often with a ceiling fan cresting the frame. But often this image would not give the viewer an integrated kinesthetic sense of the floor, feet dancing, the walls, and ceiling in a way that bound these elements to the music (examples include Simple Minds' "Don't You [Forget About Me]" and Wang Chung's "Dance Hall Days," though I can provide several exceptions).[56] In eighties videos, high heels, long legs, thick shoulder pads, and blow-dried, waxed, or sculpted hairstyling often pulled everything away from the floor, perhaps because the big glossy synth sounds provided the "true" ground.[57] In nineties hip-hop videos, the floor was essential, but it was implied, not displayed. The low-slung camera framed as a tracking wide-angle shot seemed always to be three feet above.[58]

There may be something "musical" about repressing footage of the floor, yet today, for the first time, we find directors concertedly working to create a three-dimensional space that combines the ceiling, walls, and floor. Does the music seem to call for this approach, or have directors finally figured out how to do it? Perhaps arrangements built up with digital sounds on the computer rather than through live playing create a sense of absence that must be compensated for; hence a more completely articulated space is established. Simultaneously the concrete and object-like qualities of the digital sounds may also demand clearer containers. In Justin Bieber's "I Need Somebody to Love" and Justin Timberlake's "Rock Your Body," there's a series of low-angle shots up through a glass floor—the video moves from shots of feet, toward the performer's torso, then up toward the wall, the bent background, and finally the ceiling. Francis Lawrence's "Bad Romance" articulates ceiling, walls, and floor very carefully.[59] I find Jonas Åkerlund's hybrid spaces particularly charming.

SCULPTURAL SPACES

Most music videos today need to project both on large screens and on cell phones. One way to accommodate this range is to foreground a dramatic shift in scale between figure and set. In the nineties director Mark Romanek was the master of building sets that looked simultaneously enormous and miniature, as in En Vogue's "Free Your Mind," but today there has been a renaissance. The sloping and accordion-ribbed spaces in Rihanna's "Who's That Chick?," or the Serra-like iron constructions in Nicole Scherzinger's "Whatever U Like," can be seen as canny extensions of Romanek's practice.[60] This rich play of figure and environment may well reflect an accrued understanding of the genre to be deployed and developed into the future.

PACKING THE FRAME

In many eighties videos, you could often see the seams of the barren film stage/ set or television studio; a cookie-cutter scrim produced a silhouette of a window against the wall; and a figure might be draped in silky cloth, obscured by some smoke. There weren't many items in the frame. When performers and supporting characters moved in a spookily stilted way and the blocky editing unpredictably turned harsh, there was something magical about the image with the music (for example, Kim Carnes's "Bette Davis Eyes").[61] Now, we have the reverse: with digital cameras and digital intermediate, directors can put an unprecedented number of objects in the frame, and delineate them through color, texture, and lighting. Even small objects toward the back of the frame possess distinct textures, whether they are made of softer, more malleable plastic or harder acrylic. Digital intermediate helps these elements come forward—objects pop. We can also track the shifts in spots of color from mauve to burgundy and the modulation from dark to light. Rihanna's videos seem to do this more than others. Is it her voice? Her beauty? Her Amazonian presence? In many of her videos everything projects forward. This visual strategy complements the musical scapes designed for headphones: hooks are finely manicured, stacked up, and distributed around the space. (Consider her "Who's That Chick?" "Rude Boy," and "Umbrella.")[62]

MULTIPLES AND CROWDS

Music video's prismatic proliferation of objects reflects both the digital signal and music's inherent polyphony. The image becomes buzzy as technical devices jack it up to speak to both music video's new digital technology and its nature as a polyphonic form. Also, as never before, we feel the pressure of the crowd around us as billions on the planet (many who are online at the same time) compete for the same jobs and natural resources. As Les Brill might argue, the images of multiples in the frame reflect human crowds.[63] Then again, music video has always drawn on images of multiples. Think of the crane shots that pass like wind over a field of wheat in the eighties stadium videos for rock and heavy metal, or a video like Peter Gabriel's "Sledgehammer," in which a white-speckled-on-black animated figure opens the door and walks out into a field of stars.[64]

IN DEPTH AND ON THE HORIZONTAL

The tracking shot has been an essential technique, because it supports the music's pace in relation to the video's environment and provides a respite from rapid editing. But, surprisingly, music videos have backed away from the tracking shot—and when they do deploy it, it is frequently less showy than in the past. Directors rather have started exploiting other spatial techniques, like placing performers and objects twisting from within an expanding whorl. (Examples include Justin Timberlake's "Let Me Talk To You/My Love" and Katy Perry's

Figure 10.8 The whorl in "Let Me Talk To You/ My Love."

"E.T." See figure 10.8.)[65] Today music videos are also staged more in depth and on the horizontal. Perhaps the new cameras create a greater three-dimensionality, and digital intermediate can more easily separate objects from the background, bringing some objects close while leaving others in the far distance (but all remain clearly visible through strong color demarcation). Directors shooting for the scale of cell phones, too, may coax objects to pop. With You-Tube in mind, they may sharply define edges to compete with everything around the frame. These videos may tap into primitive "fight or flight" responses: objects coming from a distance or entering from the side can seize a viewer's attention, holding her within the clip, rather than letting her dally with other engaging web attractions outside the frame. Directors and viewers may also be starting to imagine their projects in 3-D, because so many media are set for release in that format. Some visual objects are also designed for music that has been spatialized and often redistributed (panned from ear to ear) for headphones. Just as likely, the whorl could appear because it works as an inverted mirror of our lived experience: we sit at the computer and feel our presence radiating out from the mouse, through the screen, to other screens beyond it. Or it could simply be that this technique is the latest trick directors and musicians have stumbled on, a novelty to exploit, but I doubt it. Such a strong hook—something barreling down an unfurling path, calling to us, cloth whirling from an abyss at a distance—is a very powerful image. It suggests control, authority, magic, and magnetism. It claims this video is the center of our attention and the Internet.[66]

HAPTICS

Do music videos today elicit a heightened sensation of touch, or a greater sense of kinesthetic engagement? Whereas objects in recent videos may seem concrete, three-dimensional, and isolated in space, objects from earlier clips seemed more capable of existing in a generous, cohabitable space—where we might reach out and be a part of them. They seemed to belong more to the world of film critic André Bazin.

We can contrast these approaches by comparing some recent videos, like Nelly's "Just a Dream" and Justin Timberlake's "My Love," with earlier ones like Matt Mahurin and R.E.M.'s "Orange Crush" or Mark Romanek and Macy

Gray's "I Try."[67] Perhaps the older "generosity" derives from the fact that it wasn't as easy in the eighties and nineties to create a tactile sense in the image as it streamed alongside the music, so directors worked hard to find ways of using hands and objects that were expressive. In Mahurin's "Orange Crush" the hand in close-up digs into rich dirt and clasps a piece of wood. Romanek's "I Try" shows Gray holding a bouquet of flowers that perches in the frame's center for much of the video. The extra friction or work required to project a person in relation to an object may now be unnecessary. Now objects may simply be hurled at us; there is less charm in setting them off against everything else. It may also be that digital sound and image is a bit harsh, while video is softer and more capacious.[68]

In *Experiencing Music Video* I describe how objects in music videos become odd.[69] They project their own aura or voice that we recognize from the real world, but they nevertheless seem strange. It's almost as if you had inadvertently encountered your pet, suddenly feral, as it was trolling through the park, or as if you peered at a stick, as seen underwater, now twisted and bent. Objects in these videos remain strange: ring, car, violin, flower, stick, and dirt. But in recent videos, objects often seem to retain more of their real-world ordinariness, and it is difficult to pinpoint why. Perhaps each sound dutifully seeks out an object in the frame; each newly formed sound-image object is more fully rendered and separate than in the past. The sound-image connections don't seem surprising. Do we recognize these amalgams now more simply as commodities? Consider the car and ring in Nelly's "Just a Dream": they look grand and they float, but there's less sense of wonder. Directors may only now be discovering how to work with low bandwidth and a small frame in a way that compensates for what could be seen as a brittleness of the digital soundtrack and image. In "Wish You Were Here," Avril Lavigne holds a burning flower, to little effect, but such instances when a hand holds an object may resonate more strongly soon.[70]

Some objects do still seem strange, their uncanniness created through savvy use of color. In Jonas Åkerlund's "Paparazzi" the video's color arc finally leads us to Lady Gaga as a musketeer dressed in black and yellow, pouring a poisonous substance into a pale pink fizzy liquid. Suddenly everything turns uncanny. Perhaps it's because we are surprised that the video's opening spring promise—a beautiful, pale-pink rose and a rich magenta orchid, both linked to Lady Gaga—has turned sullen. The bits of purple at the video's opening and close suddenly become tainted with sickly yellow, green and black; this shift, as well as a new motor-rhythmic pulse, pushes the video into some sort of hyperdreamland where murder becomes contagious and licit.[71]

Elements in music production also have tended toward the distinct, so that they will project well on MP3s and YouTube. The attacks have become shorter, and careful equalization has sharpened the separation between sounds. Perhaps songs and images are triggering each other: the sharply defined objects in the image encourage music producers to seek sharply defined qualities in the music, and vice versa—both seem to seek a greater dimensionality. Here low-register attacks boom, each sonic event suggesting a three-dimensional object the listener can trace in space.[72] Visually, too, we can sense the other sides of objects in the frame. Like Caravaggio's chiaroscuro, in which shadows suggest fuller forms, performers now have "backs."

Sometimes a sound effect and an object can become so tightly synced that they become a three-dimensional amalgam. Look at the Dan Flavin–like fluorescent lights blinking and listen to the thumps and variously pitched cowbells in Timberlake's "Let Me Talk to You," or the exhortation of "heartbeat" and the lurid 3-D modeling of a pumping heart in Enrique Iglesias's "Heartbeat."

INTERTEXUALITY

Music video has always been self-reflexive, as well as intertextual with nearby forms and genres; the Buggles' "Video Killed the Radio Star" inaugurated music video's first broadcast in 1979, and as the song's title suggests, staked its claim against other media. My favorite historically based intertextual videos include Paula Abdul's "Rush Rush," which pays homage to *Rebel Without a Cause*, and the Blues Travelers' "Runaround," which reenacts *The Wizard of Oz*. But videos today want to say, "music video is back!" and do so in many ways. Musicians can place clips of their earlier videos in a recent one, as if to say, "I'm still around." "Know your music video history!" suggests Britney Spears's "Hold It Against Me" and Eminem and Dr. Dre's "I Need a Doctor." Another way is to intersperse references to other videos, as in Hanson's 2011 "Thinking 'Bout Somethin'."[73] The clip plays with speed; characters move a bit too fast or slow, which makes the clip seem very up-to-date, but it's also filled with a thousand references for those in the know—to Blues Brothers films, *West Side Story*, Spike Jonze and Weezer's music video "Buddy Holly" (an homage to the television show *Happy Days*), a Gap commercial, and every other "dancin' in the street" video, like the already nostalgic LMFAO's "Party Rock Anthem" and Lionel Ritchie's "All Night Long." It seems jokingly to say, "Hanson was always retro, remember when they did 'Mmmbop'? but we'll really test your knowledge of retro." Many other examples include Katy Perry's "Friday Night," which contains cameos by eighties music video stars Kenny G and Debbie Gibson, and recent YouTube viral Web star Rebecca Black. And Weezer's "Pork and Beans" video is a mashup of YouTube one-hit wonders.

REMEDIATION

Music videos frequently remediate material. They adopt images from earlier sources (films, commercials, paintings, posters) and often juxtapose them with others in the video.[74] In MTV's first half-hour in 1981, two clips exhibited extensive remediation, perhaps more than we tend to see today. Todd Rundgren's "Time Heals" featured images from paintings by Magritte, and Ph.D.'s "Little Susie's on the Up" borrowed from Fred Astaire movies (see figure 10.9). The practice of remediation continues today. In The Strokes' "Taken for a Fool," the singer wears a T-shirt with an American flag on it, while behind him flicker shadowy electric trees, lit as if they might serve as Christmas ornaments, and then the band rotates to the left as if it's on a lazy Susan.[75] We might say that the video points to multiple media: lithography (the flag stamped on the T-shirt); the coming of electricity and capitalism (electric trees); and records, record culture, and moving media (the electrified lazy Susan). The materials sort of combine into something new. A patriotic Christmastime snow globe? Whatever the intent, it's evocative and it looks good.

Music videos may remediate materials in order to work like poetry. In poems, words or phrases not normally placed together form new relations. The brain can experience a flooding, or an affective overload. In music, images serve the same function as words in poems, and the sense of overload becomes amplified by music's affective qualities, forming a potent amalgam. In the era of multitasking and the remix, our brains may more strongly crave these interactions. Remediation also makes accessible certain features of music-audiovisual relations. As Nicholas Cook and Philip Tagg argue, music presents conflicting attributes simultaneously. Music is often said to create the sense that it's immediately affective; even before culture, it goes "directly to the heart" without explanation. But in a contradictory fashion, music in an audiovisual context seems "cultural." Cook argues that music is willing to pick up associations with almost anything it encounters; it is "sticky."[76] One remembers a song because its halo of memories always trails it. All the modes of dress, performance, and paraphernalia surrounding music—its concerts, album covers—can shape our relation to a piece of music. Remediation reminds us that music still pierces us, but also that almost anything can work

Figure 10.9 Ph.D.'s "Little Suzi's on the Up" and Todd Rundgren's "Time Heals": early examples of remediation.

in an audiovisual context. One image might make associative chains with the music it is coupled with, but another might do as well.

THE FRAGMENT

Nicki Minaj sings, "boom da da da, boom da da da, super bass," and that's what the video is about. Her hands flutter, her hips pound, and speakers quiver on ice. Stuttering hooks have long been important in popular music, but earlier examples have never been so pointed, piercing, insistent.[77] Lady Gaga sings, "Ga-ga." Enrique Iglesias sings, "listen to my heart beat," and we hear a "boom, boom, boom," as we peer through his illuminated body's insides to a synchronized red heart beating (see figure 10.10).[78] Today's instances may reflect new possibilities for pinpoint control, a competitive urge with YouTube, a claim for listening now, or a desire to sync up everyone.

This chapter has embarked on a comparison of music videos from the eighties and today. I want to conclude first with a claim for the artistry of the past: with small and then adequate budgets, and with forgiving, inexpensive video incorporated into the production process, an eighties director might create a delirious environment that moved beautifully against the human figure. Video's visual softness and loose sync actually supported the big, stripped-down sound of the eighties; here, pop-music production and video technology may have tightly fitted one another.[79] The record industry also actively sought out experimental visual artists across many fields, including the graphic arts and filmmaking. Directors reported being excited by audience responses. The field was open: new programming was needed, costs could be low, and fast production schedules obliged many directors to improvise and rapidly review their ideas.

The present era also presents many exciting opportunities for music video. With digital technologies, fine sync between sound and image becomes realizable, frame by frame and pixel to pixel; more malleable, flexible relations have become possible. Though budgets have dropped, directors still find means to produce glossy work, as cameras and recording media have become cheaper. Shooting on green screen or against a studio's cyc (cyclorama) background, and paying technicians to animate backgrounds and edit on Final Cut rather

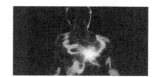

Figure 10.10 Enrique Iglesias's "Heartbeat": 3-D, haptic effects.

than shooting on location, keep costs low.[80] Placing products in videos can also raise a budget by 20 percent. On the other hand, today's audiences and their favorite venues are fragmented. Directors often feel they don't know whom they are shooting for. The relaxation of censorship rules creates new and sometimes freeing possibilities.

Which period, the eighties or today, seems richer? This chapter began with the argument that in the eighties, music and image had to work to find one another, and there was something plaintive about this (like a relationship). Some of the resistance could be found in the sync of sound and image on videotape. I suspect finer control of sync may not always be freeing today. Although today's technologies might seem capable of producing a music video sublime, where the image in its voluble fluidity can be as responsive as the song, we may not want our music video images to be so flexible that they cross over into the realm of pure animation. Rather, we may enjoy the weight of the human figure and real objects in space, in relation to more painterly elements. Technologically, today there may be less friction in creating the image or music, and it's not as exciting.

One might argue that bodies still have plenty of inertia and the digital offers all kinds of new possibilities, particularly with color. Some directors, like Romain Gavras and Melina Matsoukas, have stayed with film; others, like Mark Pellington, have embraced the digital. Even today, different approaches and aesthetics are most suited to particular technologies.

Sync may be important only for some genres of music video. On the one hand, the most popular clips on Vevo today still work "classically," hewing to the familiar mode of carefully tracking the song. On the other hand, many YouTube and Vimeo clips with 1,000 to 500,000 hits may foreground first a technical gimmick or disjunctive sound-image connections (to seem different from corporate-sponsored clips). Audiovisual aesthetics may not be as essential as we had once assumed; sync can be good enough. Directors with great visual flair can make wonderful videos even when their musicality isn't immediately apparent. Other directors, with highly developed chops in shaping music-image relations, tend to be appreciated more by connoisseurs (like directors Melina Matsoukas and Alan Ferguson).[81] Both directors use finely articulated music video contexts, what Bordwell calls "world making," and combine digital and analog technologies to create subtle audiovisual relations. Sync may boil down to taste; I like videos that encourage repeat viewings (and these tend to track the song), whereas other viewers may be drawn to punchiness or beauty in but one domain: image, music, or text.[82]

We might also be able to evaluate the eighties and the present day by considering the roles of experimentation and innovation. There are some strong early examples. In the eighties, MTV vee-jay Mark Goodman announced, "This is a wild one from R.E.M." And then he screened, both upside-down and scrolling to the left, footage of a stone quarry and bolded lyrics for the song "I'm Falling"—that's all. MTV also played clips that surprised its audience, like Peter Gabriel's "Mercy Street," which dealt with incest and suicide but lacked strong performers or identifiable figures. Today's equivalents might include clips that disrupt narrative expectations (e.g., Jonas Åkerlund's clips for Lady Gaga's "Paparazzi" and "Telephone"). Some videos experiment with hybrid forms—videos built for cell-phone apps, teasers or long-playing quasi-musicals (e.g., the work of Bjork, Britney Spears, and Kanye West), or with interactive elements that help them approach video games.[83]

But what about videos that leave us completely lost—that might reflect post-classical values, like those that have reconfigured cinema (*Eternal Sunshine of the Spotless Mind, Moulin Rouge*), or technical approaches that really stun us? I *could* claim that music video remains conservative. As noted previously, it has long showcased an image souped-up by technical effects.[84] Today, mainstream, corporate-funded music videos may cannibalize YouTube's and indie clips' technologically showy devices (trails, kaleidoscopes, sinusoidal waves) and then incorporate them as passing moments—as a means to lead into the chorus, fill in gaps among verses, or kick off the intro. But the performer's face and body must remain legible and accessible. When these effects appear, the clips find ways to explain or narrativize the devices (e.g., the trippy effects might be part of a karaoke show, or a performer's hallucination as he drives his car at night, or the whole video might adopt an art-deco sheen as if it were a segment from a Busby Berkeley musical).[85] There are some exceptions (Kanye West's "Welcome to Heartbreak," Chairlift's "Evident Utensil," and MGMT's "Time to Pretend"), but these are few and even they could be said to remain what I'd call classical.[86]

We *could* argue that mainstream music video has always been progressive and experimental, even before digital technologies saturated production practices. Music video began in the era of video editing. The technology was cumbersome and the sync was poor, but with a four- or five-minute piece, and so few constraints, a director could move material around and experiment. Techniques applied to the frame, like animation, frame-by-frame rotoscoping, and visual software and hardware, provided frisson.[87] Predigital videotape was

Figure 10.11 Solange's "Losing You": Melina Matsoukas's talent for "worldmaking." Cee-Lo's "Open Happiness": Alan Ferguson's "allover style"

already pretty weightless and buzzy. Music video is a short-form genre, and its underlying material—the pop song—has not gone through any radical transformations since the late eighties.

But then I check myself. Suddenly, anew, mainstream music video is true for me again. Beyoncé and Adria Petty's "Countdown," Rihanna and Jonas Åkerlund's "Who's That Chick," Katy Perry and Floria Sigismondi's "E.T.," Lady Gaga and Francis Lawrence's "Bad Romance," and Kanye West and Hype Williams's "All of the Lights" are as strong as or stronger than anything I have seen.

Why are these clips seductive? A sizeable cohort of music video directors have been directing for 10 to 20 years and have developed a well-honed method and mature handling of materials. Their knowledge informs these clips. Music video has also experienced competitive pressures that have forced quick adaptation, in response to both economic shifts and developments in other newly emergent media, rendering some videos tough and fleet. Mainstream music video needs to compete with or respond to indie clips[88] that appear on sites like Pitchfork and Vimeo and have their own innovations. Their music is often brutalist, compressed for the MP3 aesthetic, and the image seems overtaken by jittery, colorful, sinusoidal waves and mirroring effects that are rendered by algorithms. Surprise might play a role, too: How do Rihanna, Lady Gaga, or Katy Perry and their directors treat performance and editing when any feature can be distorted in postproduction, including an expression? Doesn't this create some uncertain tension, a new relationship among artists, practitioners, and directors? Suddenly music video has the right scale for today, and perhaps the right mode for a competitive global market (tied but loosely to language, it easily crosses national borders).

I have intimated that some of the strongest music videos arise from a nexus of evolving audiovisual relations. The image responds to pop songwriting and vice versa. Perhaps we are now witness to a new type of songwriting and directors are laboring to keep up. Some musicologists have noticed the appearance of "the soar." Many hit songs, like Katy Perry's "Teenage Dream," rely on a tiered chorus, which draws on principles of layering and "buildups" that have long been a staple of electronic dance music. Unlike a traditional pop song chorus, its chorus builds in stages. The song begins with a relatively basic, perhaps even sparse, texture, then repeats a second time with added layers that usually thicken the rhythm, along with an included propulsive dance beat. This is effectively a two-part chorus, and as the listener moves through it, she experiences a rapidly building textural crescendo. To add to this layering effect, many of these recent pop songs feature a fairly active verse that then intentionally scales back at the beginning of the prechorus or chorus, so it can make the textural layering and buildup of the chorus even more dramatic. Examples include Katy Perry's "Firework," Ke$ha's "We R Who We R," and Britney Spears's "I Wanna Go" and "Till the World Ends."[89]

Many musicologists don't like "the soar."[90] They feel listeners are forced into an automatic response—hectored into the ecstatic high of the chorus. The listener feels obliged to raise her hands (or hail the dj). But in a music video context the new songwriting technique may offer new possibilities. Against the song's regimented structure, color can adopt a contrapuntal voice, or project its own phrasing, possibly even to break free from other visual elements and the music. Watch the patches of reds, pinks, yellows, and blues in some recent videos featuring the soar, like the Black Eyed Peas' "I Gotta Feeling" and Jennifer Lopez's "On the Floor."[91] We don't know enough about how YouTube, music video, and digital cinema are influencing one another. Nor are we sufficiently tracking the ways directors draw on these media, incorporate, and refashion them while they respond to music video's history. We need to think more about this, but for now I'll say that music video is back with a vengeance.

CHAPTER 11

Digital Style

FRANCIS LAWRENCE AND DAVE MEYERS

"Music video was the most terrific sandbox, where I could try anything."
—David Fincher

While film studies has long debated the meaning and value of auteur studies and has created a canon of its own, no similar corpus exists for music video.[1] If we embrace central tenets of auteur theory like the concept of style—a director's trademark use of camera, settings, and actors along with his or her thematic preoccupations, political views or philosophy of life—we can make a case for applying these notions to music video. Initially the case of the director's auteurship may seem even stronger in music video than in film. Unlike most film and television directors, music video directors have a hand in every phase of production: the making of storyboards, the casting of extras and the selection of props, the shooting, the editing, and many other processes normally considered mostly mechanical in other genres.

An auteurist approach to music video will require some adjustments to the theory. Some questions common in film studies—about the relation of the director to collaborators and obstructionists, about finances, technology, and time constraints, about commercialism and high art—will yield unpredictable answers when asked of music video directors. Other questions are specific to music video: How does the director understand and approach a song? How does he or she work within musical genres? How does the director deal with music video's particular requirements—its short form, lack of dialogue, and need to showcase the star?

By addressing several of these questions, this chapter aims to help lay the groundwork for an auteurist study of music video.[2] The body of this essay explores two music video directors' contrasting styles and responses to songs. I will show how Francis Lawrence and Dave Meyers create structure, employ camera, relate to actors, and reflect musical features. I will also demonstrate how each director has an identity that holds consistent across works, and how each hears a song in a distinctive way. Lawrence exhibits a sense of large-scale structure, an attention to visual and musical continuity, and a concern with music video's history of representation, as well as a classicism that suggests a humanistic orientation. Meyers's work can be characterized as brash, politically playful (and sometimes questionable), star-driven, and grounded in the song's local details. Both directors show varied ways of attending to music and understanding music's role in a multimedia form. Studying the work of these directors can suggest the ways that music videos can be grouped into stylistic families.

A study of these two directors reveals something undocumented about music video practice, which is different from what has been brought to light through the study of film directors. A music video director's fingerprints on a clip creates a startling effect: a director can influence our experience of a song. This capacity to help make experience is hardly surprising when we consider that songs are multilayered. Images can bring some elements of the song to the fore and mute others. Images in music video can act like a tour guide, drawing attention to one musical parameter after another—the rhythm, a motive, a timbre, and so on.[3] Music, image, and lyrics can also function synergistically: all are transformed as they become part of a new entity.

To illuminate Lawrence's and Meyers's styles, I will adopt a parametric approach—considering, for example, how each employs large-scale form, works with elements such as rhythm, melody, and timbre, handles sets and performers, and so on.[4] Such an approach is painstaking, but it may provide the most direct way to demonstrate contrasting directorial styles and to show a director's particular way of working.[5]

The goal of this chapter is not to create a pantheon of music video directors that parallels cinema's (though a bit more respect for the genre and its directors wouldn't hurt). Auteurs across disciplines tend to explore the boundaries of what a medium makes possible. Closely examining two music directors' responses to a song can reveal unique properties of the medium, the genre's relation to technologies, and modes for understanding other videos more deeply.

The Music Videos of Francis Lawrence

One can tell immediately that Lawrence is a receptive and attentive director—a sensitive visual accompanist to the music. His softly articulated editing falls off the beat, bringing the song's rhythm to the fore, for example, and his variously sped-up and slowed-down footage showcases the music's flow.[6] He allows no element in the texture—not color, lyric, or gesture—to come too far forward.

This approach makes the song appear transparent and graspable. Repeated viewings reveal, however, that Lawrence uses camera movement and places figures in the frame in order to trace visual trajectories across the song, carrying the viewer through the video. Lawrence's response to the music coheres into a way of knowing the world.

LARGE-SCALE STRUCTURES: ALTERNATIVES
TO TRADITIONAL NARRATIVE FORMS

Lawrence's style will begin to emerge if we consider the large-scale structural devices in one of his videos. Maxwell's "Fortunate" functions well within the R&B genre: in an upscale abode, the performer sings about his lover, who appears periodically. Like most music videos, "Fortunate" eschews fully wrought narratives, for many reasons. Most significantly, pop songs tend to be nonteleological: they normally have sharp sectional divisions and much repetition—verse, chorus, verse, chorus, verse, chorus, bridge, verse, chorus. Thus, if the image were to acquire too much narrative thrust, it would force the music into the background, much as image eclipses music in Hollywood film.[7] Music videos aim to draw the viewer toward the song. Directors employ formal strategies other than those associated with narrative. One such strategy is the use of processes and threads.[8] "Fortunate" is an excellent example of tailoring such a structure to a song. The video contains seven strands. These strands interweave and echo one another in a polyphonic way.

1. In "Fortunate," the couple's progress is caught in a cross-fade—each dies and revives, or awakens and falls asleep, according to a different trajectory. Occasional stock footage of a woman's face further suggests a missed encounter or reminiscence.
2. Images of butterflies and jellyfish are carried further by the couple. Maxwell's clapping imitates the butterflies' wings in flight. A moment of visual "contagion" occurs when the lovers' lips seem to resemble those of butterfly wings.[9] The woman's unbraided hair, clinging dress, and relaxed posture suggest the hovering jellyfish.
3. Images of glass and light appear throughout the video. The city lights are picked up by banks of light that flood the bedroom. At one point an out-of-focus shot of the illuminated walls appears; at first glance, it looks as if they were the city lights, once brilliant, now dimmed. The glowing light fixtures are picked up by the butterflies' abdomens, which also radiate light—perhaps these insects turn into fireflies.
4. Glass panes pass before Maxwell (who wears sunglasses), echoing the doorways through which the couple gaze at one another.

5. The fingernail polish dripping on the bedroom carpet rhymes with the more ominous dripping of water from the bathtub's faucet.
6. Parts of the body are thematized—the eyes, fingertips, lips, and feet appear in isolation.
7. The video has a mostly cool bluish cast, which is uncommon for such a romantic R&B video. Throughout the video objects tinted in red—like lips, flowers, and the TV screen—either project brightly or dimly, but always stand out against the prevailing blue context. The red hue suggests life, death, sensuality, or mortality (see figure 11.1).

Lawrence's skill as a director derives, in part, from the ways he deploys an unusually large number of threads that seem to carry across the whole of the tape. The material within any one strand appears periodically, and will suddenly assert itself against a high point in the song. To mention three examples, the fingernail polish drips during a quiet moment in the song when a single drum hit comes to the fore; the jellyfish float in the bath on a chorus of feminine "oo's"; and the bank of wall lights first run across the room when Maxwell's chorused voice sings, "fortunate." The use of visual strands of material

Figure 11.1 "Fortunate": many visual threads.

that come to the fore and recede seems to match the musical flow—we might consider the past and future of a visual thread, as well as the transformations of a musical gesture that accompanies the heightened moment. The imagery in "Fortunate" acts like sonic elements in a pop song: a visual motif will come forward and move away; some aspect of the rhythmic arrangement or the bass line will suddenly catch the listener's attention and then drop back into the depth of the mix. Lawrence also exhibits a considerable amount of restraint with his materials. The culmination of a thread tends not to occur until a propitious moment—when the couple finally embraces.[10]

"Fortunate" does not fit into the small group of music videos that present fully wrought narratives. Lawrence also makes narrative videos, like Aerosmith's "Jaded"; the Goo Goo Dolls' "Here Is Gone"; and Lady Gaga's "Bad Romance." These hover restlessly between representations that seem natural for a short form like music video—with its lack of dialogue and responsibilities to the singer, the lyrics, and the music—as well as those connected to traditional storytelling. Lawrence's narrative videos will suggest a story but only through one or two enigmatic images. The protagonist of "Jaded" is an attractive girl residing in an opulent mansion. The verses depict doll-like handmaidens dressing and feeding her; in the choruses, the handmaidens take her to a fantastic playroom where circus performers and animals entertain her. The girl's bored expression, the dolls' stiff and repetitive movements, and the song's repetitive form encourages us to assume that she is being confined there, and wishes to leave. Music video doesn't possess a shorthand for conveying a long confinement, however: one can not simply show days and nights unfolding, leaves of the calendar falling away, or someone saying, "I'll be back next month." Even harder would be to suggest her breaking out of captivity. Lawrence's video attempts to tell us that the girl escapes by manipulating her storybook environment. When the girl sleeps, her attendants sleep. So she *pretends* to sleep, the dolls drop, and she runs away. But without dialogue or exaggerated pantomime, the video cannot quite establish the cause-and-effect relation wherein the girl's acting sleepy makes the dolls sleepy. Viewers might think everyone is bedding down for a nap (see figure 11.2).[11]

The Goo Goo Dolls' "Here Is Gone"'s plot is similarly opaque, but a hint of narrativity lingers. In the video, many extras play ghosts. One female ghost kisses a flesh-and-blood relative, and her companion becomes angry with her for transgressing the boundary between worlds. This plot development might become clear by putting wings on the characters, tinting them a different color, or giving them ghostly sounds or dialogue. To bridge the spiritual and the quotidian, Lawrence uses one postproduction effect momentarily (when characters move at different speeds within the same frame). The video relies more on mood-laden images such as broken windowpanes, old photographs, gray skies,

Figure 11.2 Aerosmith's "Jaded": music video can't describe interpersonal interactions, including the young girl's means for flight.

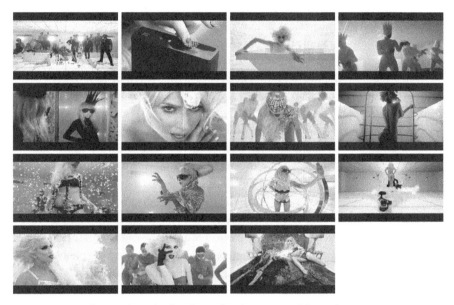

Figure 11.3 Lady Gaga's multiple roles in "Bad Romance," from chanteuse to arsonist.

and abandoned tract housing to suggest the presence of an afterlife. Though the context for this angry exchange remains unclear, a sense of story and of mystery pervades the video.

"Bad Romance" presents a convoluted narrative. Lady Gaga plays many roles, including a chanteuse; a plastic-coated, wood-nymph; a prostitute; a grande-dame in a polar-bear outfit; a witch; a kewpie doll; a chandelier; a model; a fashionista; and a bored kept woman with an entourage (see figure 11.3). The causes and effects of these transformations aren't clear, but they seem to make use of smoke, water, light, vodka, and glass. A Wikipedia entry states that Gaga's been auctioned to the Russian mafia, but then why the caskets and the bald cat and fetal-like fox headdress turned white-haired rat? Does Gaga fall in love with a man but then decide to torch him? Is she exploited, freed, made famous, swept away by love and then made murderous by her lover? Since these experiences occur out of order, the plot remains unclear. Elsewhere in this book, I argue that this new intensification of story elements is enabled by fine control of color through digital intermediary.[12] These last examples show three different ways Lawrence is able to suggest rather than tell a narrative.

SPACE, FLOW, AND THE BODY

While music video directors are not beholden to a narrative structure, they have other responsibilities. Directors must respond to a song's features. Lawrence distinguishes himself as a director through his close attention to music's processual qualities. Many directors employ heightened camera work—dollies, quick pans, finely nuanced types of camera reframing, as well as rapid cutting—to keep pace with the music. Lawrence reports that when he first hears a song, he envisions not a character, color, or setting, but how the camera might move. For Nelly Furtado's "Like A Bird," Lawrence might have imagined one camera panning 360 degrees, and another pointing up and swinging side to side. The long, dramatic pans seem specially tailored to "Like a Bird"; these camera movements differ markedly from those in "Jaded" and "Fortunate."

Videos may accentuate movement because the music video seems more capable of revealing space than place. In the cultural geographer Yi Fu Tuan's characterization, "Space is experienced directly as having room in which to move. By shifting from one place to another, a person acquires a sense of direction. Space assumes a rough coordinate frame centered on the mobile and purposive self. . . . Place is a special kind of object. Though not a valued thing that can be handled or carried about easily; it is an object in which one can dwell."[13] Always in flux as it attempts to match musical processes, the music video image rarely offers us a place to inhabit. The elaborate recording and post-production techniques of popular music create sonic environments that do not resemble lived spaces. Music videos thus depart from ordinary experience. We must throw ourselves into a video's environment if we want to guess how its spaces feel.

Music video challenges directors to explore a space while providing viewers with a sense of ground. Lawrence meets this challenge through techniques that appeal to a viewer's sense of proprioception—the body's intuitive sense of placement within and ability to control a space. His videos often begin with the star entering or waking up to a vaguely surreal environment. Soon the performer tests the space—playfully flicking a light switch or brushing her hair back so that birds fly off (as in Janet Jackson's "Son of a Gun" or Nelly Furtado's "Like a Bird"). In "Bad Romance," Gaga's gold-covered index finger triggers both sound and light; her twisted fingers drumming on the side of her pod also plumb the space. In Lawrence's videos, a hospitable corner will be revealed—a small bowl of water with a bonsai sits on a shelf, or a plump cat crouches on a dresser. There may be something psychologically cooler, like "Bad Romance's" illumination of a bank of lights and a row of vodka bottles. Next Lawrence connects viewers to the musical flow through exaggerated camera movement and the manipulation of objects. He'll often rock the camera side to side, as in "Fortunate." "Like a Bird" shows a large object moving back and forth within the frame, which creates a pumping effect. In "Bad Romance," Gaga is forced to drink an elixir, and she spins as a statue/model/icon. A third appeal to proprioception will occur past the video's midpoint: the musician—and therefore the viewer—will move into a larger space. Furtado rises up and soars through the branches of redwood trees. In "Jaded," an adolescent girl perched on a very high ladder tosses a book and it is carried 50 feet across a room (see figure 11.4). In "Bad Romance," Gaga struts across the floor in a white polar-bear cape.

To highlight a song's continuity and processual flow, Lawrence tends to move toward and then bridge across the song's sections. Like most music video directors, he presents the chorus as the song's big moment. Perhaps Lawrence's particularity lies in the ways he carefully tracks the momentary nuances within the verse, staying present in what is happening, while simultaneously projecting cues that accumulate weight and direct us toward the chorus. For example, in the Goo Goo Dolls' video, "Here Is Gone," characters and animals get ready for something: a caterpillar shakes from its thread, and tennis shoes tentatively step forward. An arc motif emerges more clearly as the verse progresses— curves appear in the fluttering plastic on windows and the brims of women's hats. Patches of light grow larger and fast-motion footage appears. People become more active: a couple initiates sex and a group of young listeners stand up and begin to move outside the scaffolding on a house. The camera too becomes livelier: it shifts between wider and closer shots of the band. The gradually increased activity in the verse brings us into the more upbeat, fully

Figure 11.4 In Lawrence's videos, the performer tests the space.

arranged chorus. Some of the ways Lawrence uses the placement and movement of the figures within the frame to build toward song sections and key
points in the video can also be seen in "Fortunate" and "Like a Bird."[14]

"Bad Romance" showcases phalanxes of dancers in its choruses. As the chorus unfolds, it places us in the immediate present and yet also reminds us we've
been brought here by historically freighted, powerful forces. Past, present, and
future seem near because we experience a pinnacle—the array of dancers—
that claims the "now," but the chorus also draws on imagery from the past as
well as presses on toward the future. The verses had shown the protagonist's
refashioning: her emergence from the casket, her digitally altered eyes and impossibly narrow waist, her release from a burlap sack, and so on. The choruses
continue to develop these transformations, intercutting them with the dance
spectacle. In chorus one Lady Gaga is pulled from a tub and forced to drink an
elixir; in chorus two she rotates, on display, surrounded by hanging precious
stones; in chorus three she torches her lover.

SENSITIVE ACCOMPANIMENT

The above description characterizes a viewer's progress through a video as well
as Lawrence's close attention to the song. His approach feels different from that
of Hype Williams, who often has characters move more quickly and erratically
than a song's materials and who uses the camera in such a way as to hover above
the music. Williams seems more improvisatory, willing to break free and
declare his own visual patterns. Lawrence reflects the song's flow of information not by mickey-mousing but rather through fine gestures that draw attention to musical shifts. He uses a variety of devices: varying the speed of the
shots and the ways they are edited; changing an object's placement in the frame
in its subsequent appearances; the handling of lyrics; and the use of color.

Lawrence's framing and editing cannot be encapsulated in a simple description of close-ups, low-angle shots, wide-angle or telephoto lenses, and so on.
Lawrence's camera placement is subtler than a strict interpretation of the 30- or
180-degree rule would be; often seated to the side of its subjects, the camera
provides elliptical points of view that disclose the space slowly over a series of
shots.[15] The frequently mobile camera sometimes moves slightly slower or faster
than the music, which paradoxically seems to draw greater attention to the
music's teleology.[16] Editing is subtly articulated—off the beat and irregular. It
makes the music the dominant voice—the image serves as a coloration or counterpoint. Like many music video directors, Lawrence frames his characters and
objects partially. This aesthetic choice can encourage the viewer to turn to the
music for additional spatial or temporal cues or to form a more unified space.
The viewer must draw upon earlier moments and anticipate later ones.[17]

Lawrence uses a small set of materials that are constantly repeated and varied in the video. This repetition of material creates a sense of continuity that matches the music's and indeed works somewhat like the use of musical motives.[18] Incubus's "Warning" accomplishes this continuity effect through the use of objects like paper, guitar strings, and chalk markings.[19] (See figure 11.5.) In the Goo Goo Dolls' "Here Is Gone," subtle connections run across the video. The gum that the girl stretches from her mouth relates to the caterpillar's thread. The crow's flight connects with the outstretched arm of the woman in a cart. Numerous windows appear, and as their appearances accrue, their presence raises questions about perception and about the boundaries between the worldly and the spiritual. Such connections keep us in the moment, but also focused on the past and future of the tape.

Lawrence reports that he focuses more on music than on words. Thus individual lyrics tend not to jut out from his videos' textures. When a lyric is underscored, it seems elliptical, almost serendipitous. Much of Incubus's "Warning" takes place in a high-rise building, but later descends to street-level. Lawrence's transparent technique may allow the viewer to remember musical moments from much earlier in the video. Once we have been on the ground for a while, we may remember an earlier line: the words "we go down" set to a descending melody, accompanied by some guitar feedback that traces the voice's contour.[20]

Lawrence's videos create arch forms, but the beginnings and ends are not identical to one another. The use of bookends works rather to strengthen a theme or continue a conversation. The opening shot of "Like a Bird" reveals Nelly Furtado lying in the hollow of a grass field—she appears to have been born there. The closing shot reveals a crowd of people—reduced to specks—holding her up to the sky. The crowd resembles the blades of grass that supported Furtado

Figure 11.5 Incubus's "Warning": visual continuity supports musical continuity.

in the opening shot. The connection between people and grass is not only formal (based on shape) but also thematic (echoing the scriptural quotation "flesh is grass"; see figure 11.4).[21] Near the end of "Bad Romance," we see a recumbent Gaga, her sparking breasts having ignited a firestorm that consumes her lover. This shot takes us back to the opening image of Gaga in recline, wearing her razor-bladed glasses, with her finger on a device, when a sudden sound and flash gives her pause. (Perhaps the sound and light are a flash-forward to her killing at the clip's end.) This compression of material and function helps to explain some of Lawrence's power as a director. The gentle return from an end to a beginning stresses the integrity of the video's large-scale structure. The video does not rely upon this return to the beginning. The closing image works only to highlight a sense of large-scale form that the video already possesses. It confirms the importance of values like integrity and wholeness: it makes clear that closure is important to this video.

PEOPLE AND PLACES

Unlike directors of narrative film, music video directors have little time, story, or text to work with. An auteurist touch shared by film and music video directors is the handling of sets and actors. Again we will find that songs elicit different responses from music video directors. Lawrence's sets differ from those of his peers in the amount of lovingly rendered detail they contain. Most music videos are relatively stripped down. Many of the highly regarded music video directors such as Mark Romanek and David Fincher employ minimalist sets. Editing shots containing a small set of objects may help the director to focus the viewer's attention: by limiting the number of objects in the frame, the director can create a visual path that works with and against musical materials. It may also be hard to construct well-defined sets because music video is such an ephemeral world, only momentarily inhabited by its characters. What are the music video characters' histories? How does one build a world for them? Lawrence's sets suggest spaces that have been inhabited for a while. He'll use unusual devices to create this effect, including combining materials from disparate locations for Maxwell's "Fortunate."[22] The set for Green Day's "Warning" is messy. The kitchen is in such a state of disrepair that the viewer may find herself fantasizing about what must be an extremely grimy floor. This cluttered environment is unusual for the way it releases the eye from a forced path through the mise en scène. (Audiovisual sync is achieved in other domains: in "Warning" Lawrence's camera makes sharp jogging movements that can resemble a painter's brush marks. These edits and camera movements provide another path through the video.)

    Settings also help to place the song within its genre. Viewers knowledgeable about music video's history will recognize the way that different modes of address correspond to different constituencies: the studio set of a living room with worn wallpaper; the industrial site with naked pipes and debris on the floor; the high-ceilinged hotel with marble staircases; and "the street." Each connotes alternative, metal, R&B, or rap, respectively. I have been impressed with Lawrence's knowledge of musical genres and sense of music video's history: his videos contain many knowing references to earlier videos and directors.[23] Lawrence is highly aware of each genre's constraints and can work within them, but also feels confident enough to stake his own claims. Maxwell's apartment recalls the swank bachelor lofts we so often see in R&B but also differs from them in important ways. "Bad Romance"'s shiny surfaces highlight this song's kinship with the coldness of techno and industrial. Do the ominous back-door bathstalls, possibly for surgery or holding women as quarry, also reveal a dark underside of the genre? The boxy lower-middle-class sets that are the hallmark of alternative videos also take on new meaning in Lawrence's hands.[24]

Lawrence's spaces depart from reality. Even when he uses a setting like an airport, a patch of meadow, and woods, or what might be described as romanticized locations from Jamaica, he'll distort the place either by elongating figures in the frame, or heavily tinting the film. By disrupting cause-and-effect relations, these strange, heightened spaces serve musical ends. The elaborate post-production techniques of today's pop songs mean that their sonic spaces do not match real physical environments. Directors like to exploit this disjunction further, playing with the illusion that objects within the space might initiate the sounds of the song and vice versa. We aren't just listening to a song in some space, but to a new world that becomes musical. The soundtrack has greater authority over this world than does sound in daily life, and much more weight than soundtracks do in film. Lawrence uses a broad range of devices to create a world in which sound engenders effects. A video may suggest that the song contains sounds the objects in the frame might make, like a musical hook that resembles the rumbling wheels in Jennifer Lopez's "Play" and Janet Jackson's "Someone to Call My Lover." Or Lawrence might also build a set wherein sounds seem to trigger the objects, as in Ginuwine's "What's So Different?," which shows stones popping up at certain moments, and Melanie C's "Things Will Never Be the Same Again," in which sounds cause Venetian blinds to shut and bulbs to flicker. He might present objects that are so closely linked to sources suggested by the song that one wonders about the relation—for example, do the water bottles in Britney Spears's "I'm a Slave for You" have anything to do with the detuned oscillators that create one of the primary hooks in the song's arrangement? (See figure 11.6.) "Bad Romance" might make one wonder whether a clinking in the soundtrack refers to dropped ice cubes or a fallen chandelier. The heavy drums and bass, with thick bands of sound in the

Figure 11.6 Melanię C's "Things Will Never Be the Same Again," and Britney Spears's "I'm a Slave for You": worlds in which sound engenders effects.

lower- to mid-register (suggestive of late 80s techno and industrial), disso-nances between voice and bassline, sinister synth touches (glissandi), and the chanting of "rah rah oo la la" establish a macabre tone.

Lawrence doesn't overuse close-ups of people, which helps his work avoid the pornographic qualities of many videos. In fact he usually keeps people rel-atively small, making the setting as important as the character. This gives his characters a bit of privacy and seems to ask for the viewer's participation. The figures are not out of reach, but we must enter into their world. Most often they seem curious about their world. Lawrence's characters engage with their set-tings and with each other. This stance suggests the possibility that a new un-derstanding of the world or closer connection among people may yet be possible. This type of inhabitation also suggests a kind of grace. The actors' highly nuanced gestures vary throughout a video, as when, in the Goo Goo Dolls' "Here Is Gone," the tentative movements of lead singer Johnny Reznik and his guitar build into wide rocking motions. These gestures are highly dif-ferentiated from the movements of lead singers in Lawrence's other videos, such as the more gentle sidestep of Brandon Boyd in Incubus's "Warning."[25]

As I have mentioned, music video's capacity for storytelling is quite attenu-ated. Without much dialogue or story time, what sorts of relations can be shown between people? In Lawrence's videos, one character will often seem to connect with another: though brief, the moment has a directness and inten-sity. When a character encounters an Other—it could be a person, animal, or animated statue—the character recognizes herself for a moment and the vid-eo's world is less strange. (Such an intimate moment can even occur between a woman and a beetle, as in "Like a Bird.") Such personal, momentary encoun-ters fit the scale of what a music video can do. There is something bittersweet here. By the video's close, these intimate moments appear to have rushed past the character. Perhaps we wish for more. Such relations speak to the ways that music and image are continually in flux, however: some encounters remain tied to unique musical events or fragile trajectories left behind in the video's unceasing flow. Even against this flow, these moments feel vital, whole, and precious.

Most haunted is "Bad Romance." We sense something meaningful has taken place, but we're behind the ball a bit, because we don't know Gaga's relation to herself, her entourage, her handmaiden/preparers, her dancers, the men who buy her, or her possible lover/purchaser/abuser. We remain curious, attentive, and open about these relationships.

If I were to place Lawrence in a class of film directors, I would place him with those humanists who also work with heightened, poised, and well-balanced relations, like Renoir and Hawks, over those who focus on relations of power and blindness, such as Lang and Welles.

Lawrence might also belong within a group of music video directors that would include David Fincher, Herb Ritts, and Mark Romanek. These directors construct large-scale visual structures that possess integrity but also are shaped to the song's form. They create paths that assist the viewer in following the song. In fact, these directors reward our efforts to follow the lines of the camera and the music as they trace across bodies and through space. They are more concerned with the relations among characters than with beguiling the viewer. During heightened moments these videos create the illusion that we can directly perceive the rhythms of the bodies before us.[26]

The Music Videos of Dave Meyers

While Lawrence's work possesses a restrained classicism, Meyers's is more Rabelaisian—bawdy, raucous, and celebratory of popular culture. Meyers's videos can illuminate the tinsel-coated surfaces of pop songs. Lawrence's videos suggest a humanistic orientation, while Meyers's often offer more visceral pleasures. Meyers's videos can seem to create a bit of an overload—like moving quickly from darkness into sunlight. As one of only three or four directors who've remained at the industry's forefront over the last twenty years, Meyers might well adopt new approaches and downplay others. His earlier videos present scintillating moments, though their political valences can be problematic. The most recent work is more fluid, nimbly working with stereotypes in ways that ricochet in unpredictable directions, finally taking them to favorable ends. Wit and ironic distance seem to transcend this difficult material. Meyers has also made politically progressive work. He'll often foreground same-sex couples in a positive light. And his and Pink's "Raise Your Glass," I've claimed, should be taken up as the Occupy movement's anthem (see figure 11.7).

Figure 11.7 "Raise Your Glass": a progressive video that the Occupy movement might claim as an anthem.

Perhaps because they are currently the industry's two most sought-after directors, Lawrence and Meyers have worked with the same coterie of stars, like Jennifer Lopez, Janet Jackson, Aerosmith, and Britney Spears. While the rest of Lawrence's roster tends toward the genteel, like Michelle Branch, Maxwell, and the Goo Goo Dolls, Meyers's other subjects, particularly in the 90s, tended to represent working class angst, like Pink, Papa Roach, and Kid Rock, and the bad boys of rap, such as Jay-Z and Method Man. Meyers, however, has also directed a range of artists, including the Christian-rock-identified Creed and the mainstream Katy Perry. Questions arise over the extent to which clients shape the director's look, and how much his personal style suits musical styles. Perhaps a generous diet of cartoons, video games, blockbusters by Spielberg and Lucas, and perhaps even soft-core T & A may have provided the ground for Meyers's aesthetic. Meyers also takes seriously the requirement that the musician be shown as a star, and that genre conventions be respected. His style seems to come readymade for the poses and moods of contemporary pop music.

SHOWCASING THE STAR

Like Lawrence's, Meyers's style comprises several interlocking features. One first notices the way the stars appear to be blown up 15 percent larger than life. I will spend some time discussing this hyperbolic frontality because the pumped-up musician against an often bold, busy background directs the viewer toward a mode of listening different from what Lawrence's videos encourage. How does Meyers create these effects? Like Hitchcock, Meyers frames his actors as big heads, but, even more than Hitchcock, Meyers uses lighting to further separate the figure from the background. The star's enormity also derives from his or her transfixing gaze. The star can seem set on hypnotizing us, as in Rihanna's most recent "Where Have You Been?" Meyers's decision so boldly to foreground the star may shape a whole series of aesthetic choices. Music videos are miniatures, and don't have much leeway to play out all possibilities. The images have an obligation to present their own integrity and flow, as well as establish a line that tracks the song. Shifting freely among a foregrounded portrait of the star as monumental and a broader depiction of many characters as they engage in complex interactions may be difficult to sustain.

Meyers's stars stand out in many ways besides their scale. The camera often tilts slightly, giving an unpredictable sense of ground and a staged quality. Though Meyers's palette has expanded from the very brash to the subdued, he'll still foreground striking isolated features. Earlier work most often featured artificial sets (frequently constructed with CGI), and colors that looked young and feminine—hot pink, magenta, lime green, light turquoise-blue. When outdoor settings were used, the sky was too blue and the trees were tinted an especially deep green. Both in recent and earlier work, Meyers's surfaces are chosen for their sensual qualities. The director likes to combine textured surfaces with glossy ones, using materials like brushed fabrics, burnished metal, fur, glass, and leather. This amplifies not only the star but also whatever objects are in the frame.

The environment in which the stars appear makes them enormous as well. And if a song's genre communicates information about the song's meanings and functions, Meyers might give this information back in spades. It is unsurprising that Jennifer Lopez's "I'm Gonna Be Alright" is set in the projects. But we may blanch at seeing her in such a stereotypical role—barefoot, bent over in front of a washing machine in a barrio Laundromat. Similarly, in "Objection (Tango)," Shakira evokes not just the role of a nightclub dancer, with high heels, tight miniskirt, ripped fishnet stockings, and rump-wiggling moves, but also that of the wanton prostitute. Jay-Z's house party in "I Just Want to Love You" is already so filled up with people partying and having sex that there is not a bathroom or closet available for a newly arrived couple seeking an intimate rendezvous. Working-class bad boy Kid Rock holds a beer and assumes the couch potato position before a big screen TV with the desert mountains as a backdrop, and later, proclaims his glory surrounded by bikers and bales of hay as he stands in front of the American flag. Papa Roach exaggerates lower-working-class disenfranchisement by flopping around in the mud with a bunch of carnies at an abandoned fairground, their bodies covered with bruises and open wounds.

But starting with Missy Elliott's "Lose Control," Meyers's work took a turn. Mashing up Southern antebellum slave culture and performance with what looks like a recent mixed-gendered b-ball cheering team "popping and locking" in the desert, the video's meanings seem unbounded and uncertain, yet historically grounded, intimately known, and funky (see figure 11.8). Rihanna's "Where Have You Been" could be seen as an African-bush-savage scenario mashed up with Asian exotic touches, but the images refuse to sit: perhaps simply the performers' movement and gazes, and the ways these claim moments alongside the music, unhinges the stereotypes. Even today, Meyers's work can give the sense that he trolls for stereotypes, but I'll argue that, though this practice might seem problematic, it doesn't always function in predictable ways. These images, in their musical contexts, can create a Brechtian distance. And dated imagery against current music can raise questions: do these memories belong to us, or have they just floated up from the backwaters of society? The images do not mesh with the music but seem rather to hover restlessly above it. These images are not so old or so obviously reprehensible that viewers will have erected a barricade of defenses or rationalizations. Perhaps they still possess some appeal.

Other devices contribute to the star's monumentality. Those background figures who seem like lesser versions of the star help to project the star further forward in the frame. (I'll return to a discussion of extras.) Placing dolls or figurines in the foreground also draws attention to the front, serving to make it the locus of value. The demonstrative enactment of a lyric also contributes to the artist's imposing stature—when Richard Patrick, lead singer of Filter, warbles "I feel like a new born babe" and we see him naked from the chest up in a pool of water, his words carry some authority. The same is true when Pink sings "I'm your operator, let me give you a ring" and she mimes the gestures of a telephone operator, or when she intones, "They'll be kissing my ass," raises a leg, throws out a hip, and points to her butt. The momentary one-to-one syncing of word and picture seems to exaggerate whatever visual material lies in the frame. But if the star seems enormous, his costume also destabilizes his authority. The costumes Meyers uses tend to be inappropriate or incongruous. In "Girls of Summer" Steven Tyler wears black and white pants among bikini-clad bathers.

Figure 11.8 "Lose Control" takes a new turn—the imagery seems both progressive and funky.

Kid Rock wears a fur-lined jacket or a red feather boa in "American Badass," despite its desert setting. One can't preclude the possibility that the stars are a bit daffy.

PROJECTING MUSICAL FEATURES

Meyers's aesthetic of overstatement helps the viewer attend to the moment at hand. This can be a successful way of listening to pop songs, which possess generous amounts of detail. As opposed to Lawrence's emphasis on seamless continuity, Meyers highlights individual visual and musical elements. His way of pulling elements in from the background does not reveal them in greater detail, however: it makes them more schematic. Imagine a soundtrack that contains a series of samples, one after another—a spoken voice, a trumpet melody and a telephone ringing—all placed against a continuous bed of street noise at a low volume. If the screen presents a cityscape, the viewer's attention may tend to wander from the solo voices; however, if this soundtrack were heard against a series of close-ups that were synced to their sources—a mouth speaking, a trumpet's bell, and a telephone receiver—these solo voices will come to the fore. There is a sense of satisfaction when sounds can be matched with objects and vice versa, both on film and in the real world. Music video can also exploit an uncertainty about whether sound or image plays the leading role.[27] Meyers's hyperbolic image offers a shock in these videos, and the viewer tries to find what might match it in the music;[28] sometimes the music forces the image to behave. Almost every music video moment seems to make a claim of "Stop. Look. Pay attention." One way Meyers keeps the viewer within the always-unfolding present is through his attention to a song's rhythm. Meyers encourages his performers to move demonstratively, more broadly than characters in other directors' videos. The ways that these figures throw their arms above their heads and perform knee bends, one wants to award them pickaxes. They really pump it. And often this will be amped up sexually—the dancers' and musicians' hands will also stray near their crotches or across their chests. Any prop can also be used to amplify the beat: a revving wheel of a motorbike, or a spigot turning off, or a fan in Justin Bieber's "Somebody to Love."

The director's camera and editing might initially be described as a bit weighty or stiff. (One of Meyers's favorite edits juxtaposes a fat calf and foot to a shoulder and big head.) However, performers can seem through their movement and placement in the frame to transcend the bluntness of the editing. His performers seem athletic, strong, and fluid. One wouldn't be surprised to see them suddenly turn a somersault, or handstand, or form an elegant line. Meyers also might begin a musical phrase by having the lead musicians make elaborate movements—flicks of the wrist and turns of the neck—while someone in the back of the frame makes different gestures in a kind of counterpoint. And in the extreme background several figures may move differently, and their number and types of movement will shift from shot to shot. Meyers also uses particular techniques to draw attention to the heterogeneity of a pop song's rhythm arrangement. The first half of a musical phrase might be ornate (as in the example just described), and the second half given over to a smother flow of images: a bevy of kids on big-wheeled bikes, or a slow-mo shot of water pouring from a pail. These two contrasting types of visual articulation—busy or drawn out—offer different vantage points. We might first listen more intently to a particular detail, and next we might hear the music as a wash. Such a pattern gives the viewer a feeling of prowess. When the pattern repeats—three or four panning or tracking shots with continuous movement against several sharply edited shots with precise gestures—the viewer has a way to experience a section and to hold onto a visual line against the music.

A similar strategy helps viewers follow phrases. Musical lines—the melody, the bass line, the inner voices—are often described graphically.[29] The shape a melody traces as it rises and falls can relate to movement within the frame. Meyers will take a musical gesture and make a visual representation of it, reduce this visual correlate to its basic elements, and then exaggerate the elements that are there. Meyers's broadly drawn and well-projected visual material can change the way we hear songs. The songs seem louder somehow. They gain a sense of clarity and immediacy. This is one of the ways Meyers's videos give off an intensity. The songs sound as if they had been compressed and pumped through enormous speakers. Near the end Pink suddenly changes from an eager socialite to a wedding-destroyer. The way she swings her cape tells us she has taken vengeance; perhaps its contours suggest our musical knowledge is now complete. As our eyes follow the moving fabric, we trace visual and aural patterns that have become familiar (see figure 11.9).[30]

Meyers further shapes phrases by drawing upon the entire reservoir of editing and postproduction effects. He will pick one or two techniques that seem apt for a particular song—it might be white solar bursts that turn into freeze-frames, as in Britney Spears's "Boyz," or the gentle, deliberate cuts that meld into zooms and dissolves in Jennifer Lopez's "I'm Gonna Be Alright." These atypical edits appear at timbral shifts, near the high points of

Figure 11.9 "Blow Me (One Last Kiss)": the viewer follows and becomes sutured into musical and visual contours.

phrases, or at the start of the song's main hook. What are in their own right highly articulated shots become even more clearly individuated through editing.

MEYERS'S PICARESQUES

Instead of foregrounding a large-scale structure, Meyers tends to work serially, moving from tableau to tableau. It often seems as if the loosest connections are the most pleasurable—a tilt up to the sky so that the camera catches the sun and then back down to earth and a different locale. So too does an instance when the character turns several revolutions, stops, and finds himself in a new costume. These casual joins suggest that viewers should go along for the ride and enjoy the scenery.[31] Music video directors like to say that there is no right setting for a song, but just so many interpretations: 20 directors will draft 20 different treatments of a given song and would go on to produce 20 differently interesting videos. Music is a heterogeneous medium in which many things happen simultaneously. The director's choice of focus reflects a personal way of experiencing the song.[32] Meyers often emphasizes quieter moments between vocal phrases, or sections in which the arrangement thins out. In Meyers's setting, the sparse bridge of Missy Elliott's "Get Ur Freak On" receives the heightened treatment it deserves, for example, as does its out-chorus. The song is produced by Timbaland, who sometimes ends a song with an extra bridge followed by a short section containing new material. While a director who aimed for a unified structure might have difficulty with this new material, Meyers's approach seems particularly suited to Timbaland's. In the final break, all the music is stripped down to the tabla and voice. Meyers's image focuses on a group dance, with the camera continually returning to stamping feet. The image possesses an intensity that's new to the video. Cutaways show Timbaland himself pretending to play the tabla on a woman stretched over his lap. (Even though there is a sexist tradition of equating a woman's body with an instrument, the coziness of their positions somehow creates a sweet image.) When an unfamiliar section follows—a slower tempo, a different vamp, new vocal material—the video shifts direction. Suddenly Missy and her crew are in a toy automobile in front of a hokey rear-screen projection of a night sky. (Earlier we had been in a subterranean grotto.) Their side-to-side rhythmic moves, tauter than before, feel like a culmination, even though the principal connection to the video as a whole is the gesture of spitting.

Meyers has a way of preparing for a change of song-section that departs from Lawrence's. While Lawrence builds gradually from verse to chorus, Meyers prefers simply to arrive. A quick join from verse to chorus will help get us there; the chorus's thicker texture then provides an excuse for a shift of scenery or scale.

Most noteworthy is when a song section foregrounds unusual timbral effects. Meyers finds excellent visual analogues. In the Filter video, a tinny reverberant sound permeates the arrangement and correspondingly the room fills with water; Creed's "One Last Breath" engulfs the star in a dust storm—the storm underscores the noisy feedback of the guitars. Even the design of the set can suggest the chorus's arrangement, as with the arching overhang in Pink's "Get the Party Started." The set design speaks to the more upbeat, fully arranged chorus, where guitar solos peel off from the solo voice's trajectory. Because these music pairs occur simultaneously and carry cultural associations based on iconicity, symbolism, and indexicality, they work to create a mutually reinforcing relationship.

Lawrence and Meyers create large-scale structure in different ways. While Lawrence uses bookends that reaffirm the importance of the video as an integral whole, Meyers works more with each moment as it unfolds, and will allow a subtle detail that appears one-quarter into the video to reappear (often in a slightly different guise) three-quarters in. This strategy plays well against his dense imagery. The question arises whether you can remember what you saw near the beginning.[33] (Note the two skulls in two heavyset women in Outkast's "Bombs over Baghdad"). Unlike Lawrence, who will take a set of materials and develop it throughout a tape, Meyers will bury a single element in the background of the frame and then push it to the foreground three to six shots later. This complements his placement of star, supporting cast, and décor, which are clearly "staged" for the viewer's consumption. The moving forward and back of planes of material within the shot adds complexity to the deployment of block-like sets. Camera work, too, helps to define Meyers's oeuvre. The camera often darts from a wide shot to a close-up and back again—a direct penetration of the space. This complements the dense imagery, the movement in depth within the single image, and the abrupt changes among tableau-like sets as the video unfolds.

A PERSONAL ICONOGRAPHY: PROPS AND PEOPLE AND HOW THEY SIGNIFY

Music video differs from film with respect to themes, visual iconography, types of shot, the use of supporting cast and their assembly, and so on. John Ford claimed that one of the most beautiful cinematic images was running horses. One doesn't find this sort of iconic imagery of movement so much in music video, at least not since the early eighties, but one often sees the performer heading down a long corridor, most often with a tracking camera. Both Lawrence and Meyers exploit the catwalk or the model's runway; perhaps because Meyers's work is more episodic, however, his use of the runway can seem arbitrary, showy, and concerted. The video proclaims, "Now, the tracking shot!" The tracking shot of a moving figure is an essential element of music video for many reasons. Such shots provide relief from a typically shallow sense of space. (We almost never reach the background or stray far from the star.) Camera movement also provides a change in point of view: instead of experiencing the music from a stationary position as it rushes past, the viewer can get the sense of running alongside the sound stream. The tracking shot embodies perfectly music video's attempt to match the energy of the song, to approach the song's rhythmic drive, even if the music remains just out of reach. The tracking shot can also constitute a distinct rhythmic element that will go in and out of synchronization with the song's other rhythmic strata.

In music video, props take on a heightened role. Human figures cannot speak: through editing, their movements become abbreviated and are rendered ambiguous; music seems to force the figure's gestures so that they become like automatons. Props take up some of the slack, taking on a more heightened and lifelike role. Meyers's props possess a vitality and monumentality. His arsenal of favored props—cars, bicycles, underwear, figurines, stuffed toys, meteors, and American flags—tug on Americans' heartstrings, complementing his high-gloss aesthetic; but they also do more. They do musical work. Some succeed because their semiotic charge equals the music's heightened affect.[34] Other props prove effective because images of locomotion reflect music's basic condition of movement.[35] The smoke, fog, wind, and pyro that frequently accompany cars, cloth, meteors, and flags also suggest transience, transition, and flow; these effects mime basic qualities of music.[36] Any prop that recurs throughout a tape helps to create continuity; this visual continuity matches the repetition of musical materials in a song.

Like the props, Meyers's supporting cast serves several functions—musical, cultural, and ideological. Some of his video's pleasures derive from puzzling out what these roles might be. Meyers can play with his charged imagery in part because the functions of his characters cannot be pinned down. A video might contain one or two shots of small children and older people early on, and this will give texture to a world that must be drawn quickly. Children also appear when a politically objectionable event takes place. Here they are a device to reassure the audience: if the content were bad, little kids wouldn't be around. Meyers will also use people for musical functions. As a musical phrase slows down, Meyers will insert a close-up of a silent couple with the woman's face turned toward us.[37] The silent representatives move at a tempo different from that of the frenetic star, and they help to slow down the speed of the imagery so that it matches music that draws toward closure.

REPRESENTATION AND MEYERS'S VIDEOS

Earlier I mentioned the sometimes questionable politics of Meyers's videos. I'd like briefly to examine the way representation works in four of Meyers's videos, looking at both older and more recent work. If one simply considers the content of these videos' images, one might rush to call the videos offensive; the manner of the depiction may make one think differently, however. Meyers's images are so overblown that they could be said to parody or lampoon their subjects. His approach places special weight on the fact that the images fall against music and text; images placed in relation to a song create new meanings.[38] When judging these images, one should note that not all receive equal emphasis. Some images take on greater importance as they occur during peak moments in the music, others because they create a fortuitous simultaneity. We must also reevaluate the performer's role. Music video's characters inhabit a strange world, one that bears some resemblance to reality but that possesses a different phenomenology: a world where sound structures events.[39] The performer is transformed in this environment. Think for example of the magical effect created when a musician grabs a prop and wields it on the beat.[40] Because music video's characters can so gracefully negotiate real and imaginary worlds, they can serve as models to emulate. When considering the political and social consequences of Meyers's work, we should take each video as it unfolds. In a few of the examples below, we'll find that music-image relations suggest retrogressive meanings. Could one redeem even these moments?

Images of gender and power (or ethnicity, sexuality, class, and so on) can be inscribed at any structural level—over the first half of a song, in a single section, measure, or phrase. The first beat can gain authority over the rest of the measure, as in the video for Jay-Z's "Just Want to Love You." At an upscale house party, the rapper and his troop pick up one woman after another and lead them around the house to have sex. Unfortunately all of the closets, bathrooms, and other potential sites are occupied. Sometimes Jay-Z bumps into an old flame and risks trouble. The video begins with some ambiguity concerning who possesses beat one, but soon the female characters start gesturing off the beat, and Jay-Z and the other men demonstratively control it. (They raise their fists or jab their elbows outward on the downbeat.) Even the middle-aged gardener, who wears a phallus-shaped chainsaw on his hips, bounces up and down and gets the first beat. Men control the sexual scenario here.

"American Badass" by Kid Rock is another video with some troublesome imagery. (My students call it "American Jackass.") This video celebrates biker culture, broadly defined. There is motorcycle racing, female mud wrestling, Kid Rock in front of an enormous American flag with bales of hay to either side, or sitting before a television set drinking beer. The video's opening suggests a quasi-progressive moment, but the video seems unable to make good on its implications. Angry prepubescent tomboys dressed like Kid Rock approach him, and he gives them high-fives. Yet these ten- to twelve-year-olds soon disappear, and the only women remaining are Playboy bunnies in bikinis. Although one might not immediately realize it, the video works to suggest that there is nowhere for the deviant girls to go when they grow up—the video provides no imaginative space for them. (*These* girls won't become Playboy models.) A video's final shot can be important for the ways that it provides closure. Porn star Ron Jeremy (a mid-40ish, sweatshirted, overweight, unshaven white male) leers at the camera. He seems to say, "Thank goodness I'm an American male."

But the most disturbing aspects of "American Badass" may arise through local audiovisual relations. The film theorist Andre Bazin pointed out that once sound film was invented, Eisensteinian montage disappeared almost completely from narrative filmmaking.[41] Montage still plays an important role in music video, however. Forming a new concept through Eisensteinian montage creates a frisson in much the way that Meyers's politically objectionable images create a jolt against the music. In "American Badass" a series of match cuts spans a long crescendo that heads toward the chorus. These match cuts move between men pounding on a furry deer carcass, and men wrapped in centerfold women. The argument is clear: women are meat. The crescendo advances inexorably as if the pounding backbeat were underscoring some moment of truth (see figure 11.10).

Other videos present more complicated portraits of race, class, and gender. Outkast's "Bombs over Baghdad" recalls Ernie Kovacs's skits with the "Nairobi Trio." In these bits, chimpanzee dolls played instruments and conked each other on the head. The video for "Bombs over Baghdad" departs from the song's political lyrics. It opens with a low-angle shot of Andre 3000, belly-up with his head dangling over the side of the bed; brilliantly colored posters cover the walls and ceiling. He bolts from the apartment and, like the pied

Figure 11.10 Kid Rock's "American Badass": an example of Meyers's earlier, perhaps less progressive work.

piper, he is followed by a large group of young African Americans. This may constitute a progressive image, since music videos have typically limited images of African Americans en masse to very set confines, like a basketball court, church, or rap show. Reflecting the imagery of the first shot, the environment turns surreal—the grass is tinted purple and the trees are lime green. As in "American Badass," a video that starts out positively may be said to take a different turn. A motorcade leads to a dance hall. On the way are intercut images of African Americans, dancing in monkey masks or posing in ape-like positions, along with monkeys. Outkast's members frolic among stereotypical images of blackness—gospel singers in purple robes, blaxploitation's dancing heroines, even orangutans and chimpanzees. Yet the music seems to serve a recuperative function. The pulse can be heard as either 80 or 160 beats per minute, and the song draws from many sources including gospel, 70s funk, and drum & bass. The rhythmic oscillation as well as the plenitude of musical materials provides ways for a listener to adopt several vantage points on the image. The speed and sound of the rapping work to overcome both the sound and visual tracks. P-Funk wrote densely referential music and appropriated shabby, neglected, and valent imagery to create a new musical-visual universe. Outkast might see themselves as inheritors of this tradition.[42]

Missy Elliott's "One Minute Man" is even more strongly culturally charged. While it is perhaps difficult to assess, it contains progressive possibilities. The video shows the rapper Ludacris rocking a woman in a giant cradle and catching her "drippings" in a pan. Meyers, always one to take advantage of the lyrics, draws upon Ludacris's rap:

> I'm big dog, havin' women seein' stripes and thangs
> They go to sleep, start snorin', countin' sheep and shit
> They so wet, that they body start to leak and shit
> Just cause I'm an ALL-nighter, shoot ALL fire
> Ludacris balance and rotate ALL tires.

"One Minute Man"'s exuberant lyrics and images could be read as celebratory rather than culturally objectionable. The commutation test works here: we take the characters and imagine changing at least one aspect about them such as race, class, gender, sexuality.[43] When we do this, we see that roles are not fixed: almost anyone (of legal age) could substitute for the video's performers and extras. One might appreciate the video's frankness about our need to police bodily functions, and the conflicting desire to both maintain and lose control during sex. Ludacris and the women appear to be given over to the music. When Ludacris raps "I rotate all tires," I hope he includes everyone's.

The reader may find it curious that I have not addressed the question of representation in Lawrence's videos. Lawrence too will use sexualized images of women. (J. Lo's "DJ" and Britney Spears's "I'm a Slave for You" are good examples.) His women, however, are shot within cinematic codes that suggest "high class." They are also grounded and have autonomy within a space; at first glance they therefore appear to possess a greater degree of agency than Meyers's.

How does one begin to make the case for Meyers's valent imagery? Like the cartoonist Robert Crumb, Meyers often complements his imaginative but objectionable world with a humor that deprecates all targets, including the stars and the director himself.[44] Almost all of Meyers's stars are at some point made to look foolish, vulnerable, or too full of themselves. It may just be the baleful gaze Kid Rock gives the camera at one point or an incongruous costume of Steve Tyler's at another. The videos also have moments that address American myths and images that deal with desires left unexpressed. For example, Meyers's stars often seem poised to ascend the ladder to success. Their positions seem precarious, and our validation crucial to them. The extras look like smaller versions of the stars: often placed lower and further back in the frame, these minions lack the means to move up. This is a kind of variation on the American musical's trope of the musician struggling for a big break.[45] While the musical shows a successful end to this struggle, Meyers's work often contains several moments of failure. Filter's "Take a Picture" and Limp Bizkit's "Boiler" show their performers drowning, and falling from a building, respectively. If these images appeared in film, one might expect to hear music that underscored the sense of suspense or alarm. Instead both songs project a gentle melancholy that, together with the images, invokes a new concept: when things have spun out of control, one should relax into one's fate. This refusal to participate in the consumption of material goods or to strive for conventional success is unacceptable in an American culture based on work speedup and competition.

Meyers also gains something from working with valent imagery. A charged image can create emotional excitement that carries over and colors the viewer's experience of subsequent edits and parts of the song. A more purely formal moment—an apt movement within the frame, a new color or texture that syncs with the music—can then carry the viewer further. I find these more formal moments, as they are experienced in a heightened emotional state, scintillating. Perhaps one feels tempted to grant Meyers some latitude surrounding questions of representation not only because one senses how he needs our attention but also because he wants to explore and try things out.[46] One might appreciate Meyers's freedom of invention, the way his imagination works with playful recombination. Sometimes his material may go outside the bounds of good taste, but then we will soon be upon another, hopefully more progressive, moment. Music video is volatile. It is hard to project exactly how the imagery will speak when cut against the music.[47] The loaded imagery does perform work for the viewer. It means that we will care, or at least that we will pay attention. I am not sure I can always stand by the politics of Meyers's videos, but I can see why the director might desire to raise the stakes so those moments of form and movement carry further.

Meyers's work is evolving, and his enthusiasm hasn't ebbed. His recent work reflects greater maturity, and so does his musicians'. The lyrics to Ludacris's "Down Low" foreground his propensity for sexual bravado. But the women are closer to the center of the video and more interested in performing for one another and solidifying their friendships than impressing Ludacris (who sometimes appears as a ghost with a deep blue tint, or with an adult's head grafted onto a child's body). A generosity extends across the tape, and many types of women with different physiques appear. One wonders whether Katy Perry's "Firework" (released a year later), which confronts social ills like the bullying of gay boys and the isolation of heavy adolescent girls, shares a similar impulse. As mentioned earlier, "Raise Your Glass" makes connections between earlier progressive movements and those of today.

Music video's aesthetic is hardly uniform. We can begin to group videos into bodies of work that reflect stylistic trends, much as has been done for cinema—for example, the tensions between realism and the fantastic of Lumière and Méliès, or that of Eisensteinian versus Bazinian space. I have characterized Lawrence and Meyers as having opposing styles; Lawrence, who presents a restrained classicism, can be placed in a humanistic tradition; Meyers's attraction to the scintillating and the local suggests a more Rabelaisian aesthetic.

I have made a claim for the work of a group of directors including Lawrence, Fincher, Ritts, and Romanek; these directors respect large-scale form, work to keep the song transparent, emphasize relations among props and people (though the type of relationship can differ; Fincher focuses on exploring the patriarchal), and trace clear paths across the tape. Dave Meyers's videos, as well as those by directors Philip Atwell, Stephane Sednaoui, and Hype Williams, hold together through a different aesthetic. These directors grasp the ever-changing surfaces of pop songs and focus on a song's momentary pleasures. Music can be heard as heterogeneous, comprised of numerous engaging events that occur simultaneously; as the image attempts to adopt the qualities of music, it may fracture into a thousand elements. At one level music video transforms itself into momentary articulation—differences are erased as the song's melodic hook, a drum hit, an edit, or jab of the elbow comes forward in the mix. In the musical multimedia context, all points become linked to pleasure. Points of connection in music videos resemble these Lacanian *objet petit a's*, tiny desirable moments for which we yearn and which are distributed like a constellation.[48] A pleasurable moment comes upon the viewer, and another, and another.

Music videos shape viewers' experiences of songs in many ways. The image may adopt an attitude toward a song. This attitude shapes our understanding of the song's unfolding. Lawrence cues us to be reflective, while Meyers demands we attend to the present "now"; against an unceasing flow these two positions give us two very different ways to hear songs. Each director tells us which people and places belong to a song, and how this music might be used. Perhaps most tellingly, a music video provides a record of a director's relations to a song. Locating a music video director's style and contribution to the genre proves difficult. A director's style emerges fleetingly in the relations among music, image, and text. Although they can be hard to catch, the traces of a director's engagement with a song are worth finding. They're one of music video's greatest pleasures. As we build a field of study for music video, we might do well to draw on the best parts of author-centered work on film and music—a respectful attentiveness to the work, an interest in style and sociopolitical context, a curiosity about the possibilities and limits of a medium—and leave aside those aspects which are less useful.

CHAPTER 12

A Music Video Canon?

Music video's reckoning seems due. Though we may not want to link its history to MTV's—depending on your predilection, you might tie Queen's "Bohemian Rhapsody" or the Scopitones to the genre's inception, and music videos have long since left MTV behind—nevertheless, in the media swirl, most of us experienced it as middle-aged. (Our parents or children watch(ed) music video.) Music video has so deeply permeated our culture it sometimes seems to be driving it: we see it in films like *The Bourne Ultimatum, Eternal Sunshine of the Spotless Mind, Hot Fuzz*, and *Moulin Rouge*; movie trailers like *Miami Vice* and *Summer of Sam*; iPod and Nike commercials; grunge and hip-hop fashion; and the "plunder phonics" of composer John Oswald and contemporary hip-hop production practices.

Nickelodeon's aim of "preserving our television heritage" aside, there are no stable archives for music video. YouTube and the MTV organization are often not responsive to inquiries from scholars. Music video history remains uncharted, even though we may feel we know video styles and our access to videos have waxed and waned: the academic literature is thin.[1] Things might be looking up, however. Music videos are making a strong showing again, as web users log time watching pixilated YouTube links while instant messaging or surreptitiously viewing them on PDAs in the classroom or at work. On streaming video sites, access to videos is greater than ever, though many of the clips are ephemeral and not downloadable.[2] If we seek more permanent objects, iTunes carries some music videos and there is always peer-to-peer file sharing, but image and audio quality rarely rises above that of MP3s.

A few megastars, including Michael Jackson and Madonna, have released music video compilation reels, but these have sold poorly and provide few aesthetic pleasures. Between 2002 and 2005, Palm Pictures assembled a "best of" series structured around the work of nine music video directors. While acknowledging the difficulty of selecting such a small set from MTV's 30-year history, I think it remains the best on music video. In this chapter, I'll analyze the work of these directors. (The music video collection stands as the most influential on DVD; many younger music video directors grew up with these as their primary source material.[3]) Regardless of the Palm series' importance, I still quarrel with Palm's choices. The company packaged four white male directors in its first box set, a single DVD of an African American male director as a second release, and most recently released another box set featuring four more white male directors. The collection, working primarily in white genres and motivated by high-art and feature film aspirations, leaves out a vast array of talent, most glaringly women and members of traditionally underrepresented groups, including Floria Sigismondi, Sophie Muller, and Paul Hunter. Even the choice of European American directors can be questioned: you wonder whether Palm will release collections by seminal directors such as David Fincher, Marcus Nispel, Matt Mahurin, Mark Pellington, Dave Meyers, Francis Lawrence, and Herb Ritts.

Nevertheless, the Palm collections provide satisfactions in ways that musicians' greatest hits albums don't, which suggests that visual style may carry as much weight as music or performance. The series is pricey at $179, but university libraries may be willing to foot the bill; individual DVDs range from $16 to $22. From a teaching standpoint, the series works wonderfully for courses in popular music, multimedia, film studies, and popular culture. Individual discs, however, are uneven. Some are lovingly produced with extensive materials; others appear slapped together. Mark Romanek's richly chronicled DVD contains 25 music videos that can be played in a variety of ways: solo, with the director's voiceover, or with one band member or another talking about the clip. The release also contains a 30-minute documentary, a "Making of the Video"; a "Romanekarian" Festschrift; and a 56-page photo flip book. By contrast, Chris Cunningham and Jonathan Glazer's DVDs contain eight music videos each and Glazer's offers almost no directorial presence. Romanek's DVD tells us several times that photographer/performance artist Erwin Wurm was thrilled that the director drew upon his artwork for inspiration. Yet in the repetition it's possible to pick up on interesting threads. So many of his musicians talk about "trust" that one might begin to suspect that Romanek fed his clients this word for Svengalian effect: here it sounds like a demand for directorial control.

Although the Palm collection does not provide an accurate representation of music video's range, style, or history, it teaches us a bit about how music videos are made as well as how power and control can shift as band members and directors conspire against the record company commissioner or vice versa. All of the DVDs feature beautiful videos, thus assuring an aesthetically stimulating experience. More strikingly, they enhance our sensitivity to music video directors as auteurs: we intuit that music video constitutes a significant realm for directors to develop style and technique and to discover a means to communicate ways of experiencing music. Directorial styles diverge because there are no film schools for making music video, no industry internship programs, nor anything like the cultural practices for learning music. Music video directors have diverse backgrounds—in dance, commercials, art photography, drawing, and sculpture—and each brings his or her training to image and music, adapting to the needs at hand. In the remainder of this essay, I will focus on this question of the music video director as auteur, drawing out some differences among the work of the Palm's eight directors.

Mark Romanek

If I were an up-and-coming music video director, Romanek's videos would serve as my model. The work is handsome and meticulously rendered, and even when the director tries to transcend his own style—for example, his homage to crime photographer Weegee in the Keith Richards "Wicked Lies" video—everything feels set in place. The power of Romanek's videos is opaque, especially because his personal voice seems nearly invisible under an ironclad technique. Details revealed in the DVD's documentary suggest that sheer labor contributes to the realization of his style. A glimpse into the background of spaces reveals elaborate preparatory sketches and models. His shoots as well as his pre- and post-production processes are also more exhaustive than standard industry practice. The shoot for Jay-Z's "99 Problems" consumed twelve days, produced twelve hours of footage, required four editors, and drew on the industry's best. Romanek pushes hard for what he wants, as do his clients; Jay-Z muses about hoofing it for what felt like hundreds of miles. For the video "Hellagood," Gwen Stefani describes catching a camera midair on its downward plunge into the ocean. Although Romanek's performers recall the wearying intensity of the shoots, they seem exceptionally grateful once their work appears on the screen.

Romanek's training is first-rate. He attended Chicago's New Trier High School, one of the best public schools in the country, and then went on to Ithaca Film School, gaining exposure to Brakhage, Warhol, and Kubrick. Like most music video directors, he is steeped in visual references, and his conversation is littered with references to high art and popular culture, from Tati, Godard, Warhol, and Wurm to Mary Poppins. I've heard other music video directors grouse that Romanek simply creates collages from tear sheets (images pulled from photo books and magazines), but these comments may reveal insider policing and peer competitiveness. Some viewers may be put off by Romanek's agonistic relationship to famous painters, sculptors, and photographers. Others may feel his level of control is antithetical to pop music. I believe the work succeeds because Romanek treats each visual and musical parameter individually and analytically.

At first glance Romanek's tactics fit standard practices. The visuals carry a semiotic wallop built to match the song's intensity. We see titillating imagery of phallic power: Linkin Park sprays water at the crowd as if it were ejaculate, Jay-Z's jacket trim resembles male briefs (to trigger anxiety about African American male sexuality?), and Fiona Apple's "Criminal" carries more than a whiff of kiddie porn. Other arresting images—Lenny Kravitz as Christ, Mick Jagger as the devil—also capture our attention. Perhaps to elicit a kinesthetic response in the viewer's body, the characters perch precariously, leap from great heights, float, or fly.[4] One trademark of Romanek's style involves holding figures in tableaux before they suddenly move to the music in showy, beautifully shaped gestures: the businessmen rising and falling from a seated position into a body wave in David Bowie's "Jump They Say"; slow-motion whirling dervishes in Madonna's "Bedtime Stories"; and Trent Reznor twirling in midair as if he were shawarma on a spit in "Closer." But what distinguishes Romanek's work is that these effects are so well integrated into the texture that they do not separate out as discrete elements.

Let's look more closely at how Romanek approaches visual parameters in service of the whole, as in his use of settings. Romanek's environments somehow suggest both the miniature and the enormous. The texture, shape, and volume of these places and their objects can imply or represent sonic properties. Imagery eliciting aural associations include resonators, such as an imposing obelisk or a microphone shaped like a breast; reflective surfaces, including curved wooden walls or spongy, protruding materials; and visual movement evoking the processual nature of sound, whether banks of lights or rushing water. His spaces—and the textures and placement of his objects within them—seem specially molded to the songs. If the sets and props were to be schematized down to CAD gridded skeins and placed against a list of songs, they could be easily matched. One feels space in Romanek's videos: a viewer's eyes seek out the set's corners and edges and quilts them to the song's features.

One such example is Romanek and Janet Jackson's "Got 'til It's Gone," a video depicting black club culture in 60s South Africa. The video's dancehall is beige and narrow. To one side a window joins its twin—a similarly long blue-tinged room; murals gird both rooms' walls, or people wearing boldly patterned earthtones line up in tiers along them. These embellishments alongside an underlying structure—tiered people, murals, and duplicated rooms—complicate the video's sense of space, evoking the aforementioned monumentality and miniaturization. "Got 'til It's Gone"'s bass and acoustic guitar, shaped into lilting, wavelike gestures that seem to roll out into a more shallow, nonrever-berant sonic and visual field, seem to match the song's space, its textures and colors. By contrast, in Lenny Kravitz's "Are You Gonna Go Way" heavy guitar riffs fit a space suggestive of an upwardly twisting vortex. Madonna's "Bedtime Stories" unrolls one tableau after another, which matches the pedal-point. Trent Reznor's "Closer" occurs within a tiny room that opens out into several cubbyholes. Such a space could be said to reflect the song's cell-like construc-tion: like the replicated set of small spaces, the song's riffs don't vary much.

Romanek has many techniques for using the body to musical ends. Hand gestures—fluttering fingers, punching fists, curling wrists—reflect a song's features. Think of the way Jay-Z slaps at the camera in "99 Problems," which fits the song's frontality. Madonna's upward-turning hands in "Bedtime Stories" speak to her quasi–Middle Eastern vocal ornaments. Similar anal-ogies can be drawn for Romanek's choreography of glances and stares.

The videos also exploit the expressive potential of the screen's edges in rela-tion to the body. Characters look upward, float or leap, or water or light pours down upon them from some unseen source. Likewise a foot steps into clay or a dead man's legs jut out from behind a low embankment. Is Romanek simply speaking about a song's ambitus or expressing hope for grace or a sense of the body's fragility? Here's one of music video's simplest means to develop a sense of drama—emotional weight accrues through the placement of people and objects within space.

Romanek loves lines and curves. (One almost imagines him sketching his videos with an architect's tools.) Note the opening shot of "Rain," with its re-iterating swoops and planes. (Romanek's interest in a precise line places his affinities closer to Ingres than Titian.) Most striking is when shapes expand and develop between shots or across sections of the video. In "Bedtime Stories" the opening circles—the platter and lights upon which Madonna lies—morph later into whirling dervishes. In "Scream" a single forked hall resembling a model's runway extends into a series of richly ornamented, paired ramps. Bodies placed within these evolving graphic designs echo and underline these shapes. Romanek turns and rotates Madonna's body and her gestures as they gradually shift from closed to open in "Bedtime Stories." Music videos' attenuated narrativity makes the exhibition of the body a pri-mary dramatic device. The movement of the body from closed to open becomes a valued technique.

Romanek's characters exhibit a heightened relation to their environments: the performers seem curious, sometimes on edge, about the places they find themselves in. Of all music video directors, only Romanek evokes a palpable sense of history in his clips. Characters seem to possess uncanny knowledge about places. Does this lie in a glance or posture, or in the characters' use of props? Or is it that the performer's grasp of her enveloping, enigmatic spaces surpasses the viewer's?

Romanek claims he tries to invest his characters with a secret, or a sense of mystery. (One recalls director Jacques Tourneur's whispering in his actors' ears; Romanek and his performers develop dense backstories before shoots begin.) Music, the image, and characters seem to engage in a private conversation.[5] But this opacity sometimes breaks: a viewer shuttles too quickly between a distanced gaze and flashes of intimacy to be grasped.

Romanek's sequences can seem even more charged when they deal with cultural flashpoints. In "Got 'til It's Gone" Romanek draws on a bevy of loaded images tied to race and myth. Imagining the video differently along parameters like race, sexuality, gender, or class would reveal how much the piece is culturally freighted. The video lacks sense when imaginatively staged as middle-class and white. A cigarette lighter flicks by a man's groin. A young child peeks behind a man as if he had been magically birthed. A one-eyed boxer poses. A couple presses up as if simulating rear-entry sex; children jump on mattresses and one is lifted as if by baptismal fire. Jackson's shadow crawls up a wall like a stalking animal. And a lone figure walks outside. Though intimated rather than placed in direct address, a viewer's situatedness in relation to race is also raised: for example, at a few points blacks and whites study one another through a stereopticon. Besides eliciting a heightened response from the viewer, "Got 'til It's Gone"'s imagery reveals a respectful gaze; however exoticizing, the directorial response vaguely acknowledges Africa as a touchstone. (Is this politically progressive?) Despite the video's loaded imagery, its mood and tone are overwhelmingly warm (as Jackson says on the DVD commentary). The song suggests a swaying motion and a restful pause performed in comforting repetition. It draws attention to Jackson's and Joni Mitchell's vocal similarities (as if Mitchell's voice were a sped up version of Jackson's; Mitchell's is more bird-like). Q-Tip's rapping is friendly and mellow. Music video can hold a number of contradictory threads without any needing to be brought to terms with the others. Even with flat representations the video's generous tone can arguably be called progressive.[6]

How Romanek achieves such coordinated effects remains mysterious. Perhaps it's because in Romanek's work, every moment is photographic. Some video directors burrow their way through songs, responding moment by moment; others, like Romanek, etch a form whose outline becomes increasingly perceptible as the video unfolds. Perhaps two techniques support Romanek's ability to connect the micro and the macro. On the micro-level, Romanek repeats and transforms visual motifs that speak to the variation of musical materials. In music, motives can resurface in new ways, with transactions occurring in the interim becoming mysterious. In music video, much like with musical motives, a series of images, separated in time, can seem well proportioned and linked together: both music and image can be similar to a series of ripples created by a stone skipping off the surface of the water. If a varied image reappears, we can be encouraged to think it has undergone some change in its absence; perhaps the music has somehow changed the nature of this image. In Nine Inch Nails' "Closer," elaborate chains of iconic connections force a consideration of the links among music and images: the black "doorman" blows dust off his hat—perhaps a reaction to something that caused the film to melt earlier; the juror's eye echoes a paper eye pasted on the arm of a metronome (à la Man Ray), and these eyes rhyme with the image of Trent Reznor's eye popping open in a still-life tableau; the salamanders hatching from eggs grow into eels that seem to stand in for the singer's genitalia while he hangs from the ceiling bound and gagged; the eviscerated heart nailed to a chair in the opening shot suggests the monkey stretched out on a surface (possibly for vivisection) and the medical drawings of arms with tendons splayed out; Reznor's microphone looks like a breast with a nipple, and his tongue seems phallic. This string of imagery culminates in the image of the doorman holding a cow's tongue in one hand.

Yet, while the viewer can close in, she can also adopt a bird's-eye view. It may help that Romanek's videos tend to hold together through single visual schemes. In "Closer" a hand-cranked Bolex produces jittery, damaged footage using a restrained palette of browns with dabs of blood reds. A bodycam strapped to the performers and luridly colored five-and-dime materials produce wildly different effects in Mick Jagger's "God Gave Me Everything."

Romanek's techniques—finding relations between lyrics and image, tuning the color scheme, using evocative gestures, spaces, and props—all work in concert to illuminate the song's formal features. This makes his videos particularly effective in the classroom. His work highlights the ways that music video's musicality differs from that of genres like Hollywood narrative film, commercials, or the American musical.

Michel Gondry

Of all the Palm directors, Michel Gondry is the wunderkind with the largest cultural cachet. Directing Hollywood films confers greater status than making music videos, and Gondry's Human Nature, Eternal Sunshine of a Spotless Mind, Dave Chappelle's Block Party, and The Science of Sleep possess the widest reach and most coveted audiences. Gondry's films and music videos shimmer between conflicting impulses. On the one hand, Gondry's work is the antithesis of Romanek's. It comes out of an exceedingly personal iconography, often linked to childhood or dreams, and constructed from the handmade: Gondry relies on materials like cardboard cutouts, Lego blocks, television noise, puppets, dolls, tinfoil, and so on. On the other hand, he possesses a mathematical mind, and integrates visual canons, palindromes, and complex graphic schema. With his background in experimental film and animation, Gondry prizes hands-on control. He also adapts mickey-mouse techniques to produce interesting effects like interweaving multiple strands of imagery, or subtly offsetting one or more of these lines to create a contrapuntal effect. If Romanek's aesthetic is Mozartian, Gondry's would be Baroque. As Gondry says on the DVD, "I saw Romanek's work and decided I had to go in a completely different direction."

Gondry aims to create a sense of enchantment: much like Romanek's the work produces dreamlike effects. He achieves this through fetishistic instances.[7] Since the edges of Gondry's *art brut* materials are meant to show, the viewer often experiences a rugged ride before suddenly things fall into place and a moment provokes a powerful emotional response. Rough-hewn details are there for the attentive viewer, like the spacemen poised to start booking in Daft Punk's "Around the World"; the hot dog truck's first entrance in "Star Guitar"; Dave Grohl's teeth gnashing while he lies in bed, and his subsequent, bored expression, at the close of the Foo Fighters' "Everlong." Respecting how a song's materials work, Gondry's visual elements repeat and vary. The crooked, L-shaped hands and arms of the bathing beauties are echoed by the jagged outlines of the two-headed puppets and the notched stairsteps in "Around the World." In "Everlong" legs morph into logs, and water streaming in the foreground (as if down a glass pane) links with a lake's rippled reflections.

The Foo Fighters' "Everlong" is a good case study of the ways visual analogues can match musical features and a dreamscape can be evoked. Hoodlums inexplicably chase singer Dave Grohl and his girlfriend (played by a fellow male band member in drag) out of a twentysomething apartment party into a *Texas Chainsaw Massacre* scenario. "Everlong" contains a thick strand of guitar within a narrow ambitus. The voice runs up and down, but fails to break the guitar's registral boundaries. Correspondingly, ceilings are low, exits barred, spaces are small, and the characters seem oppressed. The guitar riffs sound inexorable: no matter the effort expended, the song keeps finding itself back at that three-chord riff. The video presents powerful moments of audiovisual connection, such as a guitar riff accompanied by gnashing of teeth, hands swelling to baseball-bat size, legs morphing into logs, Grohl pushing a room-sized phone receiver, and band members emerging from their hooligan costumes. Gondry's camera is consistently piercing and driven; as in nightmares we encounter and move past fraught moments. We become caught in the dreamwork.[8]

Gondry develops texture in a variety of ways. A whiff of death keeps Gondry's homemade aesthetic from becoming too coy or sickly sweet. Skeletons appear in multiple guises. In "Hyper Ballad" Björk's head resembles a death mask; the light bulb nestled in her eye-socket illuminates her skull. A mix of the high-tech and handmade also creates density: the Chemical Brothers' "Star Guitar" has multiplying buildings and landscapes that might resemble the replicating effects produced with CGI, but a passing hot-dog truck makes it all seem unheimlich. Sometimes, as in Massive Attack's "Protection," Gondry's iconography becomes inscrutable. Here, we peer through cubbyhole-type apartment windows à la Hitchcock's *Rear Window* and see characters floating among 1950s and 60s bric-a-brac while they play cards, throw balls, and so on. It feels like watching an obtuse art video on a tiny screen at MoMA.

The most beautifully packaged of the Palm set, Gondry's DVD contains punch-through menus that look like pots of paint or colored pencils in a tray. On one menu Gondry plays a drum set, and children's heads wedged inside the tom-toms pop up and squeak: pressing a button takes you to another menu and stops the abuse. This show reel becomes a personal journey from childhood to adulthood, and perhaps back, as family members become momentary focal points, including Gondry's mother (who suffers from senility); Gondry's father (chronicled as a young musician in Super 8 film footage); Gondry's nine-year-old son, whose script is included; Gondry's girlfriend, who streaks in front of the camera while Gondry sits on the couch; and even Gondry's grandfather (through his landscape painting in the style of Cezanne). Seemingly every animation Gondry has made since age six has been included. Unlike Romanek's magisterial work, which makes you want to throw in the towel, Gondry's may encourage projects of self-discovery and autobiography.

Hype Williams

Hype Williams is one of the most prolific music video directors, releasing 189 videos to date. Industry insiders confide that at certain high points in his career—such as when he held four of the top ten videos—Williams would demand 15 percent rather than the industry standard 10 percent off the top of the video's total budget. Considering he lacks the art school training of his colleagues—his inspirations come from everyday materials like Eddie Murphy's *Coming to America* and Brian DePalma's *Scarface*—and did not grow up with a privileged background, such self-promotion can be seen as charming. Nor was his entrance into the industry a bed of roses: Williams painted graffiti for a TLC video, but the first show-reel so upset the producer that the videos were trashed and Williams got cursed out. Still, if Palm is footing the bill for these

DVDs, it is troubling that Williams did not receive the kind of red-carpet treatment bestowed on Romanek and Gondry, since the 10 music videos on the Williams DVD in no way reflect the range and power of his enormous output.

Williams, who sometimes goes simply by "Hype," was one of the first to secure sizable budgets for hip-hop videos and became one of the first renowned African American directors. Williams's most striking work tends to be for women artists, although it remains unclear from the DVD commentary whether Williams establishes better rapport with women or whether hip-hop provides greater latitude for depictions of female performers. Many landmark videos featuring female artists have been left out of the collection. Missy Elliott's "The Rain (Supa Dupa Fly)" has received the greatest critical acclaim, but it's not packaged here. Likewise, I love his stripped-down video for Taral Hicks's cover of Deniece Williams's "Silly." It contains his typically strong cameos—the singer in the foreground against a white cyclorama—yet what draws me in are shirtless men in the back. Neither does this DVD include Aaliyah's "Rock the Boat," which may not be novel but is one of the most sensual, free-flowing, Busby Berkeleyesque videos ever made. Instead, we have Hype's other legacy, T&A, which shows women's breasts and buttocks swelling up as enormous obstacles slightly above eye level. (One might acknowledge, though, that he has also done what could be considered progressive work with faces.) As part of his DVD commentary, which is often terse and enigmatic, Williams calls the T&A videos fun. Even with these drawbacks and omissions, the Williams DVD contains many strong pieces. The Wu-Tang Clan's "Can It Be All So Simple" reflects a very different image of black urban life from that of Romanek's "99 Problems" or Spike Jonze's video for The Notorious B.I.G.'s "Sky's the Limit."

If we consider the Palm DVD collection in relation to Williams's large oeuvre we can begin to locate his style.[9] His performers' expressions are inviting, relaxed, and legible. The figures have a comic-book monumentality, as if they'd been blown up by 15 percent. Does Williams's interest in concave and convex space contribute to this larger-than-life presence? Does camera placement and movement also help to inflate the performers? Dollies, tracks, pans, arcs, and trucks (most frequently low-angle) trace rudimentary shapes, aptly showcasing melodic contours; the camera movement against the music produces a gridding of audiovisual space, subtly "apotheosizing" the performer even as she projects an intimate charisma. Let's take a few examples: Dr. Dre's "California Love" contains a geodesic dome with a camera continually dollying around it. TLC's "No Scrubs" takes place in a horizontal tube–like environment and the camera trucks left and right but rarely presses in. There are musical corollaries here: We circle around in "California Love" because of the looping of the main hook and Roger Troutman's bird-like vocoder, which suggests circling flight.

The camera in "No Scrubs" stays at a distance because the "no" keeps us at bay. Busta Rhymes's "Woo Ha," on the other hand, repeatedly tracks in and out to highlight the song's insistent six-note rhythmic figure. Viewed silently, the stripped-down elegance of Williams's camera movement comes to the fore, along with the way a song's hook or turn toward the chorus is underscored with a somewhat different gesture. Edits come slightly off the beat, adding a bit of friction. In "No Scrubs" we sense the negative space around the sci-fi female rappers: close-up they seem godlike, but at a distance, they're like dolls.

Besides the mostly rounded spaces, Williams's colors are broadly painted primaries or pastels—shades culturally linked with women and children. Smooth and shiny surfaces bring the color to the fore. This telescoping also shows off a performer, giving them additional monumentality. As with most music video directors, Williams uses loaded imagery. His trademark is short, two- to three-shot vignettes carrying an aura of incompleteness, and high-lighting shared anxieties relating to class, sexuality, race, or gender. (Note, in LL Cool J's "Doin' It," the shots surrounding a peepshow, as well as a woman slithering on a rug.) Most strikingly Williams is sensitive to the fact that music disseminates, flows outward, and seems ever-generative (as Chion has noted as well). Images of plenitude suggest hope as well as abundance. Most signifi-cant, directors eventually become aware of their signature tropes and work to capitalize on them. Williams's early videos contain fountains or fireworks. In "Can't Tell Me Nothing," for Kanye West, Williams traces diamond-shaped, laser-like patterns across twenty edits, culminating with the diamond pin-pointed and centered within a close-up of West's ear. Rounded shapes at the beginning and end initiate this pattern.

Williams's DVD interview suggests he aims to create a different sort of working relationship with actors, one that emphasizes a sense of family and community (although he can start to sound like the Godfather). The intimacy and relaxed poise of the performers derives most likely from this collaboration.

Spike Jonze

Before directing music videos, Spike Jonze was a skateboarder and surfer who made sports documentaries. His work continues to focus on physicality and social roles. Jonze's videos incorporate gymnastics and dance competitions, as well as other demonstrations of physical prowess: performers on fire, running down streets, or delivering lyrics in reverse as they hop backward through city streets. Yet it's the opposite of Leni Riefenstahl's *Olympia*: here beauty is to be found in the body's awkwardness. Jonze depicts a wide range of movement— gawky, graceful, aggressive, vulnerable—all suggested quickly through the performer's body while the shots fall more leisurely against the music. Athleticism so permeates Jonze's ways of depicting musical experience that it becomes a part of the camera's role: the camera hugs the sidewalk like a skateboarder, or rushes forward and does a 360 as if riding a wave. Growing up as the son of a Spiegel catalog mogul, Jonze may have found conventional social roles a little strange. From his video for Fatboy Slim's "Praise You," featuring the "Torrance Community Dance Troupe," to his remake of *Happy Days* for Weezer, Jonze acts like an anthropologist in the field. Like Gondry's, his style deliberately reflects sandbox aesthetics. Jonze likes working-class uniforms as well as funny-looking trucks.

The Palm DVD collection reveals something about Jonze's relation to music. His videos often begin with a simple conceit: it might be a television sitcom trailer, or someone dressed up in a giant dog suit with a broken leg and a boombox walking around LA. These witty one-offs are charming. The mechanism is set to go, and then two-thirds into the piece there's an interesting turn. Since pop songs tend to possess a lyric rather than teleological structure (choruses, verses, and bridges), we wonder if Jonze picks up an underlying narrative curve already present in the music, or if we have the tendency to tie narrative patterns of conflict and resolution to everything we watch. One of his best videos, the Beastie Boys' "Sabotage," pays homage to the title sequence of *Kojak* as a game of role-playing and dress-up, as the band members excitedly jump across buildings and kick down doors. Another memorable effort, Fatboy Slim's "Weapon of Choice," features Christopher Walken in an empty corporate hotel as an aging Fred Astaire dancing to the music while lip-syncing to bassist Bootsy Collins's processed voice. As in many music videos, there's a suggestion that the performer has been overcome by outside forces—film, in the act of viewing, or music, in the act of listening? —and that his status has become uncertain. Is Walken a weapon of choice? What powers does he have?

Jonze's mysterious aporias stem partly from a reterritorialization of space.[10] After Jonze has set the street, the film theater entrance, and the hotel lobby to music, they suggest potentials for new use. (Who wouldn't want to prance, somersault, stalk, and fly through corporate hotels, lobbies, and escalators?) In Jonze's videos songs re-encode the ways spaces feel and bodies move. The director seems charmed as well by the strangeness of animation. What gets Christopher Walken moving or a mailbox dancing? His music videos intimate new modes of cause and effect, in which sound might be an agent.

A closer look at Björk's "Oh So Quiet" and the Beastie Boys' "Sabotage" reveals how these elements come into play. "Oh So Quiet" sets the Hollywood musical in working-class, suburban LA, within an auto parts store and outdoors in the street. The video poses questions about the nature of the musical—its format, artifice, history—as well as the musical's relation to music

video. One wonders whether the *joie de vivre* of big-band jazz derives from particular musical elements—the horn stings, the swing rhythms, the thickness
of the voicing. How much of the music's urbanity and sexual sophistication
still pertains to us? And are there gestures that would seem to work only with
this music? In Björk's remake, Jonze's dancers clump and jut out their arms and
legs, skirts and umbrellas twirling. Cunningham, Gondry, and Jonze all reference Busby Berkeley's overhead dance formations. (What in this imagery
might directors find that suits today's pop music? Of all the Hollywood musical's features, why this?) Jonze binds images to sections of music. Against shots
of Björk peeking through tires are juxtaposed the camera's swish-pans across
tires stacked horizontally in rows: the cross-cutting between this material
pulls us out of the verse and into the chorus. The chorus's enormous big-band
sounds produce streetside, explosive, giddy, collective activity, as well as overhead and crane shots. Can we find a progressive political sentiment here, or
only nostalgia? The song sections tied to slowed-down visuals of Björk walking,
as she sings to and embraces herself, present a different rhetoric, as if raising
questions about the difference between then and now—who also does Björk
sing to, and how should we respond as viewers?[11]

"Sabotage" breaks all moving elements—the camera, characters, and
objects—into two groups: those that defy gravity, and those that dart in and
freeze. These two groups of movement match corresponding musical features.
The fast yet sludgy guitar's pulse alongside the rapping conjoin with the leaping
elements, while dotted rhythms of the snare drum connect with visual elements that seek-and-hold. The video creates an impressive gestural specificity.
People don't just walk—they have a lilt to their step. Cars wing over hills. The
actors take the stairs with splayed feet; and then we lurch (the press-in-and-
hold). One notes also the ways gestures become incrementally grander as the
video unfolds: toward the end a body is hurled off a bridge and takes a long,
slow-mo dive; a camera swoops in on a split screen, zeroing in on a duct-taped
man's face and a time-bomb. Spike Jonze's paths through audiovisual relations
can sometimes lead to dangerous ends.

Chris Cunningham

Of the Palm DVD directors, Chris Cunningham projects the greatest faith in
music's powers to alter our experience and modify the material world. Aphex
Twin's "Come To Daddy" intimates that sound generates the birth of a giant
mutant who, through its screams' air blasts, nearly topples an elderly woman.
Is it a surge of electricity or of sound that fires up the video's abandoned TV
sets? Chris Cunningham's videos work by encouraging us to inhabit on-screen

bodies who possess something strange. As viewers we may bind to the musculature or mechanical structure of the figure and feel different. In "Frozen," Madonna appears in a black satin kabuki/Victorian dress and hovers in a dark sky over desert flats. Portishead's "Only You" possesses characters who float in a kind of ether between ominous, run-down buildings. Björk's "All Is Full of Love" shows two cyborgs making out. In Aphex Twin's "Windowlicker," nubile, mostly African American bikinied female bodies carry prosthetic heads or the head of the lead singer, who is not what they are: with his fatuous grin, he resembles a somewhat maniacal, slovenly European American male.

Cunningham's videos exploit a principle once observed by film composer Bernard Herrmann—film music can seek out objects and animate them. Cunningham's videos give us opportunities to reorient our bodies: testing a different tautness, a different throw. Some of his most graceful visual analogies for musical materials relate to speed and tempo. The techno-trance in "Frozen" conjoins with Madonna's suspended equipoise in the night sky, her black robes billowing out. The slow pulse of Portishead's "Only You" is stitched to people drifting underwater, while the song's fast turnarounds and record-scratching links the characters' suddenly jittery movements. In Aphex Twin's "Windowlicker" the track's punctuating attacks attach to the visual's single flash-frames. Each Palm director has a specific way of experiencing the body. Jonze's figures aim for an athletic, quirky individualism. Romanek's characters perform all kinds of activities but they almost never dance.[12] Cunningham prefers keeping figures still or having them move slowly against the music; the music streams past them or seems to flow through their bodies. Cunningham seeks a focused stillness. But Cunningham's sometimes robotic chilliness can be balanced by beauty and grace: it is the microrhythms, as Michel Chion has called them, local changes in light, water, and wind as they respond to musical changes, that define Cunningham's style.[13] In the Portishead video (shot underwater with the air bubbles excised so that we do not know where we are), hair floats like anemones; in "All Is Full of Love" sparks fly and water drips sensuously against white metal.

Without the hope of a narrative, music video directors create drama through a more limited repertoire. Cunningham suggests a sense of threat through the fracture, transformation, or faulty workings of machines and bodies. In "Frozen" ominous Dobermans and crows survey the landscape, overshadowing the human; in Björk's "All Is Full of Love" machines risk replication, repair, and failure; in Afrika Bambaataa's "Afrika Shox" body parts fall off; in Squarepusher's "Come on My Selector" limbs morph into animal appendages.

There is something disquieting about Cunningham's work—pretty, but it leaves an aftertaste. Is it that he works with taboo subject positions, or does he possess a subtle mean streak? "Windowlicker" may encourage the viewer to wonder whether music videos run mainly on images of pleasure, most readily achieved through bounteous flesh. But when pleasure is disrupted, how do we respond? The image is carefully titrated to elicit a balanced proportion between engagement and repulsion: the youthful bodies pull us in, and the grotesqueries keep us at bay. Nicholas Cook points out that music-image relations are volatile; when music and image are put together, a new, unpredictable product emerges.[14] "Windowlicker" sounds slower and prettier in the video than on its own. The video's phantasmagorical, hybridized, ambiguously raced and gendered bodies might work on the viewer like a first encounter with Godzilla on film: the gorgeous cry in tandem with the mammoth body makes us wonder, "Is this monster threatening, lovable, or of this world?" Perhaps music video is most interesting when the image offers cultural associations and affective responses different from those we associate with the music, and the viewer is asked to resolve this cultural disconnect. Can we learn to love "Windowlicker"? I can. But I need to work at it.

In some moods we may feel that music videos are not art, but commercials, or that they damage the listener's ability to forge a relationship with a song. The supplementary materials included with the Palm DVDs reveal that the directors themselves think of and experience music video as art. Even if they disrupt some sort of private listening experience, music videos also give us something: they teach us about a song. As an encapsulation of music video, Palm's contribution is only a first step. But it does provide us with a larger body of work to share and talk about.

Afterword

ACCELERATED AESTHETICS

A NEW LEXICON OF TIME, SPACE, AND RHYTHM

It can feel delirious trying to be open to everything—YouTube, cinema, music video, television, video games—wishing to know and take it all in. It's an absurd desire, of course, as media content proliferates exponentially. Across the globe populations are participating as producers, and vast quantities of historical content are being rediscovered and uploaded, every moment. The mediascape starts to resemble a world, and to see it all might be a kind of overwhelming sublime. Such a stance has rewards—it means nothing less than the dream of being interested in almost everything.

But for this chapter we might resist the lure of ubiquity and adopt a more restricted perspective: for the first time we have seemingly unlimited access to an array of digitally enhanced media that present new configurations of time and space. With our smart devices we can conjure up these media instantly, anywhere, often jarringly, with one clip up against another. We also access these heightened segments through home and work computers, or as brief moments embedded in feature films, video games, television shows, and trailers: we may become facile and fleet as we shift attention from one experiential mode to another. Now, I can't say there's an exact homology, or determine cause-and-effect relations, but I'd like to note that at the same time as we have digitally enhanced, aesthetically accelerated media, our work and leisure has become infiltrated by global financial and work flows that themselves are digitally enabled.

In other words, contemporary digital media present forms of space, time, and rhythm we haven't seen before, and these new forms bear some similarities to contemporary experiences like work speedup, multitasking, and just-in-time labor. While a Frankfurt School perspective might note that forms of entertainment replicate labor so we can better toil under our oppressive conditions, Marshall McLuhan might claim that the digital has infiltrated entertainment, finance, and labor, and hence there's a homology between them.[1] My intuition is that both perspectives grasp something. I wonder if becoming more aware of the patterns of space, time, and rhythm in media and work speedup might help us to adapt to social change. We might even work to train our forms of attention so that we can handle the shocks of contemporary society with more grace, care, and awareness.

I don't have time to fully show that we are experiencing accelerating cultural configurations, but let me offer one quick, banal example drawn from my personal experience. My adolescence lacked cell phones and computers. I occupied myself with books, played instruments, or, much worse, engaged in the low-stimulus activity of hanging out at the nearby suburban shopping mall with other teens. For entertainment we'd stand on the corner of a suburban cul-de-sac, and when a lone car passed, we'd yell, "Floor it." I doubt the driver knew what we meant. Our sense of time and horizons differed. Today, however, young people, through smart devices and multimedia forms, often take flight through the imaginarily held worlds of Facebook, texting, and video games. Theirs is a denser, more richly articulated world. YouTube clips viewed on a smart phone may provide one of the quickest, and truest, exits from the quotidian, and here's why. When we see moving media with some semblance of the human, our brain's mirror cells light up, replicating the patterns and shapes we see before us. With mirror cells, you see someone perform a gesture onscreen and somewhere in your brain, your cells model it. It's as if you've gone through the thought-motion without performing the external gesture.[2] With much media moving faster than can be biologically processed, we're leaping to catch up. Both work and leisure have become faster and more pressured.

First, what are the rhythms of today's multitasking and work speedup? If you're an IT worker laboring at the computer, your attention may be drawn along consistent paths. Sometime in your session, you might experience a hunter's drive, an attention that reaches beyond the monitor into the future. This form of attention resembles moments in recent action films and video games. At some point, you'll feel a pull back to the work at hand, and in the interim, you might experience a moment of task switching or even a stutter— the brain misfiring. Then there might be a short period of hyperfocus where you're riveted by details and your consciousness contracts to the microsecond. Soon the brain may seek to take a break and you might daydream. Or you might go into a zone of very productive work. Either way you're engaged in a different, slower form of time. Suddenly, outside pressures impinge. You have to shift tasks and it's "all at once": everything tumbles in at an instant. Though you may feel flooded you also must close this work session, so you can start again and cycle through these same modes of labor. And in the future, I suspect, our ability to control our workflow by bracketing these work sessions may diminish, and we'll become more disoriented as the borders among aesthetics, work, and leisure activities merge.

I have a dystopian picture of how multimedia and work will be coupled in the future. Then, I'll sit at the computer doing my tasks. A device will read my biological outputs and the computer will measure my workflow. An algorithm will inform me to stop and participate in a multimedia clip (for example, calisthenics in an Xbox "Kinect-like" environment). These forms, shaped to my attention, will help me break, refocus, and return to the task at hand. We'll all feel pressured to participate in these practices because we'll desire to become more employable.

In the near future, however, I think methods of working with multimedia and labor will be less uniform. I can imagine a smartphone having not just audio but also audiovisual playlists containing byte-sized clips configured for the person. These would work to call up where one wants to go or where one wants to turn back to. People may not always be aware of what they're doing, but that would be the underlying purpose of these clips. Such compendia would be as finely tuned and articulated as the enormous music and sound libraries for today's films, which allow you to choose between "graceful with a lilt," "ominous but still urbane," and so on. One might catch a clip to intervene in a cycle of rising panic or to leap into a project.

Amplifying and refashioning the self has become an increasingly prevalent theme in today's digital culture; it's called the "totally quantified life."[3] Health-conscious people wear plastic wristbands to count their steps or measure their heart rates. Others chart sleep-wake cycles or moments of insight and downtime. Positive aphorisms come chiming into cell phones throughout the day. *Wired* magazine has become one locus for sharing these forms of self-management. (One article asks whether documenting one's daily diet supports higher cognition.)[4] These protocols may become increasingly common, and the following description of how we can trace paths of attention through audiovisually intensified media provides one possible example. I place this description in the context of broader shifts, perhaps across media, away from traditional narratives to more open forms. States induced by audiovisually intensified clips might serve as a guide for creating new forms and modes of art-making. Below is one possible routine a viewer might practice and one possible way of reconfiguring a new media work.

Protocols for Practicing New Patterns of Attention:

1. Core
2. Convoluted and Extended Space
3. Stutter and Focus

4. Slo-mo and Bullet Time
5. All-at-once
6. Blurred Sectional Demarcations
7. Line

CORE

Before we consider digitally accelerated clips that reproduce features from multitasking and just-in-time labor (items 2 through 6 from the list above), let's look at a few that can establish a sense of ground, balance, and center. The first audiovisual clip I consider here is Oren Lavie's "Her Morning Elegance." The clip is characterized by a gently circling 3/4 fast waltz against a rolling hypermeter; a smoothly-flowing chord progression of vi, IV, I, V, vi; softly articulated timbres; and breathy singing seeks to please rather than demand exegesis. It seems peacefully active. The plunking bass, mumbled blasé singing, and little bells assert that the bourgeois lead a charmed life; and one little bell encourages the viewer onward. "Her Morning Elegance" has a subtly dark undertow, however. Our protagonist never emerges from sleepwalking nor makes it past her bed's confines. Also, the digital has invaded her domestic space. The quasi-two-dimensional environment resembles several computer-program screen interfaces, like the gridded windows and timelines of Avid and Pro Tools (see figure 13.1).[5]

A second clip by Anusara Yogi Bridget Woods Kramer that contains timbres with no attacks; a long, flat pedal tone articulating G major and rare appoggiatura passing tones of A and C; and a breathy voice stretched and smoothed out that suggests no change. Peaceful and passive, it feels inward but expansive (see figure 13.2).[6]

Another clip features a chakra-balancing meditation. My hunch is that many global workers including Americans will feel pressured to take designer drugs for the brain to maintain a competitive edge. An example is Adderall,

Figure 13.1 Oren Lavie's "Her Morning Elegance": a sense of grounded everydayness.

Figure 13.2 Anusara Yogi Bridget Woods Kramer's meditation clip.

which improves focus and endurance under boring labor conditions. Maybe we'll end up wired to miniature MRI biofeedback machines. And their outputs might look like the depiction in figure 13.3.[7]

CONVOLUTED AND EXTENDED SPACE

Okay. Let's be workers. Ready to rock. Let's spread out. Mark Neveldine and Brian Taylor's *Gamer* is one of my favorites for convoluted and extended space. I understand little about the body I'm supposed to identify with, where I am in space, or whether the space is 2-D or 3-D. One moment I'm in a music-video-like slide show of global cities. Next, an explosion fills the screen and I'm dropped in with some figure that is silhouetted and then stilled, fuzzed out, sped up, and slowed down, with breathing that's out of sync with the body. The camera pans much more quickly and abrasively than my muscles can respond to, and in the lag or disconnect I feel a roughness or jerkiness. Our protagonist seems to run toward a corner that's constantly expanding backward as if toward a vanishing octagonal point. The soundtrack, made up of breath, gunfire, metal, whooshes, and pitched tones, encourages us to pay attention, because we never ascertain the status of the sounds—some may have been chosen as punctuation, to create a musical line, others to define the environment.

The Wachowski siblings's *Speedracer* has a utopian, ever-expansive space, with the broad arcs and expanses that we dream by. There's no horizon. The color strips run to infinity, and I too, fingers and feet, flow out without boundary. I feel as if I cross effortlessly from hand-drawn line animation, to live action, to motion control, through an explosion, to 2-D and 3-D checkered squares. Or do I? At the clip's end, I feel uneasy. Some part of me can't assimilate the pen-and-ink mandala of red-and-white checkered squares that morphs into a tin checkerboard, becoming hard as a shiny concrete or marble showcase floor. So fast, broad, and dense I can't take it all in, but I still love it for all of its capitalistic excess (see figure 13.4).

Figure 13.3 Chakra-balancing meditation.

Figure 13.4 Speed Racer: utopian, ever-expansive space.

STUTTER AND FOCUS

Okay, let's contract. Lady Gaga's "Telephone" thematizes the problem of task-switching: right in the midst of an all-out girls-in-prison, hair-to-fist fight, you get a phone call and you don't want to take it because you're focused on getting your booty onto the dance floor (see figure 13.5). The clip has many layers of stutter, slow and fast, audio and visual. Is it that nothing is more piercing than a stutter? Does a stutter suggests mechanical failure? A brain misfiring? Recent media are so taken up by the stutter it seems like it's the central meme.[8]

Rihanna's "Rock Star 101," so digitally manipulated, is hyperembodied: note the slick viscosity of the lips; their lurid shine; the sharp points of the spiky headdress and the eyelashes with their smeared brushstroke-like traces; followed by an "rrrr" sound, which seems to smear the visual stroke into an aural blur; the smoke and digital pixels so sharply demarcated, cloaking the body. All these features meticulously placed against each other, give the sense of overwhelming tactility—ultra physical. Incessantly, points of focus rapidly direct our attention: lips, spikes, eyelashes, gun, so that only too late do we notice a trauma. Rihanna's singing, "I told you baby, I told you, uh oh," has been mutilated, the sonic envelope for "baby" abbreviated into an absence as the word "baby" smashes into the cry of "oh." This opening contains an impossible kernel, a moment suggestive of a violent act, which, in our hyperfocused, constantly moving, distracted attention we've failed to witness (see figure 13.6).[9]

We can flip media and find this hyperfocus in the soundtrack. Ke$ha may be the queen of accelerated sonic pop aesthetics. In "TiK ToK" her voice is meshed with the electronic arrangement. When she sings "tipsy" the lyrics are slowed down, and Auto-Tune is applied in special isolation to "on—the—clock." The "Oh, oh" echo's a signature trope of Gwen Stefani's. The arrangement's squeaky sounds are so tactile I can't help but activate the sensation of rubber boots on flesh. My attention can't drift from "here, here, here."

Figure 13.5 Lady Gaga's "Telephone": stutter and focus.

Figure 13.6 Rihanna's "Rock Star 101": hyperfocus in the soundtrack and image.

SLO-MO AND BULLET TIME

I'd claim that bullet time is a technology grounded in narcissism and crisis. Think of Neo dodging a bullet in *The Matrix*. We're only willing to grant bullet time to a person, not an animal or a natural event like a volcano, and the moment most often is riven with threat.[10] We can see this effect in the *CSI: Crime Scene Investigation* TV series opening credits (which uses a similar technique known as "stop time").

Bullet time's sensations may be similar to the experiential temporal elongation of a car crash; a near-death epiphany; or a long-distance plummeting to the ground. But the temporality of bullet time is uncertain. Linda Williams notes three genre-based forms of time we might attend to: (1) Melodrama, where the villain demands the maiden's rent or threatens the wife and baby, and an illicit affair produces an out-of-wedlock pregnancy—here you're too late. (2) Horror, when you've come too early, you pull the door and a knife is waiting for you. (3) Porn, which is just in time.[11] But what is the time of bullet time? Perhaps it's past tense, already remembered. Yet, paradoxically it's still unfolding in present time, so when music is added, the soundtrack is called upon to serve as a witness and provide all temporal materials, like pulse and duration. Bullet time's time may surpass our biological capabilities. Nevertheless, drawing from bullet time, I wouldn't mind having a few more moments like that in my life. I see a face, for instance, that means something to me. A taste that sweeps over me like a shock. As I pour my coffee, I would like bullet time. I would give so much to extend my life with these potholes of moments.

Nuit Blanche's slow-mo time is unusual because of its genre hybridity: it blends the human under threat with romance. It's haunted by the question of whether true love exists, or our attachments are arbitrary, simply moments of cathexis linked to some previous lost relationship. Or are we only DNA receptacles struggling for our chromosomal matter's continuance?[12] Formally *Nuit Blanche* reflects this dichotomy. It's warm and authentic, but it's artificial; almost all of it was composed from still photographs, matte-painted in Photoshop, and then stretched over texture maps. The glass never broke—it was animated. No street, building, or car existed in this space; the actors, shot in green screen, might never have met, and the music was recorded in a cathedral. Like much recent media, *Nuit Blanche* is vertiginous. Objects and people roll over and turn: the building lurches forward like the *Titanic*, and the male protagonist, buckling gently, drifts as he's hit by a car. The kiss, nestled among glass shards, starts to turn, like in Hitchcock's *Vertigo*, with both a rotation and a swerve. These large turns create a sense of disequilibrium and sleep. All this sleep, I want to argue, saturates much of contemporary media. *Nuit Blanche* literalizes McLuhan's conundrum. If we are to work with new media forms as

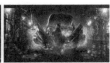

Figure 13.7 Nuit Blanche: ultra slow-mo.

prostheses, they must become natural for us. To do this, we must, at least for a while, fail to see them, undergo narcissus narcosis. But if we're building a new form of embodiment and so much of it involves sleeping or sleepwalking, we have put ourselves at risk (see figure 13.7).[13]

ALL AT ONCE

Does this "all at once" replicate our current experiences of work and play—our trying to keep up with email, instant messaging, chat windows, cell-phone calls, projects due? I can tell you that, as a professor, I'll find myself in the rush of back-logged email, preparing for a lecture, trying to submit a grant, adding a last bit of copyediting for a journal, and making a department meeting, and I'm trying to do these simultaneously. Or is "all at once" simply a response to the excitement of all the newly available media? A replica in miniature of the sublime surplus? Or is it simply what the brain delights in? "All at once" may be everywhere now because we never had as good a technology to produce this. Or is it that we like "all at once" because we feel more sharply the trajectories of other people's lives and the ones that our own lives might take? Perhaps we've made a wrong turn?

Never before *Inception* has a film asked us to hold so many separate worlds, all simultaneously, within our conscious attention for such a long duration. Director Chris Nolan felt the Edith Piaf song was so central to the film's design he couldn't decide whether to first give it to the composer or the sound designer. Each of *Inception*'s seven layers has a different set of sound effects—the way water sounds, or wind, or clocks are all particular. The Wagnerian V to flat-VI runs through the film, always hovering, never resolving. The low foghorn belongs to everything, the crashing city, the crumbling buildings, the avalanche, the car going over the bridge and nose-diving into the water. That horn suggests slumber, but it is part of the ping, the Piaf trigger, so it should be constantly waking us up. On each level, the characters are subtly different as well. Films now are not so much about story as about pathway. All I want to do is to learn the lilt, the turn of each of the characters, the way objects work in each layer, and hold these against the other layers and against the music. I'd like to learn this map or build.[14]

One more example of "all at once." Studies show that in reality people can't multitask. What we're really doing is one task at a time, with a short lag, as the brain switches focus. But multimedia say, "screw the science." Our brains are pliant. We can refigure the brain so we can follow along with this Lynyrd Sky-nyrd/Beyoncé clip, hearing both lines of music simultaneously, with equal at-tention, as two ongoing channels or streams. (The two songs are in different keys, separated by a whole step.) (See figure 13.8.)[15]

BLURRED SECTIONAL DEMARCATIONS

I've mentioned it's important to bracket work experiences into sections as a means to control the amount and flow of stimulus. In the future, however, I believe borders between leisure and work will become less clear. Santigold's "L.E.S. Artistes" points to such a future. The music video quivers between an arty, fashion-plate tableau and a narrative with current, pressing global issues, like militant activism in the face of violent repressive regimes.

Santigold's video exploits our cultural understandings about color through the fine modulations made possible by Digital Intermediary.[16] A shift from pure primaries and soft pastels to a muted burnt-sienna orange two-thirds in suddenly takes us away from a playful imaginary into a suggestively real world with tragic consequences. We have to ask: Do new technologies make it pos-sible for our politics and aesthetics to mingle this way? What does it mean for our lives when we have many streams coming in and we're not sure what's authentic and what's stylized? Santigold's clips show there are stakes here—we may be experiencing not only a shift in aesthetics and attention but also in pol-itics and community (see figure 13.9).[17]

LINE

I've started with "Core" as a technique for negotiating shifting modes of atten-tion. Let me close with another adaptive mode, which I'll call "Line." To make it in today's increasingly globalized society, we need to be "just in time," able to

Figure 13.8 Lynyrd Skynyrd/Beyoncé mashup: "all at once."

Figure 13.9 Santigold's "L.E.S. Artistes": blurring the lines between leisure, work, and politics.

work within a large organization, to retool and reconfigure our personalities and roles. Those who succeed will be "fleet"; as they move quickly through contexts, they'll no more than momentarily touch on incidents as they continue onward. An audiovisual corollary to the experience of Line is in Bekmambetov's *Day Watch*, To's *Full Time Killer*, or the trailer for *The Town* (see figure 13.10). One could argue that "the Line" is amoral, or even immoral. It's not for those who take the time to consider all perspectives, to brood over the ramifications of an event. If everyone embodies this sense of Line, it'll be another form of sleepwalking. But for someone trapped by the past or too reactive, this kind of Line might be liberatory. To travel lightly and to keep going. To not overjudge and to let go.

Justin Bieber's music video "Somebody to Love" uses the concept of Line with perhaps a positive moral valence. I've interviewed Dave Meyers, the video's director, about making it. The gig came through in two days. Meyers didn't know he'd have Usher until the night before. The backdrop was simply green screen. Meyers threw out the stalactites. He liked the choreographer and dance group, and they quickly came on board. Everyone brought unique, finely honed skills to the table, and somehow helped create a sense of community. Watch and listen to the way the video creates a finely articulated, constantly moving, yet always transitioning Line (we follow from a hand gesture by

Figure 13.10 Full Time Killer: Johnnie To's sense of line.

Figure 13.11 "Somebody To Love": ways to make it through.

Usher, to the unfolding of Japanese women's fans, to the rising and falling of dancers dressed in black moving like pistons). The video suggests that even if the context that brings people together is dissembled, a new one—also involving active, attentive, and engaged participants—might emerge. It suggests if we can find a way to go forward like this, we just might make it through (see figure 13.11.).[18]

NOTES

Introduction

1. See Lev Manovich, The Language of New Media (Cambridge, MA: MIT Press, 2001), xv, 20. David Bordwell, The Way Hollywood Tells It: Story and Style in Modern Movies (Berkeley: University of California Press, 2006), 21, 120, 121. Also Bordwell, "Intensified Continuity: Visual Style in Contemporary Hollywood Film," Film Quarterly 55, no. 3 (Spring 2002): 16–28.
2. Henri Bergson, Time and Free Will: An Essay on the Immediate Data of Consciousness (1913; Mineola, NY: Dover, 2001), 12–14.
3. Suzanne Langer, Philosophy in a New Key: A Study in the Symbolism of Art (1942; Cambridge, MA: Harvard University Press, 1957), 271.
4. I argue that intensified audiovisual aesthetics or a parametric approach can even be applied retrospectively to some director's earlier work like Vertov's and Tarkovsky's. Even some silent films, like those of Melies, can be read as embodying an intensified audiovisual approach: we feel the sonic corollaries of his puffs of smoke, performers' vanishings, and edits. These form music-video-like phrases possessing lively rhythms and articulations that come to the fore. It may be for this reason that one of the most popular music videos, the Smashing Pumpkins' "Tonight's the Night," remakes Melies's Trip to the Moon.
5. It's been shown that dreams for individuals have become both briefer and more colorful. Perhaps we now experience more media than the unconscious can process.
6. David Bordwell, The Way Hollywood Tells It: Story and Style in Modern Movies (Berkeley: University of California Press, 2006), 21, 120, 121. Also Bordwell, "Intensified Continuity: Visual Style in Contemporary Hollywood Film," Film Quarterly 55, no. 3 (Spring 2002): 16–28.
7. Eleftheria Thanouli, Post-Classical Cinema: An International Poetics of Film Narration (New York: Wallflower Press, 2009), 96, 173–182. See also Warren Buckland, Puzzle Films: Complex Storytelling in Contemporary Cinema (Malden, MA: Wiley-Blackwell, 2009); and Alan Cameron, Modular Narratives in Contemporary Cinema (Basingstoke: Palgrave Macmillan, 2008). See also Thomas Elsaesser, "The Mind-Game Film," in Puzzle Films: Complex Storytelling in Contemporary Cinema, ed. Warren Buckland (Malden MA: Wiley-Blackwell, 2009), 13-41. Edward Branigan on "multiple draft": "Nearly True: Forking Plots, Forking Interpretations," SubStance 31, no. 1 (2002): 105-114. Steve Shaviro on post-intensified continuity: "Ferrets on Crystal Meth: Post-Continuity and Post-Irony in Digital Film," paper presented at the Society for Cinema and Media Studies annual conference, Chicago, March 2013.
8. Did this sonic motif developed from the overproduced, baby-boom thuds of metal doors banging shut in contemporary cinema (which then became adopted by the editing and

frisky camera)? What is this sound trying to tell us? Think of the ways sonic and visual motifs function in *Inception, Mission Impossible, Day Watch, Never Let Me Go*, Linkin Park's "Numb," Katy Perry's "ET," and the Sony Commercial "Two Worlds."

9. Today's media may drive to coordinate and sync up. The way to achieve this may be through the smallest unit.

10. J. D. Connor also wonders about the end of the independent studios. Conversation with Connor, Spring 2011.

11. MTV has stopped playing music video and it was difficult to find clips on YouTube.

12. Daniel Goldmark has also written about the ways media and industries change as practitioners follow the best-paid gigs. Pixar started paying decent wages for soundtracks, and film music composers (who had always loved cartoons) switched fields. With better soundtracks and more fully fleshed CGI, family-oriented cartoons suddenly became popular and respectable. See Goldmark, "Pixar and the Animated Soundtrack," in *The Oxford Handbook of New Audiovisual Aesthetics*, ed. John Richardson et al. (New York and Oxford: Oxford University Press), forthcoming.

13. Contemporary media can suggest opportunities for boundless excitement without end—one simply hops from media object to the next. Many contemporary forms present great stamina, seemingly muscling their way through things. I've drawn on films like *Moulin Rouge!* and Floria Sigismondi and Katy Perry's "ET" as a way of getting through. But grief, stillness, and reflection are an important part of the human experience. As one antidote to the media swirl, I recommend watching Val Lewton's films and reading Alexander Nemerov's *Icons of Grief: Val Lewton's Home Front Pictures* (Berkeley: University of California Press, 2005).

14. The easiest way to get a "YouTube bump" is still traditional media—news articles, appearances on daytime talk shows. "Friday," however, was initially a grassroots phenomenon.

15. It's a follow-up to his Lady Gaga video, "Telephone," which is similarly large-scale, but only nine minutes long.

16. How do people respond to low-res, low-quality, intermittent footage, consciously and unconsciously? Do directors shoot and edit for YouTube's sputter? Experimental video artist Cory Archangel valorizes old videotape, analog sound, and digital and analogue artifacts, as part of a nostalgic turn, but he's probably nodding to media dysfunctions. In 2012 I kept coming across videos with solid backgrounds that became banded in thick strips of gradient colors because of too much video compression. Are people watching and making clips with this in mind?

17. Caryl Flinn, "The Mutating Musical" in Richardson, *Oxford Handbook of New Audiovisual Aesthetics*.

18. Vivian Sobchack, "When the Ear Dreams: Dolby Digital and the Imagination of Sound," *Film Quarterly* 58, no. 4 (Summer 2005): 2–15. Annette Davison, "Title Sequences for Contemporary Television Serials," in Richardson, *Oxford Handbook of New Audiovisual Aesthetics*.

19. A YouTube clip often seems to have a history and a future. It also is connected to a community. (In this way it resembles a pop song; it becomes musical.) A special shout-out to my editor Norm Hirschy for forwarding me the clip.

20. Its story reminds me of another famous pair of clips—not quite a twofer, David Fincher's and Madonna's meticulously constructed, heart-wrenching video "Oh Father," about Madonna's relation to her father in the style of *Citizen Kane*, a clip few fans saw. Almost everyone saw "Vogue," however, an inexpensive video record executives demanded after Fincher put so much money into "Oh Father" with so little gain. It was shot in a day with props found around a rented stage. The cinematographer jumped off the plane, set the light meter, and started shooting. But the contrasts between lush and stripped-down in Nava's and Beyoncé's "If I Were A Boy" and "Single Ladies," respectively, seem more extreme than the Fincher/Madonna collaborations.

21. Chapter 10 stretches further back to consider video aesthetics from the 80s.

22. Bordwell, "Intensified Continuity," 16.

23. Angela Ndalianis, *Neo-Baroque Aesthetics and Contemporary Entertainment* (Cambridge, MA: MIT Press, 2005), 27–47.

24. Conversation with Majumdar, Spring 2008. See Neepa Majumdar, "The Embodied Voice: Song Sequences and Stardom in Popular Hindi Cinema," in *Soundtrack Available*, ed. Pamela Robertson Wojcik and Arthur Knight (Durham, NC: Duke University Press, 2001), 161–181.

25. In my interviews (2012) with Jonas Åkerlund—Lady Gaga's director for videos like "Telephone"—he speaks of "animating" the performers: widening singers' mouths and turning their heads in new directions, for example.

26. Mark Augé, *Non-places: Introduction to an Anthropology of Supermodernity*, trans. John Howe (London: Verso, 1995), 19.

27. Max Horkheimer and Theodor Adorno, *Dialectic of Enlightenment (Cultural Memory in the Present)*, trans. Edmund Jephcott (Stanford, CA: Stanford University Press, 2002), 7.

28. Sianne Ngai, *Our Aesthetic Categories: Zany, Cute, Interesting* (Boston: Harvard University Press, 2012).

29. Angela Ndalianis, *Neo-Baroque Aesthetics and Contemporary Entertainment* (Cambridge, MA: MIT Press, 2005), 27–47.

30. Lauren Berlant, "Nearly Utopian, Nearly Normal: Post-Fordist Affect in La Promesse and Rosetta," *Public Culture* 19, no. 2 (2007): 279, 280.

31. Alexander Nehamas, *Nietzsche: Life as Literature* (Boston: Harvard University Press, 1987), 3-7.

32. Bordwell, *The Way Hollywood Tells It: Story and Style in Modern Movies* (Berkeley:University of California Press, 2006), 21, 120, 121. Also Bordwell, "Intensified Continuity: Visual Style in Contemporary Hollywood Film," Film Quarterly 55, no. 3 (Spring 2002): 16–28.

33. J. D. Connor, "'The Projections': Allegories of Industrial Crisis in Neoclassical Hollywood," *Representations* 71 (Summer 2000): 48–76.

Chapter 1

1. David Bordwell, *The Way Hollywood Tells It: Story and Style in Modern Movies* (Berkeley: University of California Press, 2006), 21. Eleftheria Thanouli, *Post-Classical Cinema: An International Poetics of Film Narration* (New York: Wallflower Press, 2009), 96, 173–182. See also Warren Buckland, *Puzzle Films: Complex Storytelling in Contemporary Cinema* (Malden, MA: Wiley-Blackwell, 2009). See also Elsaesser on database films, Shaviro on post-intensified continuity.

2. Or what Carole Piechota calls "audiovisual passages." Carole Piechota, "Give Me a Second Grace: Music as Absolution in *The Royal Tenenbaums*," *Senses of Cinema* 38, special issue on Movies, Musicians and Soundtracks (February 6, 2008). http://sensesofcinema.com/2006/38/music_tenenbaums/.

   For all online clips and other links mentioned in the notes to this volume: note access date of March 10, 2010.

3. In retrospect, we may find that Mexican (Inarittu, Cuaron, del Toro), Russian (Bekmambetov), and Asian (Woo) filmmakers who came to America energized the new style. Inarritu and Bekmambetov have directed music videos.

4. For strong analyses of digital audiovisual aesthetics and post-classical cinema, see Dale Chapman, "Music and the State of Exception in Alfonso Cuarón's Children of Men," Aylish Wood, "Sonic Times in Watchmen and Inception," Garrett Stewart, "Sound Thinking: Looped Time, Duped Track," Sean Cubitt, "Source Code: Eco-Criticism and Subjectivity," James Buhler, "Notes to Source Code's Soundtrack," Jay Beck, "Acoustic Auteurs and Transnational Cinema," and Miguel Mera, "Inglo(u)rious Basterdisation?

Tarantino and the War Movie Mashup," in *The Oxford Handbook of Sound and Image in Digital Media*, ed. Carol Vernallis et al. (New York and Oxford: Oxford University Press), forthcoming.

5. Mark Kerins, *Beyond Dolby (Stereo): Cinema in the Digital Sound Age* (Bloomington: Indiana University Press, 2011), 66.

6. See Richard Middleton, "'From Me to You': Popular Music As Message," in *Studying Popular Music* (Maidenhead, UK: Open University Press, 1990).

7. Lev Manovich, *Principles of New Media*, Mediamatic.net (2000), http://www.media-matic.net/5971/en/principles-of-new-media-1.   http://www.mediamatic.net/5972/en/principles-of-new-media-2. For an excellent analysis of digital audiovisual aesthetics and *The Bourne Ultimatum*, see James Buhler and Alex Newton, "Outside the Law of Action: Music and Sound in the Bourne Trilogy," in Vernallis, *Oxford Handbook of Sound and Image in Digital Media*.

8. David Bordwell, Janet Staiger, and Kristin Thompson, *The Classical Hollywood Cinema: Film Style and Mode of Production to 1960* (New York: Columbia University Press, 1985), 63.

9. See Carol Vernallis, *Experiencing Music Video: Aesthetics and Cultural Context* (New York: Columbia University Press, 2004). I've often thought that the arguments I make in this book about music video can be imported directly to post-classical cinema.

10. Stunning music-image relations place additional tears in *Bringing Out the Dead*'s fabric. An intermedia pattern: on their beat, Cage and Ving Rhames trade racial banter as streetlights rhythmically illuminate their faces; they then bob and weave into the center of a rave, again, rocking back and forth, back and forth, this time between camera movement and the electronic dance music; Rhames then raises the OD'ed Goth boy with a call and response, gospel-inflected sermon, "I be banging! I be banging! Yes God!"; the ambulance then zips off in a break-the-fifth-dimension streak of light against a heavy metal guitar solo; a heart monitor's "ding" can't slow the speed of this traversal. Too many saturated audiovisual moments claim their own time, obstructing closure for the taut five-act structure. In the film's final ten minutes Cage suddenly changes into a paramedic/mercy-killer. As with music video, we'd like to resolve this incommensurability, but the truth is partially preserved within music-image relations.

Chapter 2

1. Clifford Nass, Eyal Ophir, and Anthony D. Wagner, "Cognitive Control in Media Multitaskers," *PNAS Proceedings of the National Academy of Sciences of the United States of America* 106, no. 37 (September 15, 2009): 15583–15587. Film theorists will soon start charting the socioeconomic and cultural forces that engendered the audiovisual turn and post-classical cinema. See Wheeler Winston Dixon and Gwendolyn Audrey Foster, *21st Century Hollywood: Movies in the Era of Transformation* (New Brunswick, NJ: Rutgers University Press, 2011).

2. David Bordwell, *Poetics of Cinema* (London and New York: Routledge, 2007), 180–185.

3. David Bordwell and Kristin Thompson, *Film Art: An Introduction* (New York: McGraw-Hill, 1997), 482.

4. Michael Wedel, "Backbeat and Overlap: Time, Place, and Character Subjectivity in *Run Lola Run*," in Warren Buckland, ed., *Puzzle Films: Complex Storytelling in Contemporary Cinema* (Malden, MA : Wiley-Blackwell, 2009), 135. See also Katherine Spring, "Chance Encounters of the Musical Kind: Electronica and Audiovisual Synchronization in Three Films Directed by Tom Tykwer," in *Music and the Moving Image* 3, no. 3 (Fall 2010).

5. Joshua Landy, "Still Life in a Narrative Age: Charlie Kaufman's *Adaptation*," in *Critical Inquiry* 37, no. 3 (Chicago: University of Chicago Press, 2011), 500–503.

6. See Richard Dyer, *Se7en*, BFI Modern Classics, 1st ed. (London: British Film Institute, 2008).

7. This is something that Fincher may have learned from directing music videos.

8. Amazon commentary for the DVD rerelease of Se7en: "Colors, shadowings, sound, contrast have all been adjusted for optimum effect (one of the extras on disc 2 shows the before-and-after on several scenes). Just check out the green lamps in that library scene—WOW!"

9. See Jane Bennett, "Commodity Fetishism and Commodity Enchantment," *Theory and Event* 5, no. 1 (Winter 2001), http://muse.jhu.edu/journals/theory_and_event/v005/5.1bennett.html.

10. Story relayed to me by Jonathan Rosenbaum. Conversation with Rosenbaum, Fall 1997.

11. Manohla Dargis, "Invasion of the Robot Toys, Redux," *New York Times*, June 23, 2009.

12. See Joshua Clover, "Dream Machines: Marx and Coca-Cola," in *Film Quarterly* 61, no. 2 (2007): 6–7.

13. See Lisa Coulthard, "Torture Tunes: Tarantino, Popular Music, and New Hollywood Ultraviolence," *Music and the Moving Image* 2, no. 2 (Summer 2009): 1–6. Miguel Mera, "Inglo(u)rious Basterdization? Tarantino and the War Movie Mashup," in *The Oxford Handbook of Sound and Image in Digital Media*, ed. Carol Vernallis et al. (New York and Oxford: Oxford University Press), forthcoming.

14. The urban woman appears in the scene before and, after her death, she may project into the next. Her T-shirt's bridge insignia returns in the doubled lithographs in the following scene, which takes place in a hospital waiting room. A red line down the hallway helps us remember the skidmarks from the car crash. Black signs over doorways might suggest a memory of danger or simply breast pasties.

15. Best would be the long, careful, slow, thoughtful, close readings of someone like George Toles who can watch unflinchingly and take us through the minutiae of impact. But at this point I become frightened of the scene. See George Toles, "Auditioning Betty in Mulholland Drive," *Film Quarterly* 58, no. 1 (2004): 2–13.

16. Kristin Thompson, *Storytelling in the New Hollywood: Understanding Classical Narrative Technique* (Cambridge, MA: Harvard University Press, 1999), 36.

17. David Bordwell, *The Way Hollywood Tells It: Story and Style in Modern Movies* (Berkeley: University of California Press, 2006) 96, 97.

18. The film displays many techniques catalogued in Michel Chion's *Audio-Vision* and makes an excellent teaching text alongside it. See Michel Chion, *Audio-Vision: Sound on Screen* (New York: Columbia University Press, 1994).

19. The film's mix of elements is shaped by Russia's contemporary global situation (somewhere between East and West, capitalism and autocracy). But it also reflects problems with bootlegging and the need for Hollywood gloss. Sound design was farmed out piecemeal through a networked consortium (each workshop isolated to limit leaks); though some sounds were Russian, others were pulled from American sound libraries. Uncompressed sounds were sent via the web to Los Angeles to be given a final "big Hollywood sound" and then pieced together against a looming—and apparently unrealistic—deadline. This sharing of materials and talent on a global scale may contribute to the film's look and feel.

20. See David Bordwell, "Revisiting Planet Hong Kong," http://www.davidbordwell.net/blog/category/directors-johnnie-to-kei-fung/page/3/.

21. See Charles Kronengold, "Audiovisual Objects, Multisensory People and the Intensified Ordinary in Hong Kong Action Films," in *The Oxford Handbook of New Audiovisual Aesthetics*, ed. John Richardson et al. (New York and Oxford: Oxford University Press), forthcoming. Stephen Teo, *Director in Action: Johnnie To and the Hong Kong Action Film* (Hong Kong: University of Hong Kong Press, 2008): 215–244, 241.

22. Bordwell, *Way Hollywood Tells It*, 75–76.

23. Leonard Meyer is one of the strongest proponents of interlocking "nested" forms. He notes, for example, that Wagner's discovery of the leitmotif (a brief melodic fragment) made possible huge, sweeping pieces that, for the first time, stretched for hours. Here changes occurring at the surface shaped mid- and large-scale patterns. See Leonard Meyer, *Style and Music: Theory, History, and Ideology* (Chicago: University of Chicago Press, 1997), 19.

24. Consider the wealth of examples from Tibetan, Australian Aboriginal, and Native American art. Various periods in European history represented the figure-ground relationship so differently that we might want to focus on change over continuity. There are medieval techniques for flatly stacking figures on top of one another (Fra Angelico's angels); the Renaissance's for perspective (Botticelli's civic spaces); and 20th-century modernism's for abstract expression (Rothko's fields of color).

25. Its gravestones and houses seem to confirm my claims about post-classical film's reconfigurability. See Introduction.

26. Interview with director Timur Bekmambetov, Summer 2012.

Chapter 3

1. See Edward Wright's *Hot Fuzz*.

2. See Paul Greengrass's *Bourne Ultimatum*.

3. Marco Calavita, "'MTV Aesthetics' at the Movies: Interrogating a Film Criticism Fallacy," *Journal of Film and Video* 59, no. 3 (Fall 2007): 15–31.

4. Several music videos have since alluded to *Natural Born Killers*. Jonas Åkerlund's "Telephone" could be read as a tribute to Stone's film.

5. I was amused when one of my students claimed that Asian action films trumped music video as the important precursor, and cited a YouTube clip from *Romeo Must Die* as evidence. (Released in 2000, this film is American, with actors Jet Li and the young music video starlet Aaliyah.) I can think of one strong claim that supports Calavita's. Much as there were European directors like Godard and Nicolas Roeg, who made films that foretell much of what music video has become, there was Chinese director King Hu. These directors so clearly anticipate the new cutting style one has to wonder whether some music video directors might be aping this earlier style. I'd say no: close viewing shows music video has a style of its own. But this is still a beguiling argument.

6. David Bordwell describes "intensified continuity" in *The Way Hollywood Tells It: Story and Style in Modern Movies* (Berkeley: University of California Press, 2006), 94–97, 120–121.

7. An obvious example is the printed book. A hundred years before the book was invented, Europe had the basic tools for making books (wine press, oil-based ink, paper), but the device wasn't assembled until after the Black Plague, when new needs arose: the technology helped adjudicate land disputes after so many deaths. Once invented and disseminated, the book had uneven effects: while printed statistics assisted a new mercantile public, books also propagated much misinformation (maps were notoriously incorrect). The ways Europeans incorporated literacy differed from those of other cultures.

8. See *Director's Series Vol. 4—Work of Director Mark Romanek Starring Fiona Apple, Audioslave, Beck and Brian Bell*, director Lance Bangs, Palm Pictures/Umvd (New York, 2005).

9. See Michael Bull, *Sounding Out the City: Personal Stereos and the Management of Everyday Life* (Oxford, UK: Berg, 2000). Anahid Kassabian writes about soundscapes for websites. See Anahid Kassabian, "The End of Diegesis as We Know It?," in *The Oxford Handbook of New Audiovisual Aesthetics*, ed. John Richardson et al. (New York and Oxford: Oxford University Press), forthcoming.

10. See William Whittington, *Sound Design and Horror* (Austin: University of Texas Press, forthcoming). K. J. Donnelly, *The Spectre of Sound: Music in Film and Television* (London: British Film Institute, 2008).
11. Bordwell, *Way Hollywood Tells It*, 155.
12. Holly Rogers, *Sounding the Gallery: Video and the Rise of Art-Music (Oxford Music/ Media)* (New York: Oxford University Press, 2013). Philip Auslander, "Sound and Vision: The Audio/Visual Economy of Musical Performance," in Richardson, *Oxford Handbook of New Audiovisual Aesthetics*. Amy Herzog, *Dreams of Difference, Songs of the Same* (Minneapolis: University of Minnesota Press, 2010). John Caldwell, *Production Culture: Industrial Reflexivity and Critical Practice in Film and Television (Console-ing Passions)* (Durham, NC: Duke University Press, 2008). Murray Forman, *One Night on TV Is Worth Weeks at the Paramount: Popular Music on Early Television (Console-ing Passions)* (Raleigh, NC: Duke University Press, 2012). Norma Coates, *Rocking the Wasteland: A Cultural History of Popular Music on American Network Television from Elvis to MTV* (Raleigh, NC: Duke University Press), forthcoming.
13. See Allan Cameron, "Colour, Embodiment and Dread in High Tension and A Tale of Two Sisters," in *Horror Studies* 3, no. 1 (April 30, 2012): 87–103. John Belton, "Painting by the Numbers: The Digital Intermediate," *Film Quarterly* 61, no. 3 (Spring 2008): 58–65. J. P. Geuens, "Angels of Light," in *The Oxford Handbook of Sound and Image in Digital Media*, ed. Carol Vernallis et al. (New York and Oxford: Oxford University Press), forthcoming. Mark Kerins, *Beyond Dolby (Stereo): Cinema in the Digital Sound Age* (Bloomington: Indiana University Press, 2011). Mark Katz, *Capturing Sound: How Technology Has Changed Music* (Berkeley: University of California Press, 2004), 156. Jeff Smith, "The Sound of Intensified Continuity," in Richardson, *Oxford Handbook of New Audiovisual Aesthetics*. Melissa Ragona, "Doping the Voice," Ron Sadoff, "Scoring for Film and Video Games: Collaborative Practices and Digital Post-Production," and William Whittington, "Lost in Sensation—Reevaluating the Role of Cinematic Sound in the Digital Age," all in Vernallis, *Oxford Handbook of Sound and Image in Digital Media*.
14. See Matthew Sumera, "Understanding the Pleasures of War's Audiovision," in Vernallis, *Oxford Handbook of Sound and Image in Digital Media*. "The Ultimate Riot Collection," a 30-part YouTube series depicting violent clashes and property, http://www.youtube.com/watch?v=ZCizxpxlCNU.
15. See Thomas Elsaesser, "Digital Cinema: Convergence or Contradiction?," William Cheng, "Monstrous Noise and the Aesthetic Economies of Fear," Amy Herzog, "'Charm the Air to Give a Sound': The Uncanny Soundscape of Punchdrunk's Sleep No More," Kiri Miller, "Virtual and Visceral Experience in Music-Oriented Videogames," and Paul Morris and Susanna Paasonen, "Coming to Mind: Pornography and the Mediation of Intensity," in Vernallis, *Oxford Handbook of Sound and Image in Digital Media*. Karen Collins, *Game Sound: An Introduction to the History, Theory, and Practice of Video Game Music and Sound Design* (Cambridge, MA: MIT Press, 2008).
16. See the chapter entitled "Audiovisual Change: Viral Web Media and the Obama Campaigns." For an example of the interpenetration of high and low culture and video art, see Joanna Demers, "Discursive Accents in Some Recent Digital Media Works," in Vernallis, *Oxford Handbook of Sound and Image in Digital Media*.

"Gangnam for Freedom—Anish Kapoor and Friends (Official Video)" http://www.youtube.com/watch?v=tcjFzmWLEdQ.

"Ai Weiwei Does Gangnam Style" http://www.youtube.com/watch?v=n281GWfT1E8.

These memes seem to connect up everything. I follow "Gangnam style" because I teach YouTube. My colleague Scott Bukatman researches comic books and is working on Spiderman. Here's his book and a related link: Scott Bukatman, *The Poetics of Slumberland: Animated Spirits and the Animating Spirit* (Berkeley: University of California Press, 2012). "Deadpool vs Gangnam Style" http://www.youtube.com/watch?v=xo-tWlETq8w.

17. Alma Har'el's and Beirut's "Concubine" vimeo.com/5502040.
   Choreographed scene from *Bombay Beach* vimeo.com/23571616.
   A$AP Rocky's "Peso" http://www.youtube.com/watch?v=ob3ktDxAjWI.
   Macklemore's "Thrift Shop" http://www.youtube.com/watch?v=QK8mJJJvaes.
   For some of the best work on audiovisual aesthetics, digital media, and the documentary, see Jennifer Peterson, "Workers Leaving the Factory: Witnessing Industry in the Digital Age," John Belton, "The World in the Palm of Your Hand: Agnes Varda, Trinh T. Minh-ha, and the Digital Documentary," and Selmin Kara, "The Sonic Summons: Meditations on Nature and Anempathetic Sound in Digital Documentaries," in Vernallis, *Oxford Handbook of Sound and Image in Digital Media*. Robynn J. Stilwell, "Audio-Visual Space in an Era of Technological Convergence," in Richardson, *Oxford Handbook of New Audiovisual Aesthetics*.

Chapter 4

1. David Bordwell, for example, has catalogued new models like the database, forking-path, or multiple-draft narrative. David Bordwell, *The Way Hollywood Tells It: Story and Style in Modern Movies* (Berkeley: University of California Press, 2006), 92–93. Marsha Kinder has also described database narratives. See Marsha Kinder, "Hot Spots, Avatars, and Narrative Fields Forever: Buñuel's Legacy for New Digital Media and Interactive Database Narrative," *Film Quarterly* 55, no. 4 (Summer 2002): 2–15. Eleftheria Thanouli, *Post-Classical Cinema: An International Poetics of Film Narration* (New York: Wallflower Press, 2009), 96, 173–182. See also Warren Buckland, *Puzzle Films: Complex Storytelling in Contemporary Cinema* (Malden, MA: Wiley-Blackwell, 2009). See also Elsaesser on database films, Shaviro on post-intensified continuity.
   To date, there are two important analyses of *Moulin Rouge!*. Marsha Kinder, "Moulin Rouge," *Film Quarterly* 55, no. 3 (Spring 2002): 52–59. Pam Cook, *Baz Luhrmann* (*BFI World Directors*) (London: British Film Institute, 2010).
2. Intensified films tend to be "genres of one," where each film breaks formal and narrative classical rules in its own way. Films like *Eternal Sunshine* and *Moulin Rouge!* might seem incommensurable. I'm making an aesthetic judgment here.
3. Now 3-D and IMAX will take over with their own aesthetic requirements. 3-D must tell us where and when to look. Color is dialed down by 30 percent. Fast motion now becomes attenuated by the stereo-optic visual field.
4. Stanley Cavell, *Pursuits of Happiness: The Hollywood Comedy of Remarriage* (*Harvard Film Studies*) (Boston: Harvard University Press, 1984), 49.
5. And is this boudoir a collective space, let out by the hour, prime real estate for the highest-paid prostitute? (A flash shot of Nina during the "Can-Can" sequence suggests so.) Does Satine spend the night there after all the men leave? (Since the space contains a bath, might she have changed there, and why the shifts from a red satin, then black lace, then a red satin dress again? Such complicated seductions!)
6. "Stop-time" is a line from "Elephant Love Medley."
   What other mainstream film has such an unusual shape? (Perhaps this is a stylistic trait peculiar to Luhrmann. There's an almost full-stop cadence in the midst of *Australia* as well.)
7. Perhaps this is a species of the music video. In this genre, we often move through a dense patch to come across a close-up that feels like an opening or a clearing.
8. The first time we meet a character, it's through the eyes of another. Thus we're led through an unfolding chain. The dwarf conjures up Christian, who brings forth Lautrec and so on.
   When we witness Christian writing his and Satine's memoir, *Moulin Rouge!*, the film offers us an opportunity to think about the past and the future. But the fact that our protagonist is bound to his typewriter, locked in a garret, typing words so rhythmically

and emphatically, may give us an opportunity to opt out. We don't have to be responsible for the events unfolding because Christian is keeping a chronology. We can wander about to freely follow digressions and divertissements.

9. Sianne Ngai, *Our Aesthetic Categories: Zany, Cute, Interesting* (Boston: Harvard University Press, 2012).

10. Within *Moulin Rouge!*'s swirling mélange, there is a confusion about sex, money, art, and love. Christian's penis elicits the Bohemian's admiration of "talent," but another time it makes a cash register ring. Zidler forgets about investing, but then signs the deed and gives Satine away. Christian, role-playing the courtesan, says that he's been "cured of the ridiculous obsession with love," but with his hip thrusts, it's really sex. Lily says the Duke will get "his end in," after Christian gets "his end in." The penniless guitar player "doesn't love him." Tracking all of these associations, we become quite confused too. Are we like the audience, taken by fairytale stories when we really should be tracking the money? Perhaps Zidler and the Duke, as grand financiers, most know the story and it lies with the maharajah.

11. Our attention often stays focused on the Duke, for often no one seems to address the camera so directly as does he (in love, Christian and Satine gaze at one another). Are we encouraged to identify with him? We too might like the means to purchase the Moulin Rouge and possess Satine as one of our things. We may not have the handsomeness and charms of Christian, but, like the Duke, we hope to get our "end in." This desire, nurtured against traditional Hollywood lines, may remain illicit and repressed.

12. *Moulin Rouge!*, like many music videos, foregrounds chains of sonic and visual motifs. The elephant's trumpeting had first appeared during the "Can-Can"'s rendition of Teen Spirit. These calls were accompanied by young males in tuxes to be countered by the women dancers' descending singing.

Chapter 5

1. David Bordwell calls this style "intensified continuity" in *The Way Hollywood Tells It: Story and Style in Modern Movies* (Berkeley: University of California Press, 2006), 120–121.

2. Ibid., 147; Jean-Pierre Geuens, "The Grand Style," *Film Quarterly* 58, no. 4 (2005): 27.

3. Though the Internet makes gauging music video's current influence difficult, we should not forget that videos were once frequent viewing and topics of conversation and their effects have come to fruition. Music video's production practices are similarly central to intensified aesthetics. Since the early 1980s, music video directors have tended to film lots of footage with high shooting-to-editing ratios, use an array of camera techniques, drag the most gripping images onto the timeline, edit playfully and freely, cut and remix the soundtrack, and then re-colortime, calibrate, and generally fine-tune the image to the soundtrack, all at a breakneck pace to follow the song's path up the pop charts. But the aesthetics of music video count equally. First on video, then film, and now digitally, directors produce vast amounts of imagery within a hothouse environment densely saturated with experimentation. Technologies often appear in music video before they break into film: David Fincher's burrowing snorkel camera appeared in his Steve Winwood video "Roll with It" before his film *Fight Club* (1999).

4. Music video directors who have moved to film include Jonas Åkerlund, Michael Bay, Antoine Fuqua, Jonathan Glazer, Gary Gray, Michel Gondry, Francis Lawrence, Marcus Nispel, Mark Pellington, and Mark Romanek.

5. Stanley Cavell, *Cities of Words* (Cambridge, MA: Harvard University Press, 2004), 109.

6. The centrality of these norms is argued for in Robert McKee, *Story: Substance, Structure, Style and the Principles of Screenwriting* (New York: Harper-Collins, 1997). McKee famously appears as a character in Spike Jonze's *Adaptation* (2002). Charlie Kaufman's mock-autobiographical script shows its screenwriter protagonist reluctantly taking McKee's workshop.

7. *Eternal Sunshine*'s 1970s scenes, staged in the kitchen of Joel's childhood, illuminate his desire to possess both his mother and his girlfriend. Mierzwiak, an obstacle to these relationships, erases these memories, making such relationships impossible.

8. The film also presents a regression from recent memories back through adolescent humiliation to childhood; this might imply a clear directionality, but a shot of Joel sucking his thumb comes too early, and low-angle shots of toys, knick-knacks, and circus elephants, which suggest a child's point of view, might appear anywhere.

9. This close engagement among image, sound, and memory feels somehow musical and works like music video. See Carol Vernallis, *Experiencing Music Video: Aesthetics and Cultural Context* (New York: Columbia University Press, 2004), 20–24.

10. I am quoting from Les Brill's excellent analysis of John Huston's *Freud* (1962), with which *Eternal Sunshine* has some things in common. Huston's introductory voiceover for *Freud* narrates: "This is the story of Freud's descent into a region almost as black as hell itself, man's unconscious, and how he let in the light." Like *Eternal Sunshine*, *Freud* draws upon a large repertoire of visual and aural motifs to suggest interpersonal relationships and personal obsessions. Both films deal closely with the workings of cathexis. I would claim that *Eternal Sunshine*'s surface is more labored than *Freud*'s; Brill admires *Freud* for its humanism. Les Brill, *John Huston's Filmmaking* (Cambridge: Cambridge University Press, 1997), 175.

11. It is difficult to classify these threads or even to group them into thicker strands. A list includes the following: Charles River/Montauk, folksongs, Huckleberry Hound doll and other childhood toys, orange sweatshirt, colored hair, alcohol, mattress, pillow, posada skeletons, lamps, panties and crotch, partial faces, diary and drawings, files and mail, birds, dog, quotations, airplanes, old technology including videotapes, old tape recording machines and so on, Patrick, out-of-tune upright piano, drums and drumming, chopsticks, plaid blanket/leopardskin blanket and fur, blank, spot and birthmark, water and snow, American flags, heart, boxes with red ribbon or red wrapping paper, couples, butterflies, flowers and other plant life, figurines, white orbs, houses, fences, expanded spaces, movie theaters. and television screens.

12. A second motivic collection is tied to precomputerized literacy. *Eternal Sunshine* makes visual references to papers and filing containers (knapsacks, folders, envelopes, and so on). A television shows a shot of Grandpa from *The Munsters* passing his hand over a flying book. Stan later says: "It was here in the paper logs." We hear rustling papers at three disparate points in the film, and nothing in the image relates to these sounds.

13. David Martin-Jones argues that the appearance of the American flag underscores the film's thematic concern with the importance of taking responsibility for memories and acknowledging mistakes—a progressive post-9/11 turn. A flag turned backward is placed over the doorway as Mierzwiak runs out of the apartment after his wife. American flags decorate Clem's neighbors' yards. David Martin-Jones, *Deleuze, Cinema and National Identity: Narrative Time in National Contexts* (Edinburgh: Edinburgh University Press, 2006).

14. Here Joel crosses back from the dream of his mother's kitchen into a waking state in his living room: after his baby self gets sucked down the drain while being bathed in the kitchen sink, he reemerges, gasping for breath, as the Lacuna group hovers over him. Night scenes were shot in the studio, so the spot on the ceiling must have been deliberately painted there.

15. The spots and blanks feel Hitchcockian. See William Rothman, *Hitchcock: The Murderous Gaze* (Cambridge, MA: Harvard University Press, 1984), 260.

16. Vernallis, *Experiencing Music Video*, 20–24.

17. Richard Middleton has argued that one of the defining features of popular music is its high degree of repetition—rhythms, timbres, iconic materials, and sectional divisions repeat endlessly and build to a state of jouissance. Richard Middleton, "Over and over: Notes towards a Politics of Repetition," http://www2.hu-berlin.de/fpm/texte/middle.htm. (This article was accessed in 2008. It's no longer online.)

18. James Naremore, *Acting in the Cinema* (Indianapolis: Indiana University Press, 1998), 64–65.

19. Vernallis, *Experiencing Music Video*, 54–73. Mannequin figures appear frequently in music video because they can mediate between silence and becoming. Videos establish a continuum from stillness to flux: inanimate decor connects to the quiet out of which the song begins; still figures match the slowest rhythmic stratum; moderate physical movements such as knee-bends, heads turning to one side, or steps forward match midtempo articulations; frenetic visual elements such as the showy, fluttery gestures of the star; the rapid movement of small turning objects and shifting patterns of light speak to faster rhythmic strata. Gondry, as co-scriptwriter, may have included these depictions because they have become central to his lexicon.

20. See Charles Kronengold, "Accidents, Hooks and Theory," *Popular Music* 24, no. 3 (2005): 385–386. Music videos develop a variety of means to underscore a song's hooks.

21. Quentin Tarantino often employs these techniques.

22. In the soundtrack here, claves recall the old technique of using coconut shells to make the sound of horses' hooves. Why would we hear horses' hooves during Clem and Joel's courtship on a train? Music videos often play with diegetic sound-sources that differ from the sounds of the song. In the foreground, we might see a Slurpee machine churning away, while the song has a "squish squish" that exists at a distance from its real-world counterpart, as in the Smashing Pumpkins' "1979."

23. Joel fingers a glass with tiny daisies and Clem wears the same miniature flowers on her shirt. This doubling suggests some sort of connection. In this case the image reinforces the musical point.

24. Michel Chion, *Audiovision: Sound on Screen*, trans. Claudia Gorbman (New York: Columbia University Press, 1990), 90–91.

25. *Eternal Sunshine* borrows heavily from Hitchcock, who created novel narrative forms in films such as *Psycho* and *Vertigo*. Clem's flowery red and black dress that she wears in Barnes & Noble references Eve's dress in *North by Northwest*'s Chicago hotel room. Both women have almost killed their lovers: here, the dresses suggest death, sexuality, and rebirth. Like Eve's mothering of Thornhill, Clem mothers Joel.

26. See Carole Lyn Piechota, "Once More and Innumerable times more: Nietzsche's Eternal Return in *Eternal Sunshine of the Spotless Mind*," *Film and Philosophy* 11 (2007): 173–182.

27. The image resembles De Chirico in its empty, still, and eerie tone. The film contains other high-art allusions such as the Vermeer-like drawing of a woman in an open book on Joel's table. One thinks of the image of a seamstress on a book's open page in *Un Chien Andalou*. (The sketched woman links to the many white figurines in Joel's bedroom, as well as white orbs, some of which are deformed.) Gondry's degree of control over visual material borders on obsessive: note the anthropomorphized lamp that moves when Stan says Joel has gone off the map. The emblematic red car seen out of Joel's window (which helps build connections to the film's final montage sequence) is substituted by a tree in the film's closing scene. Perhaps the film's visually prismatic effects are not overwhelming because we are watching the workings of the unconscious, which as Freud argues is mechanical and built upon signifiers, not morals or themes.

28. See Vernallis, *Experiencing Music Video*, 10.

29. E. Ann Kaplan first noticed this phenomenon in her analysis of Madonna's "Papa Don't Preach." Even with only one performer, the video showcases two Madonnas—Madonna 1 and Madonna 2. E. Ann Kaplan, *Rocking around the Clock: MTV Postmodernism and Consumer Culture* (New York: Methuen, 1987), 130.

30. See Kobena Mercer, "Monster Metaphors: Notes on Michael Jackson's *Thriller*," in Simon Frith, Andrew Goodwin, and Lawrence Grossberg, eds., *Sound and Vision: The Music Video Reader* (New York: Routledge, 1993), 93–108.

31. Mary's embarrassment when trying to explain to Mierzwiak that "I think it's important for my job to understand the work that we do, well not that I do, but the work by the people where I work. The work of my colleagues," reveals a moment of odd entanglement between work and social relations.

32. The film does offer two or three minutes of respite within its 142-minute length, but it is only because these scenes are suffused with a sense of loss that they work effectively: Mary's reading of the quotation from Pope and her vision of elephants; Joel's weeping after being sucked through a time warp and leaving behind his mother and Clem; Joel's memory of Clem, shown as a montage of images of the couple seen out of a car's back window as it is driven into the night.

33. The film presents a relatively unexamined depiction of for-profit science in the service of cosmetic surgery for the brain. Lacuna's services do have some grounding in current medical practice: medication is now available for trauma victims that, if taken shortly after the incident, will soften the intensity of imprinted memories. New treatments for drug addiction may soon include medication with VR (virtual reality) enactments of drug consumption. The patient's emotional responses to these scenarios will become accentuated. Memory erasure seems close at hand.

34. Some of the films' representations surely invite criticism. Hard-hitting elements in the original scripts have been downplayed. Both Joel and Clem were originally depicted as depressive, with one on Prozac and the other on Zoloft. In one of the later rewrites, Mary has an abortion from a pregnancy with Mierzwiak, thus creating a stronger need to forget and a greater sense that her decision to undergo the procedure might constitute a crime of forgetting. Clem is very literate in the earlier scripts. She and Joel talk about books. In the film's closing, she's suddenly made dumb—a magazine-reading rather than a book-reading girl whom Joel notes says "li-bary" yet works at a Barnes & Noble in a fairly prosperous section of Long Island. Why these changes? Perhaps so our sympathy will stay with Joel: Clem, as a member of a lower social class, is a less valuable commodity and therefore more erasable.

35. In one of the film's abundant uses of the match cut, we move from ice to concrete. Later we will move from sand in Joel's bedroom to sand on the beach. In an aural match cut, the sounds of the timpani in the Barnes & Noble shift to thuds in Rob and Carrie's living room.

36. Recorded birdsong and dogs' cries also mark the pleasures and vicissitudes of heterosexual pairing. Dogs bark when Patrick makes an advance on Clem, or Hollis and Mierzwiak confront one another. Bird calls are linked to the romantic leads.

37. See Steve Shaviro, "Emotion Capture: Affect in Digital Film," *Projections* 1, no. 2 (2007): 37–55.

38. Nicholas Cook, *Analysing Musical Multimedia* (New York: Oxford University Press, 1998), 81–84.

Chapter 6

1. India is the largest producer of films in the world. In 2009, India produced 2,961 films on celluloid, 1,288 of which were feature films. The Indian film industry has the highest ticket sales and the second-largest revenue stream in the world. Rajesh Khanna, "The Business of Hindi Films," ed. Gulazāra et al., *Encyclopaedia of Hindi Cinema: An Enchanting Close-Up of India's Hindi Cinema* (New Delhi: Encyclopaedia Britannica, 2003), 140. See also *Annual Report 2010*, Central Board of Film Certification, Ministry of Information and Broadcasting, Government of India.

2. Hindi cinema became widely known as "Bollywood" (from combining the word Bombay and Hollywood) in the nineties. Many scholars prefer not to use the term. See Madhav Prasad, "This Thing called Bollywood," http://www.india-seminar.com/2003/525/525%20madhava%20prasad.htm. Ravi Vasudevan, "The Meanings of 'Bollywood' in Rachel Dwyer and

Jerry Pinto, eds., *Beyond the Boundaries of Bollywood: The Many Forms of Hindi Cinema* (New Delhi: Oxford University Press, 2011), 3–29.

Anna Morcom argues that Hindi Cinema has always been hybrid, with a particularly high degree of cross-cultural sharing in the post-independence era. The most recent examples reflect a merging of western global aesthetics, with A. R. Rahman and Mani Ratnam as key figures. Correspondence with Morcom, December 2012.

3. See Anna Morcom, *Hindi Film Songs and the Cinema* (*Soas Musicology Series*) (Surrey, UK: Ashgate 2007). See also Gregory D. Booth, *Behind the Curtain: Making Music in Mumbai's Film Studios* (New York: Oxford University Press, 2008).

4. M. Madhava Prasad, *Ideology of the Hindi Film: A Historical Construction* (New York: Oxford University Press, 2001), 19.

5. Anna Morcom, *Hindi Film Songs and the Cinema* (*Soas Musicology Series*) (Surrey, UK: Ashgate, 2007), 41. See also Rachel Dwyer, *All You Want Is Money, All You Need Is Love* (*Gender & Women's Studies/Literature & the Arts*) (London: Cassell, 2000).

6. Jyotika Virdi, *The Cinematic Imagination: Indian Popular Films as Social History* (Brunswick, NJ: Rutgers University Press, 2003), 28.

7. Prasad, *Ideology of the Hindi Film*, 75.

8. They help sell the soundtrack and are often viewed solo.

9. The thumbi is also called a tumbi.

Chapter 7

1. http://www.techcrunch.com/2009/06/09/YouTube-video-streams-top-1-billionday/

2. Alex Galloway, "The Unworkable Interface," *New Literary History* 39, no. 4 (Autumn 2008): 931–955.

3. "The Badger Song" http://www.youtube.com/watch?v=EIyixC9NsLI

    Some might want to call "The Badger Song" bad art and bad music, but I disagree. For future reading, see Kay Dickinson, *Off Key: When Film and Music Won't Work Together* (New York: Oxford University Press, 2008), 13–15.

    "Mango" http://www.youtube.com/watch?v=TyrRlHrgiew

    "Llama songs" http://www.youtube.com/watch?v=HbPDKHXWlLQ

    Badger song mashups: http://www.youtube.com/watch?v=BuJvqPMbMYQ, http://www.youtube.com/watch?v=B_pWTlN15bc, http://www.youtube.com/watch?v=Ddpobq4mG20, http://www.youtube.com/watch?v=kMjUf8HpnQM, http://www.youtube.com/watch?v=GCCzP70jQDw

4. In My Language http://www.youtube.com/watch?v=JnylM1hI2jc

    Cat plays with a teremin http://www.youtube.com/watch?v=0ONJfp95yoE

5. The Gummy Bear Song - Long English Version http://www.youtube.com/watch?v=astISOttCQ0

6. Crazy Frog - Axel F http://www.youtube.com/watch?v=k85mRPqvMbE

7. Alexandra Juhasz, "Learning the Five Lessons of YouTube: After Trying to Teach There, I Don't Believe the Hype," *Cinema Journal* 48, no. 2 (Winter 2009): 145–150.

8. Michael Wetsch, "An Anthropological Introduction to YouTube" (Lecture at the Library of Congress, June 23, 2008): http://www.youtube.com/watch?v=TPAO-lZ4_hU. Henry Jenkins, "If It Doesn't Spread, It's Dead (Part One): Media Viruses and Memes," Confessions of an Aca-Fan (blog), February 11, 2009, http://henryjenkins.org/2009/02/if_it_doesnt_spread_its_dead_p.html.

9. Virginia Heffernan, "The Many Tribes of YouTube" and "Pixels at Exhibition"

    "An Anthropological Introduction to YouTube" http://www.youtube.com/watch?v=TPAO-lZ4_hU

    A number of collected volumes on YouTube have come out as well. The best remains the Video Vortex, which is free to download. http://networkcultures.org/wpmu/videovortex/resources/booksbr

See *The Youtube Reader*, ed. Pelle Snickars and Patrick Vonderau (Stockholm: National Library of Sweden, 2009). *Video Vortex Reader: Responses to Youtube*, ed. Geert Lovink and Sabine Niederer (Amsterdam: Institute of Network Cultures, 2008). Michael Strangelove, *Watching Youtube: Extraordinary Videos by Ordinary People* (Toronto: University of Toronto Press, 2010). Jean Burgess and Joshua Green, *Youtube: Online Video and Participatory Culture* (Malden, MA: Polity Press, 2009). Paula Hearsum and Ian Inglis, "The Emancipation of Music Video: YouTube and the Cultural Politics of Supply and Demand," in *The Oxford Handbook of New Audiovisual Aesthetics*, ed. John Richardson et al. (New York and Oxford: Oxford University Press), forthcoming. Ken Hillis, *Online a Lot of the Time: Ritual, Fetish, Sign* (Durham, NC: Duke University Press, 2009).

10. "The Sneezing Baby Panda" http://www.youtube.com/watch?v=FzRH3iTQPrk
    "Gizmo Flushes" http://www.youtube.com/watch?v=WofFb_eOxxA

11. "Noah takes a photo of himself every day for 6 years." http://www.youtube.com/watch?v=6B26asyGKDo

12. "Hechizeros Band—El Sonidito" http://www.YouTube.com/watch?v=ih9wsbq7loo
    "Dan Deacon & Liam Lynch—Drinking Out of Cups" http://www.YouTube.com/watch?v=skCV2L0c6K0
    "cyriak's animation mix" http://www.YouTube.com/watch?v=-3JCESdFNyw
    "Shrooms: a trip experience" http://www.YouTube.com/watch?v=B4pIxnuUG1k&feature=related
    "APT Obama Obama" http://www.youtube.com/watch?v=t7RZTlzXHmo
    "Barack O'bollywood" http://www.youtube.com/watch?v=sA-451XMsuY
    "The Indian Song" http://www.youtube.com/watch?v=omVq43RhVXI
    "El Mudo—Chacarron Macarron-Crazy Music Video" http://www.youtube.com/watch?v=l12Csc_lW0Q
    "Sunday Afternoon" http://www.youtube.com/watch?v=4gx3nn6LS6g

13. Here are some examples of psychedelic reiterative clips on YouTube:
    "Dan Deacon & Liam Lynch—Drinking Out of Cups" http://www.youtube.com/watch?v=skCV2L0c6K0
    "Shrooms: a trip experience" http://www.youtube.com/watch?v=B4pIxnuUG1k&feature=related
    "Pick of Destiny Shrooms" http://www.youtube.com/watch?v=guCPHG2ys9k&feature=related
    "Get Confused" http://www.youtube.com/watch?v=9Ryypg5aB-Y

14. Robert Fink, *Repeating Ourselves: American Minimal Music as Cultural Practice* (Berkeley: University of California Press, 2005), xiii.

15. Dan Deacon and Liam Lynch, "Drinking Out of Cups" http://www.youtube.com/watch?v=skCV2L0c6K0

16. See John Richardson, *Eye for Music* (New York and Oxford: Oxford University Press, 2011), 4.

17. Simon Reynolds, *Energy Flash: A Journey through Rave Music and Dance Culture*, reprint ed. (Berkeley, CA: Soft Skull Press, 2012), xxx.

18. "Pork and Beans" http://www.youtube.com/watch?v=muP9eH2p2PI
    "South Park" http://www.youtube.com/watch?v=idZOVqdcqno

19. Lev Manovich, *The Language of New Media* (Cambridge, MA: MIT Press, 2001), xv, 20.

20. Andre Bazin, *What Is Cinema?* (Berkeley: University of California Press, 2004), 96–97.

21. Laura Mulvey, *Death 24x a Second: Stillness and the Moving Image* (London: Reaktion Books, 2006), 17–33.

22. David Rodowick, *The Virtual Life of Film* (Cambridge, MA: Harvard University Press, 2007), 119.

23. Conversation with Jonathan Sterne, Spring 2009. See Jonathan Sterne, *The Audible Past: Cultural Origins of Sound Reproduction* (Durham and London: Duke University Press, 2003), 18.

24. "Charleston Style" http://www.youtube.com/watch?v=339ixMtHrVk
    "Daft Punk—Around the World" http://www.youtube.com/watch?v=K0HSD_i2DvA
25. Carol Vernallis, *Experiencing Music Video: Aesthetics and Cultural Context* (New York: Columbia University Press, 2004), 146.
26. "Evolution of Dance" http://www.youtube.com/watch?v=dMH0bHeiRNg
    "David After Dentist" http://www.youtube.com/watch?v=txqiwrbYGrs
27. Much early photography depicted spirits. The record's spirals were also said to carry direct imprints of voices from the dead.
28. Tom Gunning's "The Cinema of Attractions: Early Film, Its Spectator and the Avant-Garde," in *Early Film*, ed. Thomas Elsaesser and Adam Barker (London: British Film Institute, 1989), 56–62.
29. "Barack Rolled" http://www.youtube.com/watch?v=65I0HNvTDH4
    "John McCain Gets BarackRoll'd" http://www.youtube.com/watch?v=_TiQCJX-pbKg
        "How To Rick Roll Somebody" http://www.youtube.com/watch?v=qmPmIJyi0sc
        "RickRoll'D" http://www.youtube.com/watch?v=oHg5SJYRHA0
        "Rick Astley - Never Gonna Give You Up" http://www.youtube.com/watch?v=dQw4w9WgXcQ
30. Obama and McCain—Dance Off! http://www.youtube.com/watch?v=wzyT9-9lUyE&feature=related
31. David Rodowick, *The Virtual Life of Film* (Cambridge, MA: Harvard University Press, 2007).
32. "Chocolate Rain," one of YouTube's most all-time popular clips, http://www.youtube.com/watch?v=EwTZ2xpQwpA
33. "Obama sings chocolate rain" http://www.youtube.com/watch?v=aD7OZZ9R6h8
34. BallsCrash http://www.youtube.com/watch?v=jlgr6MoXufU
35. Psy – Gangnam Style http://www.youtube.com/watch?v=9bZkp7q19f0
36. Mama Cat Comes to Rescue Her Little Kitten http://www.youtube.com/watch?v=S5-D0f6nHSQ
        Katy Perry ft Keenan Cahill - Teenage Dream http://www.youtube.com/watch?v=lm_n3hg-Gbg
37. Whitest Kids U' Know: Abe Lincoln http://www.youtube.com/watch?v=B4Uf9rsBbhc
38. "Barack O'bollywood" http://www.youtube.com/watch?v=sA-451XMsuY
        "LL Cool J—Mr. President (ft. Wyclef Jean)" http://www.youtube.com/watch?v=lE32yCxy87I
39. "HOT K-POP 2009 ~ special mashup pt. I ~ (23 songs in one)" http://www.youtube.com/watch?v=wyZPpwLZeag
        "Obama Mashup Tribute: He Really Deed It." http://www.youtube.com/watch?v=LBh9c8cuthQ
        "MASHUP—Obama/McCain Campaign Ads" http://www.youtube.com/watch?v=IEehKNNMq_4
        "Getting Nasty—John Bennett's entry in Campaign Mash Up" http://www.youtube.com/watch?v=DB56hlJoHN4
        "Barack Obama: Unstoppable Momentum (Led Zeppelin Mashup)" http://www.youtube.com/watch?v=g_NrAmqaShY
40. I'll describe an audiovisual hook as an image-music instance that pops out of the texture—through placement in the frame, scale, visual or sonic material.
41. Jeffrey Sconce, "Irony, Nihilism, and the New American 'Smart' Film," *Oxford Journals, Humanities, Screen* 43, no. 4 (2002): 349–369.
42. See Tim and Eric Awesome Show Great Job! episode #20, "Embarrassed" on Adult Swim. http://www.youtube.com/watch?v=AeyqS9BDPds
43. I and many of the faithful, forgoing all kinds of New Year's revelries, stayed in and recorded the year end's countdown on VHS. (Tapes had to be swapped out every two hours—we might as well have been tethered to our ovens, baking pies—it now seems so antiquated.)

44. The whole clip seems luridly, moistly covered with cellophane and ready to inspire James Rosenquist's recent series of paintings *Gift Wrapped Doll*. (In the new interpenetration of high and low, why wouldn't have Rosenquist gotten excited by "Barbie Girl"?)
    Aqua - Barbie Girl http://www.youtube.com/watch?v=ZyhrYis509A
    Avril Lavigne - Girlfriend http://www.youtube.com/watch?v=Bg59q4puhmg
45. "Pop Goes the Weasel" http://www.youtube.com/watch?v=TArfrz6pIgU
46. Garrett Stewart's high-theory analysis of the digital. See Garrett Stewart, *Framed Time: Toward a Postfilmic Cinema* (Chicago: University of Chicago Press, 2007).
47. Virginia Heffernan, "The Death of the Open Web," *New York Times*, May 21, 2010, http://www.nytimes.com/2010/05/23/magazine/23FOB-medium-t.html.
48. This image must come from getting trapped in Wal-Mart and staring distractedly at the rows of TVs perched on shelves or late-night TV advertisements showing the same.
49. I'd claim Gizmo's clip—not Pachelbel's "Canon" —is YouTube's first mega-milestone. YouTube fans go bananas for animals and Gizmo was the first superstar. (Gizmo's been out for so many years and recently I couldn't find him on YouTube.)
50. Lawrence Lessig has written provocatively on this: *Code: And Other Laws of Cyberspace, Version 2.0* (New York: Basic Books, 2006); and Lessig, *Free Culture: The Nature and Future of Creativity* (New York: Penguin Group, 2004).
51. My skill at being able to sit through a feature—say a repeat viewing of Hitchcock's *Vertigo*— is gone, *it's shot*.
52. Okay, I found it: "Tim and Eric I Sit on You" http://www.adultswim.com/video/?episodeID=8a25c3921691a4b30116924a730f0085
53. I've tried all available avenues—emailing several sources both through Google and the YouTube website, calling on the phone, trying third-party references, just to find out basic facts about the service. Finally, one staff person spoke to me on the phone for a good bit and promised to get back to me as well as send clips. The trail went cold. It's in the public interest to make such a site transparent to all of us.
54. I became enamored with the Jack Smith clip because I had assigned it along with a chapter by Laura Marks in an upper-division course. See Laura Marks, "Loving a Disappearing Image," in *Touch: Sensuous Theory and Multisensory Media* (Minneapolis: University of Minnesota Press, 2002), 91–110.
55. "Asian Backstreet Boys" http://www.youtube.com/watch?v=D2BZwwgKF2s
56. Conversation with William Rothman, Spring 2010.

Chapter 8

1. "'McCain Wins!' Guilt Your Friends into Voting with Video Prank," Huffington Post, November 24, 2008, http://www.huffingtonpost.com/2008/10/24/mccain-wins-guilt-your-fr_n_137705.html. An earlier version of this chapter appeared in Cinema Journal, Vol. 5, no. 4 (2011).
2. Viral media are web-based media made popular through user-to-user sharing (through email, blogs, Facebook, etc.). Corporations like viral media because consumers do the work of disseminating the message. Media scholar Henry Jenkins prefers the terms "spreadable" and "sticky" to "viral" web media. These terms avoid the metaphor of infection and acknowledge a consumer's agency. "Spreadability" describes the way consumers remake, sample, remix, and repurpose content. "Stickiness" is associated with the content's ability to attract and hold viewer interest. Henry Jenkins, "If It Doesn't Spread, It's Dead (Part One): Media Viruses and Memes," Confessions of an Aca-Fan (blog), February 11, 2009, http://henryjenkins.org/2009/02/if_it_doesnt_spread_its_dead_p.html. See also Geert Lovink and Sabine Niederer, eds., *The Video Vortex Reader: Responses to YouTube* (Amsterdam: Institute of Network Cultures, 2008).
3. Fred Aun, "Over Long Campaign, Obama Views Drew Nearly a Billion Views," Clickz, November 7, 2008, http://www.clickz.com/3631604.

4. "Scott Thomas: Designing the Obama Campaign," 99 percent, http://the99percent.com/videos/5821/scott-thomas-designing-the-obama-campaign%3E; Jim Stanton, "The Man Behind Obama's Online Election Campaign," Web 2.0 Convergence (blog), April 20, 2009, http://www.digitalcommunitiesblogs.com/web_20_convergence/2009/04/the-man-behind-obamas-online-e.php.

5. According to Max Harper, Obama's chief staffperson for online video, clips were central to microtargeting. A music video would be made for a particular demographic like the Asian American Pacific Islander community, and people would receive an email with a subject line like "VIDEO: Maya Soetoro-Ng Will Tell You About Her Brother Barack." The body would contain a short description of the video, why you should click on it, and a thumbnail photo that would take you to a MyBo blog. Shown to produce a 5 percent increased open rate, video clips, according to Harper, increased participation, engagement, and financial donations. "Obama's Campaign Video Strategist: Forget Viral, It's All About Targeted Impact," Beet.TV, July 15, 2009, http://www.beet.tv/2009/07/obamas-campaign-video-strategist-forget-viral-its-about-targeted-impact.html; Meetu Chilana, "Changes" music video, http://www.youtube.com/watch?v=8FX7bKHjC04.

6. "Auto-Tune the News #2: pirates. drugs. gay marriage," April 20, 2009, http://www.youtube.com/watch?v=tBb4cjjj1gI.

7. Prince, Whitney Houston, Bobby Brown, P. Diddy, Public Enemy, Queen Latifah, Alicia Keys, Janet and Michael Jackson, Tribe Called Quest, to name a few.

8. Michael Luo, "In Job Hunt, College Degree Can't Close Racial Gap," *New York Times*, November 30, 2009.

9. E. A. Phelps, K. J. O'Connor, W. A. Cunningham, and E. S. Funayama, "Performance on Indirect Measures of Race Evaluation Predicts Amygdala Activation," *Journal of Cognitive Neuroscience* 12, no. 5 (September 2000): 729–738.

10. Benedict Carey, "Tolerance over Race Can Spread, Studies Find," *New York Times*, November 6, 2008.

11. See Alicia Keys and Jack White, "Another Way to Die," October 21, 2008, http://www.youtube.com/watch?v=hM5UJvnbbuY; Ludacris, "Obama Is Here (MUSIC VIDEO)," http://www.youtube.com/watch?v=ulcGldJlKiA.

12. Pink "Dear Mr. President" http://www.youtube.com/watch?v=9eDJ3cuXKV4
    Wyclef Jean; Canibus "Gone Till November" http://www.youtube.com/watch?v=17cmBnziQw4

13. "We must not again make manifest the 'apathy' label. . . . Our country will not be okay if Obama loses." Danyel Smith, EdNote, *Vibe*, November 2008, 20.

14. Angela Balakrishnan, "Presidential Playlist: Obama Opens Up His iPod," *guardian.co.uk*, June 25, 2008, http://www.guardian.co.uk/world/2008/jun/25/barackobama.uselections2008.

15. "Entrainment occurs when two oscillators come to oscillate together. . . . [E]ntrainment is the coordinating of the timing of our behaviors and the synchronizing of our attentional resources." Gill Satinder, "Entrainment and Musicality in the Human System Interface," *AI & Soc* (June 25, 2007): 567–605.

16. Suzanne Langer, *Philosophy in a New Key: A Study in the Symbolism of Art* (1942; Cambridge, MA: Harvard University Press, 1957), 271.

17. See Katie Overy and Istvan Molnar-Szakacs, "Being Together in Time: Musical Experience and the Mirror Neuron System," *Music Perception* 26, no. 5 (June 2009): 489–491.

18. George Mather, http://www.michaelbach.de/ot/mot_biomot/index.html

19. George Mather, "Biological Motion," http://www.lifesci.sussex.ac.uk/home/George_Mather/Motion/BM.html.

20. Bernard Herrmann, quoted in Roger Manvell and John Huntley, eds., *Technique of Film Music*, 2nd ed. (New York: Focal Press, 1975), 244.

21. Carol Vernallis, *Experiencing Music Video: Aesthetics and Cultural Context* (New York: Columbia University Press, 2004), 48–67.

22. Rudolf Arnheim, *The Power of the Center* (Berkeley: University of California Press, 1988), 53–55.

23. Warren Buckland, *Directed by Steven Spielberg: Poetics of the Contemporary Hollywood Blockbuster* (New York: Continuum, 2006), 193–212.

24. Jane Feuer, *The Hollywood Musical* (Bloomington: Indiana University Press, 1982), 3–5.

25. Vernallis, *Experiencing Music Video*, 307.

26. Beyoncé, "If I Were a Boy" (music video), http://new.music.yahoo.com/videos/Beyonc/If-I-Were-A-Boy—201579307. Music video doesn't always do this: a more distanced camera or an ironic performance, such as we sometimes see in alternative videos, creates different sorts of engagement and detachment.

27. The video for and commentary about "Yes We Can" are at http://yeswecan.dipdive.com/.

28. Most YouTube clips garner a few hundred views; only rarely does one surpass a thousand. Blogs picked up "Yes We Can," MyBo hosted it, and Michelle Obama emailed it to everyone she knew. A clip's biggest bump often stems from traditional media. ABC News blurbed "Yes We Can," "Obama Girl," and "The Real John McCain," but "Yes We Can" was different. The clip steadily gained view counts throughout the election cycle. John Kelly, conversation with the author, December 13, 2009.

29. "John Rich—Raisin' McCain Music Video," August 14, 2008, http://www.youtube.com/watch?v=qmKgITJejfg. As of December 31, 2010, the official posting of "Raisin' McCain" had garnered just over 206,000 views.

30. TheONECampaign, "ONE TV Spot," April 24, 2007, http://www.youtube.com/watch?v=Jkf5oVtYCeM.

31. This streak of light is suggested earlier in the video. Many of the performers wear a white tie or shirt, which creates an energetic, upward flow, most markedly with the first singer's blouse at the beginning of the second verse.

32. David Bordwell, *Poetics of Cinema* (New York: Routledge, 2007), 118, 119.

33. Laura Mulvey, *Death 24x a Second: Stillness and the Moving Image* (London: Reaktion Books, 2006), 70.

34. Esthero's wink and her skull tattoo also form the out-of-focus spot in relation to anamorphic viewing, the moment when the video stares back threateningly at us. See Slavoj Žižek, "Looking Awry," *October* (Fall 1989): 30–55.

35. In the soundtrack it's stunning, though this time the image doesn't give the music equal weight, instead seeking out other moments for emphasis. This is a common music video device. The heterogeneous, multifaceted soundtrack presents too much for the image to attend to. All it can do is point and say "look at this," "now this," like a tour guide. See Vernallis, *Experiencing Music Video*, 156.

36. See Vernallis, *Experiencing Music Video*, 213.

37. Arnold Schoenberg, *Style and Idea*, ed. Leonard Stein (Berkeley: University of California Press, 1975), 288.

38. George Lakoff and Mark Johnson, *Philosophy in the Flesh: The Embodied Mind and Its Challenge to Western Thought* (New York: Basic Books, 1999), 32.

39. Justin London, *Hearing in Time: Psychological Aspects of Meter* (Oxford: Oxford University Press, 2004), 6, 12, 154.

40. Johansson's and will.i.am's gaze toward the top and bottom of the screen reflect the contours of the guitar strumming. Their blinks help define contour as well. See Vernallis, *Experiencing Music Video*, 213.

41. Lyrics underscore the harmony's sentiment, for example, the Beatles' "Let It Be": "When I find myself in times of trouble / Mother Mary comes to me"; as well as their "Blackbird": "Take these broken wings and learn to fly." See also Journey's "Don't Stop Believin'":

"Just a small-town girl / Living in a lonely world . . . ." Marc Evans, Charles Kronengold, and Jesse Rodin contributed to this harmonic analysis. See also Philip Tagg's analysis, "The 'Yes We Can' chords," http://tagg.org/xpdfs/YesWeCanChords.pdf.

42. Pornographer Paul Morris said in a December 28, 2008, phone conversation that the videos discussed in this paper offer little for gay subjects. (There are no identifiable gay performers nor signs of same-sex intimacy.) With no address to a gay viewership, the lyrics' aggressiveness ("Yes we can"), intense looks, and folky music might feel oppressive. While the lyrics for "If I Were a Boy" open a space for a youthful, shifting, not yet fully formed sexual identity, the lyric "boy" rather than "man" suggests a distance from black masculinity. Adequately depicting a minority group in a music video can prove difficult. See Hillary Clinton's "Hillary4U&Me" campaign music video, which worked hard (though not altogether successfully) to appeal to the gay community.

   "Hillary4U&Me," September 28, 2007, http://www.youtube.com/watch?v=5FvyG ydc8no.

43. Recently a significant portion of African pop performers have embraced the folk guitar, Beyoncé's newest album, "I am . . . Sasha Fierce," being one such example. Historical precedents include Hootie and the Blowfish and Prince, both of whom performed with interracial bands. And of course, folk and blues have interconnected roots, with black performers like Huddie "Lead Belly" Ledbetter influencing many later singer-songwriters.

44. The shot has an afterimage—an African American female singer wears a silk headband and gold necklace forming a shining perfect circle centered on the screen.

45. There are several competing videos of the Corrigan Brothers' "There's No One as Irish as Barack Obama," partly because of an authorship dispute between former members of the band. The current "official" version is here: http://www.youtube.com/watch?v=HplZ_taHXLM; Dirk Powell, "Oui, On Peut," October 21, 2008, http://www.youtube.com/watch?v=FLvgwHGlpdQ.

46. "Yes We Can" produced strong reactions. Perhaps these derived, in part, from the video's performances. Most performers flew in the day before taping from various legs of the campaign trail. Their expressions may reflect their recent, highly charged encounters with people they worked with, tried to convince, met at rallies, and so on. Director Jesse Dylan says that "Yes We Can" "caught a vapor," something in the air, and that he could never recreate its moment.

47. *MADtv* "Yes We Can" spoof, http://www.youtube.com/watch?v=kUpjvLGiSmM.

48. Ayo Jackson Dancers, "Yes We Can-Dance," March 1, 2008, http://www.youtube.com/watch?v=T2Bfjze-ymQ.

49. Hugh Atkin, "Barack Rolled," August 29, 2008, http://www.youtube.com/watch?v=wzSVOcgKq04; "John McCain Gets BarackRoll'd," http://www.youtube.com/watch?v=8XIJeIzSwYo; VideoJug, "How To "Rick Roll Somebody," September 16, 2008, http://www.youtube.com/watch?v=qmPmIJyi0sc; Cotter548, "RickRoll'D," May 15, 2007, http://www.youtube.com/watch?v=oHg5SJYRHA0.

50. I couldn't believe it. I use a lot of YouTube in my courses. I could find almost no links on film music temp tracks for my "Music Video and Its Siblings" class this Spring. Standing before my students while working with Blackboard, I noticed a student had posted a link that said, "The temp track in film music." Excitedly I exclaimed, "Look! Joe found a link for me!" and I clicked on it. I was "rickrolled."

51. Janet M. Box-Steffensmeier and Steven E. Schier, *The American Elections of 2008* (New York: Rowman & Littlefield, 2009) 16–17, 22–24. Clay Shossow, "Top 10 Most Important Online Political Events of 2008," December 30, 2008, New Media Campaigns, http://www.newmediacampaigns.com/page/top-10-most-important-online-political-events-of-2008.

52. John Legend, "Green Light" (music video), http://new.music.yahoo.com/videos/John-Legend/Green-Light—184533 177.

53. On its November 5, 2008 homepage, the website Launch showcased an enormous ad for an Obama tribute album with a link to "Green Light." In a YouTube clip posted on November 5, a nine- or ten-year-old African American boy, from behind a large cardboard life-sized cutout of Obama, elatedly sings "Green Light." "Obama singing Green Light, ft. Me," http://www.youtube.com/watch?v=GEeFDiHmV9Q.

54. In a preelection interview with *Vibe Magazine*, Robin Thicke claimed he titled his album "Something Else" as a message of hope for political change. After Obama was elected, one of the most popular YouTube links connected to Obama was Kool and the Gang's "Celebration." http://www.youtube.com/watch?v=YwEMxYggoKQ

55. E. Bonilla-Silva, C. Goar, and D. G. Embrick, "When Whites Flock Together: The Social Psychology of White Habitus," *Critical Sociology* 32, nos. 2–3 (2006): 229–253.

56. Besides "Green Light," T. Pain's "Can't Believe It" works similarly. TPainVEVO, October 24, 2009, http://www.youtube.com/watch?v=kWBE0sQC5L8.

57. Thomas Elsaesser, "Real Location, Fantasy Space, Performative Place: Double Occupancy and Mutual Interference in European Cinema," in *European Film Theory*, ed. Temenuga Trifonova (New York: Routledge, 2009), 56–57.

58. Patrice Evans, "The Bump Heard 'Round the World," *The Root*, June 2, 2009, http://www.theroot.com/views/bump-heard-round-world.

59. Andre 3000 acknowledges the latter, saying, "even Stevie Wonder got down sometimes."

60. The sexualized string of motifs (the dog, couple having sex, and woman bent forward provocatively); the engaged glances among performers; and the green stoplight and expansive declaration "I'm ready to go right now" offer the viewer nonhierarchical points of entry into the video.

61. Obama claims Earth, Wind & Fire as one of his favorite groups; the rival seventies funk group Parliament suggested EWF was too corporate. "Green Light" alludes to earlier empowered moments in African American pop music. Obama's rallies ended similarly with several "upwardly mobile" sixties Motown hits.

62. Conversation with Bambi Haggins, author of *Laughing Mad: The Black Comic Persona in Post-Soul America* (New Brunswick, NJ: Rutgers University Press, 2007).

63. The video's opening ambient music is a quarter-tone off and in a distant key from the song proper, and then the harmony takes a while to resolve, making it difficult for viewers to get their bearings. Who maintains authority here—the music, Legend (who slammed down the piano's lid), or the director? Such unclear forces provide an opportunity for us to seek our own way through the video.

64. BarackObama.com, "Barack Obama in Raleigh, NC," April 17, 2008, http://www.youtube.com/watch?v=FlR9DNfq GD4.

65. will.i.am & John Legend sing "Yes We Can," http://www.youtube.com/watch?v=247mUV0cjbI.

66. The live performer/rearscreen projection of Obama may also echo the Rickrolled series. The camera picks out two or three audience members—one shot is of a European American father holding his child, here reminiscent of "Yes We Can"'s Madonna and child.

67. The term "prosumer" blends "professional" or "producer" with "consumer."

68. Michael Stevens, "Barack O'bollywood," http://www.youtube.com/watch?v=Whx-0sBRks8; Amigos de Obama, "VIVA OBAMA 2008," February 19, 2008, http://www.youtube.com/watch?v=0fd-MVU4 vtU; Dave Stewart, "American Prayer" (music video), August 21, 2008, http://www.youtube.com/watch?v=oVi4rUzf-0Q.

69. Triple Spiral Productions, "Barack Obama Is IRISH!" September 26, 2008, http://www.youtube.com/watch?v=EADUQWKoVek; APT, "'Obama Obama': A Milli Obama Remix," http://www.youtube.com/watch?v=t7RZTlzXHmo.

70. Obama supporters decided that jokes about McCain's age were fair game because even though the candidate might not suffer from cognitive deficits, statistics showed that

most people in his age bracket did. Since the rates of cognition loss among the elderly are unpredictable, it was a topic worthy of discussion.

71. "McCain vs. Madonna: Grey Ambition," http://www.youtube.com/watch?v=8G9jA-FGGd8; "Star Trek McCain," http://www.youtube.com/watch?v=rpXKDAPX2Jc.

72. Sirened, "McCain Checks Out Palin's Ass While Fiddling with Wedding Ring," September 1, 2008, http://www.sirened.com/mccain-checks-out-palins-ass-while-fiddling-with-wedding-ring.

73. Illuminati TV, "Obama Citizenship: I Invented the Internet (Ep. 6: October Surprise)," October 10, 2008, http://www.youtube.com/watch?v=gA6_k3NtXZs.

74. "The Official Hillary Clinton Campaign Song Video You And I" http://www.youtube.com/watch?v=ionFwC1UUUw

75. "Obama/McCain 3rd Debate, Part 8—Joe the Plumber," October 15, 2008, http://www.youtube.com/watch?v=9BtcQIq-acY. Though Obama and McCain urged free dissemination of debate footage, this clip has been repeatedly removed by YouTube before being reposted by various users. John Eggerton, "Obama, McCain Back Public Re-use of Debate Footage," *Broadcasting and Cable*, October 7, 2008, http://www.broadcastingcable.com/article/115756-Obama_McCain_Back_Public_Re_use_Of_Debate_Footage.php; TPM, "McCain's Freaky Eyebrow Moment," October 15, 2008, http://www.youtube.com/watch?v=yxi8xIeK1II. The "official" posting of the full debate is available as well: C-SPAN, "Third 2008 Presidential debate (Full Video)," October 15, 2008, http://www.youtube.com/watch?v=DvdfO0lq4rQ.

76. Allan Cameron, *Modular Narratives in Contemporary Cinema* (New York: Palgrave Macmillan, 2008).

77. Might watching too much YouTube engender an irreverent response to the debates? Consider clips like the dramatic chipmunk and the hamster on a piano. "Dramatic Look" (http://www.youtube.com/watch?v=y8Kyi0WNg40) and "THE LEGEND of Hamster on a piano and pop corn! 5,9 MILLION VIEWS! THANKYOU ALL!" (http://www.youtube.com/watch?v=rfqNXADl3kU).

   Some candidates found YouTube too undignified—Mitt Romney refused to respond to a YouTube clip featuring a snowman querying him about global warming during a national debate. "Snowman vs. Romney—CNN reports" http://www.youtube.com/watch?v=NmVImJRHH4.

78. Joseph Romm, "McCain Blinks: How Obama Did It," *Huffington Post*, September 26, 2008, http://www.huffingtonpost.com/joseph-romm/mccain-blinks-how-obama-d_b_129635.html.

79. David McNeill, *Gesture and Thought* (Chicago: University of Chicago Press, 2005), 17.

80. Caleb Crain, "Twilight of the Books," *New Yorker*, December 2007.

81. Virginia Heffernan, "The Many Tribes of YouTube," *New York Times*, May 27, 2007.

82. My undergraduates initially attributed an authenticity to McCain's videos and a lack of content to Obama's. Class discussion helped the students come to a deeper understanding of these clips. It enriched my analysis. I teach in a red state where many students were pro-McCain. The students perceived the video "Yes We Can" as a video about the "almost famous," a group different from them, while McCain's "Joe the Plumber" was shot for and made by "real people like us." In truth, McCain's video, even though it looks amateurish, was almost surely made by professionals. Its imagery of wealthy, middle-class, and lower-income groups is highly coded through music and mise en scène. My students also claimed that "Yes We Can"'s lyrics were contentless (for them, the video said nothing more than "We want change"). When we more closely considered the lyrics for "Raisin' McCain" and "Yes We Can" the discussion became richer. From there we were able to move onto a larger discussion about American values. "I am Joe" http://www.youtube.com/watch?v=ZS0OYjMKCdc.

83. Barack Obama, "Weekly Address: On the 4th of July, Overcoming America's Challenges," July 3, 2009, http://www.whitehouse.gov/blog/2009/07/03/weekly-address-4th-july-overcoming-americarsquos-challenges.

84. Larry Rohter, "Real Deal on 'Joe the Plumber' Reveals New Slant," *New York Times,* October 16, 2008.

85. *Saturday Night Live,* "Palin/Hillary Open," September 13, 2008, http://www.hulu.com/watch/34465/saturday-night-live-palin-hillary-open.

Chapter 9

1. Some stylistic techniques common in 80s music videos recur today: simple cyclorama backgrounds, primary colors, clothes changes, limited props, and a stripped-down premise.

2. Email correspondence with Amy E., executive director, Music Video Production Association, Fall 2008.

3. Conversation with Aaron Retica, staff at the *New York Times,* Fall 2008. See also: Richard Perez-Pena, "New York Times Plans to Cut 100 Newsroom Jobs," *New York Times,* February, 14, 2008, http://www.nytimes.com/2008/02/14/business/media/14cnd-times.html?_r=0 and Jack Mirkinson, "NY Times Layoffs Looming; Jill Abramson 'Begging' Top Editors To Take Buyouts: NY Mag," *Huffington Post,* January, 11, 2013, http://www.huffingtonpost.com/2013/01/11/ny-times-layoffs-jill-abramson-buyouts_n_2457520.html

4. Carol Vernallis, *Experiencing Music Video: Aesthetics and Cultural Context* (New York: Columbia University Press, 2004), 6.

5. This, of course, is the title of Katy Perry's smash-hit from 2008.

6. *Auto-Tune the News* is a series of clips, available on YouTube, where the Brooklyn musician Michael Gregory has taken a number of evening news broadcast snippets that he comments upon by turning them into R&B pieces. His own voice as well as the voices of the people appearing in the news clips (such as news presenters, politicians, etc.) are electronically altered with the help of the software program "Auto-Tune," which normally is used in order to help singers' voices to achieve "perfect pitch." See as an example "Auto-Tune the News #2: pirates. drugs. gay marriage": http://www.youtube.com/watch?v=tBb4cjjj1gI.

7. "The Duck Song," music by Bryant Oden, animation by Forrest Whaley (2009): http://www.youtube.com/watch?v=MtN1YnoL46Q. "The Gummy Bear Song – Long English Version" http://www.youtube.com/watch?v=astISOttCQ0.

8. Oden has even released a CD that he sells on http://www.cdbaby.com/cd/bryantoden2.

9. For "Haha Baby," a clip of a laughing baby, responding to the noises made by a male adult, see: http://www.youtube.com/watch?v=NzQUtElQXX0.

10. For "Kung Fu Baby," a clip of a baby making kung-fu-like moves being accompanied by music, see: http://www.youtube.com/watch?v=bxAirY-5QCQ, for "Dramatic Chipmunk," the clip of a chipmunk accompanied by a dramatic and rousing score, see: http://www.youtube.com/watch?v=a1Y73sPHKxw. Mishka the husky dog has her own channel, numerous clips, and a wide following. See Husky Dog Talking - "I Love You" http://www.youtube.com/watch?v=qXo3NFqkaRM.

11. For "Evolution of Dance," showing the performance of comedian Judson Laipply, who dances his way through the history of popular dances, see: http://www.youtube.com/watch?v=dMH0bHeiRNg; for "Charlie Bit My Finger," showing a baby biting an older boy's finger (one of the most viewed videos in YouTube), see: http://www.youtube.com/watch?v=he5fpsmH_2g.

12. Liminal videos existing near the genre's borders include "Automatic Mario: Queen's 'Don't Stop Me Now,'" "Alice," and South Park's remake of "Pork and Beans" (a response to Weezer's original "Pork and Beans"). For "Automatic Mario: Queen's 'Don't Stop Me Now,'" an online advertisement, matching four parallel levels from

Super Mario World levels with the pitch and beat of the Queen song, see: http://www. break.com/game-trailers/game/new-super-mario-bros/automatic-mario-queens-dont-stop-me-now.html; for "Alice" see: Alice (tiled) http://www.yooouuutuuube. com/v/?rows=36&cols=36&id=pAwR6w2TgxY&startZoom=1, Alice http://www. youtube.com/watch?v=zP7bI8JJIVA; for the South Park characters Kyle and Stan performing "Pork and Beans" see http://www.youtube.com/watch?v=kekmyVT9HRs.

13. Over the last few years, music video has hit several nadirs. (Post-2000, many music video fans could only view music videos through high-tiered cable. Regular cable programming like MTV had switched to reality shows.) During YouTube's first years, music video sites like Launch, AOL, and MTV streamed videos but bandwidth was narrow and budgets were low. As advertising moves to the web, music video budgets will most likely continue to grow. Currently directors gain higher budgets by including product placement. During MTV's reign, product placement was not permitted.

14. Michael Arrington, "YouTube Video Streams Top 1.2 Billion/Day": http://techcrunch. com/2009/06/09/youtube-video-streams-top-1-billionday.

15. For Carly Rae Jepsen "Call Me Maybe" see http://www.youtube.com/watch?v=fWNaR-rxAic. For "Harlem Shake v3 (office edition)" see http://www.youtube.com/watch?v=0IJoKuTlvuM. For Psy "Gangnam Style" see http://www.youtube.com/watch?v=9bZkp7q19f0.

16. I've spoken twice with a staff person in PR at YouTube, but still have many questions about the site.

17. Alexandra Juhasz, "Learning the Five Lessons of YouTube: After Trying to Teach There, I Don't Believe the Hype," *Cinema Journal* 48, no. 2 (Winter 2009): 145–150. See also Alexander Juhasz, *AIDS TV: Identity, Community and Alternative Video*, (Raleigh, NC: Duke University Press, 1996).

18. Henry Jenkins, "If It Doesn't Spread, It's Dead (Part One): Media Viruses and Memes," Confessions of an Aca-Fan (blog), February 11, 2009, http://henryjenkins. org/2009/02/if_it_doesnt_spread_its_dead_p.html. Michael Wetsch, "An Anthropological Introduction to YouTube" (Lecture at the Library of Congress, June 23, 2008): http://www.youtube.com/watch?v=TPAO-lZ4_hU

19. Julie Levin Russo, "User-Penetrated Content: Fan Videos in the Age of Convergence," *Cinema Journal* 48, no. 4 (Summer 2009): 125–130.

20. David Gurney, "Recombinant Comedy, Transmedial Mobility, and Viral Video," *Velvet Light Trap* 68 (2011): 3–13.

21. For a close analysis of "Video Phone" that nicely complements mine, see Lori Burns and Marc Lafrance, "Gender, Sexuality, and the Politics of Looking in Beyoncé's 'Videophone,'" paper presented at The Ghost in the Machine conference, McGill University, February 2–3, 2011 and at the International Conference on Feminist Theory and Music, Phoenix, Arizona, September 2011. See Judith Jack Halberstam, *Gaga Feminism: Sex, Gender, and the End of Normal (Queer Action/Queer Ideas)* (Boston: Beacon Press, 2012). See also Stan Hawkins, "Aesthetics and Hyperembodiment in Pop Videos: Rihanna's 'Umbrella,'" in *The Oxford Handbook of New Audiovisual Aesthetics*, ed. John Richardson et al. (New York and Oxford: Oxford University Press), forthcoming. An earlier version of this chapter appeared in Henry Keazor and Thorsten Wübbena, *Rewind, Play, Fast Forward: The Past, Present and Future of the Music Video* (Bielefeld: Transcript Verlag, 2010).

22. A prosumer is a person in postindustrial society who combines the economic roles of producer and consumer—the notion was coined by futurologist Alvin Toffler in his 1980 book *The Third Wave*.

23. For "The Sneezing Baby Panda" see: http://www.youtube.com/watch?v=FzRH3i TQPrk; for the "Gizmo Flushes" (a clip, showing the obsession of the cat Gizmo with toilet flushes) see: http://www.youtube.com/watch?v=WofFb_eOxxA.

24. For a political reiterative clip, see the "APT Obama Obama" (a remake of Lil' Wayne's "A Milli") http://www.youtube.com/watch?v=t7RZTlzXHmo. Here are some examples of psychedelic reiterative clips on YouTube: "Dan Deacon & Liam Lynch—Drinking Out of Cups," see: http://www.youtube.com/watch?v=skCV2L0c6K0; for "Shrooms: a trip experience," see: http://www.youtube.com/watch?v=B4pIxnuUG1k&feature=related; for "Pick of Destiny Shrooms," see: http://www.youtube.com/watch?v=guCPHG2ys9k&feature=related; for Fischerspooner, "Get Confused," see: http://www.youtube.com/watch?v=tIjmpp1wot4.

25. For Hechizeros Band, "El Sonidito," see http://www.youtube.com/watch?v=-XgN-FLo5WOI; for El Mudo, "Chacarron Macarron" (Crazy Music Video), see: http://www.youtube.com/watch?v=l12Csc_lW0Q; for Jon Lajoie, "Sunday Afternoon," see: http://www.youtube.com/watch?v=4gx3nn6LS6g.

26. Here are some examples of very punchy YouTube clips that reiterate. "The New Llama Song !!!!!" http://www.youtube.com/watch?v=HbPDKHXWlLQ. "Reading and Time: A Dialectic Between Academic Expectation and Academic Frustration" http://www.youtube.com/watch?v=uSdHoNJu5fU. "Two Talking Cats: Two in One" http://www.youtube.com/watch?v=v4SJVN0Zn5U

27. When music videos first appeared, many theorists and critics complained that they were incoherent or schizophrenic. At the time it seemed difficult to decipher what music videos might be saying or what their effects were. As mentioned earlier, music video on television has become less and less important, though more and more people are watching videos on the web. Strangely, part of the aesthetics of web-based music video lies in its grounding function. Clicking among sites and multitasking so regularly, a three- to five-minute moment of music can actually provide both ground and respite—a moment of emotional connection. Shared with others, videos take on a social dimension.

28. For "Shoes" (directed and interpreted by the comedian Liam Kyle Sullivan) see: http://www.youtube.com/watch?v=wCF3ywukQYA.

29. Gilles Deleuze, *Difference and Repetition* (New York: Columbia University Press, 1995), 75.

30. My book *Experiencing Music Video* shows the ways such repetition also becomes manifest in the music-video image, as well as in audiovisual relations among music, image, and lyrics.

31. "Nyan Cat" [original] http://www.youtube.com/watch?v=QH2-TGUlwu4.
    "The Annoying Orange" http://www.youtube.com/watch?v=ZN5PoW7_kdA.

32. "Earworms!": http://www.freedomgen.com/index.php/community/groups/viewdiscussion?groupid=38&;topicid=53; "Dig those earworms out": http://www.herald-mail.com/blogs/schelle/?p=59.
    Beyoncé "Single Ladies" http://www.youtube.com/watch?v=4m1EFMoRFvY

33. Lev Manovich, *The Language of New Media* (Cambridge, MA: MIT Press, 2001), xv, 20.

34. Andre Bazin, *What Is Cinema?* (Berkeley: University of California Press, 2004), 96–97.

35. Laura Mulvey, *Death 24x a Second: Stillness and the Moving Image* (London: Reaktion Books, 2006), 17–33.

36. David Rodowick, *The Virtual Life of Film* (Cambridge, MA: Harvard University Press, 2007), 93–99, 163.

37. Conversation with Jonathan Sterne, Spring 2009. See Jonathan Sterne, *The Audible Past: Cultural Origins of Sound Reproduction* (Durham, NC, and London: Duke University Press, 2003), 18.

38. "Felix Baumgartner's Supersonic Freefall from 128k' -Mission Highlights" http://www.youtube.com/watch?v=FHtvDA0W34I

39. Walk off the Earth's cover of Gotye's "Somebody that I Used to Know" http://www.youtube.com/watch?v=d9NF2edxy-M.

40. Vernallis, *Experiencing Music Video*, 6.

41. David Rodowick, *The Virtual Life of Film* (Cambridge, MA: Harvard University Press, 2007), 151.
42. For the clip, showing a webcam video from 2004 of Gary Brolsma, who filmed himself while himself miming to the song "Dragostea din tei" by the Moldovan pop band O-Zone and thus gained worldwide cult status as the "Numa Numa Guy," see: http://www.youtube.com/watch?v=60og9gwKh1o&feature=fvst. For "LEAVE BRITNEY ALONE!" (by Chris Crocker) see:http://www.youtube.com/watch?v=kHmvkRoEowc; for "Fred Loses His Meds" see: http://www.youtube.com/watch?v=m9MA0eW8yyw.
43. In an email from 2011, Alan Finke offered: "Did you watch it on a video phone? I did. They told me to. It takes on a different quality. The minimalism becomes very sharp and clear, the 8-bit casio sound becomes very appropriate in a GameBoy way and the most interesting thing is the lighting. It turns an iPhone into a little box of light that you hold in your hand. There's a sort of 3d quality with a depth that extends behind the phone into your hand, and there's a cool moment near the end where a burst of fire from a gun breaks the frame (another penetration reference?) And there's a whole other quality to being able to hold the performers in your hand. You can possess them, but you can't touch them. They're in a flat frame, but they're in a 3d world and you can tap on the glass."
44. Enter Kazoo Man: Metallica Enter Sandman performed on KAZOO by Mister Tim (multitrack) http://www.youtube.com/watch?v=iC65ufGUvKM, "Michael Jackson Medley" http://www.youtube.com/watch?v=R12QVtuB0_Q.
45. Walk off the Earth's cover of Gotye's "Somebody that I Used to Know" http://www.youtube.com/watch?v=d9NF2edxy-M. "Crystallize - Lindsey Stirling (Dubstep Violin Original Song)" http://www.youtube.com/watch?v=aHjpOzsQ9YI&list=PLSTz8jpJdr5pkXfNu3IQAOYIQjjTY0DMj
46. For "Tick-Toxic: Mashup of Britney Spears and Gwen Stefani," which combines the music and the visuals from the videos for their songs "Toxic" (video directed in 2004 by Joseph Kahn) and "What You Waiting For?" (clip directed in 2004 by Francis Lawrence), see http://www.youtube.com/watch?v=gRHfd9Yto0A. For mashups see also "HOT K-POP 2009 ~ special mashup pt. I ~ (23 songs in one)": http://www.youtube.com/watch?v=wyZPpwLZeag, which features 23 Korean hit songs from 2009. For "Obama Mashup Tribute: He Really Deed It," see:,http://www.youtube.com/watch?v=LBh9c8cuthQ; See also "MASHUP—Obama/McCain Campaign Ads": http://www.youtube.com/watch?v=IEehKNNMq_4, "Getting Nasty—John Bennett's entry in Campaign Mash Up": http://www.youtube.com/watch?v=DB56hlJoHN4 and "Barack Obama: Unstoppable Momentum (Led Zeppelin Mashup)": http://www.youtube.com/watch?v=g_NrAmqaShY.
47. "Lady Gaga—Telephone (Official Explicit Version) ft. Beyoncé" http://www.ladygaga.com/telephone/#.
48. See the section on condensation for more discussion of "Video Phone"'s intertextuality. "Telephone" references *Kill Bill*, *Thelma and Louise*, noir, B-movies and YouTube fan culture.
49. See Richard Dyer, *Pastiche* (London: Routledge, 2007). Jeffrey Sconce, "Irony, Nihilism, and the New American 'Smart' Film," *Screen* 43, no.4 (2002): 349–369.
50. MeTube: August Sings Carmen 'Habanera' http://www.youtube.com/watch?v=P2jn_lxrrPg. Thomas Grey coined the mashup description of the clip—"postmodern retro-digital Germanopunk crypto-geriatric Eurotrash parody."
51. See for example the "Video Phone Remix Beyoncé and Lady Gaga (Cordless Phone Spoof)": http://www.youtube.com/watch?v=DfHh8jHsF0w. "I look at photos of myself, and I look like such a tranny! It's amazing! I look like Grace Jones, androgynous, robo, future fashion queen. It's not what is sexy. It's graphic, and it's art." See http://popwatch.ew.com/2009/02/09/lady-gaga-inter.

   There are also ample references from gay sources citing Gaga as a gay icon. For example, her profile in *OUT* magazine says: "A life of glamour is an ethos to which every gay—from the 17-year-old Dominican tranny voguing in his bedroom to the tanorexic middle-aged Miami circuit queen—can relate. It's one reason we love Gaga. Another, of course, is that Gaga loves us back. Gayness is in Gaga's DNA." And: "Her devotion to gay culture is unparalleled by any other artist operating at her level of visibility or success." See for this: http://www.out.com/detail.asp?page=2&id=25720. See also a YouTube video alleging her transsexuality (1,231,978 views): "Breaking news: Lady GaGa is actually a MAN!": http://www.youtube.com/watch?v=P36i5BaAP6w.

52. Zoe Alsop, "Uganda's Anti-Gay Bill: Inspired by the U.S.," *Time* (December 2009), http://www.time.com/time/world/article/0,8599,1946645,00.html?xid=rss-topstories. It doesn't seem unreasonable to me that Williams, Beyoncé, and Lady Gaga or the clip's costume designers and other technicians might have added a subtle detail like this to the video. Many of my friends and colleagues in the gay community follow international gay rights closely. Choreographer Michael Peter's finger snaps in Michael Jackson's "Thriller" is one example of a touch added to speak to the gay community.

I'm most curious about the big t-shirt, the Barbados accent, and the surveillance interrogation footage. I'll be sure to footnote you if you'd like to contribute. With Guantanamo still a locus of inhumanity, I wonder if I might say that at least the clip helps keep the questions present. Like *Source Code,* there's an odd transposition of characters (it's okay to torture our own or to be a torturer). I don't know what this transposition is about. For a discussion of U.S. involvement in terrorism in the third world see Hector Hoyos, "Aftershock," *Third Text* 26:2, (April, 2012): 217–228. I wonder about Beyoncé and Jay-Z's 2013 wedding anniversary trip to Cuba and the non-first world imagery in the video. The Right was much alarmed by this visit.

53. Interview, December 3, 2009.

54. The line "Can you handle it" is at the same time a clear reference to the song "Bootylicious," interpreted in 2001 by Beyoncé's former group Destiny's Child.

55. Vernallis, *Experiencing Music Video,* 43, 129.

56. Watch the video from 3 minutes 10 seconds.

57. Note the fourth shot into "Video Phone"'s opening. The blonde-haloed man enters left of frame at :29 and exits at :37.

58. Conversation about the song and musical analysis offered by Jesse Rodin, December 10, 2009.

59. See Chapter 8 for an analysis of "Yes We Can" and its direct appeal to a solitary viewer.

60. 1alexandra12: "horrible . . . Beyoncé you dissapointed me . . . and lady gaga you are an ugly slut." shakirap483: "Beyoncé owns the stage not lady gaga she's wired in head in so many ways." taytaygurl09: "this is a unique video, but what's with all the toy guns?" 1111GENESIS: "@taytaygurl09 the video is symbolic for the gay revolution." MrSweetJuice: "lady ga ga is the worst fucking singer or w.e she is on the planet. . . . i mean the bitch is fucking terrible and all her songs sound the same and im pretty sure shes a fucking guy. . . . fucking tranny cunt nigger, FUCK HER!! and honestly fuck her gay faggot homosexual fanbase, all you HIV carrying monkeys need to be put to death right along with niggers and Lady ga ga the fuckign tranny cunt!! oh and all u faggot fudge packers better not message my profile with homo messages OR ELSE!!!"

LiteSkin87: "Beyoncé is bad, thick, and delicious looking, but man, she is straight sleazy. She's married, for shit's sake. Stop talking about how niggas is hitting you up and you're assuming the position. Sit your ass down and have a kid somewhere."

norhophobia: "yep she's an official whore now. i wouldn't want my man or my daughters watchn her vids now . . . and would feel uncomfortable watchn w/my momma around or anybody for that matter @liteskin87 i agree she's married wth this is disgusting. . . . it's sad cuz she's so talented u can see she is pretty and "sexy" w/o her acting and lookn like a street walker in all her vids smh"

nautigirl2774: "apparently sex sells, but this a totally crap video. I used to think that Beyoncé had class, but now see that she'll do anything to make a buck. So much for being a role model to young girls, she looks like a tramp."

cobra902001: "Please Wake up people, this video is about Beyoncé and Lady Gaga promoting bi-sexuality, don't let the elite brain wash you any longer" rainbowskies400: "Umm . . . not sure how to feel about this video. haha"

All of which are from just one copy of "Video Phone": http://www.youtube.com/watch?v=btuRgzIaZsohttp://www.youtube.com/watch?v=btuRgzIaZso.

61. See this, e.g., "Thomas the Taxi Driver": http://www.youtube.com/watch?v=usfkj bsjNtk.

62. Mark Fisher, *Capitalist Realism: Is There No Alternative?* (Winchester: Zero Books: 2009), 2. Providing another explanation for boredom, Saikat Majumdar might claim that with the hidden 1 percent and global capital we might all feel like we are in the provinces. See Saikat Majumdar, *Prose of the World* (New York: Columbia Univeristy Press: 2013), 33.

63. Examples include the videos for Beyoncé's "If I Were A Boy" (directed in 2008 by Jake Nava); "Irreplaceable" (directed in 2006 by Anthony Mandler); and Hype Williams's "Diamonds from Sierra Leone" for Kanye West (2005) and "The Rain (Supa Dupa Fly)" for Missy Elliott (1997).

64. See for example those for Ne-Yo, "Go On Girl" (2007), Wu-Tang Clan, "Can It Be All So Simple" (1994), and Taral Hicks, "Silly" (1997).

65. The video by Francis Lawrence for Lady Gaga's "Bad Romance" (2009) suggests this might be so.

Chapter 10

1. Music video is financially viable again as directors and musicians embed product placement in clips, and YouTube clips link directly to the industry-driven site VEVO. Though music video has not received the scholarly attention it deserves (compared to television, film, or video games), insightful analysis exists. See Andrew Goodwin, *Dancing in the Distraction Factory: Music Television and Popular Culture* (Minneapolis: University of Minnesota Press, 1992) and *Sound and Vision: The Music Video Reader*, ed. Simon Frith et al. (London and New York: Routledge, 1993). Carol Vernallis, *Experiencing Music Video: Aesthetics and Cultural Context* (New York: Columbia University Press, 2004). Kevin Williams, *Why I [Still] Want My MTV: Music Video and Aesthetic Communication* (Cresskill, NJ: Hampton Press, 2003). Henry Keazor and Thorsten Wübbena, *Rewind, Play, Fast Forward: The Past, Present and Future of the Music Video* (Bielefeld: Transcript Verlag, 2010). Diane Railton and Paul Watson, *Music Video and the Politics of Representation* (Edinburgh: Edinburgh University Press, 2011). Joachim Strand, *The Cinesthetic Montage of Music-Video: Hearing the Image and Seeing the Sound* (Saarbrücken: VDM Verlag Dr. Müller, 2008). John Richardson, *An Eye for Music: Popular Music and the Audiovisual Surreal (The Oxford Music/Media)* (New York: Oxford University Press, 2011).

2. At least the Hays Office distributed a highly codified list of what was disallowed. Francis Lawrence reported that after 9/11 the censors got so anxious, there was a question whether his and Janet Jackson's "Son of a Gun (I Betcha Think This Song Is About You)" could be aired. In the clip, she and five women strut in an underground parking lot, chasing an ex-paramour. Janet earlier walked down a corridor, wielding a baseball bat (interview with the director, 2001). All links searched on October 11, 2011. http://www.dailymotion.com/video/x8dpej_janet-jackson-ft-missy-elliott-son_music#.UNEPL28qaAg

   But MTV's censors have sometimes had positive effects. Around 2005 the company made a progressive move—if a woman's buttocks were to be shown, her face would need to appear in the following shot.

3. My friend who's a gay pornographer has been able to do so. You embed the footage in the clip's center. A prosumer is a consumer who does production. The work can be semiprofessional.

4. My students post their children's first performance in bands, for example. A tween in the basement with friends—the lighting and camera's pretty bad. Let me give a shout out to my student Shannon Kleinjans, for example, who made a music video for her daughter's band, Anorexic Cookie's "Spilt Milk," at http://www.youtube.com/watch?v=7XHO5sr0CD4

5. La Fura del Baus with Zubin Mehta's YouTube clips of Wagner's *The Ring*, at http://www.youtube.com/watch?v=osoKrvetnpU seem very music video–like.

6. TV On the Radio's album-length music video collection, R Kelly's opera-length "Trapped in the Closet," at http://www.youtube.com/watch?v=_Ch4dKpBJmU, and Kanye West's "Runaway," at http://www.youtube.com/watch?v=Jg5wkZ-dJXA.

7. Like Bjork's project *Biophilia*.

8. There's even my favorite outliers, like "Captain Underpants" and "The Duck Song" (which look like children's cartoons), and "Auto-Tune the News" (which foregrounds newscasters' voices remixed through Auto-Tunes so they sing their stories).
   Captain Underpants, at http://www.youtube.com/watch?v=3jPLGgaHMwo
   The Duck Song, at http://www.youtube.com/watch?v=MtN1YnoL46Q
   Auto-Tune the News, at http://www.youtube.com/watch?v=bduQaCRkgg4

9. The definition of music video I advanced in *Experiencing Music Video* also seems obsolete. There I argued that music video imagery seeks to sell a song by showing off musical features in a serial fashion (because one can't reveal all of them simultaneously). This careful tracking of musical features largely holds true for the industry-funded music videos of big-name artists, but not for today's music videos more broadly. Carol Vernallis, *Experiencing Music Video: Aesthetics and Cultural Context* (New York: Columbia University Press, 2004), 68.
   Mathias Korsgaard has collected a large group of videos produced by independent and small labels with different functions and different audiovisual relations that take preeminence over musical ones. A profusion of signs (remediation), a business in the frame, and a foregrounding of technological devices (like image trailing and kaleidoscopic patterning) show off the sounds' and images' digital signal and reflect music's polyphony in total rather than anything closely related to an individual song's features. Korsgaard's indie clips' aesthetics are tied to their function. They sell not the song, but T-shirts and concert tickets and they aim to position themselves as antimainstream, hence casual sync is a virtue different from today's. Should we create new genres or subclasses for music video? Mathias Korsgaard, "Creation and Erasure: Music Video as a Signaletic Form of Practice," *Journal of Aesthetics & Culture* 4 (Stockholm: Co-Action Publishing, 2012), http://www.aestheticsandculture.net/index.php/jac/article/view/18151/22823
   Philip Auslander points out that sixties light shows for rock concerts had engaging music-image relations. Oil blobs projected through color wheels while a band jammed made loose audiovisual relations, but if you had taken a lot of drugs and were in an expanded frame of mind, this was pretty cool. And as clips on YouTube they kind of look like music videos, and the same is true of clips from musicals and operas, especially if they've been remixed or mashed up. Korsgaard's clips, with their buzzy, busy technology, and 1,000 hits, may work similarly. Philip Auslander, "Sound and Vision: The Audio/Visual Economy of Musical Performance," in *The Oxford Handbook of New Audiovisual Aesthetics*, ed. John Richardson et al. (New York and Oxford: Oxford University Press), forthcoming.

10. Nicholas Cook, *Analysing Musical Multimedia* (New York and Oxford: Oxford University Press, 1998), 98–106. Michel Chion, *Audio-Vision: Sound on Screen* (New York: Columbia University Press, 1994), 5. Claudia Gorbman in "Aesthetics and Rhetoric," *American Music* 22, no.1 (Spring 2004): 14–26, cites Bernard Herrmann's famous quote, drawing from Cook's *Analysing Musical Multimedia* (New York and Oxford: Oxford University Press, 1998), 104.

Gorbman's *Unheard Melodies: Narrative Film Music* (London: BFI, 1987), 2, 57, is considered the first major scholarly work on film scoring. She discusses many topics including what music does in the movies and how it does it. She notes that music relaxes the "psychic sensor" and provides interpretive assistance to combat the ambiguity of visual cues. Nevertheless, what I value most is the ways she considers what music and image do together and apart. Drawing on film scenes, for example, bicyclists on a holiday in Truffaut's *Jules and Jim*, she queries the ways music shapes our attention to the image.

11. Kay Dickinson's approach, which considers music-image relations that have gone bad, seems particularly relevant here. See her book *Off Key: When Film and Music Won't Work Together* (New York and Oxford: Oxford University Press, 2008).

12. Sigur Rós's "Untitled," at http://www.vevo.com/watch/sigur-ros-1/untitled/GBK 680300010

    Lady Gaga's "Born This Way," at http://www.vevo.com/watch/lady-gaga/born-this-way/USUV71100098?source=ap Kanye West's "Power," at http://www.vevo.com/watch/kanye-west/power/USUV71001422?source=ap

13. Siegfried Kracauer, "Girls und Krise," *Frankfurter Zeitung*, May 27, 1931.

14. Pam Belluck, "To Tug Hearts, Music First Must Tickle the Neurons," *New York Times*, April 18, 2011.

15. A-Ha's "Take on Me," at http://www.youtube.com/watch?v=djV11Xbc914

    Meiert Avis and U2's "With or Without You" at http://www.youtube.com/watch?v=XmSdTa9kaiQ&ob=av3e

    Andy Morahan and George Michael's "Father Figure," at http://www.vevo.com/watch/george-michael/father-figure/GB0200202150

    Beyoncé's "1 + 1," at http://www.youtube.com/watch?v=KaasJ44O5lI

16. I'd like to thank John Richardson for coining this phrase. For more on contemporary audiovisual aesthetics see his *An Eye for Music: Popular Music and the Audiovisual Surreal* (New York and Oxford: Oxford University Press, 2011).

17. Mathias Korsgaard, "'Creation and Erasure': Music Video as a Signaletic Form of Practice," *Journal of Aesthetics & Culture* 4 (Stockholm: Co-Action Publishing, 2012). http://www.aestheticsandculture.net/index.php/jac/article/view/18151/22823

18. David Byrne's "Once in a Lifetime," at http://www.youtube.com/watch?v=I1wg1 DNHbNU

    Prince's "When Doves Cry," at http://www.slack-time.com/music-video-6416-Prince-When-Doves-Cry

    Queen's "Bohemian Rhapsody," at http://www.vevo.com/watch/queen/bohemian-rhapsody/GB0400201412

    Steve Winwood's "Roll with It," at http://www.youtube.com/watch?v=fWpt XUblA4E

    Cutting Crew's "I Just Died in Your Arms Tonight," at http://www.youtube.com/watch?v=Ua26qTEK25U

    One of the oddest things about improvements in technology and media is that in a multimedia context, each medium can be out of step. An improvement in sound reproduction can leave the image looking small and wan (as Jay Beck has noted, Dolby momentarily made the screen image look like a postage stamp). Conversation with Jay Beck, Spring 2011. See William Whittington, "Lost in Sensation—Reevaluating the Role of Cinematic Sound in the Digital Age," Melissa Ragona, "Doping the Voice," J. P. Geuens, "Angels of Light," Eric Lyon, "The Absent Image in Electronic Music," Jessica Aldred, "'I Am Beowulf! Now, It's Your Turn': Playing With (and as) the Digital Convergence Character," all in *The Oxford Handbook of Sound and Image in Digital Media*, ed. Carol Vernallis et al. (New York and Oxford: Oxford University Press), forthcoming.

19. Selena Gomez and the Scene's "Naturally," at http://www.vevo.com/watch/selena-gomez-and-the-scene/naturally/USH5V0920974

    Gnarls Barkley's "Crazy," at http://www.youtube.com/watch?v=7W2KR_z9P0M

Michael Jackson's "Billie Jean," at http://www.vevo.com/watch/michael-jackson/billie-jean/USSM20301088. Other examples of quadrants include Asia's "Heat of the Moment," at http://www.youtube.com/watch?v=wlTvWvfEMxE

20. Michael Jackson's "Black or White," at http://www.vevo.com/watch/michael-jackson/black-or-white/USSM20300985

For a historical description of morphing in cinema, see Mark J. P. Wolf, "A Brief History of Morphing," in *Visual Transformation Meta Morphing and the Culture of Quick-Change,* ed. Vivian Sobchack (Minneapolis: University of Minnesota Press, 2000), 91. For bullet time, see Bob Rehak, "The Migration of Forms: Bullet Time as Microgenre," *Film Criticism* 32, no. 1 (Fall 2007): 26–47.

Lady Gaga's "Bad Romance," at http://www.vevo.com/watch/lady-gaga/bad-romance/USUV70903493

21. The Police's "Every Breath You Take," at http://www.vevo.com/watch/the-police/every-breath-you-take/GBF060300032

OK Go's "WTF?," at http://www.youtube.com/watch?v=12zJw9varYE

Kanye West's "Welcome to Heartbreak," at http://www.youtube.com/watch?v=wMH0e8kIZtE

David Bowie's "Ashes to Ashes," at http://www.youtube.com/watch?v=CMThz7eQ6K0&ob=av2n

22. Azis's "Bulgaria +18 [Tits and Penis]" at http://www.youtube.com/watch?v=78g5AAWtRQw

23. Linkin Park's "Iridescent," at http://www.youtube.com/watch?v=xLYiIBCN9ec&ob=av2e

Selena Gomez and the Scene's "Naturally," at http://www.vevo.com/watch/selena-gomez-and-the-scene/naturally/USH5V0920974

24. I've argued in *Experiencing Music Video* for the ways the image reflects music's processual nature and its heterogeneity. Vernallis, *Experiencing Music Video,* 68.

25. Radiohead's "House of Cards," at http://www.youtube.com/watch?v=8nTFjVm9sTQ

Erasure's "A Little Respect," at http://www.youtube.com/watch?v=65lyoDUDWQg

Michael Jackson's "Rock with You," at http://www.vevo.com/watch/michael-jackson/rock-with-you/USSM20301087

One of the earliest examples is Loie Fuller's work in silent film. A dancer, she wore huge sheets of cloth sewn together, and through waving her arms rapidly in figure-eight patterns, transformed herself into some sort of phantasmagorical hybrid hummingbird-dragonfly crossed with a rotating, voluptuously unfolding tulip. She and her outfit made shifting, swishing, flying shapes. Upon them were projected colored lights that briskly turned shades. Perhaps this might make us think of OK Go's "WTF?"

Consider Vincent Morisset's interactive homage to Fuller. Music videos remember their history. Arcade Fire's "Sprawl" at http://www.sprawl2.com/

26. The Gatorade commercial—in black and white except the Gatorade—made its debut in 1994. http://articles.chicagotribune.com/1994-04-13/business/9404130237_1_isotonic-beverage-boston-chicken-fluid-absorption

27. The Outfield's "Since You've Been Gone," at http://www.vevo.com/watch/the-outfield/since-youve-been-gone/USSM20400831

INXS's "What You Need," at http://www.youtube.com/watch?v=vSME53nL8tg

Belinda Carlisle's "I Get Weak," at http://www.youtube.com/watch?v=nmMCXLdNrz8&ob=av2n, is another video that uses the isolation of color for expressive effects.

28. Katy Perry featuring Kanye West's "E.T.," at http://www.youtube.com/watch?v=t5Sd5c4o9UM&ob=av2e.

Perry's "E.T." provides a twist on Garrett Stewart's trope of the digital eruption, where filmic images suddenly comment on the transformation to the new technology—now in the midst of the digital we have analog eruptions, where analog, as if through a time machine, asserts its ghostly power, claiming for itself more charisma than the digital.

David Guetta featuring Ludacris and Taio Cruz's "Little Bad Girl," at http://www.vevo.com/watch/david-guetta/little-bad-girl/GB28K1120016

29. Lady Gaga's "Judas," at http://www.youtube.com/watch?v=wagn8Wrmzuc&ob=av2e
   Mika's "We Are Golden," at http://www.youtube.com/watch?v=hEhutIEUq8k&ob=av2e
   Britney Spears's "Hold It Against Me," at http://www.youtube.com/watch?v=-Edv8Onsrgg&ob=av2e

30. See Vernallis, *Experiencing Music Video*, 125.

31. Katy Perry featuring Kanye West's "E.T.," at http://www.youtube.com/watch?v=t5Sd5c4o9UM&ob=av2e

32. Michel Chion, *Audiovision: Sound on Screen*, trans. Claudia Gorbman (New York: Columbia University Press, 1990), 16

33. Janet Jackson's "Make Me," at http://www.youtube.com/watch?v=ZwQyUTkGOew, foregrounds the way director Michael Hales isolates and brings to the fore various musical elements—easier to do now with digital technologies.

34. U2's "With or Without You," at http://www.youtube.com/watch?v=XmSdTa9kaiQ&ob=av2e
   Adele's "Rolling in the Deep," at http://www.youtube.com/watch?v=rYEDA3JcQqw&ob=av2e
   The Human League's "Human," at http://www.vevo.com/watch/the-human-league/human/GB1200301690, is another eighties example. Janet Jackson's and Busta Rhymes's "What's It Gonna Be," http://www.youtube.com/watch?v=P4PFClnMkOU, is a nineties one.

35. Beyoncé's "Best Thing I Never Had," at http://www.youtube.com/watch?v=FHp2Kgy QUFk&ob=av2e; Chris Isaak's "Wicked Games," at http://www.youtube.com/watch?v=UAOxCqSxRD0. Conversation with director David Fincher, Spring 1998.

36. While editing on video you might also accidentally "break your control track" by hitting the wrong button: this would abruptly interrupt the videotape's strip of information. You'd then have to start anew, from before the rupture, or drop down a tape generation. All of your footage would reside on different tapes, and if you'd like to make a change, you'd have to refer back to the log, pull out a Bible-sized tape, drop it in the deck, and scroll to the moment you needed. When I was doing much video production, I was always changing my project's scale, breaking control track, and wearing my workprints down to almost nothing—after dropping a generation more than once, I'd be editing to a very pale and grainy image.

37. Taio Cruz's "Take a Dirty Picture of Me," at http://www.youtube.com/watch?v=RgnXl7fz0Bc
   Pink's "Sober," at http://www.youtube.com/watch?v=nJ3ZM8FDBlg

38. This aesthetic was both technologically and musically driven. A video with different concerns, R.E.M.'s "Driver 8," showcased folk guitar and nostalgia and featured grainy Super-8 footage of trains.

39. The clips include Mark Pellington and Pearl Jam's "Jeremy"; at http://www.youtube.com/watch?v=MS91knuzoOA&ob=av2e
   Marcus Nispel and C&C Factory's "Everybody Dance Now"; at http://www.youtube.com/watch?v=N2VQQEoWlTg
   Amy Grant's "House of Love"; at http://www.youtube.com/watch?v=aXxXj7rzZy4&ob=av2n
   Tarsem Singh and R.E.M.'s "Losing My Religion"; at http://www.youtube.com/watch?v=if-UzXIQ5vw&ob=av2e
   Hype Williams and Missy Elliott's "The Rain (Supa Dupa Fly)"; at http://www.youtube.com/watch?v=hHcyJPTTn9w
   The Notorious B.I.G., "Big Poppa," at http://www.youtube.com/watch?v=phaJXp_zMYM

Floria Sigismondi and Marilyn Manson's "The Beautiful People"; at http://www.youtube.com/watch?v=Ypkv0HeUvTc&ob=av2e

Alan Ferguson and Cee-Lo's "Open Happiness," at http://www.youtube.com/watch?v=Cxfkg3RaRjs

40. Rihanna's "Rude Boy," at http://www.youtube.com/watch?v=e82VE8UtW8A&ob=av2e.

INXS's "What You Need," at http://www.youtube.com/watch?v=vSME53nL8tg. But then when I look at videos like Marcus Nispel and C + C Music Factory's "Everybody Dance Now," at http://www.youtube.com/watch?v=N2VQQEoWlTg or ABC's "Be Near Me," at http://www.youtube.com/watch?v=fEkRAC98SnA, I think today has nothing on the eighties. Some of the shots and uses of space are so stunning in these videos. These are ways of experiencing space that are no longer available to us. They cannot be recaptured—other forms of knowledge have taken their place.

41. Lady Gaga and Beyoncé's "Telephone," at http://www.youtube.com/watch?v=EVBsypHzF3U

42. Madonna and David Fincher's "Bad Girl," at http://www.youtube.com/watch?v=JUII7DTACf4

Aerosmith and David Fincher's "Janie's Got a Gun," at http://www.youtube.com/watch?v=bvFeqUQcBOE

43. Katy Perry and Floria Sigismondi's "E.T.," at http://www.youtube.com/watch?v=t5Sd5c4o9UM&ob=av2e

Vladimir Yakovlevich Propp, *Morphology of the Folktale*, trans. T. R. Laurence Scott (Austin: University of Texas Press, 1968).

44. Gibson and Lady Gaga's "You and I," at http://www.youtube.com/watch?v=X9YMU0WeBwU&ob=av2e

Madonna's "Papa Don't Preach," at http://www.youtube.com/watch?v=RkxqxWgEEz4&ob=av2n

E. Ann Kaplan, *Rocking Around the Clock: Music Television, Post Modernism and Consumer Culture* (New York and London: Routledge, 1987), 130.

45. Lady Gaga and Francis Lawrence's "Bad Romance," at http://www.youtube.com/watch?v=qrO4YZeyl0I

46. See Vernallis, *Experiencing Music Video*, 286.

Gary Numan's "Cars," (http://www.youtube.com/watch?v=Ldyx3KHOFXw) is one example.

47. Think of the 70s Earth, Wind, and Fire's "After the Love Is Gone" at http://www.youtube.com/watch?v=B0lpityVOiE compared to the 80s Human League's "Don't You Want Me," at http://www.youtube.com/watch?v=uPudE8nDog0&ob=av2e

48. Though there are some exceptions, like Young MC's "Bust a Move," at http://www.youtube.com/watch?v=tZQQGX24Teg

49. See Jean-Pierre Geuens's chapter on the coming of digital intermediate and the end of art, "Angels of Light," in Vernallis, *Oxford Handbook of Sound and Image in Digital Media*.

50. Sinead O'Connor's "Nothing Compares 2U," at http://www.youtube.com/watch?v=iUiTQvT0W_0

Justin Timberlake's "Cry Me a River," at http://www.youtube.com/watch?v=DksSPZTZES0&ob=av2e. And sure enough Timberlake became an actor—but I'd argue his best performance was in this music video.

51. Vernallis, *Experiencing Music Video*, 54–72.

52. For a description of background characters in feature films, see Will Straw, "Scales of Presence: Bess Flowers and the Hollywood Extra," *Screen* 52 (2011): 121–127. Ph.D.'s "Little Susie's on the Up," at http://www.youtube.com/watch?v=JKgzYLBV_cc

Lady Gaga, "Paparazzi," at http://www.youtube.com/watch?v=d2smz_1L2_0&ob=av3e

53. Nicole Scherzinger's "Poison," at http://www.youtube.com/watch?v=9joqPp3peLg
    See Nina Eidsheim, "Voice as a Technology of Selfhood: Towards an Analysis of Racialized Timbre and Vocal Performance," Ph.D. diss., University of California San Diego, 2008.

54. Steve Winwood's "Higher Love," at http://lockerz.com/u/20542314/decalz/6159090/steve_winwood_higher_love

55. See Vernallis, *Experiencing Music Video*, 32. For a historical perspective on music and levitation, see Thomas Grey, "'On Wings of Song': Representing Music as Agency in Nineteenth-Century Culture," in *Representation in Western Music*, ed. Joshua S. Walden (Cambridge: Cambridge University Press, 2012), 103–126.

56. Wang Chung's "Dance Hall Days," at http://www.youtube.com/watch?v=V-xpJRwIA-Q&ob=av2e, and Flock of Seagulls "I Ran," at http://www.youtube.com/watch?v=0_Pq0xYr3L4
    Paula Abdul's "Cold Hearted Snake," at http://www.youtube.com/watch?v=o7aShcmEksw&ob=av2e, is a good example: staged as a Bob Fosse number, it draws from traditional dance editing. Lionel Ritchie's "Dancing in the Streets" similarly references the musical.

57. "En Vogue's "Free Your Mind," at http://www.youtube.com/watch?v=i7iQbBbMAFE
    Rihanna's "Who's That Chick?," at www.youtube.com/watch?v=jbghbznr26U

58. In hip-hop videos, the expensive, fancy car moving in slow motion with a focus on the hubcaps was a common trope. Ron Isley and R. Kelly's "Down Low," at http://www.youtube.com/watch?v=fXdu3pwT4ps&ob=av2e is a good example.

59. Justin Bieber's "Somebody to Love," at http://www.youtube.com/watch?v=SOI4OF7iIr4&ob=av2e
    Justin Timberlake's "Rock Your Body," at http://www.youtube.com/watch?v=TSVHoHyErBQ&ob=av2e Francis Lawrence's "Bad Romance," at http://www.youtube.com/watch?v=qrO4YZeyl0I

60. En Vogue's "Free Your Mind," at http://www.youtube.com/watch?v=i7iQbBbMAFE
    Rihanna's "Who's That Chick?," at http://www.youtube.com/watch?v=D4_U2Zq-FLeM
    Nicole Scherzinger's "Whatever U Like," at http://www.youtube.com/watch?v=JX-1q_Lpzp8&ob=av2e

61. Kim Carnes's "Bette Davis Eyes," at http://www.youtube.com/watch?v=EPOIS5taqA8&ob=av2e

62. Rihanna's "Who's That Chick?" at http://www.youtube.com/watch?v=vDgT0kR6770&feature=fvwrel. Rihanna's "Umbrella," at http://www.youtube.com/watch?v=PXvauXKo2hU. Stan Hawkins has written about what he calls the "hyperembodiment" of the figure. Each thing including bodies seems more extremely realized.

63. Les Brill, *Crowds, Power, and Transformation in Cinema (Contemporary Approaches to Film and Television)* (Detroit: Wayne State University Press, 2006), 3.

64. Peter Gabriel's "Sledgehammer," at http://www.youtube.com/watch?v=hqyc37aOqT0
    George Michael's "Monkey," at http://www.youtube.com/watch?v=CHb2XYeXcJI&ob=av2e, is a good example of a crane shot documenting a stadium performance with masses of concertgoers.

65. For example, Lady Gaga's "Bad Romance," at http://www.youtube.com/watch?v=qrO4YZeyl0I&ob=av2e, and "Telephone," at http://www.youtube.com/watch?v=EVBsypHzF3U&ob=av2e use very discreet tracking shots.

66. It appears in Floria Sigismondi and Katy Perry's "E.T.," at http://www.youtube.com/watch?v=t5Sd5c4o9UM&ob=av2e,
    Kanye West's "Power," at http://www.youtube.com/watch?v=L53gjP-TtGE&ob=av2e, and Lady Gaga's "Born This Way," at http://www.youtube.com/watch?v=wV1FrqwZyKw&ob=av2e, for example. Consider an early Hall and Oates music video with string instruments distributed around the foyer of a two-story house; it feels a bit

322 Notes to Pages 225–227

Alice in Wonderlandish—violins, cellos, violas—and these bow themselves through their own woody extended arms. The instruments float down the stairs and across the ceilings. Yet they never take on the approaching whorl-like patterns we find in Justin Timberlake's "Let Me Talk To You/My Love," at http://www.youtube.com/watch?v=OVvIWkgJ12g. Nor in any other video. "Let Me Talk To You"'s violins start gliding forward from a vanishing point at the extreme distance in the frame accelerating onward until they nearly pass us near the frame's sides at what looks like full scale and nearly full force. We can grasp the shift in production strategies by looking at David Fincher and George Michael's "Freedom," at http://www.youtube.com/watch?v=diYAc7gB-0A. The pieces of brick and wood coming at us in the "Freedom" video have poor definition and we viewers may have little kinesthetic response to them. Sending something down the X-axis in the past made little sense. The now graspable whorl-like shape is perfect for cell phones. Is music video doing this because it's musical, or will we start seeing this everywhere; like many innovations, is it a technique first to be tried out here? If it's hot it'll be picked up in advertising—its charm then used up, the whorl will quickly be abandoned.

67. Nelly's "Just a Dream," at http://www.youtube.com/watch?v=N6O2ncUKvlg&ob=av2e
     Justin Timberlake's "My Love," at http://www.youtube.com/watch?v=OVvI WkgJ12g
     Matt Mahurin and R.E.M.'s "Orange Crush," at http://www.youtube.com/watch?v=_mSmOcmk7uQ&ob=av2n
     Mark Romanek and Macy Gray's "I Try," at http://www.youtube.com/watch?v=Lz vbiFR95gM&feature=related

68. Marshall McLuhan argued that the television screen elicited a greater sense of touch than sight. McLuhan, "The Playboy Interview: Marshall McLuhan," *Playboy Magazine*, March (1969) 1994, 11. Perhaps a combination of factors at any historical moment shapes our relation to space and objects. Factors might include technologies, economics, and culture. Concerning popular music, the blissful, wanton sexuality of Led Zeppelin or Jimmy Hendrix, where elements mingle and blur, can never be returned to again. Now we tend to isolate and prissify everything. Today's search for manicured sonic perfection comes with some losses.

69. Vernallis, *Experiencing Music Video*, 99.

70. Avril Lavigne's "Wish You Were Here," at http://www.youtube.com/watch?v=VT1-sitWRtY&ob=av2e But consider another example by the same director, Dave Meyers. In his video for Pink's "Fuckin' Perfect," a Teddy Bear is affectively potent but creates little haptic response even though it's tossed back and forth from the back to the front of the frame. Later, a razor blade slashed against the woman's wrist in the tub does create a visceral response. But is it because of the curling and unfurling blood drifting through the water? The digital may be good for some elements and not others. It's best for smoke and liquids. It's good also for objects that might as easily be animated, like in another of Dave Meyers's videos, Justin Bieber and Usher's "Somebody to Love," at http://www.youtube.com/watch?v=SOI4OF7iIr4 Pink, "Fuckin' Perfect," at http://www.youtube.com/watch?v=K3GkSo3ujSY

71. Lady Gaga, "Paparazzi," at http://www.youtube.com/watch?v=d2smz_1L2_0&ob=av3e

72. So have musical and visual elements, as suggested above, become more individuated and particularized today? In Rihanna's "Who's That Chick?" I notice a mass of piled-high men's shirts, a mini-throne upon which Rihanna climbs and then perches. Each shirt has integrity, each is different, made possible through some judicious preproduction choices of texture and color, and postproduction decisions linked to digital intermediate and after effects. As a bundled heap from the back of the frame, the shirts come forward the right amount. Think also of Adele's "Rolling in the Deep."

73. Paula Abdul's "Rush Rush," at http://www.youtube.com/watch?v=yqyIaNWP0T0

Britney Spears's "Hold It Against Me," at http://www.youtube.com/watch?v=-Edv8Onsrgg&ob=av2e

Hanson's "Thinking 'Bout Somethin'," at http://www.youtube.com/watch?v=Tm G0DqhfDbY

74. Korsgaard suggests that more of this takes place in the digital era than in the past. This is an interesting claim, but it might be hard to prove. Mathias Korsgaard, "Creation and Erasure: Music Video as a Signaletic Form of Practice," *Journal of Aesthetics & Culture* 4 (Stockholm: Co-Action Publishing, 2012). http://www.aestheticsandculture.net/index.php/jac/article/view/18151/22823

75. Ph.D.'s "Little Susie's on the Up," at http://www.youtube.com/watch?v=JKgzYLBV_cc

The Strokes' "Taken for a Fool," at http://www.youtube.com/watch?v=0U_jGVE Kr9s&ob=av2e

Queen and David Bowie's "Under Pressure," at http://www.youtube.com/watch?v=xtrEN-YKLBM, is another example of an eighties video that uses much remediation.

Lady Gaga's "Paparazzi," at http://www.youtube.com/watch?v=d2smz_1L2_0&ob=av2e

76. Research backs this up: we tend to recognize many forms of music—lullaby, sex, dance, or fighting—through rhythm, melodic contour, and harmony (and these can be recognized across cultures; infants seem to respond differently to these as patterns at birth). When images are placed against the music, they may match the music, complement or contradict it, but the music's hailings to elicit bodily comportment and its strong affective pulls still projects regardless of what images are placed against it. In other words, music still pierces. Yet music is also capacious and can accept many types of imagery. (One might remember a song from a moment first heard on the radio or in concert.) See Nicholas Cook, "Theorizing Musical Meaning," *Music Theory Spectrum* 23, no. 2 (Autumn 2001): 170–195; and Phillip Tagg, "Gestural Interconversion and Connotative Precision," *Film International* 3, no. 13 (January 2005): 20–31.

77. One of my favorites is the seventies "ba-ba-ba-baby you ain't seen nothing yet" by Bachman-Turner Overdrive.

78. Nicki Minaj's "Super Bass," at http://www.youtube.com/watch?v=4JipHEz53sU&ob=av2e

Enrique Iglesias's "Heartbeat," at http://www.youtube.com/watch?v=NVk4vENO biI&ob=av2e

79. Eighties synthesizer sounds were often glacial—enormous and dramatic. The stiff and low-res image and resistant edits help show off the music.

80. Directors complain about the tedium of green screen, however. It's hard on the performers and hard on everyone's eyes. One gets tired from the green and the constant photoshopping.

81. Alan Ferguson (who has made music videos for Fall Out Boy and Katy Perry) is one of the most musical directors. He's the most sophisticated in terms of rendering complex music-image relations that finely reflect the musical features in music video (a classical guitarist, he holds degrees in music from Howard). Ferguson's art might escape many of his viewers; they simply might not see and hear all his level of craft. This may be a function of eye trace rhythms—one needs to pass over the entire frame to appreciate the work. I've claimed Alan Fergusons's all-over style resembles painter Peter Paul Rubens. He uses all of the frame from the center to the borders. He tries to catch and follow every musical detail. It's delicate, fine work.

Bordwell claims recent film directors are better at "world making" (*The Way Hollywood Tells It*, 19). Films can be more densely narrated, because directors have gotten better at suggesting the worlds in which their actors exist. The same is true for music video directors, but their "world making" involves building musical worlds. Directors like Melina Matsoukas and Alan Ferguson use a variety of costumes and props to richly articulate textured, colorful people and places.

82. I cordon off a large body of clips that are more likely to appear on Pitchfork and Vimeo as their own subgenre, arguing that they're for "alt" kids—I call them the "1,000 hit subgenre." Perhaps all of the polyphonic, hallucinogenic effects they possess help them stand apart from mainstream corporate ones. These videos don't need to foreground the song: their responsibility first is to help sell T-shirts and concerts (examples include Fake Blood's "I Think I Like It" and The Presets' "My People"). Their musicality can derive from indirect methods. When watching, a weird state of mind sets in that leads you to engage with the music (like if you'd smoked too much pot). But these are old tricks. Multiples have long been used to stun thinking. (Consider the eerie twins in Kubrick's *The Shining*, Diane Arbus's photography, or the Talking Heads' music video "Once in a Lifetime.") Stamping repeated figures like buildings and light poles into the music video's frames does similar things (for example Chemical Brothers' "Star Guitar"). Early music videos loved duplicates and twins.

83. See Mathias Korsgaard, "Music Video Transformed," and Nicola Dibben, "Inventing the App Album in Björk's Biophilia," in Vernallis, *Oxford Handbook of Sound and Image in Digital Media.*

84. For example, Gary Numan's "Cars," at http://www.youtube.com/watch?v=Ldyx3KH OFXw, or The Buggle's "Video Killed the Radio Star," at http://www.youtube.com/watch?v=Iwuy4hHO3YQ, screened in music video's infancy.

85. Here my argument follows David Bordwell's understanding of post-classical cinema. For Bordwell intensified continuity is tamed and rationalized in traditional Hollywood films, which retain their traditional character arcs and three-act structures. Similarly, music videos in corporate clips assimilate novel techniques while still focusing on showing off features of the song. David Bordwell describes "intensified continuity" in *The Way Hollywood Tells It: Story and Style in Modern Movies* (Berkeley: University of California Press, 2006), 120–121.

   Selena Gomez & the Scene's "Naturally," at http://www.youtube.com/watch?v=a_YR4dKArgo

86. Kanye West's "Welcome to Heartbreak," at http://www.youtube.com/watch?v=wMH0 e8kIZtE&ob=av2e

   MGMT's "Time to Pretend," at http://www.youtube.com/watch?v=B9dSYgd5Elk&ob=av2n

   Though Beyoncé's "Countdown," at http://www.youtube.com/watch?v=2XY3Av VgDns&ob=av2e, is very mannerist! Technique subsumes all.

87. Like the Quantel and the toaster in the eighties, and the flame in the nineties.

88. Health's "Die Slow," at http://www.youtube.com/watch?v=EWZxThGh5wQ

89. I'd like to thank Theo Cateforis for describing "the soar" for me.

90. See Simon Reynolds, who also connects "the soar" to dance music: http://www.guardian.co.uk/music/musicblog/2011/apr/14/balearics-ibiza-pop and Daniel Barrow's critique of the soar. http://thequietus.com/articles/06073-a-plague-of-soars-warps-in-the-fabric-of-pop/

91. The Black Eyed Peas' "I Gotta Feeling," at http://www.youtube.com/watch?v=uSD4 vsh1zDA

   Jennifer Lopez and Pitbull's "On the Floor (featuring Pitbull)," at http://www.youtube.com/watch?v=t4H_Zoh7G5A.

Chapter 11

1. David Fincher, personal interview, October 1998.

   Lawrence's and Meyers's videos can be seen on the web. Readers can go to www.launch.com, type in the title of the song, and then stream or download the video. Alex Garcia's website at www.mvdb.com maintains a somewhat current list of Lawrence's and Meyers's output. Typing "music video download" and the director's name in Google will bring up what is current. Meyers's website is http://www.davemeyers.com. Lawrence's company website is http://www.dnala.com/director/?director=Francis-Lawrence.

2. It is beyond this chapter's scope to enter the debate on the merits of auteur studies. Virginia Wexman acknowledges the good arguments against auteur studies, including the elevation of mediocre work by famous directors over exemplary works by lesser-known ones, the downplaying of genre, and the doubts about whether authors can be said to exist for films. She suggests, however, that auteur studies still have relevance. See her *Film and Authorship* (Brunswick, NJ: Rutgers University Press, 2002). So little has been written on music video directors that it is good to start *somewhere*. The question of style has been particularly neglected.

3. One could argue that music video is a medium distinct from its predecessors—film, television, photography—a medium with its own ways of organizing materials, exploring themes, and dealing with time. I take the song and director's response to it in the music video most seriously, for a simple reason: music videos derive from the songs they set. The music comes first—the song is produced before the video is conceived—and the director normally designs images with the song as a guide. Moreover, the video must sell the song; it is therefore responsible to the song in the eyes of the artist and the record company. Music videos develop many ways of following a song. They often reflect a song's structure and pick up on specific visual and musical features in the domains of melody, rhythm, and timbre. The image can even seem to imitate sonic properties like ebb, flow, and indeterminacy of boundaries.

    Roger Beebe has a chapter forthcoming in the book *Music Video/Music Television/ MTV* (Duke University Press) which claims that the addition of director's credits to music videos in 1987 *did* increase audience recognition of directors and seemed to have a positive effect on music video as a whole. To date, no article on music video directors and their styles exists.

4. Optimally, an auteurist approach should be coupled with a study of the industrial and economic processes of the industry. However, such studies don't exist. Jack Banks's *Monopoly Television: MTV's Quest to Control the Music* is derived from trade magazines like Variety and Billboard, sources which devote almost no attention to music video production. Banks, *Monopoly Television: MTV's Quest to Control the Music* (Boulder, CO: Westview Press, 1996). I am currently working on a book entitled *Transmedia Directors: Mavericks of Music Video, Commercials and Film* (Durham, NC: Duke University Press). This book includes interviews with music video directors, editors, set designers, producers, and musicians. Interlaced among these interviews are chapters on technology, censorship, genres, directorial style, intertextuality, and music video's history. The fieldwork I have done colors this chapter.

    A director's style emerges from the backdrop of a common practice of techniques within the genre. My first book, *Experiencing Music Video: Aesthetics and Cultural Context* (New York: Columbia University Press, 2004), describes the common practice within the field as well as providing close readings of particular music videos. To understand the music video genre one would wish to augment studies of industrial and economic processes, auteurship, and the medium's common practice with a consideration of audience reception and genre history.

5. To best illuminate a director's style, this discussion begins with a director's predominant stylistic features and traces others as they cluster around these. It's important to acknowledge that many of the stylistic devices discussed here can be found in the work of other music video directors, though some remain unique to the director. A director's *orchestration* of these techniques produces a unifying style.

6. By flow I refer to succession, continuity, the piece's ability to help a viewer predict what will happen. A pop song's sense of flow can be difficult to characterize: it most likely is constructed through the simultaneous functioning of many musical elements. Similarly the way a music video image relates to a song's flow would be hard to measure. Nicholas Cook and Alf Bjornberg have tried to describe the flow of music video images against the song through quantitative analysis. Nicholas Cook, *Analyzing Musical Multimedia* (New York: Oxford University Press, 1998); Alf Bjornberg, "Structural Relationships of Music and Images in Music Video," *Popular Music* 13, no. 1 (1994).

How might one parameter—editing—underscore a song's processual drive? We might look to a visual analogy. Several critics commented that Christo's placement of his Gates helped to highlight the sinuous contours of walkways, hills, and valleys through Central Park. The Gates' placement seemed to possess a regularity, an attention to the park's shifts in terrain, as well as a capacity to appear slightly before or behind prominent landmarks. (In our analogy, the land is the musical structure, and the Gates are edit points.) A focused close examination (incorporating quantitative measurements) of where edits fall against a song would give us new insights into how this parameter works in music video.

7. Music video presents a range all the way from extremely abstract videos emphasizing color and movement to those that convey a story. But most videos tend to be nonnarrative. An Aristotelian definition—characters with defined personality traits, goals, and a sense of agency encounter obstacles and are changed by them—describes only a small fraction of videos, perhaps one in fifty. Still fewer meet the criteria that David Bordwell and Kristin Thompson require for a story: that all of the events we see and hear, plus those we infer or assume to have occurred, can be arranged according to their presumed causal relations, chronological order, duration, frequency, and spatial locations. Even if we have a sense of a music video's story, we may not feel that we can reconstruct the tale in the manner that Bordwell and Thompson's criteria demand. David Bordwell and Kristin Thompson, *Film Art: An Introduction* (New York: McGraw-Hill, 1997), 482.

8. If narrative models fail to capture a large portion of music video, what models can we put in their stead? Many videos are devoted to completing a single process: getting everyone to the party on time, ensuring that the plane gets off the ground or that the baby is born, and so on. (Here, we might define "process" as the act of carrying on or going on, a series of actions, changes, or functions bringing about a result, or a series of operations performed in the making or treatment of a product.) Such music video projects do not feel like narratives, in part because they are arbitrary; one activity might have been picked as well as another. In addition, the focus on a single task often becomes apparent only in retrospect. The presentation of this process is fragmented, attenuated abruptly by images of the band performing or lip-syncing against an amorphous background. The sustained treatment of the activity comes suddenly, at a time when we do not expect it, and its duration may be unusually prolonged or drastically abbreviated. The video's main project is dispersed across a number of the song's sections. When footage of this material appears over the course of the video, carrying the process forward, these appearances gain an uncanny sense of return. In such videos, the emblematic characters, appearing intermittently with ferocious attention to a simple task, create qualities of volition and determination befitting musical materials that function similarly. Other types of means of structuring a video include catalogues, "slices of life," and tableaux. I use the term "thread" to signify the successive iterations of a visual motive. These motives can appear and recede while still seeming connected.

9. Many music videos work on the principle of contagion: an element in one of the strands seeps into another—it might be a color, a particular prop, a way of feeling or moving. For example, in Ben Folds Five's "Brick," the splashes of red that appear in the performance space (which function purely as an arbitrary, decorative touch) gradually invade the story space (we see a red Christmas bulb). This visual process can match a musical one. In a song, a guitar melody might modify its pitch content or timbre so that it echoes the voice.

10. The tone of Lawrence's videos is interesting as well. "Fortunate" contains something attractive and inviting and yet a subtly darker undertow remains. The couple's embrace is one of the most tender in music video, but the woman on the bathroom floor disturbs us. The video is haunted by loss. In "Fortunate" there is some ambiguity whether the singer might be dreaming of or witnessing a lover's death.

11. This is what I assumed was occurring. In a 2001 interview Lawrence explained to me the video's backstory.

12. Some other details related to color: Do the green flashing laptop screens projecting bids to purchase Gaga echo her strobe-lit, ultra-sequined green outfit? Does the smoke surrounding Gaga's red-laced dancing troupe suggests they're celebrating her lover's incineration? We don't know it yet, but most likely their dancing reflects a flash-forward to events transpiring after the clip's ending.

13. Yi-Fu Tuan, *Space and Place: The Perspective of Experience* (Minneapolis: University of Minnesota Press, 1977), 12.

14. One way music video directors create form is through the placement of figures and objects in the frame. Francis Lawrence will often begin a video with a character placed low in the frame. By the song's apex, she will have moved up. David Fincher reported that "Vogue" starts with a shot from Madonna's back so that it has somewhere to build from.

15. When videos showcase a performer like Maxwell, Melanie C, or J-Lo, some shots will be frontal, but many will be placed slightly to the side, or close and high over one shoulder or lower from the back, creating a sense not of mastery of the space but of coming to know this space over time.

16. Can a moving camera match a song's tempo? The objects depicted in the frame, the steadiness and placement of the camera, the shot's color and the types of editing that surround it all shape our sense of a shot's speed. Nevertheless, a tracking shot at the speed of a person walking seems to match a song's tempo of 60 beats per minute. Sped-up footage works well with music with a fast pulse and conversely slowed-down footage works well with her slow tempi. Some videos contain footage that seems to run slightly faster or slower than the song; the mismatch creates an interesting friction. Because songs tend to possess numerous rhythmic strata, as does an image, correspondences can occur at several levels. See "Musical Parameters" in Vernallis, *Experiencing Music Video*.

17. For a detailed description of the types of relation possible between music and image, see Vernallis, *Experiencing Music Video*, 18–19.

18. Philosophers have long been interested in music's ability to suggest a sense of time not as broken up, but rather wherein the past flows seamlessly into the present, and the present into the future: "hearing a melody is hearing, having heard, and being about to hear, all at once." Music derives its temporal flexibility in part through its continual change and momentum, even as it repeats itself. Richard Middleton has pointed to the repetition in pop music and how it might return us to some sort of preoedipal bliss. Victor Zuckerkandl, *Sound and Symbol: Music and the External World*, trans. Willard R. Trask (London: Routledge, 1956), 234–235. Middleton, "Over and Over: Notes Towards a Politics of Repetition," http://www2.huberlin.de/fpm/middle.htm.

19. Incubus's "Warning" features a postapocalyptic landscape in which all of the people in a city suddenly disappear. Repetition and variation blend seamlessly into the visual texture: one chalkboard resembles the sky, while shapes on another chalkboard recall the office building and the sun. Chalk dust blows past a girl's bedroom window, and something like the obsessive notes pasted to her wall reappear on the walls of the classroom. The spaces—office, hallway, grocery store, church, and classroom—resemble the inside of the bus. People we see resemble each other, which creates an opportunity for another visual rhyme.

20. Lineages of visual and aural ideas might be traced. Incubus's "Warning" seems to reference Mark Pellington and Pearl Jam's music video "Jeremy" and foreshadows David Fincher's *Girl with the Dragon Tattoo*.

21. Can a music video image suggest a verbal metaphor? Eisenstein's theory of montage suggests it can. See the later discussion of Meyers's "An American Badass." Men pound slabs of meat and strippers pour forward in the next few shots. Masculine aggression and women are linked.

22. Lawrence claims that the set was modeled on the layout of a room at the fancy Chateau Marmont in Hollywood but the ceiling was inspired by a public library.

23. Incubus's "Warning" has a reference to director Matt Mahurin, and Brittany Spears's "I'm a Slave For You" echoes Paula Abdul's "Cold Hearted Snake."

24. In a 2001 interview, Lawrence claimed that he wanted to break the rules for rap and R&B in his videos for Maxwell's "Fortunate" and Ginuwine's "Oh So Different." I've often heard such a response from directors, but I've never heard them express the desire to break the rules for alternative, pop, or heavy metal.

25. Preferring understatement to melodrama, Lawrence often asks his characters to keep their expressions blank. They can trust that the music will help to fill in their emotional state. When Lawrence works with actors, he obtains highly nuanced gestures that vary throughout the course of a video. He shoots a lot of footage to ensure that he has enough material to edit, and requests that his actors move in particular ways, but he tries never to ask them to do something that feels unnatural or uncomfortable. (Conversation with director 2001.)

    Meyers's approach is different. He speaks about obtaining exaggeratively heroic and glamorous performances from his musicians. He might jump from behind the camera to suggest how a performer should move.

26. "The Aesthetics of Music Video: An Analysis of Madonna's 'Cherish,'" in Vernallis, *Experiencing Music Video*, contains a longer discussion of this aesthetic.

27. A filmmaker or music video director can provide a path through the images or soundtrack. David Bordwell draws attention to the way Jacques Tati draws the viewer's attention to particular areas within the scene by use of sound. In *Monsieur Hulot's Holiday*, vacationers relax at a resort hotel. In the foreground of the shot, some guests quietly play cards, while in the background, M. Hulot plays ping-pong. Early in the scene, the guests in the foreground are murmuring softly and Hulot's ping-pong game is louder. The sound encourages us to watch Hulot. As the guests become louder and we hear less of Hulot's ping-pong ball, our attention shifts to the front of the set. Bordwell and Kristin Thompson, *Film Art* (New York: McGraw-Hill, 1997), 280–281.

    Let me now give a similar example from music video. In a video, our attention to the song shapes the way we perceive the image, but, to an equal extent, what we attend to in the image helps to determine how we hear the music. When a star jams his face in front of the camera, or when a hand or foot threatens to break through the viewing plane, we suddenly hear the music in a different way. We become aware that we should pay attention right now. If the same moment in the song were accompanied by a less assertive image—say, a long shot—we would more likely attend to the overall arrangement of the song than focus on any particular element. This experiment can work in reverse, with the music influencing our attention to the image. Imagine a scenario with two types of music. The first contains a city scene, shot in slow motion, with people walking down a busy street; a medium shot in slow motion is cropped so that we see the people from their knees to just above their eyebrows. Let us say that the song contains a pounding jungle beat and short synthesizer flurries. We might notice the intensity of the pedestrians' faces or the muscular armature of one or two people. On the other hand, if we hear a flowing synthesizer pad with a minimal rhythm arrangement, perhaps some innocuous "CD jazz," we might attend instead to the spring and sweep of the bodies in motion, and to the flow of the crowd as a whole. Music videos frequently crop images such as the example above, breaking bodies at the joint or rendering them partially, so that more of the context must be supplied by the music than by the image.

28. Many scholars have focused on the interdependence of music and image in a musical multimedia context. Bernard Herrmann notes that in movie soundtracks, "the music seems to seek out and intensify the inner thoughts of the characters" as well as to "invest a scene with terror, grandeur, gaiety, or misery." Nicholas Cook argues that a musical multimedia relation does not only "engender meanings of its own" (20); "the coupling

of image and sound contextualizes, clarifies, and in a sense analyses the music" (74). Music and image provide a "two-way interaction of commensurability and heterogeneity, similarity and difference" (81). Quoted in Cook, *Analyzing Musical Multimedia*.

I argue that a slight disjuncture between music and image may encourage more attentive listening and viewing, hence the playful, tangential relations between music and image that occur so frequently in music video. When a viewer cannot get her bearings, she may attend more closely to the soundtrack.

29. In music video the shape of the musical line can correlate to the shape of the visual image. See Vernallis, *Experiencing Music Video*, 160–162, 213–214.

30. Teaching the viewer the song's contours and then interpolating her into them is a strong music video technique. Alan Ferguson and Beyoncé's "Party" works similarly. Note the moment when Kelly Rowland and Beyoncé dance side by side and then Beyoncé runs her fingers along the trailer's side.

    Beyoncé, Party ft. J. Cole http://www.youtube.com/watch?v=XWCwcl_sYMY

31. Meyers's disparate imagery and picaresque storytelling can leave the viewer lost in the song's structure. Lawrence helps the viewer grasp the overall song structure.

32. When setting the image for Madonna's "Cherish," heterocentric directors might choose to emphasize the IV-chord suspension, say through imagery of unrequited love. Music video director Herb Ritts moves past this suspension and draws attention to the verse fragment, thereby underscoring the mermen's collective identity. See Vernallis, *Experiencing Music Video*, 223–228.

33. This is often a musical question: can you identify the ways the bridge's material resembles that of the introduction?

34. Many theorists argue that music has physiological roots. Robert Frances states, "The kinship between rhythmic and melodic pattern in music, and the patterns of gestures that accompany behaviour, represents one of the basic elements of music's expressive language . . . the basic psychological states (calm, excitation, tension, relaxation, exaltation, despair) normally translate themselves as gestural forms that have a given rhythm, as tendencies and ascents, as modalities for organizing the fragmentary forms within global forms (constant repetition, diversity, periodicity, evolution)." Robert Frances, *La Perception de la Musique* (Paris: Vrin, 1958), 299, quoted and translated in Jay Dowling, *The Perception of Music* (Hillsdale, NJ: Lawrence Erlbaum, 1998), 19.

35. Philosophers of music have noticed that music seems like movement in time— movement that ironically goes nowhere. Eduard Hanslick describes music as "tonally moving forms," and Suzanne Langer makes the claim that music's primary illusion is "an order of virtual time, in which its sonorous forms move in relation to each other." "Music is the sonorous image of passage." Hanslick, *On the Musically Beautiful*, trans. Geoffrey Payzant (Indianapolis: Hackett, 1986), 29. Langer, *Mind: An Essay on Human Feeling*, vol. 1 (Baltimore: Johns Hopkins University Press, 1967), 109, 113.

36. Michel Chion notes that while images have a static aspect, sounds present a trajectory: "All sounds consist of an attack and a slight fading resonance, a finite story, oriented in time in a precise and irreversible manner." He goes on to refine the comparison, and considers both sound and image as following a kind of trajectory. He offers that sound might be thought of as having properties like those of a gas, while image might be compared to directed lines. Sound is characterized by gradual diffusion, by a progressive loss of clarity and grip. Michel Chion, *Audiovision: Sound on Screen*, trans. Claudia Gorbman (New York: Columbia University Press, 1990), 19, 144.

37. As John Berger notes, this is a common device from painting and advertising aimed to flatter the viewer. John Berger, *Ways of Seeing* (New York: Viking Press, 1995).

38. See Nicholas Cook for a good description of how media interact in a musical multimedia context. Cook, *Analyzing Musical Multimedia*, 100.

39. The music video's unfolding landscape appears to reflect the music's teleology. Objects like pixie dust, cloth, and tumbleweeds fall away after musical entrances, suggesting a cause-and-effect relation. A wandering camera turns in response to the music.

40. The satisfaction derives from multiple sources. First, in the strange world of music video, many of the sights and sounds fail to do what we expect of them in everyday life; we no longer have a sense of what sounds and images mean. By wielding a prop to mark the beat, the performer fills in the gap, telling us how to feel the weight and quality of the percussion. Second, we do not have enough information about the characters in a music video—what animates them remains unclear. The sound, setting, and performer belong to one another; for a moment, a distance has been broached. Third, the synchronization of performers, music, and props is a triumph for the director and for the video itself. Music rarely represents real things in the world—with few exceptions like cuckoo clocks, trains, and ringing telephones. The pleasure of music video, therefore, derives in part from the ways that the performer can negotiate two worlds—one like ours, and the other a parallel musical universe in which the performer becomes a musician who moves through a musical landscape. Wielding a prop, a star functions as an actor as well as a musician. The question is, for how long can the performer straddle both roles well, or will he lapse into only one?

41. Andre Bazin observes that the use of the graphic match atrophied once sound became used in film. He notes that the shots of women talking and then chickens clucking in Fritz Lang's *Fury* are a holdover from silent filmmaking. Andre Bazin, *What Is Cinema?* (Berkeley: University of California Press, 1971), 34.

42. We can continue to find progressive moments here. We should remember that the politics of the bedroom, the family, the neighborhood, and larger spheres such as the political do not always cohere; this video focuses on the bedroom. Music videos can be built up through a series of isolated moments, each with its own integrity. Without a strong narrative arc, clear progression or definite closure, an early moment in a music video can stand up to a later one. Given the unpredictability of the video's outcome, the viewer might hope for and even expect a revolutionary moment. The opening shots of "Bombs over Baghdad" seem to linger, waiting for a moment to reassert themselves.

43. John O. Thompson, "Screen Acting and the Commutation Test," *Screen* 19, no. 2 (1978): 55–70.

44. In Terry Zwigoff's documentary *Crumb*, art historian Robert Hughes describes Crumb as the Hieronymus Bosch of our time. Several ex-girlfriends testify that the cartoonist's work emerges from a deep personal need; therefore they feel all right about it. Terry Zwigoff, *Crumb*, VHS (Columbia/TriStar Studios, 1997).

45. See Rick Altman, *The American Film Musical* (Bloomington: Indiana University Press, 1999); and Jane Feuer, *The Hollywood Musical* (Bloomington: Indiana University Press, 1982).

46. Lawrence's work may attract viewers for its classicism and restraint. But there is something to be said for the bawdy and raw in Meyers's work. If nothing else, it is at least interesting to see someone like Missy Elliott shoot a spit wad that travels across the room into a man's mouth. And it may surprise us to see women pulling up their skirts after taking a piss. Other imagery I can't quite endorse. I don't know what to say about Meyers's frequent staging of a woman taking a shower with a young boy, suited up for a Norman Rockwell painting, voyeuristically watching her.

47. One of Nicholas Cook's most significant contributions is to emphasize the frequently volatile nature of multimedia. Earlier theorists have assumed that "music in the film simply represents a meaning that already exists, rather than participating in the construction of that meaning. . . . Language that suggests that music reinforces, emphasizes, contradicts, or alters the image falls into this trap" (115). Instead, Cook argues, multimedia has "a dynamic, processive character" (67). "The result is qualitatively distinguishable from each component element viewed separately" (84). He cites Eisenstein's line that "multimedia had effects we were totally unprepared for" (84). Cook, *Analyzing Musical Multimedia*. In both "Bombs over Baghdad" and "One Minute Man" music, image, and lyrics become newly inflected as a result of the relations among media.

One senses how different each director is in relation to music video by looking at how they deal with closure. Lawrence's videos are elegantly shaped, well-formed miniatures, while Meyers's reflect a more fundamental greediness: he seems reluctant to encounter an ending in the hopes that the video might keep running and he will be able to keep on following the trajectory of the song. As a song progresses, he continually throws in more and more densely constructed images and types of music-image relations.

48. Lacan never directly explores how sounds, music, and rhythm might function as *objets petit a*, objects fetishized for the plenitude they represent for the subject and for the suggestion they bring of bygone wholeness. Other psychoanalytic critics have, however. Gerard Blanchard, *Images de la musique de cinema* (Paris: Edilig, 1984), 101–102.

Chapter 12

1. See Carol Vernallis, *Experiencing Music Video: Aesthetics and Cultural Context* (New York: Columbia University Press, 2004); and "Teaching Music Video: Aesthetics, Politics and Pedagogy," *Journal of Popular Music Studies* 12 (November 2000): 93–101.
2. Vevo's, Yahoo's, and AOL's play lists cycle quickly; YouTube is best for sheer breadth, though audiovisual sync and image quality can be poor, and the record industry can legally remove the videos.
3. Director Abteen Bagheri told me the Palm DVD series was the inspiration for his going into music videos. Interview with Bagheri, Fall 2012.
4. Elegance, lucidity, classical style, and technique—perhaps Romanek could have stood-in for Jørgen Leth in Lars Von Trier's *The Five Obstructions*. Like Jørgen Leth's and Stanley Kubrick's aesthetic, Romanek's is structured around a distanced eye. One wonders about this: is he hiding something, or is homage to and conversation with other visual media practitioners the most rewarding? Or perhaps distance and respect provide greater room for the song to come forward. Since Romanek's films like *One Hour Photo* and *Never Let Me Go* are emotionally laden, I assume his approach to music videos reflects a particular response to the genre.
5. One might claim that the relation between film music and image can suggest an intimate conversation that the viewer isn't fully privy to. This can leave the viewer, at some level, on the outside, as a witness rather than participant. Being left out of audiovisual relations isn't much different from being left out of relations between one's parents, which always harks back to the primal scene—here our parents literally turn their backs to us. To my knowledge a concept of viewership, the primal scene, film music, and the image hasn't yet been theorized. See Judith Butler, *Giving an Account of Oneself* (New York: Fordham University Press, 2005).
6. In my interviews with music video directors, I've discovered they often have a personal, gradually evolving visual iconography. In Romanek's later "Can't Stop the Feeling" for the Red Hot Chili Peppers, the band frolics with Aaron Worm–inspired readymades (clothes hangers, nerf balls, wastepaper baskets, plastic tubing) in an abandoned, cement-box-like warehouse. Suddenly one of the band members wears a fuzzy, purple, hippo headdress, and peers from behind an office potted fern. The shot cuts to singer Anthony Kiedis humping the drum set. Many directors describe their relation to music video as dreamlike, and ideas come late at night. I wonder. Is this cut psychic residue from "Got 'til It's Gone"? (Africa is where sexuality happens?) Is this a conscious or unconscious touch on the director's part, or rather an affecting moment discovered during editing?
7. These instances seem to work like Barthes's punctums.
8. In "Around the World" musical lines are taken up by a figure or a flashing light. Similarly, in "Hyper Ballad," every musical element aligns with an object or a lighting effect.
9. Clips are available through websites like YouTube, Google, Launch, and AOL, and searchable by director.

10. One could take this in the Deleuzian sense.

11. One might also wonder if music video has penetrated more deeply into films, television shows, and websites than can be traced. Did "Oh So Quiet"'s authentically gritty, working-class, automobile-inspired environments and allusion to the joyous gleam of 40s musicals inspire Von Trier's *Dancer in the Dark*?

12. When they do it can be explained by the song's status as or the musician's reputation as a conveyor of dance music (i.e., Janet and Michael Jackson's "Scream").

13. Michel Chion, *Audiovision: Sound on Screen*, trans. Claudia Gorbman (New York: Columbia University Press, 1990), 16.

14. Nicholas Cook, *Analyzing Musical Multimedia* (New York: Oxford University Press, 1998), 81–84.

Afterword

1. Max Horkheimer and Theodor Adorno, *Dialectic of Enlightenment (Cultural Memory in the Present)*, trans. Edmund Jephcott (Stanford, CA: Stanford University Press, 2002), 7. See also Marshall McLuhan, "The Playboy Interview: Marshall McLuhan," *Playboy Magazine*, March 1969, repr. 1994, 11. Lauren Berlant gives one of the most moving analyses of present-day life/work conditions. Because of "hyperexploitive entrepreneurial atomism that has been variously dubbed globalization, liberal sovereignty, late capitalism, post-Fordism, or neoliberalism," so many of us are living "a life dedicated to moving toward the good life's normative/utopian zone but [are] actually stuck in what we might call survival time, the time of struggling, drowning, holding on to the ledge, treading water, not-stopping." Lauren Berlant, "Nearly Utopian, Nearly Normal: Post-Fordist Affect in La Promesse and Rosetta," *Public Culture* 19, no. 2 (2007): 279, 280.

2. R. C. Miall, "Connecting Mirror Neurons and Forward Models," *Neuroreport* 14, no. 17 (2003): 2135–2137.
   "Entrainment occurs when two oscillators come to oscillate together . . . entrainment is the coordinating of the timing of our behaviors and the synchronizing of our attentional resources." Satinder P. Gill, "Entrainment and Musicality in the Human System Interface," *AI & Society* 25 (2007): 567–605.

3. See "QS: Quantified Self, Self Knowledge Through Numbers," http://quantifiedself.com/.

4. Gary Wolf, "The Data-Driven Life," in *New York Times*, April 28, 2010, http://www.nytimes.com/2010/05/02/magazine/02self-measurement-t.html?pagewanted=all&_r=0

5. Oren Lavie, "Her Morning Elegance," http://www.youtube.com/watch?v=2_HXUh-ShhmY

6. Many people experience weird YouTube vortices, where they're not only moving laterally, clicking from link to link, but also trying to pursue some sort of connoisseurly obscure topic like abrasive, gauche regional carpet-cleaning commercials from the seventies. I've started collecting meditation clips, in part for their oxymoronic qualities. There's little Benjaminian aura here. The ads blare, and the low-res images compete with the snarky commentary. Some person may be reaching out, but just as well she might be trying to peddle a DVD, and in the middle of the viewer's vulnerably hypnotic meditative state, an intrusive, loud, blaring sound might appear. (I've kept one eye for such complaints in the commentary.) People before me have come and gone leaving little trace, so the "sacred" of meditation is tainted with that of a peepshow. But some of it actually works. Perhaps yoga is so popular today because it's effective at combating social and economic demands. Anusara Yogi Bridget Woods Kramer, "Meditation," http://www.youtube.com/watch?v=Tu-qZugHXfc

7. "Chakra Balancing Meditation music Very Intense NO ADVERT," http://www.youtube.com/watch?v=9P_hgfiSmLM

8. Audiovisual stutter has historical precedents, and what's exciting about new media is that my intertextual precursors for this effect most likely differs from yours. Mine features the 1970s Purina Cat Chow commercials in which (with primitive video editing) the cat goes, "Chow chow chow." Today, perhaps nearly everyone enters a clip from a different vantage point. Perhaps we're less in sync than we thought. For new research on the glitch and the stutter, see Laura Marks, "A Noisy Brush with the Infinite: Noise in Enfolding-Unfolding Aesthetics," and Caetlin Benson-Allott, "Going Gaga for Glitch: Digital Failure @nd Feminist Spectacle in Twenty-F1rst Century Music Video," in *The Oxford Handbook of Sound and Image in Digital Media*, ed. Carol Vernallis et al. (New York and Oxford: Oxford University Press, forthcoming). Lady Gaga, "Telephone ft. Beyoncé," http://www.youtube.com/watch?v=EVBsypHzF3U

9. Film theorists have recently become obsessed with the digital versus analog. Digital and analog can sometimes be understood as a state of mind or experience—something can seem digitalish or analogish based on context. (In a scene in a very digitally embodied film, *Inception*, the femme fatale Mal sits in her mission house and the sun glints on a knife and cut, glowing, golden tomatoes. The digital should feel cold, abstracted, nonearthly, but this is one of the most quotidian and holy of scenes—notably warm.) With accelerated aesthetics, categorical attributes attributed to the digital and analogue can confound us. See D. N. Rodowick, *The Virtual Life of Film* (Cambridge, MA: Harvard University Press 2007). Rihanna, "Rockstar 101 ft. Slash," http://www.youtube.com/watch?v=eMOIUUS8GWo

10. Technologically for bullet time, still cameras are placed around the circumference of the profilmic event and then recombined into a moving image.

11. Linda Williams, "Film Bodies: Gender, Genre, and Excess," in *Film Theory and Criticism*, ed. Leo Braudy and Marshall Cohen, 5th ed. (New York: Oxford University Press, 1999), 711.

12. Several recent films such as *Fifty First Dates* (2004), *Eternal Sunshine of the Spotless Mind* (2004), and *(500) Days of Summer* (2009) reflect the same themes.

13. Is a possible subspecies or genre-blending of "slow-mo" and "all at once" the scroll? If we're watching a television newscaster in a dazed state, the scroll can seem to pull our distracted attention in a flow terminating nowhere. This two-state, split configuration is inassimilable. *Nuit Blanche*, http://vimeo.com/9078364

14. In contemporary film, we often follow an avatar-like character against a shifting landscape; sometimes this character itself changes. In these archipelago-like forms, we cleave to sound-image relations. We simply want the feel and pattern, a kinesthetic response we can match with the film's own routines comprised of varied forms of time, space, and rhythm. Consider, for example, *Moulin Rouge!* (2001), *Bourne Ultimatum* (2007), and *Life Aquatic* (2004).

15. Eclectic Method, "Beyoncé VS Lynyrd Skynrd" http://www.youtube.com/watch?v=tinOCcOzLf4

16. In the case of "L.E.S. Artistes," I'll argue the driver's simply digital intermediary, or in industry parlance, DI. DI functions like Photoshop's processes for altering images, but it works with real-time moving media. You can tweak an individual pixel's color, isolate it, and modulate it, thereby fracturing the moving image, pulling it away from its referent in the world. Even if the Santigold video had not been designed with digital intermediary, I'd say it relies on DI's safety net: that a piece can be "made in post." Santigold, "L.E.S. Artistes," http://www.youtube.com/watch?v=ciJDA0tcQfs

17. Epochs in the throes of change may produce their own antidotes and remedies. The *New York Times* published a study recently suggesting that IT workers who multitasked were deskilling. They were over-responding to a surfeit of stimulus, and failing to identify important elements within a field of information. I took the test and was pleased at how well I'd done. I've spent years studying music video, however, and have learned to hunt and track one item at a time as it threads through the material. I've also taught and done

production. The benefits of participating in media (through criticism, teaching, or production) may be also why so many of my students, regardless of their discipline, now turn to video production. Production practice provides a way to make manageable and find patterns within an onslaught of stimuli, and to begin to articulate one's own dreams rather than more simply re-envisioning the dreams of others. Part of me is hopeful about new media. We will become more shotgun, staccato-like readers, but also listeners and viewers who might, through new configurations of the senses, take part in a public conversation.

18. Justin Bieber, "Somebody to Love," http://www.youtube.com/watch?v=SOI4OF7iIr4.

INDEX

Heffernan, Virginia, 130, 150, 153, 179
"Hellagood" (Stefani), 264
Hellboy 2, 137
Hello Dolly, 28
Hendrix, Jimmy, 322n68
"Here Is Gone" (Goo Goo Dolls), 238–39, 241, 243, 246
"Her Morning Elegance" (Lavie), 280, 280f
heroin, 134
Herrmann, Bernard, 39, 107, 159, 328n28
Herzog, Amy, 74
Herzog, Werner, 18
heteronormativity, 110
Hicks, Taral, 203, 271
"Higher Love" (Winwood), 222
Hillis, Ken, 302n9
"The Hills Are Alive," 81, 86
Hindemith, Paul, 107
hip-hop, 262
    rhythm in, 154
"Hips Don't Lie" (Shakira), 23
Hirschbiegel, Oliver, 18
Hitchcock, Alfred, 144, 248
    Psycho, 136, 299n25
    Vertigo, 84, 89, 108, 283, 299n25
"Hold it Against Me" (Spears), 19, 216, 227
homosexuality, 198, 307n42, 313n51, 314n52
Hong Kong action films, 4, 36, 70, 71
Hootie and the Blowfish, 307n43
Horkheimer, Max, 332n1
Horne, Lena, 199
horror film music, 73
Hot Fuzz, 7, 33, 38, 262
House of Cards (Fincher), 20
"House of Cards" (Radiohead), 214
Houston, Whitney, 187
Hoyos, Hector, 314n52
Hu, King, 63, 294n5
    A Touch of Zen, 71
Hughes, Robert, 330n44
Hughes, Tim, 74
Hulk, 28
Hulu, 143, 208
Human Nature (Gondry), 268
"Human Nature" (Madonna), 192
Hunter, Paul, 263
Hussey, David, 215
Huston, John, 298n10
"Hyper Ballad" (Björk), 270, 331n8

"I am . . . Sasha Fierce" (Beyoncé), 307n43
"I Am That Name," 152
If, 70
"If I Were a Boy" (Beyoncé), 18, 160, 160f, 203, 290n20
Iglesias, Enrique, 227, 229, 229f
"I Gotta Feeling" (Black Eyed Peas), 233

"I Just Died in Your Arms Tonight" (Cutting Crew), 212
"I Just Want to Love You" (Jay-Z), 249, 256
"I'm a Slave for You" (Spears), 245, 259
IMAX, 138, 296n3
IMDb, 43
"I'm Falling" (R.E.M.), 231
"I'm Gonna Be Alright" (Lopez), 249, 252
I'm Not There (Haynes), 66
iMovie, 150
Inception (Nolan), 8, 13, 284, 333n9
Incubus, 243, 243f, 246, 327n19
Independence Day, 8
Inglis, Ian, 302n9
Inglourious Basterds, 8
Ingres, Jean Auguste Dominique, 266
"In My Language," 128
Inner Space, 40
inset narratives, 43–45, 113
intensified audiovisual aesthetics, 38, 45, 72, 94
    cross platform, 12–13
    of digital cinema, 7–8
    of music video, 11–12, 297n3
    of YouTube, 9–10
intensified continuity, 22, 33–36, 117, 136
    in music video, 71
intermediality, 143–46. *See also* cross-mediality
    mashups and, 193
intertextuality, 9, 14, 23, 28, 104, 183
    music video and, 227
    on YouTube, 24, 155, 171–73, 192–93
INXS, 215, 219
iPhone, 10, 16, 174
iPod, 132, 138
    audiovisual aesthetics and, 73
"Iridescent" (Linkin Park), 214
Isaak, Chris, 217
"I Sit on You," 151
I Spy, 202
"I Think I Like It" (Fake Blood), 324n82
"I Try" (Gray), 225–26
"I Wanna Dance with Somebody" (Houston), 187
"I Wanna Go" (Spears), 232

Jackson, Janet, 248
    "Got 'til It's Gone," 265, 267
    "Someone to Call My Lover," 245
    "Son of a Gun," 240, 315n2
Jackson, Michael, 262
    "Billie Jean," 148, 157
    "Black or White," 213
    "Rock with You," 214
    "Thriller," 40, 219, 314n52
"Jaded" (Aerosmith), 238, 238f, 239f, 240
Jagger, Mick, 265
    "God Gave Me Everything," 268
"Jai Ho" (Pussycat Dolls), 23

media
  cross-genre aesthetics, 12–13
  genre competition, 19
  platform confusions in, 15–16
  trajectory of, 13–14
media swirl, 3–4, 14
Melancholia, 18, 34
Melanie C, 245, 327n15
Méliès, Georges, 139, 260
melody, 12, 79, 91, 105, 117, 121, 182, 187, 235,
    243, 251–52
Memento, 14
memes, 18
memory, 38–39
Mera, Miguel, 53
Mercer, Kobena, 299n30
"Mercy Street" (Gabriel), 231
Merendino, James, 22, 42–45, 66
merengue, 39
Method Man, 248
Metropolis (Lang), 214
Metropolitan Opera, 4
"MeTube: August sings Carmen 'Habanera,'" 195–96
Meyer, Leonard, 294n23
Meyers, Dave, 25, 215, 247–61, 263, 286,
    322n70, 330n46
  editing of, 251–52
  large-scale structures in work of, 253
  Lawrence compared to, 234–35, 248, 260–61
  personal iconography of, 254–55
  picaresques of, 253–55
  props used by, 254–55
  representation, 256–61
  stars in work of, 248–51
MGMT, 231
Miami Vice, 145, 262
Michael, George
  "Father Figure," 210f, 211
  "Freedom," 214, 322n66
"Michael Bay so fast your eyeballs burn," 16, 17, 18
"Michael Jackson Medley," 193
microtargeting, 305n5
Middleton, Richard, 74, 298n17, 327n18
Midsummer Night's Dream, 80
Mika, 216
Milk, Chris, 75
Miller, Frank, 144, 145f, 193
Miller Lite, 174
Minaj, Nicki, 75, 229
minimalism, 154
Minority Report (Spielberg), 159
mise en abyme, 60
Mission Impossible, 202
Mitchell, Joni, 267
Mixalot, Sir, 148
mixing-board aesthetic, 4–5, 34
"Mmmbop" (Hanson), 227

Mondino, Jean-Baptiste, 192
*Monopoly Television: MTV's Quest to Control the
    Music* (Banks), 325n4
Monroe, Marilyn, 79
Monsieur Hulot's Holiday, 328n27
montage, 327n21
  in *Eternal Sunshine*, 98, 100, 107, 114–15, 299n27
  in music video, 257
  narrative and, 113
Moore, Alan, 74
Morahan, Andy, 317n15
Morcom, Anna, 118, 300n2, 301n3
Morisset, Vincent, 75, 318n25
Morning Masume, 153
morphing, 213
Morricone, Ennio, 40, 198, 199
Morris, Mark, 52
Morris, Mitchell, 74
Morris, Paul, 198, 307n42
Mothersbaugh, Mark, 40
motifs, 36, 63, 121
  death, 92
  in *Eternal Sunshine*, 22, 94–95, 97–102, 107–9
  Lawrence using, 238, 241
  in music video, 109
  in Romanek, 267
Moulin Rouge! (Luhrmann), 5, 7, 14, 22, 26, 33,
    68, 146, 231, 290n13, 333n14
  characters, 89–90
  design in, 80
  editing in, 85–88
  form of, 83–85
  geography in, 80–82
  improvisation in, 89–90
  love in, 80, 84f
  multiple narrators in, 77–79, 79f
  musicality of, 83, 85–88, 91–93
  music in, 91–93
  performance in, 89–90
  relationships in, 90–91
  soundtrack of, 91–93
  story of, 82
  synopsis, 76–77
  tropes in, 88–89
movement, 117
moveon.org, 155
"Moves like Jagger" (Maroon 5), 18
MP3, 226
"Mr. Ott's sneeze," 139
"Mr. President" (LL Cool J), 145
MTV, 11, 69, 219
  history of, 207–8
  shows on, 70
Mughal-e-Azam, 118, 118f
Mulholland Drive (Lynch), 66
Muller, Sophie, 263
multitasking, 277–78, 333n17

Pellington, Mark, 72, 218, 230, 263, 327n20
Penderecki, Krzysztof, 107
"Penny Lane," 79
Perez, Rosie, 179
performance
   in Moulin Rouge!, 89–90
   in music video, 221–22
   in post-classical cinema, 38
   YouTube and, 197
Performance (Roeg), 71
Perry, Katy, 12, 187, 248, 323n81
   "E.T.," 215, 220–22, 224–25, 290n13
   "Firework," 232, 260
   "Friday Night," 15, 227
   "Teenage Dream," 143, 232
Perry, Steve, 138
"Peso" (A$AP Rocky), 75
Peter, Michael, 314n52
Peter, Paul & Mary, 168
Peterson, Jennifer, 296n17
Pet Shop Boys, 221
   "West End Girls," 221*f*
Petty, Adria, 232
P-Funk, 258
Ph.D., 222, 228, 228*f*
The Philadelphia Story, 63
Photoshop, 130
Piaf, Edith, 284
Picasso, Pablo, 50
Pickett, Ben, 138
Piechota, Carole, 291n2
Pineda, Arnel, 139
Pink, 250
   "Fuckin' Perfect," 322n70
   "Get the Party Started," 254
   "Raise Your Glass," 248, 248*f*
   "Sober," 217
Pitchfork, 150, 208, 232, 324n82
Pixar, 129, 290n12
"Play" (Lopez), 245
PlentyOfFish, 14
poetry, 228
"Poison" (Scherzinger), 222
Poitier, Sydney Tamiia, 59
Polaroid, 14
The Police, 213
"Pop Goes the Weasel," 148
"Pork and Beans" (Weezer), 135, 227, 310n12
Portishead, 275
post-classical cinema, 3, 5
   accelerated aesthetics of, 33, 71, 79
   Bordwell on, 7, 33, 60, 67, 84, 324n85
   color in, 38
   costumes in, 38
   defined, 7
   economics and, 34
   editing in, 33

gesture in, 38
graphic typography in, 38
lighting in, 38
memory and, 38–39
musicality of, 67
music video's influence on, 34, 69–74
pacing of, 38
performance in, 38
sets in, 38
sound in, 38
soundtracks in, 22–23, 28–29, 35–40
structural qualities of, 38–39
"Power" (West), 210
"Praise You" (Fatboy Slim), 273
Prassad, M. Madhava, 117
The Presets, 324n82
presidential debates, 178–79
Presley, Elvis, 148
Prince, 212, 307n43
production tools
   Avid, 22, 34, 35, 94, 109, 136, 280
   digital intermediary, 4, 35, 37, 94, 136,
      215–16, 221, 224, 285
   Logic, 35, 94
   Pro Tools, 11, 22, 35, 94, 136, 280
   videotape, 4, 70, 73, 188, 211, 230, 231,
      290n16, 303n43
product placement, 230
Prokofiev, Sergei, 63
prosumer, 16, 17, 28, 74, 139, 145, 185, 208, 311n22
   defined, 308n67
   populist clips and, 177
   professionalism and, 154
   technology, 149–50
   on YouTube, 130, 132, 149–50
"Protection" (Massive Attack), 270
Pro Tools, 11, 22, 35, 94, 136, 280
Psy, 73, 74, 142, 183, 186, 190, 193, 295n16
Psycho (Hitchcock), 136, 299n25
Public Enemy, 154
"Puff the Magic Dragon" (Peter, Paul & Mary), 168
Purcer, Justin, 17
Pussycat Dolls, 161, 167
   "Jai Ho," 23
puzzle films, 7, 33–34

Q-Tip, 267
Quantel, 35, 214
Queen, 212, 262

race, 6, 25, 92, 158, 160, 162, 174, 178, 199, 216,
   258, 260, 267, 272, 276
   in "Yes We Can," 170–71
racism, 157
Radiohead, 214
Ragona, Melissa, 74
Rahman, A. R., 117, 120, 122